PAUL ROBESON

Frontispiece. Paul Robeson as "The Emperor Jones." 1933.
Photo by Edward Steichen. Courtesy George Eastman House. Reprinted with permission of Joanna T. Steichen.

PAUL ROBESON
Artist and Citizen

Edited and with an introduction by
Jeffrey C. Stewart

RUTGERS UNIVERSITY PRESS,
NEW BRUNSWICK, NEW JERSEY, AND LONDON
AND
THE PAUL ROBESON CULTURAL CENTER

This book has been published in conjunction with the Paul Robeson Centennial Project, organized by the Paul Robeson Cultural Center of Rutgers University.

STAFF OF THE PAUL ROBESON CULTURAL CENTER
FOR THE CENTENNIAL PROJECT:

Rae Alexander-Minter, Project Director
Jeffrey C. Stewart, Exhibition Curator and Volume Editor
Janet Greenberg, Project Manager and Editorial Consultant

ITINERARY OF THE MULTIMEDIA TRAVELING EXHIBITION,
PAUL ROBESON: ARTIST AND CITIZEN:

The Jane Voorhees Zimmerli Art Museum of Rutgers,
The State University of New Jersey, New Brunswick
April–July 1998

The California African-American Museum, Los Angeles
September–December 1998

The National Portrait Gallery of the Smithsonian Institution, Washington, D.C.
February–April 1999

The Museum of the City of New York
June–September 1999

Funding for major components of the Paul Robeson Centennial Project was provided, in part, by the National Endowment for the Humanities, the Vice President for Academic Affairs and the Provost's Fund of Rutgers University, the William Penn Foundation, The Rockefeller Foundation, the New Jersey State Council on the Arts/Department of State, the American Express Philanthropic Program, Allen and Joan Bildner and the Bildner Family Foundation, the Geraldine R. Dodge Foundation, and Sony Music Entertainment.

Interior design and typesetting by Ellen C. Dawson.

Manufactured in the United States of America

Library of Congress Cataloging-in-Publication Data

Paul Robeson : artist and citizen / edited with an introduction by Jeffrey C. Stewart.
　　p.　　cm.
　　Includes bibliographical references (p.) and index.
　　ISBN 0-8135-2510-1 (alk. paper). — ISBN 0-8135-2511-X (pbk. : alk. paper)
　　1. Robeson, Paul, 1898–1976. 2. Afro-Americans—Biography. 3. Singers—United States—Biography. 4. Actors—United States—Biography. 5. Political Activists—United States—Biography. I. Stewart, Jeffrey C., 1950–　　.
　　E185.97.R63P37　　1998
　　782'.0092—dc21
　　[B]　　　　　　　　　　　　　　　　　　　　　　　　　　　　　　　97-31660
　　　　　　　　　　　　　　　　　　　　　　　　　　　　　　　　　　　　CIP

British Cataloging-in-Publication data for this book is available from the British Library

CONTENTS

ILLUSTRATIONS

COLOR PLATES

Rae Alexander-Minter

PREFACE

Many years ago when I was a child living in Philadelphia, Paul Robeson was an occasional visitor to my parents' home. To one so young, it mattered little that he was my paternal grandfather's nephew by marriage; rather, it was his majestic appeal that impressed me beyond kinship. A few of those indelible memories recurred when I became Director of the Paul Robeson Cultural Center in 1993.

Robeson's presence at Rutgers College—where he was a two-time All-American and from which he graduated with honors in 1919—is widely evidenced but no more so than at the Cultural Center, which was established in 1969 and renamed for Robeson in 1971. As the embodiment of Robeson's legacy and a reflection of his dauntless nobility, the Center provides leadership, vision, and support for 5,000 African American, African, and Caribbean students on campus. The Center's lecture series, conferences, and course development have resonated beyond the campus, influencing 40,000 members of the general community and in the New Jersey public schools each year, as well as offering cultural programming for broad audiences in the tristate area.

As I assumed my position as Director of the Cultural Center, the possibility of a Robeson centennial was foremost in my thinking. More fortuitous than my personal reunion with the Robeson aura is the significance of this project for millions of Americans of all races and ethnicities.

It has taken an advisory committee of esteemed scholars, each well-versed in a facet of Robeson's life, and a curator of rare ability to nurture the concept closer to full bloom, that righteous epiphany. With the encouragement and support of the administration at Rutgers University and the largess of corporations, foundations, and federal and state governments, the exhibition, *Paul Robeson: Artist and Citizen*, its accompanying book and public programs are offered to an enthusiastic national audience. The various components of the Robeson Centennial Project will enable adults and young people to view Paul Robeson in all of his magnificent diversity and to witness the supreme importance of his legacy within the context of American and African American art, music, history, and politics of the twentieth century.

This book includes never-before-published photographs from the Julius Lazarus Archives and Collection, a veritable treasure trove of 70,000 photographs and negatives and 20,000 other books and printed materials that serves as a valuable resource and record of public life in action in both the United States and Europe, as well as a compendium of interracial relations within progressive causes in the years immediately after World War II. Paul Robeson has a place of prominence throughout the Lazarus Archives and Collection. We are deeply indebted to Julius Lazarus for the generous donation to Rutgers University of his rich photographic archives and collection.

Given the special balance of text and images, this book is much more than a collection of data and memorabilia to inspire and educate viewers; it is a living document to the degree that Robeson's legacy is unending and ever evolving. The rich contours of his life will always create other ways for us to celebrate his triumphant passage, other ways for us to realize our own possibilities through his example. For older Americans, the thought-provoking essays and riveting photographs will evoke memories of Robeson as symbolic of an emerging civil- and human-rights movement that presaged Dr. Martin Luther King, Jr., and Malcolm X. And younger Americans, particularly those of color, will relish Robeson's strength and stamina, and find in him an enduring role model upon which to fasten their own hopes and aspirations.

The glorious odyssey of Robeson's life will be shared vicariously by all Americans interested in justice and fair play. He was indeed "the tallest tree in the forest," a man of unshakable conviction who was determined not to concede an inch to the forces of repression and fascism. Such a bold stance created a powerful reaction that practically rendered Robeson invisible, but it was impossible to curtail his influence, to muffle his relentless voice for social change and human decency. No amount of vilification or nullification by his enemies could stifle his magic at the podium, his gift of language, his international appeal in the realms of theater, film, and political thought. To impede Robeson's majesty, to subdue his resolve for the downtrodden, required much more clout than the state could muster. All of this is now before us within the pages of this book.

It has also been interpreted through the many components of this centennial project which are being presented in four major urban areas in the United States in 1998 and 1999. From the traveling exhibition to the series of public programs for diverse adult and youth audiences, this project has coordinated a complete retrospective of Robeson's films; a new, interdisciplinary curriculum for middle school and high school students; the presentation of Ossie Davis's new play about Robeson to young audiences in New Jersey; and a photographic exhibit focused on Robeson's political activism. The programs of the centennial project were built progressively over four years in response to interest expressed by many people and organizations across the country.

————

I wish to thank Jeffrey C. Stewart, the curator of the exhibition and editor of this volume, whose vision and comprehension of Robeson and his time served to give us a new understanding of this extraordinary person; and Rutgers University, especially Joseph J. Seneca, University Vice President for Academic Affairs, who was unwavering in his belief in me and the project. Very special thanks go to Janet Greenberg, who served as project manager and editorial consultant on this volume. Her contribution to the conceptual and fund development of this mammoth project, and her commitment to maintaining its organizational integrity, were crucial to its successful realization.

Also important to the realization of this project were Joan Sandler, a friend and colleague in the arts, who sparked my thinking about the centennial in 1993; and Robin Merle, formerly of the Rutgers University Foundation, who was generous in her support.

Each component of the project was developed in collaboration with generous and creative individuals and organizations. We are pleased that the exhibition, *Paul Robeson: Artist and Citizen,* will be seen by many thousands of people when it travels across the country. The committed efforts of four museum directors made the tour possible: Phillip Dennis Cate, Director, the Jane Voorhees Zimmerli Art Museum of Rutgers University, New Brunswick; Jamesina E. Henderson, Executive Director, California African-American Museum in Los Angeles; Alan Fern, Director, National Portrait Gallery of the Smithsonian Institution, Washington, D.C.; and Robert R. McDonald, Director, Museum of the City of New York. The design services firm Douglas/Gallagher, represented by Veronica Jackson, Senior Exhibit Designer, and Randy Anderson, Senior Project Manager, designed the traveling exhibition. They worked closely with Melissa Rachleff and Judy Mannes, the scriptwriters, and Design and Production, Incorporated, whose development of the audiovisual components made the exhibit a truly multimedia experience that engages wide audiences of all ages.

Our partners in curating and presenting the film series include, in New York City, the Museum of Modern Art and the Schomburg Center for Research in Black Culture of the New York Public Library; in Los Angeles, the Academy of Motion Picture Arts and Sciences, the University of California, Los Angeles, the Los Angeles County Museum of Art, and the Pan African Film Festival; and the Library of Congress in Washington, D.C. A team of three film scholars curated the film program: Charles Musser, Ed Guerrero, and Mark A. Reid.

The public school districts of New Brunswick and Camden, New Jersey, were energetic partners in developing and piloting a multidisciplinary curriculum for inclusion in courses in African American studies, American history, music, and language arts. The curriculum project was greatly facilitated by the leadership of Penelope E. Lattimer, Assistant Superintendent of Curriculum and Instruction of the New Brunswick Public Schools, and Wilma J. Farmer, Director of Region II of the Camden Public Schools. V. P. Franklin, Professor of History, Drexel University, developed the two-part curriculum. Our presentation of the new play by Ossie Davis about Paul Robeson is the result of close collaboration with Charles Hull, Managing Director, Theatreworks/U.S.A., and with creative leaders of three major theaters in New Jersey, which will host performances for several thousand youth in 1998: Ricardo Khan, Co-founder and Artistic Director, Crossroads Theatre Company in New Brunswick; Philip S. Thomas, Vice President–Arts Education, New Jersey Performing Arts Center in Newark; and Barbara S. Fenhagen, Executive Director, South Jersey Performing Arts Center in Camden.

Within the Rutgers community, colleagues in many departments and units worked together to make the exhibition and public programs possible. Staff of the Zimmerli Art Museum, especially Phillip Dennis Cate, Director; Barbara Trelstad, Registrar; and Clare Savard, Assistant Registrar, were crucial to the development of the exhibition and the book. The acquisition and cataloging of the Julius Lazarus Archives and Collection by the Rutgers University Libraries and Special Collections were tremendously facilitated by Ronald L. Becker, Head of Special Collections, and Albert C. King, Manuscripts Librarian. The Stedman Gallery, Rutgers University–Camden Center for the Arts, produced an exhibition of selections from the Julius Lazarus Archives and Collection, and the Walter K. Gordon Theater presented performances, films, and lectures. In addition, an extensive series of arts and cultural education programs benefited Camden school children. With the Center for the Study of Jewish Life, we designed a public symposium series for several venues across the country; in collaboration with the Mason Gross School of the Arts, music and dance performances will be presented in New Jersey. We extend our gratitude to each of these organizations for joining with us to ensure that the exhibition and the public programs reach a wide audience across the United States.

A number of important grants made it possible to realize the centennial plan: my gratitude and thanks for major funding must go to The National Endowment for the Humanities, whose Division of Public Programs showed early and continuous confidence in this challenging project by providing a crucial planning grant in 1994 and a major implementation grant for the exhibition in 1997. Generous funding for the exhibition and this book was also provided by The Rockefeller Foundation. The William Penn Foundation, the New Jersey State Council on the Arts, and the Geraldine R. Dodge Foundation generously contributed to the public school programs in both the Stedman Art Gallery and the Walter K. Gordon Theater on the Rutgers-Camden campus. For curriculum development in the New Brunswick, New Jersey, schools, funding was provided by the Geraldine R. Dodge Foundation. To present to youth in New Jersey an original play about Paul Robeson by Ossie Davis, major funding was provided by the William Penn Foundation, as well as by the New Jersey State Council on the Arts/Department of State, which also contributed to centennial programs at Rutgers-Camden. To mount a complete retrospective of Robeson's films in each exhibition city, funding was provided by the American Express Philanthropic Program. Crucial support for components of the centennial project was also provided by Allen I. and Joan Bildner and Sony Music Entertainment.

The dedicated staff of the Paul Robeson Cultural Center—especially Dion W. Lewis, assistant to the director; Linda Workman, personal secretary; and Anita M. Christian and Cherie Foster, assistant project coordinators—worked with unfailing energy to sustain ongoing programs while building this project over several years.

And finally, let me extend my deepest appreciation to the students and alumni of the Paul Robeson Cultural Center, who understood my vision and supported me at every point toward the completion of this project, which I have watched grow and become a source of empowerment for thousands of people. It has been a collective effort and worthy of the universal praise it has received.

Jeffrey C. Stewart

ACKNOWLEDGMENTS

No publication such as this happens without a number of people working together to make a vision into a reality. This book and the exhibition that it accompanies have been blessed by the kind of teamwork and collaboration among lenders, researchers, scholars, administrators, and museum professionals that is rare in today's highly specialized and increasingly distinct provinces of public history. In pulling together this team of personnel, Rae Alexander-Minter, Director of the Paul Robeson Cultural Center at Rutgers University, deserves the first and highest acknowledgment. When Dr. Alexander-Minter telephoned me in 1994 and asked me to curate this Paul Robeson Centennial Exhibition, I initially demurred—not because I have not revered Paul Robeson for a number of years. Through family stories about his contributions and reading about him in the biographies over the years, and having written notes to a National Portrait Gallery production of *Ballad for Americans* in 1985, I have always had a fascination for Robeson. But at the time, I had a full plate, given that I was working on two books and teaching full time at George Mason University, more than three hundred miles away from Rutgers University, the site of the celebration. But Rae continued to call and the prospect of fully investigating the life of one of America's most outstanding citizens was too much for me to resist. Such an opportunity for me—and for others whose work is collected in this volume—to give Robeson sustained attention would not have existed without her. For in addition to running a cultural center at Rutgers, Rae Alexander-Minter has raised the funding, selected the essayists in this volume, and functioned as a liaison among several Rutgers University units, including the Rutgers University Press, the Jane Voorhees Zimmerli Art Museum, and the University Libraries. Throughout it all she has maintained the enthusiasm that motivated her original idea—that Rutgers University owed Paul Robeson, perhaps its most distinguished alumnus, a comprehensive celebration of his life and work on the hundredth anniversary of his birth.

Translating such an idea into a reality is a challenging research undertaking, and it would not have been possible without the assistance of a number of excellent scholars and research assistants. First the fourteen scholars who have contributed essays to this volume have brought both new information and new insights to the study of Paul Robeson. I owe thanks to my fellow contributors Derrick Bell, Charles L. Blockson, Lloyd L. Brown, Martin Duberman, John Hope Franklin, Ed Guerrero, Francis C. Harris, Gerald Horne, David Levering Lewis, Julianne Malveaux, Doris Evans McGinty, Mark D. Naison, Mark A. Reid, Wayne Shirley, and Deborah Willis for their participation on this project and their struggle with the challenging topic of Paul Robeson. Beyond her contribution as an author, Deborah Willis, photography historian and Smithsonian Institution curator, deserves special thanks for locating numerous photographs and artifacts, recommending key personnel to assist the exhibition, helping me select photographs and the design for the exhibit, and providing invaluable advice and support along the way.

Similarly, my research for the exhibition and this book was greatly assisted by several others. Helen Shannon, an art historian, who visited a number of archives, was invaluable. She made photocopies of artwork, took copious, detailed notes on what she found, and hunted down difficult-to-find photographs and artifacts. I also greatly benefited from the willingness of Nnenna Ugwunna, on her way to graduate work at the London School of Economics, to conduct research in the Hulton Getty Picture Collection, Ltd., for this project. Lisa Epstein at the Academy of Motion Picture Arts and Sciences Margaret Herrick Library was very helpful in locating information on Robeson's films. Cheryl Finley provided invaluable assistance in locating photographs and printed materials at Yale University and participated in cataloging the Julius Lazarus Archives and Collection. I also benefited greatly from the insight of Veronica Jackson for photographic, artifactual, and design assistance, the advice and counsel of Fath Davis Ruffins, the commentary of Marilyn Sanders Mobley and Claudia Tate, the research and secretarial assistance of Cheryl Simmons, Stefanie Tildon, and Corey Holt, and the excellent support of Clare Savard, Assistant Registrar for this project, who wrote letters, processed permissions, and performed numerous other duties with tact and good humor. Beverly Cox, Curator of Exhibitions at the National Portrait Gallery, kindly gave of her time to review the photographs and artifacts at key moments in this process, and Alan Fern, Director of the National Portrait Gallery, provided me with valuable insight and advice. At the Zimmerli Art Museum, I am tremendously indebted to Barbara Trelstad, Registrar, for supervision of the registration and permissions work on this project, and to Phillip Dennis Cate, Director, for his support. I also wish to thank Rae Graham for her assistance early in the project. Of course, this project would not have been realized without generous financial support from its conception. My thanks here go to those who supported the curatorial research and planning stages, and the production of this volume: Early curatorial research and planning was supported by a National Endowment for the Humanities planning grant in 1995. Additional support for research and development was provided in 1997 by the Rockefeller Foundation. Tomás Ybarra-Frausto, Associate Director of Arts and Humanities, deserves our special thanks for his enthusiasm and support. Most important all along the way has been the support of Joseph J. Seneca, Rutgers University Vice President for Academic Affairs, who provided the day-to-day funding that was necessary to initiate the project and enable it to develop over these several years.

Vital to this project are the lenders to this exhibition and volume of essays. Special thanks and gratitude are extended to such fine institutions as the Academy of Motion Picture Arts and Sciences; the Archives of American Art, Smithsonian Institution; the Art Museum, Princeton University; the Charles L. Blockson Afro-American Collection, Temple University; the Corbis-Bettmann Archives; the Boston Museum of Fine Arts; the Hulton Getty Picture Collection, Ltd.; the Museum of the City of New York; the National Archives; the National Museum of American History and the National Portrait Gallery, Smithsonian Institution; the New York Public Library for the Performing Arts; the Paul Robeson Student Center, Rutgers University–Newark; the Phillips Collection; Rutgers University Libraries, Special Collections; the Schomburg Center for Research in Black Culture of the New York Public Library; and such exemplary individuals as Charles L. Blockson, Lloyd L. Brown, Esther Jackson (for *Freedomways* photographs), Julius Lazarus, Ed and Monife Love, Irving Salk, Tony Schwartz, Jean Sieroty, Robert Smith, and Danny Tisdale. Special thanks are extended to Charles L. Blockson, Lloyd L. Brown, and Robert Smith not only for opening their extensive private collections to me and the project, but also for educating me about Paul Robeson and the location of information, artifacts, and photographs I have needed during this project. My very special thanks go to Julius Lazarus, who in 1995 donated his huge collection to the university, which now holds the Julius Lazarus Archives and Collection in the Special Collections of the Rutgers University Libraries, in part because of his enthusiasm and support for this book. In addition, he spent hundreds of hours identifying and organizing his photographs in Special Collections at Rutgers, assisted in the selection and arranged for the printing of his photographs, and devoted considerable time during a trip to Europe in the fall of 1996 to collect and bring back additional photographs, videos, films, and records from his colleagues, some of which have become part of this volume of essays. I would also like to thank all of those who assisted Mr. Lazarus: Christine Nauman, the former curator (from 1982 to 1991) of the Paul Robeson Archives, Academy of Arts–Berlin; Gerhard Kiesling, a photographer in Berlin, who provided free of charge photographs of Paul Robeson receiving an honorary doctorate in philosophy from Humboldt University in Berlin, October 12, 1960; the Bildarchiv Neues Deutschland, Berlin, for permission to reproduce several photographs in this book; and Dr. Alfred Katzenstein for providing photographs and negatives, taken by Franz Loeser, of Paul and Eslanda Robeson during his stay at the Buch Hospital in Berlin in the summer of 1963. The acquisition, rehousing, and cataloguing of the Julius Lazarus Archives and Collection into the Special Collections of Alexander Library, Rutgers University, was a tremendous job. We wish to thank Ronald L. Becker, Head of Special Collections, who managed the acquisition; Albert C. King, Manuscript Librarian, who coordinated the rehousing and cataloguing; and Michelle Anastasia, Courtney

Brown, Anita M. Christian, Cherie Foster, Rae Graham, Lisa Groppe, Mary A. Kennedy, Troy Simmons, Rachael S. Tomori, Dionya S. Webb, and all the others who helped rehouse thousands of photographs and negatives. For five months while Mr. Lazarus worked on this project he stayed at the Continuing Education Center at Rutgers University–New Brunswick. We thank the staff of the Center, especially Elinor Berrey, Thelma P. N. Collins, Daphne V. Johnson-Jones, Franklin Lugo, Steven Lione, Melissa Lomanoh, Thomas Parker, Nona Sanchez, and Michael Salpas, for the room, board, and companionship they provided Mr. Lazarus. For work on the exhibiton of Lazarus photographs on Paul Robeson's activism, March 9 to May 2, 1998, at the Stedman Gallery, Rutgers University–Camden Center for the Arts, we thank especially Virginia Oberlin Steel, Director and Curator; Nancy Maguire, Curator of Exhibitions; Noreen Scott Garrity, Curator of Education; and Capucine Jackson Grimes, Theater Programs and Marketing Coordinator. Finally, we thank Eva Lazarus, Julius's wife of forty years, for supporting him not only during this project but also through all the years of his effort to record and preserve Paul Robeson's life and work.

Several individuals have been crucial to the publication of this book. Janet Greenberg, Manager of the Paul Robeson Centennial Project and Editorial Consultant, played a key role in the book's development and coordinated the flow of information among the many contributors and key collaborating units of the University from inception to the final months of production. She and Mark Kempson did excellent work in handling computer text files of the manuscript, bringing the components of the book together, and moving the manuscript from the Paul Robeson Cultural Center into production by the Press. The work of the staff of the Paul Robeson Cultural Center, especially Dion W. Lewis, Linda Workman, and Anita M. Christian, was crucial all along the way. At the Rutgers University Libraries, Ronald L. Becker, Head of Special Collections, and Albert C. King, Manuscript Librarian, Special Collections, have been enormously supportive. At Rutgers University Press, Leslie Mitchner, Editor in Chief and Associate Director; Tricia Politi, Senior Production Coordinator; Marilyn Campbell, Managing Editor; and the copyeditor of the manuscript, Robert E. Brown, have patiently cooperated with and steered a project that became increasingly demanding. I would especially like to thank Leslie Mitchner for her good advice, needed encouragement, and generosity in stepping forward to resolve many problems. We all thank you for making this book happen.

I am especially grateful for the support of my wife, Marta Reid Stewart, who gave me not only her unflagging support, but her expertise as an art historian in selection of the photographs. I am indebted to the intellectual input of Imamu Amiri Baraka, Cynthia Fuchs, and Melanie McAlister. I also want to thank my friends: Reginald Clark, for providing me access to his office, staff, and equipment in Montclair, in California; Lawrence Lee Jones, who provided a house in Malibu where I could finish work on the book; and Marie Brown, who helped solve contractual difficulties on the project; Stanley Sanders, Alan Sieroty, Anthony Ruiz, and Suzanne Zada, Ellen Harrington, Winston Kennedy, and Thomas and Page Richards provided moral support. I also want to thank those who helped with the project but whose names are not mentioned individually here. Their help is greatly appreciated.

CHRONOLOGY

1898   Born to William Drew Robeson and Maria Louisa Robeson, April 9, in Princeton, NJ. He is the youngest of five children.

1901   Father, twenty-year pastor of Witherspoon Street Presbyterian Church, Princeton, is forced to resign by the Presbytery's investigating commission.

1904   Mother dies in accidental kitchen fire, but he is not home when tragedy strikes.

1906   Father joins the African Methodist Episcopal (A.M.E) Zion Church, an independent African American denomination.

1907–1908   Family moves to Westfield, NJ, and lives above a grocery store, where father works. Paul attends integrated public school for the first time. Father builds a small church, Downer Street St. Luke A.M.E. Zion, and a parsonage.

1910–1912   Family moves to Somerville, NJ, where father assumes pastorate of St. Thomas A.M.E. Zion Church. In 1911, graduates from James L. Jamison's "Colored School" and delivers declamation of Patrick Henry's "An Appeal to Arms." Enters Somerville High School in 1912, where he is one of a dozen African Americans in a school of 200.

1915   Performs Shakespeare's title character Othello in a high school theatrical medley, "Shakespeare at the Water Cure" (db, 13; lb, 48). Wins statewide written examination competition for four-year scholarship at Rutgers College, New Brunswick, NJ (pf, 27; db, 17). Graduates from Somerville High School, an honor student at age seventeen (pf, 27). Finishes third in statewide oratorical contest (pf, 27). That summer, waits tables in restaurant of the Imperial Hotel, a whites-only hotel with all-Black staff, Narragansett Pier, RI (pf, 27; db, 11). Enters Rutgers College that fall (pf, 27).

This chronology was compiled by Khalil G. Muhammad, doctoral student in American History at Rutgers University.

The following sources were consulted: db = Martin Duberman, *Paul Robeson: A Biography* (New York: The New Press, 1995); dll = David Levering Lewis, *When Harlem Was in Vogue* (New York: Oxford University Press, 1981); lb = Lloyd L. Brown, *The Young Paul Robeson: "On My Journey Now"* (Boulder, CO: Westview Press, 1997); pf = Philip S. Foner, ed., *Paul Robeson Speaks: Writings, Speeches, Interviews* (Secaucus, NJ: Citadel Press, 1978).

1917   Stars on Rutgers football team. Chosen an All-American by many sports writers, but not by Walter Camp who, in response to US entry into World War I, publishes instead an All-Service team of players in the armed forces. Dates Geraldine Maimie Neale, high school senior from Freehold, NJ, who later attends Teachers Normal School, Trenton, NJ.

1918–1919   Father dies in 1918 at seventy-three. Honoring father's last requests, wins oratorical contests. Named to Camp's All-American football team. Will receive fifteen varsity letters at Rutgers, in football, basketball, baseball, and track and field. Elected to Phi Beta Kappa as a junior. Hears W.E.B. Du Bois for the first time at a banquet for Assistant District Attorney F. Q. Morton at the Terrace Garden. In Rutgers senior year, 1919, chosen for Cap and Skull Honor Society, Ann Van Nest Bussing Prize in Extemporaneous Speaking, Valedictorian of the class. Gives 153rd Commencement Address, "The New Idealism." In July moves to Harlem, NY.

1920   Starts at Columbia University Law School (pf, 28; lb, 107) in February, and plays professional football with Frank Nied's Akron Pros. With Fritz Pollard, the Black All-American from Brown, assistant coach of football at Lincoln University (js, 5; db, 34). Makes stage debut in *Simon the Cyrenian*, one of *Three Plays for a Negro Theater* by white poet Ridgely Torrence (pf, 28; db 43). Begins dating Eslanda "Essie" Goode, a pathology technician at New York's Presbyterian Hospital, where Robeson spent several weeks recuperating from a football injury (db, 39).

1921   His marriage proposal rejected by Geraldine Neale in Freehold, NJ, he marries Eslanda Goode on August 17 in Port Chester, New York. Continues to play professional football with the Akron Pros (db, 40).

1922   In April, makes professional acting debut as Jim in *Taboo*, Mary Hoyt Wiborg's play. (In July, a London production of the play, renamed *Voodoo*, will feature him and Mrs. Patrick Campbell) (pf, 28; db, 43, 47; dll, 91). He also joins cast of Eubie Blake's *Shuffle Along* (db, 44). In England that summer, he meets Lawrence Brown at Regents Park Road flat of John Payne, African American singer (pf, 28; db, 49), and tours British provinces with Mrs. Campbell (pf, 28; db 49), later returning to New York to be with Essie during her illness. In the fall he assists Coach Sanford of Rutgers football to help make ends meet and plays last year of professional football with the Milwaukee Badgers. He scores both touchdowns in shutout victory over the Oorang Indians, whose star, the legendary Jim Thorpe, Robeson allegedly punches out in self-defense on the field (db, 52). Eubie Blake, Noble Sissle, and others perform with him that November (db, 52).

1923   After graduating from Columbia Law School in February, he will not find work in law until later that spring. Meanwhile, he sings in Harlem's Cotton Club (pf, 28; db, 54), and appears in Lew Leslie's *Plantation Revue*, starring Florence Mills (db, 52). He clerks in Post Office to help meet expenses (db, 52), but declines a fight promoter's offer to challenge Henry Wills and Jack Dempsey (db, 52). By March, he makes first appeal to Otto H. Kahn, a wealthy art patron, for assistance in getting other theatrical parts (db, 53). Rutgers alumnus Louis William Stotesbury hires Robeson as the only African American at Stotesbury and Miner, a New York law office, where he starts work as an attorney that June (pf, 28; db, 54). By the fall, he resigns from the firm owing to the limited opportunity for African Americans to get work or respect as lawyers (db, 55).

1924   Sings at a Brooklyn YMCA banquet for the St. Christopher basketball team, and at the request of Walter White during an NAACP function (db, 56, 76). March through June, he stars in a Black revival of white playwright Nan Bagby Stevens's *Roseanne*, at the Lafayette in Harlem (db, 56–57), and later that June in Philadelphia (pf, 28; db, 57). That spring, accepts lead role in Eugene O'Neill's *All God's Chillun Got Wings*. Racial bigots, including journalists and critics, begin uproar over white actress Mary Blair kissing Robeson's hand in *All God's Chillun*. On May 5, Ku Klux Klan threatens Robeson over the act (pf, 28). Accepts lead as Brutus Jones in *The Emperor Jones* (pf, 28; db 57), which opens May 6 to divert attention from *All God's Chillun*. Will perform *Emperor Jones* from May through June. *Chillun* opens May 15 and is otherwise a success (it will close on October 24 after 100 performances). The Robesons become friends with Gladys and Walter White and Grace Nail and James Weldon Johnson. Mr. Johnson and Mr. White are both officers of the NAACP (db, 71). That fall, Robeson makes the silent movie *Body and Soul* for Oscar Micheaux, an independent African American filmmaker (pf, 29; db, 77). In

November he sings in first formal concert at Copley Plaza Hotel, Boston, and also on December 17 at Rutgers (db, 77). In a December 24 article in National Urban League's *Opportunity* magazine, he defends *All God's Chilluns*'s ambitious racial perspective and Eugene O'Neill's unique ability to "read the negro soul" (db, 66 and fn 70, 588).

1925 The Robesons meet Carl Van Vechten and his wife, actress Fania Marinoff (db, 73). He again stars in *The Emperor Jones* on Broadway. That January, gives concert at the Highland Park (NJ) Reformed Church (db, fn, 32, 594), and appears at Rutgers functions in February and March: as speaker for the Freshman Banquet, and as Junior Banquet's guest of honor (db, 76). He negotiates a contract to give performances with friend and accompanist Lawrence Brown (db, 78), the first of which are at Greenwich Village Theatre, April 19 and May 3 (pf, 29; db, 79, fn31, 594), and later in May at the Dutch Treat Club, for artists and authors. He and Brown sign with agent James B. Pond, and an exclusive one-year contract with Victor Talking Machine Company (db, 82). However, he refuses to appear in David Belasco's play *Lulu Belle*, because of its "stereotyped format" (db, 83). After Essie appeals again to Otto H. Kahn for help in getting Paul roles, on June 28 Kahn becomes a patron of Robeson's career with a $5,000 loan (db, 53, 84). Appears in a London production of *The Emperor Jones*, which opens in September, is critically acclaimed, but closes after only five weeks. London critics praise Robeson's performances, but not the play (db, 91). He begins vocal training with Flora Arnold (db, 91). That winter, the Robesons visit Paris, Nice, and Villefrance, establishing friendships with Claude McKay, Max Eastman, and others (db, 93–97), then return to New York (db, 97). His first recordings, four double-sided albums, are released: "Joshua Fit de Battle" and "Bye and Bye" are best-sellers (db, 98).

1926 In January, makes second recordings for Victor Company (db, 98), and begins a seven-concert tour in New York (db, 98). Italian American sculptor Antonio Salemmé unveils his nude statue of Robeson, a two-year project. While on tour, February–March, Robeson is denied hotel accommodations in cities such as Green Bay, WI, and Boston, MA (db, 99, 100). On October 6, he stars in *Black Boy,* a play based roughly on life of Jack Johnson, at New York's Comedy Theater. Although his performance receives raves, the play does not; it closes after a few weeks (pf, 29; db 103–104). After he turns down role in Paul Green's play *In Abraham's Bosom,* which he considers too negative to be popular or profitable, the play wins Pulitzer Prize in 1927 (db, 105).

1927–1928 Begins singing tour with Lawrence Brown, and they sign a new agent, Walter K. Varney, who had managed the Fisk Jubilee Singers (db, 105, 106). On October 27, Robeson departs with Brown for year-long concert tour of Europe, beginning in Paris (pf, 29; db, 106). On November 2, son, Paul Robeson, Jr., is born (pf, 29; db, 110), and he returns to New York on December 26 to see Eslanda and baby (db, 112). "All Time All-American College Eleven" votes in Robeson (pf, 29). In March and April, performs in two plays: as Crown in *Porgy,* by Du Bose and Dorothy Heyward; and as Joe in London production of *Show Boat,* by Jerome Kern and Oscar Hammerstein II, where he creates sensation singing "Ol' Man River" (pf, 29; db, 113). (He will continue in *Show Boat* through March 1929, despite Equity Association's one-month suspension of him in August for failing to honor contract with producer Caroline Dudley Reagan; dispute will be settled by $8,000 fine the following summer [db, 117, 118].) July 3, performs concert with Lawrence Brown at the Drury Lane theater in London. Concert is sensational. In September, Eslanda's mother and Paul, Jr., move to England (db, 118).

1929 Signs on for Lionel Powell's Celebrity Concert Tour in Europe. Begins first concert tour of British cities and Central Europe with Lawrence Brown (pf, 29; db, 120–121). Despite invitation by top London society, encounters racial discrimination and is refused admission to London hotels (through 1930). Creates furor, and major hotels state they will not refuse admission or service to Black people (pf, 29). Gives concert with Lawrence Brown at Albert Hall in London (pf, 29; db, 121). In November, returns to US to begin first full-scale American concert tour. Sings inaugural concert to sell-out audience at Carnegie Hall (pf, 29; db, 125).

1930 Begins second concert tour with Lawrence Brown of British Isles and Central Europe (db, 129). March 20–30, appears in experimental silent film *Borderline* with Eslanda, made in Switzerland (pf, 30; db 130). In April, opens to raves in the title role of Shakespeare's

Othello at Savoy Theatre, London (pf, 29). In June, performs two shows of *The Emperor Jones* in Berlin (pf, 30; db, 132). Back in US, Art Alliance of Philadelphia refuses to display Antonio Salemme's statue of nude Robeson in Rittenhouse Square (pf, 30; db 69). Eslanda publishes the first biography of her husband, *Paul Robeson, Negro* (Doubleday and Doran Publishing Company) (pf, 30; db, 121), and Robeson appears in British *Who's Who* (pf, 30). In October to December, he again tours British provinces (db, 143).

1931–1932   On May 11, returns to London, but falls ill from strain of touring followed immediately by rehearsals for O'Neill's play *The Hairy Ape*, which he is to perform at the Ambassador Theater (db, 148, pf, 30). He is bedridden for a week; the play closes after five shows (db, 149). By December 30, sails on the *Olympic* for the US (db, 155). On January 18, performs first concert of new two-month US tour at Town Hall, New York. His new repertoire of songs in Russian (a language he sang in because he felt there was a "kinship" between Russians and people of African descent) is well received (db, 149, 156, 157). On May 20, he stars in a *Show Boat* revival on Broadway, which receives much praise (db, 159). He receives $1,500 a week. By June 1932, the Robesons announce their plans to divorce, but reconcile after Robeson's mistress, Yolande Jackson, breaks off their engagement (db, 160, 163). Receives Honorary Master's Degree from Rutgers (pf, 30; db, 161). In September, returns to England (db, 162).

1933   Between rehearsals for *All God's Chillun* in London (db, 165), he returns in May to New York and stars in his first talkie and commercial film of *The Emperor Jones* (pf, 30; db, 167). In August, studies singing and languages in London, and meets African students there, including Kwame Nkrumah and Jomo Kenyatta. The Robesons become honorary members of the West African Student's Union. After he performs benefit of *All God's Chillun* for Jewish refugees, Robeson comments that this marked the beginning of his political awareness (pf, 30). In September speaks at Socialist Club of Cambridge University (pf, 30). Tells reporter for *Film Weekly* that American culture is distinct because of Black contribution (js, 1; db, 169).

1934   In January declares publicly that Nazi oppression is horrible (db, 178). He enrolls in the School of Oriental Studies at London University, to study African linguistics. Also focuses on phonetics and African folk songs (pf, 30; db, 170), and extends repertoire beyond Negro spirituals to include Mexican, Scottish, Hebrew, Slavonic, and Russian folk songs (pf, 30; db 178). That summer he plays Bosambo, an African tribal chief, in film of Edgar Wallace's *Sanders of the River*, directed by Zoltan Korda. However, Robeson is disgusted by the final version of the film, which glorifies British imperialism (pf, 30; db 178–179). In December, tells the press that he will someday move to Africa (db, 176). In keeping with his new appreciation for his African past, he announces he will no longer sing classical music, but will focus on "trying to find an Art that is purely Negro, that is not dependent on Western and European influences" (db, 176). In December, the Robesons visit the Soviet Union to witness the Soviets' treatment of minorities and to discuss making a film (pf, 31; db, 183).

1935   Begins two-month concert tour in Europe, including the English provinces, Scotland, Ireland, and Wales (db, 191). April through May, performs in two plays: the title role in *Basalik*, about an African chief who defies European advances (db, 192); and in Paul Peters and George Sklar's *Stevedore*, about interracial labor unity (pf, 31; db, 192). Declines honorary position of Lord Rectorship at Edinburgh University, due to travel plans in Africa and Asia (db, 193). In September, returns to US to make Hollywood film production of *Show Boat* (pf, 31; db, 194).

1936   In January returns to London. Records song for Joseph Bust's *Africa Looks Up*, a documentary on South Africa (js, 1; db 202). In March, performs as Toussaint L'Ouverture in C.L.R. James's *Black Majesty* (pf, 31; db, 197). Starts reading socialist and Africanist writings (js, 1; db, 198). He begins making two films: *The Song of Freedom*, based on Claude Williams and Dorothy Holloway's *The Kingdom of the Zinga*; and *King Solomon's Mines*, based on H. Rider Haggard's novel (pf, 31; db, 203, 207). *Show Boat* opens internationally and is praised in the mainstream press, but criticized by the Black press and leftists. Robeson later vacations alone in the Soviet Union, planning to improve his Russian (db, 205). December to January, in travels to Soviet Asia and Caucasus, is impressed by racial minorities' progress in these areas. Also performs four-city concert tour in Moscow,

Leningrad, Kiev, and Odessa (pf, 31; db, 208). Paul, Jr., enters a Soviet Model School after his father insists that his son will not be subjected to the racial oppression he experienced as a child (db, 208). *Song of Freedom* opens to mixed reviews.

1937 In January, founds with Max Yergan the Council on African Affairs, to aid national-liberation struggles in Africa (pf, 31). Performs in two films: J. Elder Wills's *Big Fella*, based on Claude McKay's *Banjo* (pf, 31; db, 207), and *Jericho* (released in US as *Dark Sands*) in Cairo, Egypt, about an American soldier who remains in Africa after World War I (pf, 31; db, 209). Sings in and contributes prologue to Joseph Best's documentary *My Song Goes Forth*. April, appears in concert at the Victoria Place, London, to assist homeless children and women in Spain (db, 210). In Soviet Union most of summer (db, 210); he supports several causes: for Spain's Republicans against Franco's fascists; appears at London concert to benefit Basque refugee children (pf, 31; db, 212). In August, back in US, speaks against Japanese aggression in China. Attends benefits for the *Daily Worker* and the Friends of the Soviet Union (db, 212). That fall, announces he will perform theater only in the working-class Unity Theatre, ". . . it gives me the chance to act in plays that say something I want to say about things that must be emphasized" (db, 213). *King Solomon's Mines* opens to mixed reviews. In December, makes several more appearances in support of the Republic while the civil war in Spain rages (db, 213).

1938 From January in Spain, supports the Republic, and sings in three hospitals for troops of International Brigade in Benicasim (pf, 32; db, 216, 217). Paul, Jr., transfers to Soviet School in London (db, 221), where his father sings at several political rallies (db, 222). Through June, appears in Ben Bengal's play *Plant in the Sun*, about a successful interracial sit-down strike, produced by Unity Theatre under auspices of British Labour Party (pf, 32; db, 223). Sings Soviet Anthem at a rally organized by the Emergency Youth Peace Campaign (db, 222). June 27, speaks out at a rally to welcome Jawaharlal Nehru to London (db, 225). August, on tour with Lawrence Brown in British provinces (db, 226). September, announces in London: "I am tired of playing Stepin Fetchit comics and savages with leopard skin and spear" (db, 227). December, sings for the Welsh National Memorial Meeting at Mountain Ash for Welsh members of International Brigade fighting in Spain (pf, 32; db, 227).

1939 In January, participates in mass meeting at Empress Hall, London, greeting two British battalions that had fought for Republican Spain (pf, 32). In April, with Brown performs concerts in Oslo, Copenhagen, and Stockholm that are anti-Nazi demonstrations (db, 228). Returns in June to US, where he makes two appearances: in short-run revival of *The Emperor Jones* in White Plains, NY (pf, 32; db, 228), and in concert supporting Spanish Intellectual Aid (Spanish Culture in Exile) in New York City (db, fn 42, 646). Meets with Benjamin Davis, Jr., a Black Communist, to help register Black voters in Birmingham, AL (db, 230). Returns to London in July for four-weeks at a "nature-cure" rest home improving his health. He supports Soviets even after Nazi-Soviet Pact (db, 231). September to October, having finished filming *The Proud Valley* (to be released in 1940 in UK and 1941 in US), about Black miner in Welsh mines (pf 32; db, 28, 232, 239), heads for New York. Announces that Britain and Western Europe intend on saving Germany from Hitler's plans and collectively joining against the Soviet Union. Robeson condemns "those Munich Men" for abetting fascism in Spain and Czechoslovakia, and describes the Soviet Union's march into Poland and Finland as defensive responses to the encroachments of Western imperialists (db, 234). November 5, appears in *Ballad for Americans* in CBS radio's "Pursuit of Happiness" series, a huge success (pf, 32; db 237).

1940 In January, records *Ballad for Americans* for Victor Talking Machine (db, 237), stars in Roark Bradford's play *John Henry* (db, 238), and receives an honorary Doctor of Humane Letters from Hamilton College (pf, 32; db, 238). May through August performs in revival of *Show Boat* with the Los Angeles Civic Light Opera Association (cast facilities are segregated) and at the Lewisohn Stadium in New York (db, 239, 240); in *Ballad for Americans* at Hollywood Bowl, to crowd of 30,000, an attendance record there (pf, 32; db, 240); in two-week revival of *The Emperor Jones*, directed by Jimmy Light (db, 240); and in song at interracial Camp Wo-Chi-Ca, for children of workers who had established a Paul Robeson Day (db, fn. 17, 649). In September, joins board of eight, including Richard Wright, Max Yergan, Alain Locke, and others, to establish Negro Playwrights Company. Sings at inaugural celebration with pianist Hazel Scott before 5,000 at the Golden Gate Ballroom,

Harlem (pf, 33; db, 243). That fall, begins concert tour with Clara Rockmore, leading theremin player (db, 243). In October, records blues hit "King Joe" with Count Basie Band (a rare blues attempt) (db, 177), and sings at Carnegie Hall, first indoor concert in nearly five years (db, fn 17, 649). In November, sues San Francisco restaurant Vanessi's for racial discrimination, but case is never tried (db, 244).

1941   Becomes Chairman of the Council of African Affairs; Max Yergan is Executive Director (db, 257). In January, FBI agent reports that Robeson is "reputedly a member of the Communist party" (db, 253). Signs recording contract with Columbia Masterworks (db, 239). March through December, several public appearances: "Free Earl Browder" rally, Madison Square Garden (Browder, CPUSA party leader, had recently been sentenced to prison for violating passport regulations) (db, 249); April 25, sings to 6,000 at the Uline Auditorium, Washington, DC, to support the Washington Committee for Aid to China, sponsored by the National Negro Congress (NNC) (db, 252); May 19, at United Auto Workers, CIO organizing drive, downtown Detroit, days before "showdown" with Henry Ford (pf, 33; db, 249); December, sings for inmates at San Quentin Prison (db, 51, 654), and speaks at a "Defend America Rally," Los Angeles, sponsored by the NNC and with the assistance of "100 leading Negro citizens." In July 7, is made honorary member of the National Maritime Union (pf, 33). September, radio broadcast "Salute to the Champions," supported American troops in World War II (db, fn 51, 654).

1942   January, attends a "Salute to Negro Troops" to honor African American war heroes at the Cosmopolitan Opera, New York (db, fn 51, 654). February 20, midway through a concert in Kansas City, he stops to note the segregation of the audience, announces he is continuing under protest (pf, 33; db, 256). March through April, public appearances include: March 7, Bethel A.M.E. Church, to support Black families of Sojourner Truth Housing Project, Detroit (pf, 33); March 22, guest of honor at dinner "in tribute to Anti-fascist fighters," Biltmore Hotel, New York (db, fn 51, 654); April, with Eleanor Roosevelt to honor Mary McLeod Bethune, director of the Black division of the National Youth Administration, at the Southern Conference for Human Welfare event in Nashville (db, 259); April 8, addresses mass meeting in New York to organize African Americans and colonial people against Fascism (pf, 33). Performance in film *Tales of Manhattan*, controversial Hollywood depiction of poor Black sharecroppers, leads Robeson to announce later he will no longer act in Hollywood movies (db, 260). Narrates documentary *Native Land*, film reenacting civil-liberties violations by government officials (pf, 33; db, 261); joins celebrities, including Marian Anderson and Joe Louis, at the first interracial war bonds rally in Detroit (db, fn 51, 654). In May 17, he receives citation from Henry Morgenthau, Jr., Secretary of the Treasury, for "distinguished and patriotic service to our Country" (db, fn 51, 654). On June 22, participates in a Madison Square Garden rally to support Russian War Relief (db, 253). Performances July through August include: Robin Hood Dell concert, Philadelphia, where he refuses to sing a requested song because it offends the "colored race" (db, fn 53, 655); and two *Othello*s, his first US performance of it at Brattle Hall, Cambridge, MA (pf, 33; db, 263), and at McCarter Theater, Princeton, NJ (db, fn 9, 658). In September, Earl Schenck Miers's novel *Big Ben*, based on Robeson's life, is published (pf, 33). Martin Dies, head of House Un-American Activities Committee (HUAC), includes Robeson on a list of presumed "Communists" (db, 261). Throughout September and October, he appears at several rallies: September 2 in Manhattan to support the Free India movement, sponsored by the Council on African Affairs (db, 266); September 15, sings and speaks to aircraft workers of Local 887, UAW-CIO, at the North American Aviation plant in Englewood, CA (pf, 33; db, 266); at Booker T. Washington School in New Orleans, LA (db, 266); and again, at mass rally, "Salute to Our Russian Ally," in Madison Square Garden (db, fn 12, 659). In October, he, Lawrence Brown, and Clara Rockmore begin longest US concert tour, through April 5 (db, 267).

1943   In January and February, receives honors: Abraham Lincoln Medal for notable and distinguished service in human relations (pf, 34; db, 281), and along with eighteen others, a distinguished service award from the Schomburg Collection of Negro Literature (NYPL) (db, fn 13, 659). April 30, FBI issues a card for the custodial detention of Robeson (subject to immediate arrest in case of national emergency) (db, 254). In May and June, appears at two rallies: Labor for Victory Rally, Yankee Stadium (with Mayor La Guardia participating) (db, 267), and Negro Freedom Rally at Madison Square Garden (pf, 34). On

June 2, receives honorary degree of Doctor of Humane Letters from Morehouse College, Atlanta (pf, 33; db, 267), and on June 10 delivers commencement speech at the Manual Training School, urging Blacks to support interracial unionism (db, fn 36, 652). In July, performs with Robert Shaw's Collegiate Chorale and the Philharmonic Orchestra, at Lewisohn Stadium (db, 268). Rallies through August include singing and speaking at a Production for Victory rally, Apex Smelting Co. plant in Chicago (db, 268); a rally to benefit the Joint Anti-Fascist Refuge Committee in Los Angeles (db, 268); and a CIO-sponsored conference on national and racial minorities in San Francisco (db, 268). That August, FBI labels Robeson a "leading figure in the Communist Party" (db, 254). In September and October, takes *Othello* to New Haven, Boston, Philadelphia, before opening on Broadway, October 19, in Theatre Guild production (pf, 34; db, 275). November 12, receives honorary lifetime membership in International Longshoremen's and Warehousemen's Union (pf, 34). November 16, addresses the first session of the New York *Herald-Tribune* Forum on Current Problems as chairman of Council of African Affairs (pf, 34). December 3, presents plea before Baseball Commissioner Kenesaw Mountain Landis to remove ban against African Americans in major leagues (pf, 34; db, 282).

1944   In January, made honorary member of State, County and Municipal Workers of America, CIO, who in May create the Paul Robeson Scholarship Fund at New York University to educate Black students in business management (pf, 34). April 9, celebrates 46th birthday with 7,000 guests at 17th Regiment Armory in New York City (pf, 34; db, 284). April 14, delivers opening statement at a conference on "African—New Perspectives," sponsored by the Council on African Affairs (pf, 34; db, fn 6, 666). Will begin seven-month cross-country tour with *Othello* in September, except to segregated audiences (pf 34; db, 286, 294, 295). Honors include Gold Medal from the American Academy of Arts and Sciences in May (pf, 34; db 281; fn 3, 665), and on July 4 *Billboard* magazine's Donaldson Award for Outstanding Lead Performance in *Othello* (pf, 34; db, 281, fn 3, 665).

1945   In April, becomes co-chairman of the National Committee to Win the Peace (db, 304). Honored in: May, award from the Negro Newspaper Publishers Association (db, fn 28, 669); June, honorary degree, Howard University, Washington, DC (pf, 34; db, 294); and October, NAACP's annual Spingarn Medal, the highest award to a Black person (pf, 35; db 301). Rally appearances include: Madison Square Garden, June 25, to support Fair Employment Practices Committee (pf, 34), and again, November 14, for World Freedom Rally (db, 301). Performance tours are: August, first overseas interracial USO tour, singing for American troops in Germany, France, and Czechoslovakia (during the tour he is disturbed at seeing Nazi concentration camps) (pf, 35; db, 297–298); and September, seven-month American concert tour with Lawrence Brown (db, 302). In November, addresses Central Conference of American Rabbis at the Institute on Judaism (pf, 35; db, 301). Eslanda Robeson's book, *African Journey*, is published (db, 295).

1946   Appears with Marian Anderson at rally for South African famine relief at Harlem's Abyssinian Baptist Church (pf, 35; db, 304). In spring, Council on African Affairs condemns Churchill's "Iron Curtain" speech (db, 305). Joins pickets, July 17, at Dodge plant, Windsor, Ontario (pf, 35). In September, active against lynching: September 12, condemns it at a Madison Square Garden rally, where he states: "The leaders of this country can call out the Army and Navy to stop the railroad workers, and to stop the maritime workers—why can't they stop the lynchers?" (db, 305); September 23, leads Crusade Against Lynching, Washington, DC, with 3,000 African Americans and sympathetic whites (pf, 35; db, 306); he and seven others meet with President Truman to discuss antilynching legislation (db, 307). October, becomes vice president of the Civil Rights Congress. William L. Patterson, longtime friend and CPUSA member, is executive secretary (pf, 35; db, 311). Visits West Coast with Revels Cayton on behalf of the National Negro Congress (db, 310). In October, testifies before Senator Jack B. Tenney's Joint Fact-Finding Committee on Un-American Activities in the California Legislature (pf, 35; db, 307), and addresses strike meeting as co-chairman of National Committee to Win the Peace, sponsored by Committee for Maritime Unity in San Francisco, CA (pf, 35). In December addresses national Convention of Alpha Phi Alpha Fraternity, Incorporated, criticizes Western imperialism and suggests possibility for a new third party (db, fn 23, 673).

1947   In January, begins four-month concert tour with Lawrence Brown (db, 316). In March, announces he will stop giving concerts for two years and will sing only for unions and college friends (pf, 35; db, 317). His HUAC citing creates problems: in February, his car wheel is loosened and flies off car in St. Louis (db, 317); in Peoria in April, he is prevented from singing (db, 318); but next month, a Supreme Court ruling says the Albany Board of Education cannot deny him permission to sing at Philip Livingston Junior High (pf, 36; db, 319). In June performs four concerts in Panama Canal Zone for United Public Workers of America, CIO (UPW). Subsequently establishes Canal Zone scholarship fund for the education of Black teachers (pf, 36; db, 320). Continues union activities, picketing in January with the Civil Rights Congress (CRC) of St. Louis against segregated facilities in the city's theaters (db, 317), and in June speaking on behalf of predominantly African American Local 22, Food and Tobacco Workers, in Winston-Salem, NC (pf, 36). Also that month, speaks to Southern Negro Youth Congress in Miami, FL (db, 320). He is honored in October with award from Artists, Writers, and Printing Workers Congress of Bucharest, Romania (pf, 36). In November, presides over meeting of eighteen Black leaders in the Harlem branch of the NAACP to coordinate antilynching efforts (db, 323). On December 20, supports Henry A. Wallace for US presidency (pf, 36; db, 324).

1948   In January, joins Henry Wallace on a Chicago platform after Wallace announces his presidential candidacy from the newly formed Progressive Party. At Progressive Party nominating convention in July, he turns down calls of "Robeson for vice president" (pf, 36; db, 324). But he travels the South with Wallace's campaign, in the face of lynching threats (pf, 37; db, 326–327), shares platform with Wallace at Madison Square Garden in September (db, 321), and speaks at Progressive Party rally in Chicago, condemning the NAACP for dismissing Du Bois (db, 334). During spring, he is active against Mundt-Nixon Bill, which requires registering Communist Party members and "Communist Front" organizations: testifies at US Senate Judiciary Committee hearings on it, and joins picketers outside the White House to protest the bill (pf, 36; db, 328, 330). Later in June, entreats artists and writers at a Manhattan Center dinner, sponsored by *Masses & Mainstream* magazine, to oppose the bill, which does not come to a vote in Senate (pf, 36). March, tours Hawaiian Islands for International Longshoremen's and Warehousemen's Union accompanied by Earl Robinson (pf, 36; db, 327). His spring appearances include: concerts at Symphony Hall, Boston, and Lewisohn Stadium, New York City, both to large crowds (db, 321). However, several places deny Robeson the opportunity to speak (db, 327). May 26, Council of African Affairs suspends cofounder Max Yergan after he accuses the organization of being run by Communists (db, 333). June 2, National Non-Partisan Mass Delegation to Washington is launched (out of the eighteen men who met in November 1947). More prominent leaders come aboard, including Mary Church Terrell, Benjamin E. Mays, and Coleman Young; however, the NAACP remains disinterested (db, 324). In August, joins Du Bois and others to establish the Committee to End the Jim Crow "Silver-Gold" System in the Panama Canal Zone (db, fn 12, 680).

1949   In January attends legislative conference of Civil Rights Congress in Washington, DC (db, 337). January 28, at protest meeting called by the Negro Youth Builders Institute, Inc., speaks out on the widespread hostility against the colored minority (pf, 37). February, starts four-month concert tour in England because US tour canceled due to red-baiting (pf, 37; db, 338). March 25, Participates in conference sponsored by the South African Committee of India League to protest apartheid in South Africa, held at Friend's House, London (pf, 37; db, 340). His April 20 speech at World Congress of Partisans of Peace in Paris has lasting repercussions: his remarks are distorted by the US press, quoting him as saying African Americans should not fight in a war against the Soviet Union. Anti-Communists are hostile to him and a host of Black leaders repudiate him, including, notably, Jackie Robinson, who tells a July 18 HUAC meeting Robeson's remarks seem "silly" (pf, 37, 38; db, 341, 360). In a Stockholm concert, Robeson explains poor treatment of Blacks in America, following a Soviet song that is booed (db, 349). April 30, Walter White, Executive Secretary of the NAACP, tells the State Department of Blacks' basic patriotism, but suggests Robeson exemplifies extreme disappointment among African Americans toward the US government's civil rights efforts (pf, 37; db, 343). Other African American leaders, headed by A. Philip Randolph and Bayard Rustin, organize a meeting to denounce Robeson's statements (db, 344). That July prominent Blacks, including Charles S. Johnson, Fisk University President, and Lester Granger of the Urban League, will testify before the HUAC, declaring Robeson did not speak for his race at Paris. NAACP denounces hearings (pf, 38; db, 359). In May travels to Warsaw, Poland, singing at two factory concerts and before a large stadium crowd (pf, 37; db, 352). Speaks five times in Oslo for groups like the Norwegian-Russian Society and the World Federation of Women for Peace (db, 350). June, in Moscow, becomes aware of arrests of Jewish friends and in concert declares the deep cultural ties between American Jews and Soviet Jews (db, 353). June 14–16, publishes three-part series, "Two Worlds," in *Komsomolskaya Pravda*, journal of Communist Youth in USSR (pf, 37). On return to US, he condemns press for distorting his statements while he was overseas. Announces his support for the Communist leaders on trial in Foley Square. June 19, Paul Robeson, Jr., marries Marilyn Paula Greenberg (pf, 38, db, 355), and Paul Sr. hurts a press agent in trying to push him out of the wedding-party car (db, 356). At his welcome home rally of 5,000, sponsored by the Council on African Affairs, he denounces American leadership and politics in dealing with Blacks at the Rockland Palace in Harlem (pf, 38; db, 357–358). In a *Time* June 27 interview, he "praises [the] beauty of Moscow" and emphasizes that "Africans will liberate themselves in near future" (pf, 38). June 29, participates in protest rally at Madison Square Garden sponsored by the Civil Rights Congress (pf, 38). August 4, joins UPW, CIO, picketing the White House to protest employment discrimination by Bureau of Engraving and Printing (pf, 38; db, 363). August 27, riots begin at Robeson concert in Peekskill, NY, and he is prevented from singing; many in audience are injured by rock throwers (pf, 38; db, 364). August 28, Westchester Committee for Law and Order is formed to protect subsequent performance (db, 366). August 30, participates in Golden Gate Ballroom rally in Harlem to protest Peekskill riots. September 2, two effigies of Robeson are hung at night by Peekskill rioters (db, 368). September 4, Peekskill concert is successful, but afterward chaos ensues and 140 are injured. In response to the lack of protection offered by police, Robeson condemns the attack as fascist, considering lack of police protection; he will sue rioters in November (pf, 38; db, 369, 372). Testifies at trial of eleven Communist leaders in Foley Square, however, is prevented from saying more than that he knows the defendants (pf, 38; db, 372). September 25, begins speaking and singing tour sponsored by Council on African Affairs (pf, 38; db, 375). His relations with Soviets warm: October, USSR names Mount Robeson in his honor (pf, 39); November 10, speaks at a banquet sponsored by National Council of American-Soviet Friendship, favoring peaceful relations with Soviets, Waldorf-Astoria, New York City (pf, 39; db,381).

1950   In February, delivers address at Progressive Party national convention in Chicago (pf, 39; db, 383). March, Robeson becomes first American banned from TV when NBC prevents him from appearing on Eleanor Roosevelt's scheduled program, *Today with Mrs. Roosevelt* (pf, 39; db, 384). May, speaks and sings to 20,000 at a meeting of the World Peace Council at Lincoln's Inn Fields in London (db, 386). May 6, *Afro-American* 1950 National Honor Roll, sponsored by Afro-American Newspapers, selects Robeson (pf, 39; db, 385). June 10, addresses delegates at Chicago meeting of National Labor Conference for Negro Rights (later published as pamphlet, *Forge Negro-Labor Unity for Peace and Jobs*) (pf, 39; db, 387). June 28, speaks out against US participation in Korean War at Madison Square Garden rally (pf, 39; db, 388). June–August, passport struggles: Refuses to yield passport as requested by agents of State Department. In response to his counsel's query, chief of the passport division states: "The Department considers that Robeson's travel abroad at this time would be contrary to best interests of the United States." Meets with State Department officials, but he will not be allowed passport unless he signs affidavit denying he is a Communist; he refuses. That December, he will file civil suit in US District Court in Washington, DC, against the State Department in the name of Secretary of State Dean Acheson demanding the return of his passport and claiming that the cancellation of it prevented him from making a living abroad (pf, 39; db, 388, 389, 393). December, first column in Robeson's monthly newspaper, *Freedom*, appears (pf, 39; db, 392). Cables greetings with W.E.B. Du Bois, William Patterson, Ben Davis, and others to Joseph Stalin during his seventieth birthday (db, 383).

1951   In January, becomes honorary member of the National Negro Labor Council (newly founded in Cincinnati to fight for jobs and against segregation) (db, fn 47, 714). Sponsors the American Peace Crusade with Thomas Mann and others (pf, 39). Black criticism of Robeson: in February, Walter White, NAACP executive, writes negatively on him in *Ebony* magazine (pf, 40; db, 394). In December, NAACP's publication, *The Crisis*, attacks Robeson (Roy Wilkins later admits being editorial's author (db, 395), and New York *Amsterdam News* omits him from a list of previous Spingarn Medal winners (db, 396). Passport troubles continue: in April, US District Court upholds State Department's ruling and dismisses Robeson's suit; he will appeal the decision in August (pf, 40; db, 396). June 5, his grandson, David Paul Robeson, is born (db, 397). Active speaker at rallies: June 29–July 1, addresses 5,000 in Chicago rally hosted by the American Peoples Congress for Peace, where he criticizes the First Amendment violations of the Smith Act and US action in Korea (db, 397); in November, speaks at a Conference for Equal Rights for Blacks in the Arts, Sciences, and Professions, and in a rally for world peace with Soviet Ambassador Alexander S. Panyushin and Corlis Lamont, sponsored by National Council of American-Soviet Friendship, both in New York City (pf, 40). December 17, presents petition to UN as head of New York delegation of Civil Rights Congress, charging the US with genocide against Black people (pf, 40; db, 398).

1952   January 31, under orders of the State Department, Immigration and Naturalization Service officials prevent Robeson from crossing the Canadian border from Blaine, WA, in order to speak at a meeting of the Mine, Mill and Smelter Workers' Union in Vancouver, BC. Facing stiff penalties, he speaks and sings to the meeting by telephone from Seattle (pf, 40; db, 399). April 6–June 2, birthday tour raises $1,500 to aid National Negro Labor Council, Council on African Affairs, and *Freedom* (pf, 40; db, 403). May 18, performs for as many as 40,000 listeners at a Peace Arch Park on US-Canada border (pf, 40; db, 400). In July, attends Progressive Party's national convention in Chicago (db, 405). On October 15, Peace Liaison Committee for Asian and Pacific Peace, chaired by Madame Sun Yat Yen, elects Robeson vice chairman (pf, 40). In December, Othello Recording Company, managed by Paul Robeson, Jr., and Lloyd Brown, releases the album *Robeson Sings* (db, 409); and he receives 1952 Stalin Peace Prize, but State Department denies him permission to travel to accept it (pf, 40; db, 406).

1953   Granddaughter, Susan Robeson, is born (db, 408). In January, the National Church of Nigeria names him "Champion of African Freedom" (pf, 41). In February, he and six others appeal to parole board for release of Benjamin J. Davis, a Black Communist imprisoned under the Smith Act (pf, 41). His wife's mother, Eslanda Goode, dies in the spring, and he sells his house in Enfield, CT (db, 412). His performances continue: in April speaks and sings to 6,000 at Sacred Cross Baptist Church in Detroit under sponsorship of Freedom Associates of Detroit (pf, 41), and in June begins second nationwide concert tour to benefit Freedom Association (pf, 41; db, 409). July 5, performs outdoor concert for 25,000, sponsored by Freedom Associates of Chicago, in Washington Park, Chicago (pf, 41). While he is on tour, Eslanda testifies before Senator Joseph McCarthy's Senate Investigating Committee (db, 412). In August, Passport Office denies him permission to travel to European engagements (pf, 41; db, 414).

1954   Othello Recording Company releases new album, *Let Freedom Sing* (db, fn 47, 714). Robeson sings in the film *Song of the Rivers*. March, denounces to the press US intervention in Guatemala and in African countries (db, 424). A campaign on his behalf: spring, "Let Robeson Sing" begins in England (db, 424–4255); May 24, artists, including Thelonious Monk, Pete Seeger, and Lorraine Hansberry, sponsor a "Salute to Paul Robeson" at the Renaissance Casino (db, 425). Passport troubles: July, State Department rejects his application. Hires new lawyers, plans to appeal to the Supreme Court (db, 425); in November he will again be denied passport to attend Soviet Congress of Writers Conference in Moscow (pf, 41). In August, performs at Third Annual Peace Arch Concert (db, 425). Moves into brother Ben Robeson's parsonage in Harlem that winter (db, 427).

1955   Othello Recording Company releases new album, *Solid Rock: Favorite Hymns of My People* (db, fn 47, 714). In February, testifies before a joint state legislative committee, investigating "Communist-front" organizations (db, 430). Several performances: March, two sold-out shows at the First Unitarian Church of Los Angeles (front wheel of car flies off while driving in Los Angeles, the second apparent attempt on his life, to be followed by two more mysteriously unhinged wheels in 1958); and in April, performs and speaks at City College of New York (having been prevented four years earlier), and at Swarthmore College, Pennsylvania (pf, 41; db, 431); and in summer sings at Fourth Annual Peace Arch Concert (db, 433). Passport difficulties continue: May 10 application is denied because he will not sign an affidavit stating he is not a member of the Communist Party. He reapplies in June, in the wake of a US Court of Appeals decision to reinstate passport of Max Schachtman, of the Independent Socialist League (db, 432). Although State Department promises "careful and prompt" attention, on August 16, US District Judge Burnita S. Matthews of Washington, DC, refuses to order the State Department to issue passport to Robeson without his signing a non-Communist affidavit. Robeson refuses (pf, 41; db, 433). In June, the Council on African Affairs and *Freedom* are disbanded (pf, 41; db, 437). In fall, he has prostate surgery (db, 435).

1956 In February, leaves US for first time in six years, attending the national Mine, Mill convention in Sudbury, Ontario, and performing to a capacity crowd in Massey Hall, Toronto (pf, 41; db, 437). In March, suffers a urinary-tract infection and emotional collapse (db, 437). Throughout year, passport troubles persist: July 13, testifies under subpoena before the HUAC, investigating "passport irregularities by Communist sympathizers." Committee tries to cite him for contempt when he calls them "the real Un-Americans" (pf, 41; db, 442). In November, Supreme Court refuses to hear his arguments for an appeal of the Appellate Court decision on his passport, arguing he has not exhausted all "administrative remedies" to reinstate it (i.e., he has not signed the non-Communist affidavit) (db, 444). Suffers indignities: in August, he is attacked by mostly Hungarian "egg-and-tomato-hurling hecklers"at a peace rally sponsored by the National Council of American-Soviet Friendship (db, 443); and in November newest edition of *College Football and All-American* omits him from a list of players on the 1918 Walter Camp All-American team (pf, 42). His public appearances include several with Black political groups on a three-day visit to New Jersey; and November at the 39th Anniversary of the October Revolution at the Soviet Embassy, Washington, DC (db, 443), a celebratory event he will repeat in 1957 (db, 453).

1957 In spring through fall, active supporting school desegregation: attends Prayer Pilgrimage in Washington, DC, celebrating 1954 *Brown v. Board of Education* decision; in July tells press he supports Martin Luther King, Jr., and the Montgomery Bus Boycott; in September, demands that federal government defend Constitution against segregationists in Little Rock, AR (pf, 42; db, 447). Uses technology to give concerts despite his passport problems: May 26 performance for a London audience, sponsored by the National "Let Paul Robeson Sing" Committee, and December 19 for Welsh at 1957 Eisteddfod, he sings via transatlantic cable connections (pf, 42; db, 449). May 29, attends State Department hearing to discuss passport, and that summer is allowed to travel where passport is unnecessary in Western Hemisphere (db, 450, 451). In summer, six-week California tour for left-wing concerts (db, 448), including Comeback Concert to a packed audience at the Third Baptist Church, San Francisco (pf, 42). In December, speaks at American-Soviet Friendship annual event, Carnegie Hall (db, 453).

1958 His sixtieth-birthday year marked by celebratory events: in February attends 20th Anniversary of the publication *People's World,* and gives Negro History Week speech before Local 6 of International Longshoremen's and Warehousemen's Union (pf, 42). On March 17, Indira Ghandi, Indian Prime Minister Jawaharlal Nehru's daughter, organizes "Paul Robeson Day" in Delhi, despite US Embassy attempts to prevent it (pf, 42; db, 461). The day itself is celebrated in several foreign countries (pf, 42; db, 461). April marked by performances for African American churches in Pittsburgh (db, 455), and a social event in Chicago sponsored by Alpha Phi Alpha Fraternity Inc. (db, 436), as well as a public meeting in Chicago's Parkway Ballroom (db, 457). May concerts are at Ben Robeson's church, Mother A.M.E. Zion (db, 462), and first New York concert in ten years to capacity crowd at Carnegie Hall, following which he tells audience that he has won his passport battle (pf, 42). With passport restriction lifted in June by Supreme Court ruling in a related case (db, 463), makes concerts and appearances abroad for rest of 1958: In July, agrees to two TV concert series, and holds a press conference at the Empress Club in West End to large turnout (pf, 42, db, 464–466). In early August, Lawrence Brown arrives to join Robeson in an Albert Hall concert and later British tour (db, 476), and performs in National Eisteddfod in Ebbw Vale, Wales. Autobiography *Here I Stand* published in four countries after no noteworthy American publisher would publish it (pf, 43; db, 458). Mid-August, begins Soviet tour, greeted by enthusiastic crowds at Vnukovo Airport and the Metropole Hotel, and is interviewed on Moscow TV (pf, 42; db, 467). Sings at Lenin Sports Stadium,

Moscow, to 18,000 (pf, 42, 43; db, 467, 468). August 26–September 14, meets with Premier Nikita Khrushchev near Yalta, and receives honorary professorship at the Moscow State Conservatory of Music (pf, 43; db, 469). British tour with Lawrence Brown, September 17–October 11 (pf, 43; db, 470), ends with historic service at St. Paul's Cathedral. Appearing before an audience of 4,000 plus 5,000 standing outside, Robeson sings the first secular song at the Cathedral and is the first person of African descent to stand at the lectern (pf, 43; db, 471). In winter, Vanguard Records re-signs Robeson (db, 460). On December 29, flies to Moscow with Eslanda, W.E.B. Du Bois, and Shirley Graham Du Bois (db, 473).

1959   Attends gala dinner at the Kremlin New Year's Ball hosted by Khrushchev (pf 43; db, 473). In mid-January, begins three-week Kremlin Hospital stay for exhaustion and circulatory problems, followed by month's recuperation at Barveekha Sanatorium, then departure for London (pf, 43; db, 473, 474, 475). In April, starts highly successful seven-month run of *Othello* at Stratford-on-Avon, ending November 26 (pf, 43; db, 477, 482). While in London, participates in the African Freedom Day concert in April, sponsored by the Movement for Colonial Freedom; in May, appears on two BBC TV programs and is featured on ten Sunday-night radio broadcasts (db, 479, 481). Sales of *Here I Stand* reach 25,000 copies (db, 460). May 11, Becomes vice president of the British-Soviet Friendship Society (pf, 43). Summer travels in Europe: to attend the Congress of Socialist Culture in Prague; the World Youth Festival in Vienna with his son and daughter-in-law, an event attended by 17,000 from 82 countries (pf, 43; db, 479); and gives an interview to the Hungarian Telegraph Office en route back to London (db, 480).

1960   January–February, three-week Moscow visit with Eslanda, including one-week stay at Barveekha Sanatorium. Also participates in World Peace Committee sessions. Speaking and singing appearance for workers at Ball Bearing Plant No. 1 in Moscow (pf, 43; db, 482). On return to London in February, makes a second series of BBC radio broadcasts (db, 483), and participates in a ban-the-bomb rally in Trafalgar Square (db, fn 47, 737). February 21, begins thirty-two-city British concert tour with Lawrence Brown, attends the London *Daily Worker*'s 30th anniversary celebration, and May Day Miners' Gala in Edinburgh, Scotland, where he receives Scottish Miners Lamp (pf, 43; db, 483). June–October appearances and awards in Europe: press festival in East Berlin, sponsored by *Neues Deutschland*, organ of Communist Party (db, 483), and in Paris, for 40th anniversary of the Communist paper *L'Humanité* (db, 486). In October, receives honorary Doctor of Philosophy, Humboldt University, German Democratic Republic (GDR), and prizes from East German peace movement (pf, 43; db, 486). Attends gala of 5,000 at the Central Youth Club, GDR, and is first person to receive the Order of the Star of International Friendship, pinned on him by Chairman Walter Ulbricht. October–November, final concert tour with Lawrence Brown to Australia and New Zealand (pf, 43; db, 487). Peace reception in his honor in Sydney (db, 490). Views a fifteen-minute film about the plight of the aborigines in the Warburton Ranges. Later comments: "The indigenous people of Australia are my brothers and sisters" (db, 490). On return to London in December, declares his singing-tour days are nearly over (db, 491).

1961   In January, meets privately with Kwame Nkrumah (db, 492). March 5, sings and speaks at the 31st anniversary of the *Daily Worker* at Albert Hall (db, fn 67, 741). March–April, solo visit to Moscow, where he begins stay at hospital due to serious illness, and at Barveekha Sanatorium (pf, 44; db, 500). May, brief visit from Chinese Ambassador to the USSR. Back in London following month, begins work with Lawrence Brown on their music (db, 500). Kwame Nkrumah's invitation for Robeson to chair music and drama at the University of Accra, Ghana, must eventually be turned down (db, 500–501). Summer, back in Barveekha Sanatorium for three months (db, 502), Robeson remains sick and in treatment for depression through the next year.

1962–1963   Following his wife, and pressured by friend John Apt (CPUSA member), Robeson signs non-Communist affidavit, under the McCarran Act, to protect his right to remain in London (db, 510). False article appears the following January in *The National Insider*, purportedly by Robeson, claiming he was Communist, Socialist, and Fascist at various times (db, 512). February, Robert Rockmore, friend and business manager (since 1932), dies suddenly. In May, Eslanda writes an official rebuttal of the bogus article (db, 513). In July, his brother, Rev. Benjamin C. Robeson, pastor for twenty-seven years of Mother

A.M.E. Zion Church, Harlem, dies at seventy (pf, 44; db, 519). August 25, London *Sunday Telegraph* article claims Robeson had "broken with Moscow" and was about to be kidnapped and detained in East Berlin indefinitely (db, 515). He and Eslanda depart for East Berlin's Buch Clinic, seeking special medical attention. A *Sunday Telegraph* reporter intercepts Robeson, asks him about claim, and about the March on Washington. Robeson sends his congratulations for the successful march (db, 516). August 26, Harry Francis, close friend, denies Robeson is disillusioned with Socialist countries, calls *Telegraph* article "sheer nonsense"(pf, 44;db, fn 47, 749). September–October, Buch doctors diagnose Paget's disease (a bone disorder) in Robeson, though it is unclear how much the disease stems from a physical or psychological condition (db, fn 50, 751), and in Eslanda, terminal cancer. Robeson is not informed of his wife's fatal condition (db, 518). December 7, tells Eslanda that he wants to return to the US to assist the Black struggle and spend time with his grandchildren (db, 520). December 22, returns to US after five years and five months abroad (pf, 44; db, 521).

1964   January, FBI, under J. Edgar Hoover's instructions, renews investigation into Robeson's activities (db, 522). August 22, Benjamin J. Davis, close friend and Communist leader in Harlem, dies at sixty of cancer. Robeson speaks at his funeral (pf, 44; db, 525). August 28, first public statements following his return to the US, on the anniversary of 1963 March on Washington, he states: "We're moving" (pf, 44; db, 525). November, attends a USSR reception at the United Nations, and makes surprise appearance at a National Council for American-Soviet Friendship celebration at Carnegie Hall (db, 526). Speaks briefly and receives a five-minute standing ovation from the audience. Gives a short speech at the seventieth birthday party of John Howard Lawson, the "dean of the Hollywood Ten" (db, 527).

1965   January–February: makes public statements about the death of Claudia Jones, Black Communist leader (db, 527); appears at celebration of Alexander Trachtenberg's eightieth birthday and the fortieth anniversary of the International Publishers at the Statler-Hilton dinner; delivers eulogy at playwright Lorraine Hansberry's funeral. Speaks at fund-raising party of the Upper West Side W.E.B. Du Bois Club, a Marxist youth group of the New Left (db, fn 15, 755). March, at celebration of *Freedomways'* publishing Robeson's "The Legacy of W.E.B. Du Bois" (pf, 44; db, 527), sings for the first time in four years. April 22, *Freedomways* hosts a "Salute to Paul Robeson," a sixty-seventh-birthday celebration at the Hotel Americana, New York (pf, 44; db, 527). John Lewis, chairman of the Student Non-Violent Coordinating Committee (SNCC), delivers a statement: "We of SNCC are Paul Robeson's spiritual children. We too have rejected gradualism and moderation. We are also being accused of radicalism, of communist infiltration" (db, 528). May, Robeson travels to Los Angeles with Eslanda. Several appearances: speaks and sings at a celebration in his and Eslanda's honor at Stephen Fritchman's First Unitarian Church (db, 530), attends packed meeting at Mt. Sinai Baptist Church, a fund-raiser for *People's World* (db, 531), and for Du Bois in San Francisco (db, 532). By June, Robeson and Eslanda, too ill to make more appearances, return to New York, where he suffers psychological setbacks (db, 532). June 11–July 1, Robeson at Gracie Square psychiatric hospital (db, 533). Eslanda enters Beth Israel Hospital for cobalt treatments, and on August 10, surgery. With cancer rampant, she is given only months to live (db, 534, 535). August 7, Robeson returns to Gracie Square psychiatric hospital (db, 535); suffering near-death experience with double pneumonia, kidney blockage, and reaction to medication, he is transferred to the superior University Hospital. September, Robeson and Eslanda return home (db, 537). October, Robeson enters Vanderbilt Clinic, Presbyterian Hospital, for facial lacerations and other bruises, after being found unconscious near Highbridge Park. Leaves the hospital days later (pf, 44; db, 538). November 23, Eslanda enters Beth Israel Hospital, where she dies on December 13, two days before her seventieth birthday (pf, 44; db, 538). In December, Robeson moves to Philadelphia to live with his sister, Marian Robeson Forsythe, a retired schoolteacher (db, 539).

1966   February, returns to New York to live with Paul, Jr., and Marilyn (db, 540). March, attends a benefit dinner for SNCC, where James Farmer celebrates him: "We all know of your part in the struggle for Freedom and it was a great privilege to be able to tell you how much you mean to all of us" (db, 540). Spring–fall, alternates living with sister Marian in Philadelphia and Paul, Jr., and Marilyn in Manhattan, finally settling with Marian (db, 541).

1967–1968   In winter, *Who's Who in American History* includes Robeson's biography. He enters University Hospital in Philadelphia (db, 542). Following April, Robeson's birthday is celebrated internationally in Britain, GDR, and the USSR (db, 543).

1969–1970   Rutgers University dedicates new student building, the Paul Robeson Music and Arts Lounge in April (pf, 45; db, fn 12, 760). The following February, receives the Ira Aldridge Award from the New York Chapter of the Association for the Study of Negro Life and History (db, 543). April, Paul, Jr., speaks at rededication ceremony for the Paul Robeson Music and Arts Lounge, sponsored by the Eastern Region of Alpha Phi Alpha Fraternity, Inc., and Rutgers Student Center (pf, 45; db, fn, 760). November honors: *Black World* publishes C.L.R. James's tribute, "Paul Robeson: Black Star"; receives the Zhitlovsky Award by Zhitlovsky Foundation for Jewish Education (pf, 45). Local 1199, Martin Luther King, Jr., Labor Center sponsors the opening of its new headquarters with "A Tribute to Paul Robeson." Artists such as Ossie Davis, Ruby Dee, and Pete Seeger participate (pf, 45; db, fn, 12, 761).

1971   Beacon Press reprints *Here I Stand* with preface by Lloyd Brown (pf 45; db, 543). In spring, Columbia Records releases *Paul Robeson in Live Performance* (db, fn 12, 761). April 8–9, speakers, including William L. Patterson and Lloyd Brown, participate in a two-day Paul Robeson symposium to celebrate his seventy-third birthday in Berlin, GDR (pf, 45; db, fn 12, 761). April 9, Rutgers University President Edward J. Bloustein announces the renaming of the Newark-Rutgers Student Center to the Paul Robeson Student Center, through efforts of the Harambee Organization, a Black student group (pf, 45; db, fn 12, 760). The Black House, on the Rutgers–New Brunswick campus, is renamed the Paul Robeson Cultural Center. December, Dizzy Gillespie hosts a "Tribute to Paul Robeson and Black Culture" at the Princeton University Chapel (db, fn, 12, 761). December 25, Lawrence Brown, Robeson's accompanist and companion for many years, dies in Harlem Hospital (pf, 45; db, 547).

1972   In April, Association of Black Psychiatrists honors Robeson for being a role model to Black youth (pf, 45; db 544). August, *Ebony* magazine lists Robeson as one of "ten most important Black men in American history" (pf, 45; db, fn 12, 761). Awards: Whitney M. Young Memorial Award from the New York Urban League (pf, 45; db, 544); the Ellington Medal from Yale University for outstanding Black musicians and singers (db, fn 12, 761); NAACP's Image Award for "brotherhood" (db, 544).

1973   In April, Rutgers University holds a symposium on Robeson's life (db, 547). On April 19, Rutgers confers an honorary Doctor of Humane Letters degree upon Robeson; Paul, Jr., accepts for his father. April 15, Paul, Jr., organizes "Salute to Paul Robeson" to celebrate Robeson's seventy-fifth birthday before a capacity audience at Carnegie Hall (pf, 45; db, 546). April 16, Gallery 1199 of Drug and Hospital Workers' Union opens a "Salute to Paul Robeson" Exhibition (pf, 45). June 3, honorary Doctor of Law from Lincoln University, first Black college in US and father's alma mater; Paul, Jr., accepts the award (pf, 46; db, 547). July, Black Sports Hall of Fame honors Robeson for his athletic achievements (db, 547).

1974   FBI reports "no further investigation is warranted" of Robeson (db, 547). Congressional Black Caucus honors Robeson with its Special Award of Merit (db, fn 20, 762). June, receives first annual award named for him by the Actor's Equity Association, AFL-CIO (pf, 46; db, fn 12, 761).

1975   In June, Charles H. Wright's book, *Robeson, Labor's Forgotten Champion,* is published. December 28, Robeson enters Presbyterian Medical Center in Philadelphia after mild stroke. With his condition deteriorating daily, a second and final stroke follows less than a month later.

1976   On January 23, Paul Robeson dies at seventy-seven (pf, 46; db, 548). January 27, 5,000 attend funeral service at Mother A.M.E. Zion Church in Harlem (pf, 46; db, 549). Buried at Ferncliff Cemetery, Hartsdale, NY, adjoining graves of Eslanda Goode Robeson and Lawrence Brown.

PAUL ROBESON

1. Paul Robeson speaking at the American Labor Conference. New York. 1954.
Photo © by Julius Lazarus.

Jeffrey C. Stewart

INTRODUCTION

Something beyond the watch and din of Cold War warriors and politically correct radicals has occurred in the scholarship of Paul Robeson (1898–1976) in recent months, and the first fruits of this new approach to this African American artist and McCarthy era martyr are collected in this volume of essays. For decades, the serious study of Paul Robeson's life and career has been mired in heated controversies between attackers from the Right who have claimed that Robeson's unswerving support of the Stalinist Soviet Union obliterated everything of value that existed in his career and defenders from the Left who remembered him as a political hero whose life and career were above investigation or reproach. Now, however, with the Cold War over and the former Soviet Union again an ally (though in capitalist development not antifascism this time around), the politically charged climate of opinion that demanded we demonize or deify Paul Robeson has abated. Moreover, a new and fresher interest in Robeson has emerged in the interdisciplinary work of a new generation of scholars, artists, and political analysts who approach Robeson and his accomplishments from the vantage point of their work in art history, film criticism, musicology, cultural studies, legal and political theory, and the New Labor History. Under the auspices of Rutgers University's Paul Robeson Cultural Center and a National Endowment for the Humanities research grant, some of these scholars came together with other historians, collectors, and personal friends of Robeson to begin an intergenerational, interracial, and multidisciplinary discussion about the place and significance of the life of Paul Robeson in American culture. The first fruits of that discussion are this volume of essays, *Paul Robeson: Artist and Citizen.*

Even by today's standards, Paul Robeson, the All-American football player, Phi Beta Kappa Rutgers College graduate, and world-renowned actor, singer, and motion picture star was one of the most talented Americans of the twentieth century. Enormously versatile, Robeson played three years of professional football after college, earned a law degree from Columbia University, and then starred in Eugene O'Neill's plays, sang his way onto the most prestigious American and European concert stages, headlined three productions of *Othello*, and created enduring roles in such movies as *The Emperor Jones* (1933), *The Song of Freedom* (1936), and *Proud Valley* (1940). But Robeson was also an African American, who reacted against negative representations of Blacks[1] in his films *Sanders of the River* (1935) and *Tales of Manhattan* (1942) by criticizing racism in the media and ultimately refusing to make more films. But what made Robeson controversial was his willingness to step outside the frame which usually contains the work of artists and use his status as an artist to advance a complex program of civil and human rights changes around the world and in the United States. Not only was Robeson motivated by a desire to excel at whatever he did, whether it was the intricacies of catching a pass as a tight end in football or the particular pronunciation of English during Shakespeare's time, but he was also propelled by a desire for humane treatment of all people, which formed the basis of his commitment to socialism, to the African Liberation Movement, and to exposing racism and human-rights violations in the United States. As such, Robeson became, in the 1930s, a robust political intellectual, who shaped the Leftist critique of fascism, capitalism, and the Cold War, and ultimately sacrificed his success and his health to continue to speak out against injustice during the McCarthy era. His commitment to speaking out about the plight of Black people in America and the nature of oppression worldwide became a symbol of the activism of the Civil Rights movement and the anti–Vietnam War movement that followed in his footsteps.

On one level, this volume of essays serves as a catalog to the interpretive exhibition, retrospective film series, and other outreach programs Rutgers University has inaugurated to celebrate the centennial anniversary of Robeson's birth. But in another sense, the authors in this collection, while celebrating Robeson's outstanding life and accomplishments, want this book to be something more. We wish this volume to inaugurate a new openness in the discussion of the life and the meaning of the life of Paul Robeson, more than has existed before. For most of the years since his death in 1976, Paul Robeson has been more of a problem than a person, a thing to be debated, argued and fought over, rather than a life to be understood.

Philip Dean Hayes's play about Paul Robeson, starring James Earl Jones and produced on Broadway, was picketed and protested by a cadre of Black artists, friends, and family members who deemed the play "unrepresentative" of Robeson.[2] In 1976, Harold Cruse's critique of Robeson for performing in relatively few plays written by Black playwrights launched a vitriolic exchange of articles between him and another historian, Sterling Stuckey, who debated publicly whether or not Paul Robeson was a Black nationalist.[3] Even as recently as 1988, when Martin Duberman's meticulously researched *Paul Robeson: A Biography,* appeared, it was criticized by a few for not capturing the "true" or "real" Paul Robeson. Such controversy is certainly understandable when one has a larger-than-life African American personality like Robeson's, who was vilified by large sections of the white American public, harassed by federal and state government agencies in the United States, and condemned by the Black establishment during his most difficult years. With such a figure, it is legitimate to feel protective, but such policing of Robeson's memory has made it difficult to understand the process by which Robeson became such a pivotal figure in the culture and politics of mid-twentieth-century America.

How should we proceed to achieve that greater understanding? We believe that the best way is to have a discussion devoid of censorship of what the scholars, friends, and associates of Paul Robeson are allowed to say in this volume. Here the reader enters a conversation that has gone on for several months now among honest people who value the memory of Paul Robeson, but acknowledge that they approach that memory in different ways, and believe that it is in that difference that something of the diversity of Paul Robeson can be sought. For such a man's life raises more questions than can be answered in any book, let alone a volume of essays. As the historian Page Smith wrote in his biography of John Adams, "a book is at best a poor contrivance to catch a life in." What we aim to catch, however, is some of the spirit of interrogation which is Robeson's legacy, a willingness, an intellectual quality characteristic of his mind, to investigate, to uncover, and to probe each issue that came before him. We see ourselves as heirs to Robeson not in following any particular ideology that he espoused, but in practicing the intellectual integrity he lived, to follow out to the inevitable conclusion the logic of our ideas. Hence, in this volume is a chorus of diverse voices, not all of whom sing Robeson's praises, but which rather raise the kinds of concerns that he himself voiced during his long and fruitful life.

Over the course of our discussions, three broad themes surfaced that are recorded in this volume of essays. First, there was a group of us who see Robeson as a hero, especially to the African American community, and as Charles Blockson suggests in his essay, "Paul Robeson as a Bibliophile," as a hero to a generation of African American men for whom he was a symbol of self-conscious and courageous Black manhood, a man who "stood up to the man" with integrity and honor, despite the horrific pressure brought to bear on him. This sense of Robeson as a hero also essays in the first section of the book, "Early Life, Athletics, and Citizenship," especially in the excerpted chapter, "Happy Black Boy," from Lloyd

Brown's recent biography, *The Young Paul Robeson* (1996). Brown, a novelist, an ally, and a close friend of Paul Robeson, captures the closeness of Robeson's ties to the Black community, and the valuation of him by the community of his origin, which recognized something special in him from his early youth. Black people early perceived that he would be, in one sense or another, a representative for them in the larger society; and Robeson, as Brown suggests, never forgot that obligation, never let them down. The sense of Robeson as the Hero in History also shapes some of the evaluation of Robeson's importance as a scholar-athlete in Francis C. Harris's essay, "Paul Robeson: An Athlete's Legacy," in which he chronicles the formative process by which Robeson became an athletic hero at Rutgers and a scholarly hero in the classroom. In this sense, Robeson was a hero of a type that we seldom see today—a man who was both a superlative athlete and a superlative intellectual. Further evidence for some of these sentiments about Robeson's rising to the challenge posed to all heroes to meet the terrors of their journey comes through in Derrick Bell's essay on "Doing the State Some Service," as one of our foremost legal minds of the late twentieth century details the role of moral leadership and engaged citizenship that such athletes as Robeson, John Carlos, and Tommie Smith have provided to our nation. Bell's essay, along with Julianne Malveaux's "What Is Robeson's Contemporary Legacy?" provide us with an opportunity to examine what Robeson's case has to tell us about the plight of talented African Americans, especially athletes and entertainers, who face a moment of decision as to whether to use their celebrity to advance a social agenda. What these authors suggest is that whatever the ideological positions and transitions of Robeson's public identity vis-à-vis the Soviet Union or Communism, a strong element in the African American community viewed him as a hero and continues to view him as a hero today, in large part for his courage in representing the interest of Black peoples, as he conceived it, honestly and with integrity throughout his life.

Related to the role that superlative Black athletes and celebrities have played in our culture is a second theme that emerged among our discussants, and that is the concept of representation, that is, the notion that how we are seen in the media determines how we are treated in the larger society. They investigate this theme by considering Robeson's struggle with the reality that this concept signifies, from the 1910s through the 1970s. Here, in the second section of the book, "Visual Arts, Drama, Music, and Film Contribution," the newer note in this approach to Robeson comes from scholars, influenced by recent trends of poststructuralism, postcolonialism, and deconstruction in media studies, who are more interested in the interrogation of Robeson's films, photographs, and dramatic performances for what they reveal about the problem of representation for African American actors and celebrities throughout the twentieth century. Robeson rose to stardom in the 1920s and 1930s in a system of representation by which Black people were portrayed using dehumanizing stereotypes, meaning fixed, recurring images of people of African descent as lazy, stupid, comic, and uncivilized, in popular American and European culture. Robeson was the first African

American intellectual of the twentieth century to struggle self-consciously against this system of representation of minorities in American popular culture as a practicing performing artist himself whose livelihood was directly dependent on the media he was critical of. Photography historian Deborah Willis shows in her essay, "The Image and Paul Robeson," what Robeson was up against. For Willis suggests a tension exists between the notion of Robeson as a man, as a heroic leader of his people, and some of the images of Robeson that have come down from us from his photographs, his plays, and his films, especially those from the 1920s and 1930s. In seeking to understand the source of that tension, Willis reads Robeson's images for what they say about the racial dynamics of "performing the primitive" in the 1920s and 1930s, a requirement of Black actors of the time that Robeson entered into and ultimately rebelled against. Film historian Charles Musser elaborates on that struggle in his essay, "Troubled Relations: Robeson, Eugene O'Neill, and Oscar Micheaux" by considering Robeson's controversial role in Eugene O'Neill's play and film, *The Emperor Jones,* by contrasting it with Robeson's experience working with African American film director Oscar Micheaux on *Body and Soul,* Robeson's first motion picture. Musser shows that some members of the African American community of the 1920s were critical of Robeson's performance in *The Emperor Jones,* partly because of O'Neill's characterization of African Americans, and partly because some saw Robeson as less resistant to O'Neill's misconceptions of Negroes than was Charles Gilpin, the originator of the role. As evidence of this discontent, Musser reveals the extent to which Micheaux's film, *Body and Soul,* can be read as a critique not only of *The Emperor Jones,* but also of Robeson's role in it, and suggests that the not-so-subtle critique by Micheaux of Robeson was one of the factors in the Robesons', both Paul and his wife Eslanda's, not referring to that film afterward. That helps explain one of the puzzles I came across while curating this exhibition: in the materials for *Borderline,* the experimental film the Robesons made in Switzerland in 1930, there is a reference to the effect that *Borderline* was Robeson's first film! Musser's analysis provides a convincing explanation of how that misrepresentation came to exist.

Music historians Doris Evans McGinty and Wayne Shirley show in their essay, "Paul Robeson, Musician," how Robeson's performance of his first solo concert devoted to spirituals affected the representation of that musical genre in the larger culture. Here the issue is more than simply making the spirituals into a more acceptable concert item. What Robeson did was not only validate the spirituals as fine art, but also validate African American folk culture as itself the centerpiece of American culture at a time in our cultural history when the search for an authentic, native, and vibrant American national culture had reached a fever pitch. Even more subtly, Robeson also represented himself as a Black intellectual in this choice of concert material, for he affirmed his own roots as the son of a former slave who was proud of and preserving that heritage in the act of performing it. Similarly, Martin Duberman, the author of the critically acclaimed biography, *Paul Robeson: A Biography,* strikes a similar note in the chapter excerpted here, "Robeson and *Othello,*" from his book on Robeson's performance of *Othello,* especially in London in 1930. For that performance was, in the words of the Delany sisters who saw Robeson perform in 1930, the first time that *Othello* had been performed in the twentieth century as a Black play, as expressive of the Black condition in modern life, again echoing Derrick Bell's title, of the Black "doing the state some service," as a citizen for his nation, and then being betrayed by one of its citizens, because of race.[4] That interpretation of Shakespeare's play as essentially a commentary on the modern racial condition is something that Robeson, and Ira Aldridge before him, brought to the role.

In his essay on Robeson's British films entitled "Race, Working-Class Consciousness, and Dreaming in Africa: *Song of Freedom* and *Jericho,*" film historian Mark A. Reid addresses the underlying problem faced by Robeson and other Black actors when they sought out tragic roles in film. Reid acknowledges that Robeson's performances in such films as *Sanders of the River* (1935) and *King Solomon's Mines* (1937), which even Robeson later admitted were justifications for colonialism, were problematical. But Reid suggests that in two British films, *Song of Freedom* (1936) and *Jericho* (1937), Robeson did find heroic roles that matched his own aspirations for representing Black people on film. But Robeson ultimately failed to find many other roles on film that matched his already enormous stature in real life as an international personality. As Reid states, the problem was larger than Robeson. By the 1930s, the motion picture industry had become in the United States and Europe such a highly capitalized structure of production and distribution that no actor, certainly no Black actor, could really bend it to his or her social agenda. Robeson was a performing artist at a crucial moment in American cultural history, when technological innovation transformed entertainment in America from a participatory to a consumer industry, when the primacy in American culture shifted from the manipulation of words to the manipulation of images, and the prevailing role of art as a mirror of society gave way to the primacy of entertainment delivered to thousands and eventually millions of people through the economics of cultural production in the motion picture, concert singing, and legitimate theater world. Reid suggests, therefore, that we try and understand Robeson's image—his representations—in the context of the structures he struggled within as a performing artist on film in the 1930s and 1940s. In my essay, "The Black Body," I take up the issue of how a performing artist tries to appropriate the representations that the culture has imposed on him or her and to manipulate them in such a way that they can be turned into ideological weapons for a different agenda, one that became increasingly important for Robeson in the late 1930s and early 1940s—a transformative social agenda.

That leads us into the third theme that emerged among our group, the theme of citizenship as it relates to Paul Robeson, raised throughout the book, but specifically addressed in the essays collected under "Political Activism and Final Years" and "Robeson's Contemporary Significance." The newest political interest in Robeson is away from his pro-Sovietism and more toward a recovery of Robeson's contribution to a redefinition of

American citizenship as an adherence to the founding principles of American democracy and solidarity with a multiethnic labor community that has built this country. This renewed interest is a response to the political and economic situation of African Americans at the end of the century. The problem today is no longer whether or not Robeson was a Black nationalist. The reality of late-twentieth-century America is that neither liberal integrationist nor Black separatist ideologies have brought freedom to the masses of Black people in America. The failure of liberal integrationism to improve the quality of life for lower-class African Americans is well known, although today's National Association for the Advancement of Colored People (NAACP), the organization which led the attack against Robeson in the Black community during the 1950s, still champions that ideology in the face of nationwide resegregation in American schools, churches, and neighborhoods. And though the recent ascendancy of Louis Farrakhan with the Million Man March has resurrected Black religious separatism as a utopic solution, the pervasive poverty, social decay, and psychological malaise of America's sprawling Black ghettos suggest that self-segregation of America's largest colored minority cannot lift that community out of the cellar of America's economy. The new interest in Robeson, therefore, comes out of a recognition, belated in some quarters, that something else, whether something new or something old, needs to be tried to break the cycle of optimistic integrationism and nihilistic separatism that dominates America's racial politics. Thus, rather than emphasizing Robeson's Sovietism, the newer political interest focuses on the kind of interracial, labor-based, multiethnic, economic-structure-altering movement that Robeson argued was required to solve America's most intractable racial problems. However impractical sounding, one of Robeson's contributions as a citizen of the United States was to work through a series of ideological solutions to the problem of race in America and to advance a solution that was consistently antiracist, antiseparatist, and anticolonialist in its orientation.

Historian Mark D. Naison leads off our discussion of Robeson's twentieth-century politics in his essay, "Paul Robeson and the American Labor Movement," by shifting the evaluation of Robeson's contribution as a political thinker away from the question of whether he was correct in his analysis of the Soviet Union and its treatment of minorities under Stalin (which we now know was deeply flawed) and toward a more important question: how did Robeson's work for labor and democracy in America during the 1940s and 1950s reinterpret what it means to be a citizen? What Naison finds is that rather than being a hopeless romantic about the Soviet Union, Robeson returned to the United States in 1939 after an extensive residence in London with a coherent and comprehensive vision of American citizenship as based on the labor of those African American, Mexican American, Asian, and European immigrant peoples who have built this country with tears and the sweat of their brows. The tragedy of Robeson for Naison is that his articulation of this radical labor notion of American democracy was derailed in the 1950s by the Communist witch hunts, riots, and harassment, which extended not only to Robeson, but to all those—African

American, Jewish, Catholic, unionist, and antiracist—who found a place under Robeson's multicultural, multiracial, economically democratic tent. In a subtle way, Naison also contributes to our discourse on representation, for his essay is an attempt to transform the representation of Robeson and by doing so to reignite the kind of prolabor, pro–African American, pro-collective-struggle movement toward a more tolerant notion of American citizenship than that which dominates in 1990s America, with its demands that, for example, English be made the official language of the United States.

In his essay, "Comrades and Friends," Gerald Horne also revises our conception of Robeson as an isolated individual, who acted alone when he articulated the vision of America that Naison describes. Horne details how Robeson was part of a cadre, really a generation of African American intellectuals, who were born around the turn of the century, grew up during the Black Progressivism of the NAACP and W.E.B. Du Bois's *Crisis* magazine editorials in the 1910s, matured during the Harlem Renaissance of the 1920s, and moved to embrace the Marxist interpretation of modern history that became popular among almost all American intellectuals during the 1930s Depression. It was the group of intellectuals around Robeson whom Horne credits as serving as a critical intellectual community that challenged him about his representations of African peoples in his films, and moved his consciousness toward a radical conception of himself as a cultural worker who could employ his international prestige as an artist to advance a radical egalitarian social agenda. Moreover, Horne, like Bell, suggests that Robeson and his colleagues performed a generally unacknowledged role in the Civil Rights movement of the 1940s and 1950s by serving as the bogeymen for the NAACP and other gradualist organizations to scare President Harry Truman and the Warren Supreme Court into granting modest Civil Rights concessions in order to thwart the so-called Black Communist threat. Recent revelations about the effort of then NAACP legal counsel and later Supreme Court Justice Thurgood Marshall's attempt to meet with FBI Director J. Edgar Hoover to alert him to the "Communist threat in the Civil Rights movement," lend credence to the notion that Robeson and other Black leftists were used to advance the cause of a broader and more just American citizenship at the same time that they were defined by both white and Black leaders as disloyal to their country.

Robeson's Achilles heel as a political leader in the 1940s and 1950s was his love affair with the Soviet Union, which David Levering Lewis probes in his essay, "Paul Robeson and the U.S.S.R." Lewis shows that the core of that love affair derived from the same emotional sources in Robeson as it did for other African American intellectuals infatuated with Russia during the 1930s—a sense that the Soviet Union had advanced far beyond the United States in its treatment of Black folk, at least the Black artists and intellectuals like Robeson who traveled there beginning in the 1930s. What made Robeson different from other Soviet sympathizers like Langston Hughes and Adam Clayton Powell, Jr., among others, was that Robeson remained loyal to the Soviet Union after it was no longer fashionable, after the end of the Second World War, when the demand from Truman and other leaders of what President Eisenhower later termed the military-industrial complex was that all true American citizens suddenly start hating the Soviet Union after being told to love it during the war. The problem was that Robeson did not desert friends when it was no longer convenient to have them and that quality, normally considered exemplary in a citizen, became a noose around Robeson's neck in the 1940s. As Lewis points out, Robeson was never convicted or even accused of any act of sabotage, conspiracy, or threat against the United States, at a time when he was probably the most heavily wiretapped, monitored, and invaded human being in the United States. All that he did was to speak his mind, reputedly a right of American citizenship.

In some respects, the closing essays by Julianne Malveaux, Ed Guerrero, and John Hope Franklin combine and renarrate the themes that have been introduced so far. Not only does Malveaux, in her essay, "What Is Robeson's Contemporary Legacy?" consider Robeson a hero because he was willing to sacrifice his career to fight for social justice, but she also engages the question of citizenship in a provocative way, suggesting that Robeson was precisely the kind of globally minded citizen that America needs to remember today. Rather than the kind of globalism that affirms the right of the Kathie Lee Giffords and the Michael Jordans to lend their names to companies that exploit the cheap labor of children in foreign countries to leverage celebrity careers in the United States, Robeson, Malveaux suggests, was the kind of Black athlete, artist, and icon who identified with the workers of the world as part of a transnational community that deserves the same kind of moral respect of rights that American citizens are promised. Indeed, Malveaux sees Robeson's embrace of a class analysis of oppression as key to his ability to break out of the prisonhouse of racial self-glorification that has entrapped the analysis of many other so-called "radical" Black leaders and to forge links with oppressed peoples around the world. Thus, Robeson emerges here as a symbol of the kind of responsible citizenship and global self-consciousness that is as desperately needed by America's rich African American athletes and celebrities as by anyone else in America.

Indeed, the irony of the O. J. Simpson case and the excommunicated Black celebrity who is not particularly concerned about the larger Black community or his representation of it in the media prompts film historian Ed Guerrero to see, in "Black Stars in Exile," parallels between the public excoriation of Robeson and Simpson, despite their ideological and intellectual differences. Robeson's career is a narrative of the price of celebrity and fame for all Americans, but also, specifically, for African American celebrities, who make a number of compromises in their lives and dignity in order to become the popular icons that America celebrates, but just as quickly assassinates when they deviate from very narrowly prescribed social and cultural norms. Guerrero suggests what it means to be a fallen hero in the race wars of celebrity that have become a symbol of the larger racial conflict that still grips the culture, a conflict over what place to allow the Negro to occupy in a society that is rapidly experiencing change and transformation in its cultural hierarchies. As African

Americans become more and more prominent as producers of twentieth- and twenty-first-century culture, Guerrero suggests, the costs of making oneself into a consumable commodity will increase; and those who venture into that cauldron of America's racial remaking ought to study the case of Robeson as a warning and a model.

Eminent historian John Hope Franklin poses Robeson as an "Icon for the Twenty-first Century" in his essay, as a model of engaged citizenship and moral responsibility that is sorely needed and desperately undersupplied in the role models of contemporary Americans. On the eve of the twenty-first century, America is again face-to-face with the problem of the color line, but also with something more—a sense and a need to re-create the moral commitment and social idealism that underlay the spirit of the Declaration of Independence, but was thwarted by the reality of American enslavement and racial practice after the Revolution. Where can America look to re-create a sense of integrity in the American Idea, that all men and women are created equal, with an equal right to fair and just treatment not only by America's institutions but also by all Americans themselves? Robeson, Franklin suggests, is a good place to start.

ARTIST AND CITIZEN: A BRIEF HISTORY

Paul Robeson's life story epitomizes what it means to be an American citizen. His maternal great-great grandfather, Cyrus Bustill, was a free-born African American merchant who supplied General George Washington's forces with food during the American Revolution. Robeson's father, William Robeson, on the other hand, was born a slave, who ran away from his plantation in North Carolina, and returned to fight in another American war, the Civil War. Two wars, two legacies, the one of the drama of fighting for American freedom, the other the reality of American slavery, define the twin poles of American citizenship, indeed, speak to the irony of what it means to be an American: all of us who call ourselves Americans are part of a country that is celebrated worldwide for its freedoms, but also a country known historically for the most devastating forms of enslavement. Paul Robeson's career as an engaged citizen was to try to force the nation of his birth to put into practice the ideals of its revolutionary beginnings, especially in its treatment of America's most abused citizens, the African Americans.

Born on April 9, 1898, into this twin legacy of his family, Paul Robeson spent his childhood in Princeton, New Jersey, where African Americans could not vote and where he attended segregated elementary schools. While in those schools, he witnessed his father losing his ministry of the Witherspoon Street Presbyterian Church because the elder Robeson would not bow and scrape to satisfy the southern traditions of deference in Princeton. But the younger Robeson also saw a father who moved his family to a new locale, built a new church, and maintained himself and his family in poverty but also in great dignity rather than give in to the powers of racial subordination in early-twentieth-century America. From his father's example, Paul Robeson learned a powerful lesson of American citizenship—that the real citizen is the man or woman willing to sacrifice everything for the sake of principle.

Paul Robeson's bond with his father strengthened as Paul met the challenges of race in school, particularly at Rutgers College, where he enrolled in 1915. There his experience in football was formative. Trying out for the team, he was stomped, beaten, and gang-tackled by white team members determined to discourage the "giant" Negro from joining the team. In one sense, this was simply the fact of segregation in American life in the 1910s, but it was also something more: college sports had emerged by the second decade of the twentieth century as a site of masculine conflict in which white men proved their Darwinian superiority over other men. By 1915, the masculine ideal in popular culture was no longer the Victorian gentleman, but the muscular and aggressive football player, whose ability to endure pain, destroy the opposition, and work together with other players epitomized the notion of life as a field of organized conflict between blindly goal-centered muscular men. And here was Robeson, a six-foot, two-inch, one-hundred-and-ninety-pound young man who was muscular, a swift and aggressive runner, an excellent catcher of the football, a superb blocker, whose body was hard as nails—a masculine ideal, who had to be kept out of the arena, lest he overturn the notion that whites were biologically superior to Blacks. Robeson faced the first major challenge of his life after his first practice, during which players had broken his nose and dislocated his shoulder. Robeson went home severely injured and thought of quitting the team. But the male coterie of his father and brother emboldened him to return. And to the inner Paul, the father's image of courage had been internalized—he would not bend, he would not be broken. When his hand was stomped on during the next practice, Robeson began knocking players to the ground and picked up one with the intent to body-slam him to the ground. Then, the coach yelled, "Robeson, you're on the team." In that moment, Robeson also manifested the character attributes of the new masculinity popularized by Theodore Roosevelt that the true man exhibited courage in the face of enormous odds. By fighting back, Robeson dispelled white supremacist notions that because they had been slaves, all Blacks were cowards. In this step, Robeson's action embodied the generational consciousness of the "New Negro," and anticipated the "fighting back" attitude of northern Blacks during the attacks on their communities by whites in the 1919 race riots. In this step, Paul Robeson had himself become a hero.

I have often asked myself, what did it feel like to be Paul Robeson? What did it feel like to be the best football player of one's day, to letter in basketball, baseball, and track, to dominate not only the field but also the classroom at Rutgers, being one of four undergraduates to qualify for admission to Phi Beta Kappa in his junior year, to be the best on the varsity debating team, to win the class oratorical prize four years in succession, to be elected to the Cap and Skull honor society in his senior year, to be valedictorian of his class, and yet to be treated as a man apart, even at Rutgers and at the same time that Rutgers celebrated his presence on campus? What did it feel like to dominate the Glee Club with his bass-baritone voice, and yet to be prevented from attending the social activities after the concerts because he was Black? Or even after Rutgers, what did it feel like to earn a law degree from Columbia University in 1923, and have a secretary at the law firm he was employed at refuse, in her words, to take dictation from a "nigger"? Certainly such things hurt, because Robeson was a sensitive man and they produced in him feelings of anger and frustration. But such feelings were counterbalanced by an internal faith in the American Ideal, as expressed in his senior thesis at Rutgers on "The Fourteenth Amendment," where he opined that if the Fourteenth Amendment "be duly observed," then "the American people shall develop a higher sense of constitutional morality." Pessimism about America was held in check by his fundamental idealism, the belief that if you simply worked hard and showed America your talent, America would accept and reward you. That idealism, really the ideology of liberal integrationism, was made plain in his valedictory address, "The New Idealism," where he stated that "We of this less favored race realize that our future lies chiefly in our own hands," but warned that white Americans must accept Blacks when they achieve. Hidden in the breast of the speaker was the rage that would ensue if a generation of talented African Americans actually believed the American ideal of inclusion of the talented, only to find their access blocked by racism. For the dashing of their idealism could lead to the kind of revolutionary rage that had inspired the Founding Fathers to overthrow their government because it did not live up to its promise.

Supplemented with the 1920s cultural pluralist ideology of the Harlem Renaissance that one can celebrate one's ethnic identity in the marketplace of American culture, Robeson's idealism carried Robeson through a successful acting career in Eugene O'Neill's plays and into a successful singing career, after his magnificent interpretations of the spirituals were discovered and vetted by Carl Van Vechten and the Greenwich Village bohemian set. But when he embarked on a nationwide singing tour in 1926, he encountered virulent racial epithets, exclusion from hotels because he was Black, and dilapidated, second-class railroad service that weakened his health and his idealism. He left us for London, which he and his wife, Eslanda (Essie) Cardozo Goode, made their home from 1928 to 1939. Eslanda, whom he had married in 1921, had a B.S. iin practical science from Teachers College, Columbia, and was granddaughter of Reconstruction leader Francis L. Cardozo. In England he could escape American racism and star in a London production of Shakespeare's *Othello* at a time when a Black could not perform that play on stage in America. But a bout with racism in London, when he was refused service at a hotel, let him know that racism was a global, not simply an American, problem. His eyes were further opened when he starred in *Sanders of the River,* an English motion picture that he believed would present a positive view of African life and custom, but was actually a deeply racist film that legitimated British colonialism by arguing that only through the intervention of a white man, Sanders, could African chieftans stop killing one another. Robeson realized that simply pursuing his art and displaying his talent would not result in movies and performances that would honor the Black experience. He learned that he could not escape the reality of race by going abroad or by confining himself to his art.

Precisely at the moment in his life when his idealism began to dim and his anger and frustration about race began to grow, he was exposed to a global political consciousness that began to allow him to make sense of his own experience and relate his feelings and experience to those of other peoples. It was in England, for example, that he was invited to sing before working-class audiences, and to realize that the plight of the English miners was analogous to that of Black miners and sharecroppers in the United States. It was in England that he saw Jewish refugees pouring in from Germany and realized that fascism was an international force as profound and as genocidal as anything he had heard about in the American South. It was in England, finally, I believe, that Robeson was exposed to an adult education and trade-union movement that the historian Raymond Williams recalled as the germination of the Cultural Studies movement, that fostered an educational awakening among workers to change their lives.[5] It was in this intellectual context, in dialogue with European and African American and African intellectuals, that Robeson began to understand the way in which cultural products, such as his films, were inextricably bound up with the broader social relations of American and British societies, and that awareness led him to realize that only by changing the social relations of modern society could an artist like himself achieve real cultural freedom. It was because he was an artist that Robeson became an activist citizen.

For unlike many others who learned these things, Robeson leapt into action: he raised money by singing for Jewish refugees; he traveled to Spain during the Spanish Civil War to sing to the Republican troops; and he returned to the United States in 1939 to work to defeat fascism and create a new vision of Americanism. Robeson electrified radio listening audiences with his performance of *Ballad for Americans*, which wedded patriotism to an appeal for racial democracy. But Robeson's patriotism was a social patriotism, grounded in a vision of an America in which people of color were allied with second- and third-generation European immigrants to build a multiracial, multiethnic, economically democratic America. During the Second World War, he sang and spoke at numerous government-sponsored rallies to encourage Black support for the war, but he also spoke at numerous rallies, concerts, and meetings of unions where he defined his vision of Americanism, one informed by his globalism, and in the process he redefined what and who is an American citizen. And Robeson was a very effective activist citizen because he was an artist—an actor, singer, and presence who moved crowds to dream and to act.

Unfortunately for Robeson, the end of the war brought a change in the political climate in America as the Truman administration identified the Soviet Union as the new threat to American freedom. Robeson, who loved the Soviet Union, refused, like his father before him, to desert principle, despite increasing evidence that Stalin was carrying out pogroms on the Russian people. As relations between the United States and the Soviet Union worsened,

American "citizens" terrorized his concerts, forced cancellation of concert bookings, snatched his records from stores, and sought to make him a nonperson. In 1950, the State Department took away his passport, ostensibly because of his Communist affiliations, but actually, as it was later revealed in a secret memo, to keep Robeson from criticizing colonialism in Africa on trips abroad. Condemnation of Robeson was so pervasive that his name was removed from the list of All-Americans in 1950. A McCarthy-led America tried to make Robeson disappear, but he would not disappear. Then, in 1956, two years before the Supreme Court ruled that the State Department denial of passports to dissidents was unconstitutional, the House's Committee on Un-American Activities hauled him before them to accuse him of being a member of the Communist Party, which he was not. His rebuttal to that committee gives a sense of the vision of this man, even in his darkest hour.

> *Mr. Arens:* Did you write an article . . . [in which you said] "Moscow is very dear to me and close to my heart. I want to emphasize that only here, in the Soviet Union, did I feel that I was a real man with a capital 'M.'"? Did you say that? . . .
>
> *Mr. Robeson:* In Russia I felt for the first time like a full human being. No color prejudice like in Mississippi, and no color prejudice like in Washington. It was the first time I felt like a human being. Where I did not feel the pressure of color as I feel [it] in this Committee today.
>
> *Mr. Scherer:* Why do you not stay in Russia?
>
> *Mr. Robeson:* Because my father was a slave, and my people died to build this country, and I am going to stay here, and have a part of it just like you. And no Fascist-minded people will drive me from it. Is that clear?[6]

Notice, here, that he did not say white people or resort to any simplistic racial formations of what was wrong with America. Instead of attacking his inquisitors because of the color of their skins, he attacked them for the content of their minds. They, he retorted, were the real UN-Americans. Robeson had been able to make the leap from his own experience to identify with other peoples' experience, from looking at the world purely through the lens of race to seeing race as part of a larger systemic problem and the solution to that problem as larger than simply a racial solution. I think that whether we agree with his particular solution or not, that he could transcend his own experience, yet hold on to it, use it, and see the commonalities with other peoples' experiences of oppression, is a triumph of the human consciousness and an example of the kind of citizenship we will need to make our own leap to the next century.

2. Paul Robeson at the *National Guardian*. c. 1947–1948.

EARLY LIFE, ATHLETICS, AND CITIZENSHIP

3. Paul Robeson. 1918.
*Courtesy of Esther Jackson/*Freedomways *magazine.*

Lloyd L. Brown

HAPPY BLACK BOY

Paul Robeson, born on April 9, 1898, in Princeton, New Jersey, was the seventh and last child born to William Drew Robeson and Maria Louisa Robeson twenty years after their marriage. (Two earlier children had died in infancy.) As a teenager, Paul's father had escaped from slavery in Martin County, North Carolina, become an honor graduate from Lincoln University in Pennsylvania, entered the Presbyterian ministry, and married Maria Louisa Bustill, a schoolteacher and member of a noted Philadelphia family of free black abolitionists. When Paul was three years old, a devastating blow came to his family: after serving twenty-two years as pastor of the Witherspoon Street Presbyterian Church, the Reverend Robeson was summarily removed from that position of community leadership by the local Establishment and had to earn his living hauling ashes for the townsfolk. A more grievous loss, occurring when Paul was six, was the death of his mother in a household accident. Nevertheless, despite those tragic events in his earliest years, there were other circumstances that made his childhood a time of carefree happiness, as recounted in this chapter from *The Young Paul Robeson: "On My Journey Now."*

4. Witherspoon Street Presbyterian Church, William Robeson's Princeton, New Jersey, church. 1952.
Photo by Betty Millard. Lloyd Brown Collection.

5. Early twentieth-century group portrait of about fifty members of the Bustill family, Paul Robeson's maternal extended family. The young boy standing in front row center may be a young Paul Robeson.
The Bustill-Bowser-Asbury Papers, Moorland-Spingarn Research Center, Howard University.

6. Parsonage of Witherspoon Street Presbyterian Church where Paul Robeson was born. Princeton. 1976. *Photo by Betty Millard. Lloyd Brown Collection.*

The ashman's youngest son was a happy child. If Paul ever grieved at the loss of the mother he did not remember, he could never have felt "a long ways from home," as did the mother-less child in the plaintive Negro spiritual he would sing in concerts. In Paul's case "home" was all around him in the black community where he was born, and indeed, as Paul said, if one were to list all of the people who helped raise him, "it would read like the roster of Negro Princeton."[1] In addition to all of those who called one another "brother" and "sis-ter" as church members and treated with avuncular fondness their former pastor's little boy, Paul was surrounded by many actual relatives in the neighborhood of Green Street. And not only were there the children of Uncle Ben and Uncle John, but there were also numerous cousins surnamed Carraway and Chance, whose parents had followed their Robeson rela-tives from Martin County to Princeton. As Paul remembered: "My early youth was spent hugged to the hearts and bosoms of my hard-working relatives. Mother died when I was six, but just across the street were my cousins the Carraways, with many children—Sam, Martha, Cecelia. And I remember the cornmeal, greens, yams, and the peanuts and other goodies sent up in bags from down in North Carolina."[2] And whenever his father's work as a coachman took him out of town (it was more than forty miles to the seaside resorts of Long Beach or Asbury Park), Paul would be left in the care of any one of a dozen different households that were like home to him.

One of those homes was visited by Paul Robeson in 1952—almost fifty years after his mother's death—when he undertook to show this writer the scenes of his childhood that he himself had not seen for many years. One of the persons on Green Street who stopped to shake his hand told him that a certain Mrs. Staton was doing poorly and asked if he would like to see her. Of course he would, he said; he was then led to a small frame house nearby, wherein a very old woman lay. So frail she barely made a mound beneath the blanket, Mrs. Staton looked up at the visitor, whose massive bulk seemed to fill the tiny bedroom, and cried out: "Paul! Paul! Oh, come here, boy!" And as he went over to kiss her, she slowly raised her arms, so thin, dry-brown, and withered, to gently embrace him. "Paul, boy," she whispered weakly, "I could crush every bone in your body!" Then as she sank back she looked at him with loving wonder and murmured, "You know, I used to hold you in my arms when you was just a little baby." Later Paul explained to me that Mrs. Staton was the sister of his Uncle Ben's wife, Huldah, and that the old lady was one of those who had cared for him as a child.

However, at the center of everything for the boy was his father's gentle love and firm direction. After the death of his wife, the Reverend Robeson sent his son Ben and daughter, Marian, to boarding schools in North Carolina, where except for vacations Ben would stay through high school and college, and Marian through high school. (Marian would later attend a training school for teachers in Pennsylvania.) Thus, with his two oldest brothers—Bill and Reeve—away at college, only Paul was always at home with his father. Under that circumstance a close bond developed between the boy and the man who was old enough to be his grandfather. Everything about the man he called "Pop" was a shining glory to Paul, whose eyes would fill with tears whenever he spoke of the man he remembered as the embodiment of human goodness. Pop's character was of "rocklike strength and dignity," and he had "the greatest speaking voice I have ever heard . . . a deep sonorous basso, richly melodic and refined."[3] Paul's lifelong habit of identifying every achievement with thoughts of his father no doubt began in childhood when he was filled with pride to walk hand in hand with Pop and to share the glow of respect and love that flashed on people's faces as they greeted the pair.

The communal love that came to Paul was also a legacy from his mother—the "Aunt Lou" of the neighborhood—who had for many years been the Reverend Robeson's active partner in the various duties they assumed in the absence of other social agencies—visiting the sick and bedridden; collecting food, clothing, and fuel for the destitute; interceding with the authorities on behalf of juvenile offenders; and finding jobs for the steady stream of refugees from the land of terror in the South. Maria Louisa Robeson had, like her husband, been greatly respected for her book-learning; she had also been a schoolteacher, an occupation that was exceeded in prestige only by the positions of pastor and school principal.

As Paul remembered it, there was something mystical and strangely prophetic in the community's attitude toward him. The people seemed to feel that there was something special about him, that he was somehow destined for big things in life. Apart from any intuitive foresight that may have been involved (and Paul would always give great weight to intuition), the people had doubtlessly come to the stock conclusion that an obedient, dutiful, and respectful child like Paul, who was being raised by a man who preached and practiced "doing right," was bound to grow up to "amount to something"—the highest level of which was to become "a credit to the race." Folk wisdom in such matters has, of course, the infallibility of "heads I win, tails you lose," because that body of knowledge encompasses many mutually contradictory ideas. Thus the black community of Princeton, which was sure the preacher's son Paul was bound for earthly glory, no doubt also firmly held to the folklore of such communities that foretold that a preacher's son was certain to go wrong. And sure enough, John Bunyan Reeve Robeson, the second oldest son in the family, did become an example to prove that rule.

When Reeve (he was nicknamed "Reed" by his family and friends) decided as a child to drop the churchly "John Bunyan" part of his name,[4] it may have been a foreboding to the Reverend Robeson that he would have trouble in keeping that independent-minded boy on the path of righteousness. For a youngster to be righteous, public school was no less important than Sunday school in the dogma of William Robeson's generation, to whom education, like Jesus, was "the truth, the light and the way." Rising from the depths of chattel slavery and aspiring to the heights of full equality, the freedmen were strong in their belief that the enforced ignorance of enslavement was a bond to be broken along with the physical shackles. Thus to the Reverend Robeson it must have been not only a keen personal disappointment but the rankest of heresies for Reeve to leave college and not graduate with the Class of 1907, with which he had started.

The circumstances of Reeve's failure are not known. If, as may happen with a preacher's son, Reeve had become surfeited with the religious environment at home, he would have found no change at college. Lincoln University, like other church-sponsored colleges for blacks, made chapel attendance compulsory, and there was little exaggeration in the complaint of students that chapel was three times every day and all day Sunday. Then too, if Reeve for certain lacked his father's do-or-die motivation to master the difficult curriculum, he may also have lacked the aptitude for study that characterized the other Lincoln graduate in the family—his brother Bill.

When the prodigal son came home, he probably did not dare say to his father that without a college diploma he was just as qualified for the work available to a black man in Princeton as was the Reverend Robeson with all three of his degrees. That obvious truth was quickly demonstrated when, with the help of his father, Reeve got a horse and carriage and became

7. "And the migrants suffered deep privation in housing." Panel 47 of *The Migration of the Negro* series by Jacob Lawrence. 1940–41. Tempera on masonite. 18 x 12 in. *The Phillips Collection, Washington, D.C.*

a hack driver. But Reeve lacked the iron self-control that such a job required. A former slave like his father had had to learn early in life that to survive he must close his mind to verbal abuse by a master. But when Ol' Massa's student-sons at Princeton spoke abusively to him, Reeve would seek to teach self-control rather than to practice it. A passenger who directed some racist epithet to that driver or sought to make him the object of some joke about "darkies" could quickly find himself hauled from his seat and reprimanded by Reeve's fists. And if a group of offenders was involved, Reeve would vigorously lay about him with the bag of rocks he always carried under his seat.

Scorning the social laws of caste behavior, the rebellious Reeve became increasingly scornful of law in general, and from time to time it became the embarrassing duty of the dignified Reverend Robeson to go to court and try to get his son out of trouble. To young Paul that wayward brother, so quick with his fists to challenge any slight, was as admirable as Bill, who was always best in his classes, or Ben, the star of the neighborhood with a baseball and bat.

As a scholar and a clergyman, the Reverend Robeson was, of course, a man of peace. He would lead community actions against injustices, but to him individual acts of violence

8. Paul Robeson on the set of *Show Boat* (Universal, 1936). c. 1935. *Courtesy of the Academy of Motion Picture Arts and Sciences. Copyright renewed 1963, Universal Pictures.*

were both futile and immoral; and Reeve must often have heard him cite Matthew 26:52, wherein the Master counseled: "Put up again thy sword into his place: for all they that take the sword shall perish with the sword." And the Old Testament made things very clear when it advised Reeve that "A wise son *heareth* his father's instruction: but a scorner heareth not rebuke" (Proverbs 13:1). The Bible likewise advised his father what to do about a heedless son: "Cast out the scorner, and contention shall go out" (Proverbs 22:10).

Reeve had to be cast out. Not mainly because of the contention caused by Reeve's scofflaw ways, but because of the Reverend Robeson's worry that his second-oldest son would be a bad example for his innocent youngest. At his father's insistence, Reeve left town.[5] Paul would never forget the advice Reeve once gave him: "Don't ever take low. Stand up to them and hit back harder than they hit you." And years after the brother's death Paul would note that though Reeve "won no honors in classroom, pulpit or platform . . . I remember him with love."[6]

When Paul was eight and a pupil at the segregated public school that his brothers and sisters had attended, his father made a momentous decision: In 1906 the Reverend Robeson changed his church affiliation from the Presbytery of New Brunswick, which had removed him as pastor five years earlier, to the New Jersey Conference of the African Methodist Episcopal (A.M.E.) Zion Church—an independent black denomination founded in New York in 1796.[7] The following year the Reverend Robeson, at the age of sixty-two (which was far beyond the average life expectancy at the time) decided to leave Princeton, where he had lived for nearly thirty years, and build elsewhere a new church in his new denomination, beginning all over again as a pastor among his people. Taking young Paul with him, the old man moved to the town of Westfield, New Jersey, which happily for his son was only about thirty miles from all his uncles, aunts, cousins, and friends in Princeton.

Westfield, though larger than Princeton, had a much smaller black population, of whom fewer than a dozen were adherents of the A.M.E. Zion denomination. Together with that little band of followers, the Reverend Robeson dug the foundation for the church building that would rise when and if the money could be raised. As the bishop who assigned him to that unpromising post must have known, William Robeson was a remarkable fund-raiser. (In their farewell tribute to him, his old congregation in Princeton had noted that he was "an excellent financier" who "in many instances came to the relief of officers and congregation when the raising of needful funds seemed an impossibility."[8]) The seemingly impossible task in Westfield was also accomplished, and in 1908, a year after the Reverend Robeson's arrival, the St. Luke's A.M.E. Zion Church was erected, together with a parsonage for the wonder-working pastor.[9]

The enormous pride and joy that must have filled the heart of the recent ashman-coachman as he rose again to a leading position did not manifest itself in any outward jubilation, and to his sensitive young son, Pop seemed as calmly impassive in his triumph as he had been in defeat. The two newcomers to the town where they would live for three years (Westfield would never seem like home to Paul as Princeton had been and Somerville would be) grew even closer together. As they had done in Princeton, the old man and the boy spent many evenings together in the parlor, playing checkers—a game that the old man loved. They would play for hours with little talk but a warm sense of companionship.

It was in Westfield that there occurred the one instance Paul could recall when he had disobeyed his father. It was a crucial event to him, and on two occasions he published an account of that boyhood transgression and its lasting effect.

> I remember . . . he told me to do something. I didn't do it, and he said, "Come here." I ran away. He ran after me. I darted across the road. He followed, stumbled and fell. I was horrified. I hurried back, helped Pop to his feet. He had knocked out one of his most needed teeth. I shall never forget my feeling. It has remained ever present. As I write, I experience horror, shame, ingratitude, selfishness all over again. For I loved my Pop like no one in all the world. I adored him, looked up to him, would have given my life for him in a flash—and here I had hurt him, had disobeyed him.
>
> Never in all his life (though this was in 1908 and I was ten; he died in 1918) did he have to admonish me again. This incident became a source of tremendous discipline which has lasted until this day [April 1952].[10]

There were too few blacks in that town to allow for a segregated public school, which was the general pattern in New Jersey, and in Westfield Paul attended school with white children for the first time. His relationship with his white classmates was peacefully uneventful. Paul was a big boy, always the largest in his class, and strong and agile—obviously not one to be bullied. "Bunny" Gordon, one of his black schoolmates, remembered Paul as a very good athlete who was well liked by all the children, never got into any fights, never used any bad language, and had a very strict father. Gordon, interviewed when he was a seventy-seven-year-old retired postal worker in New York, shook his head sadly as he recalled the meager lunches that he and Paul took to school: "Nothing but two little old slices of bread, with butter and sugar."[11]

Hard times were all the time at the Robeson parsonage. Though the Reverend Robeson was an "excellent financier," his former Princeton congregation had also noted that his "sympathy reached out to all sufferers and in his efforts to give needed relief . . . he often suffered himself in consequence."[12] But despite their father's poverty-level income, William Robeson's children did not feel impoverished, as his daughter, Marian, who spent her summer vacations at home, explained:

> As short as the money was, I never remember us going hungry. Pop always had a garden and we ate good. He was always too kind[13]—to us and everybody. One time there was a doll I saw that I wanted. I think it was one dollar, or sometimes

I think it was three dollars, but the one dollar keeps coming to mind. A dollar was a lot of money in those days, and for my father it was even more. When I asked him could I have that doll, he said, no—I should try to do without it. But you know what? That really must have bothered him and he got me that doll! He really took care of us.

As I was saying, Pop was too kind. There was this preacher who wasn't doing too well and Pop would have him come once in a while to preach the sermon [and get the collection]. And this preacher would come on Saturday morning, for break-fast. Imagine, coming *Saturday* morning to preach a sermon! [Question: Your father didn't mind?] Not Pop—I was the one that didn't like it. For him, the more the merrier.

There were always a lot of people at the table.[14]

And for the poor pastor's son, Paul, there was the richness of a happy boyhood. Life was fun. School was fun. And play—that was the main fun. Because his lessons came easy to him, Paul would quickly finish his homework and dash out to play baseball, football, or anything else that came to mind. The cry of "Who wants to play?" would always bring Paul running, and he would play until it was too dark to see. The only cloud in his sunny life was the rule that a good boy helped with the chores, and arms that could swing a baseball bat were also expected to wield a rug beater on the parlor carpet hung on the backyard clothesline. Such outdoor chores were not too painful to Paul, because quitting time could be set by his own permissive conscience; but he hated all indoor tasks. His hands, so quick and sure in scooping up a bad hop at shortstop (and on the rough playing field of the corner lot nearly all ground balls would bounce erratically), seemed hopelessly awkward at work in the kitchen. "He acted," said his sister—and it must have been one of his most persuasive bits of acting—"as if he never could learn how to wash the dishes, though of course he had to do them when I wasn't home."

That aversion to any kind of household work would be cultivated throughout Paul's life; and in the film version of the musical comedy *Show Boat,* Paul's own feelings on the subject were expressed by the character he portrayed, who in his song "I Still Suits Me" scorn-fully rejects his nagging wife's complaint that he never does the dishes or any other domes-tic chores.

When Paul's brothers, Bill and Ben, and his sister, Marian, were home from school, the family members frequently entertained themselves with parlor performances rather than with games. (For one thing, card playing was then frowned upon in truly Christian homes: whist playing could lead to gambling, which led straight to Hell.) In an account of those days written when Ben was the Reverend B. C. Robeson, a prominent Harlem clergyman, it was Bill who first discovered that Paul had a talent for singing. The discovery was said to have been made one day at the parsonage when the three brothers were singing popular ballads in harmony: "We were making one of those minors known only to homeloving groups; Paul was bearing down on it with boyish glee; in fact, all of us were. Out of all the discord, Bill yelled: 'Wait a minute, hit that note again, Paul.' Paul hit it out of the lot [the baseball expression for a home run still came naturally to the former boyhood baseball star], and Bill said: 'Paul, you can sing.'"[15] Paul ridiculed the idea at first, but at Bill's insistence he began to sing with the church choir and at their home performances. Ben recalled: "Entertainments were always numerous, and the law of the parsonage was that every child must do something. The rest of us had recourse to nothing but a recitation or essay, and Paul, to be different, was forced to sing."

Paul Robeson remarked upon the important influence of that home environment at the time of his greatest success in the American theater. Observing that he had been "appearing before audiences since I was eight—in Sunday school and in my father's church," he told an interviewer in 1944:

> My interest in language goes back to my childhood. . . . From my earliest days
> I have been conscious of the potentialities of the voice to interest, entertain, and
> particularly to move people deeply. I was brought up in a *vocal* household. My
> father was the finest speaker I have ever heard. My brothers were all fine, expe-
> rienced public speakers. In my home, all through my childhood we "orated," recited,
> or debated. With the single exception of my sister, we all belonged to debating
> teams in grade, high school and college. We all "tried out" our speeches at home
> before the highly critical audience of the family.[16]

Paul's homegrown beginnings as a singer, orator, and athlete would first come to public attention in Somerville, New Jersey, where his father was transferred in 1910. That town, about fifteen miles from Princeton, had a more numerous black population than Westfield, and a larger congregation was enrolled in the St. Thomas A.M.E. Zion Church in Somerville, where William Robeson would serve his last pastorate. The parsonage there would be Paul's home through high school and college.

Paul first became noticed by the townspeople when he was still in grade school. (He finished part of seventh grade when he came to Somerville, and that fall he began his last year of grammar school.) As it happened, the pride of each town in the area rested on the success of the local high school baseball team in the fiercely fought contests with the enemy (not merely rival) teams. That Paul was a pupil in Somerville's "colored school" (there were enough of his color in town to have a separate grade school) and not yet a student at the racially integrated high school, was conveniently overlooked. As a good ballplayer he was "drafted" to help the town's high school in its crucial battles against the other towns, whose players and fans would never suspect that the big black kid at shortstop was not yet in high school.

Within a year of his arrival in town there appeared what must have been Paul Robeson's first press notice. The item, which demonstrated that he had indeed learned early "the potentialities of the voice to . . . move people deeply," was published in a Somerville newspaper when Paul, age thirteen, graduated from the eighth grade.

Colored School Commencement

The closing exercises of the local colored school were held Friday evening [June 23, 1911] in the St. Thomas A.M.E. Zion Church.

The graduates were Paul Leroy Robeson, Margaret Frances Potter and Elsie Victoria Rogers.

The oratorical efforts would well have graced any high school stage, and so impressive were the speakers that many tears were in evidence. To Paul Robeson belongs the credit of a rendition whose excellence has seldom been surpassed by a public school pupil.[17]

Margaret (Potter) Gibbons, who would also graduate with Paul from high school, would not later recall the subject of her own oration on that long-ago summer day in the church where the Reverend Robeson was pastor and her mother was the organist.[18] But she was certain nearly sixty years later that Paul's rendition on that occasion was Patrick Henry's famous speech.

If the Muse of Drama would have been pleasantly surprised to see that the earnest young orator could move an audience to tears with such shopworn material, the Muse of History would have pondered the irony involved: That impassioned appeal for freedom, voiced in 1775 by a white slaveholder in Virginia, now in 1911 stirred the hearts of the people assembled in Somerville's black church, whose slave-born pastor listened with quiet pride as his youngest son declaimed: *I know not what course others may take, but as for me, give me liberty or give me death!*

9. Paul Robeson. c. 1924.
Photo by Doris Ulmann. Platinum print. National Portrait Gallery, Smithsonian Institution.

10. Paul Robeson wearing helmet. c. 1917.
Robert Smith Collection.

Francis C. Harris

PAUL ROBESON

An Athlete's Legacy

In today's society the term "student-athlete" has a different meaning than it did eighty years ago. In our present society collegiate athletes sometimes are allowed to take any courses that they wish to keep their athletic eligibility. When Paul Robeson graduated from Rutgers College in 1919, he had defined the true meaning of the term "student-athlete."

Paul Leroy Robeson was born the youngest of seven children (five survived childbirth) on April 9, 1898, in Princeton, New Jersey, to William Drew and Maria Louisa Robeson. His father was born a slave on July 27, 1845, in Martin County, North Carolina. At the age of seventeen William Robeson escaped from slavery and joined the Union Army as a laborer. After the Civil War he attended Lincoln University, the first black university, founded in Pennsylvania in 1854. William Robeson earned an A.B. degree from Lincoln in 1873, and a Bachelor of Sacred Theology degree in 1876. He met his wife, Maria Louisa Bustill, while he was attending Lincoln, and they were married in 1878. In 1904, when Paul Robeson was six years old, his mother died of severe burns. Maria

Robeson's dress caught fire when a coal stove in the Robesons' home tipped over and ignited her dress.

The Reverend William Robeson was the pastor of the Witherspoon Street Presbyterian Church in Princeton, New Jersey, when his youngest son was born. In 1907 he became the pastor of the Downer Street St. Luke's African Methodist Episcopal (A.M.E.) Zion Church in Westfield, New Jersey. Three years later in 1910 the Robeson family moved to Somerville, New Jersey, when the Reverend Robeson became the pastor of the St. Thomas A.M.E. Church in Somerville.

The Reverend Robeson was a man who stressed the importance of education to all of his children. Paul Robeson's brothers Bill, Reeve, and Ben, and his sister Marian attended college (Reeve was the only one who did not graduate). By the time the family had moved to Somerville, the Reverend Robeson's youngest son was the only child living at home.

After graduating from the James L. Jamison Colored School in Somerville in June 1911, Paul Robeson attended the Washington School in Westfield, New Jersey, for part of the seventh grade. The eighth grade was spent at an all-black school in Somerville before he enrolled at Somerville High School. The high school had an enrollment of 250 students, and the young Robeson was one of eight students in his class enrolled in college preparatory courses. He was also one of three African American students in the entire school. Robeson became known as an outstanding athlete while attending Somerville High School, playing fullback on the football team, forward on the basketball team, shortstop and catcher on the baseball team, javelin and discus thrower on the track and field team, and he was the sports editor of *The Valkyrie,* the Somerville High School student newspaper. J. Douglas "Doug" Brown, who played halfback with Paul Robeson at Somerville High School and later became provost and dean of faculty at Princeton University, remembered how outstanding Robeson was on the football field. "Paul was three quarters of our team," said Brown. "I remember

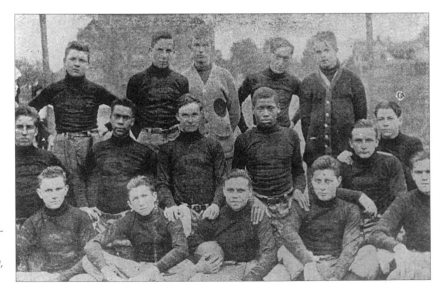

11. Somerville High School football team. 1913.
Courtesy of Akademie der Künste, Berlin.

our concern about him. When we played Phillipsburg we really tried to protect him because they were a rough bunch of kids. He broke his collarbone in a game against Bound Brook, but that was an accident."[1] In the game against arch rival Bound Brook High School in November 1913, Paul Robeson scored the only touchdown of the game to help Somerville to a 6–0 victory.

His athletic ability came from practice and tutoring in the correct technique from his brother Ben. He credited his brother in *Here I Stand,* his autobiography published in 1958, by saying, "It was my brother Ben who most inspired my interest in sports. Ben was an outstanding athlete by any standards, and had he attended one of the prominent colleges I'm convinced he would have been chosen All-American. Certainly he ranked in ability with many of the famous stars I encountered in college games and professional football. Ben was also a remarkable baseball player, fleet of foot and a power at bat, and had Negroes been permitted to play in the major leagues, I think Ben was one of those who could have made the grade."[2]

Between his studies and athletics at Somerville High School he was also a member of the drama and glee clubs, and the debating team. During his summers, starting at the age of fourteen, he worked as a waiter at a resort hotel at Narragansett Pier in Rhode Island. He would continue to work as a waiter in the summer during his college years.

An outstanding scholar (he maintained a 98 grade point average), he took a statewide examination sponsored by the State of New Jersey in June 1915. Students who got a high score on the examination were offered four-year scholarships to Rutgers College. Although Robeson was forced to take an exam focusing on four years of high school studies, while his classmates took the same exam that focused on three years of study, he passed and accepted a scholarship to Rutgers.

When he matriculated in 1915 Paul Robeson was only the third African American to attend Rutgers since it was founded in 1766. He attended at a time when the United States was a deeply segregated country, and the majority of African Americans attended historically black colleges and universities. Only a handful of African Americans went to predominantly white colleges and universities. That policy of token integration for a talented few but pervasive segregation for most African Americans prevailed until the 1940s, when the ideology of democracy that exists in America was under attack from Communist sympathizers. The social and economic conditions that existed for African Americans made them targets for anyone promoting communism. When the American media began to launch their anti-Communist campaign, a handful of African Americans who had gained success in their careers were used as evidence that America did not discriminate regardless of race, creed or color. This was entirely untrue. The majority of African Americans lived with discrimination every day of their lives.

In the fall of 1915, Robeson stood 6 feet 2 inches tall and weighed 190 pounds. His reputation as an outstanding athlete was known to Rutgers head football coach George Foster Sanford. Ralph White, who was a senior on the 1915 Rutgers College football team when

12. Paul Robeson with football team. c. 1915.
Special Collections, Rutgers University Libraries.

Paul Robeson was a freshman, remembers Coach Sanford calling a team meeting to say a Negro was coming out for the team. "We said 'send him out—we'll kill him.' "[3]

For Paul Robeson the memories of his first Rutgers football practice were very vivid. In an interview with Robert Van Gelder in the Sunday *New York Times* in 1944 he recalled what happened:

> I was seventeen years old and I was a freshman trying to make the football team. Rutgers had a great team that year, but the boys—well—they didn't want a Negro on their team, they just didn't want me on it.
>
> Later they became my friends, but every word of this is true, and though they are my friends I think they won't mind me telling it. On the first day of scrimmage they set about making sure that I wouldn't get on their team. One boy slugged me in the face and smashed my nose. That's been a trouble to me as a singer every day since. And then when I was down, flat on my back, another boy got me with his knee, just came over and fell on me. He managed to dislocate my right shoulder.
>
> Well, that night I was a very, very sorry boy. Broken nose, shoulder thrown out, and plenty of other cuts and bruises. I didn't know whether I could take any more. Seventeen years old, it was tough going for that age. But my father—my father

was born into slavery in 1843 down in North Carolina, and all his life he'd worked hard—was a good man, and a strong man. He had impressed upon me that when I was out on a football field or in a classroom or anywhere else I wasn't there just on my own. I was the representative of a lot of Negro boys who wanted to play football and wanted to go to college, and as their representative, I had to show that I could take whatever was handed out.

Well, I didn't know. My brother Bill came to see me, and he said, "Kid, I know what it is, I went through it at Pennsylvania. If you want to quit school go ahead, but I wouldn't like to think, and our father wouldn't like to think, that our family had a quitter in it."

So I stayed. I had ten days in bed, a few days at the training table, and then out for another scrimmage. I made a tackle and was on the ground. A boy came over and stepped hard on my hand. He meant to break the bones. The bones held, but his cleats took every single one of the fingernails off my right hand. That's when I knew rage!

The next play came around my end, the whole first string backfield came at me. I swept out my arms, and the three men running interference went down. The ball carrier was a first-class back named Kelly. I got Kelly in my two hands and I got him up over my head. I was going to smash him so hard to the ground that I'd break him right in two, and I could have done it. But just then Coach Sanford yelled: "Robey, you're on the varsity!" That brought me around.[4]

His freshman season, Robeson began as a substitute tackle. He did not play in the first two games of the season. His first collegiate game was against Rensselaer Polytechnic Institute on October 9, 1915 (Rutgers won 96–0). He got the first start of his collegiate career against Stevens Tech on November 20, 1915 (Rutgers won 39–3). Altogether he played in four of the eight games that Rutgers played during the 1915 season. The 1916 season he played first-string tackle and guard in six of the seven games that Rutgers played (Rutgers had a record of 3–2–2 in 1916). The only game that he did not play came October 14, 1916, against Washington and Lee University (of Virginia). Washington and Lee refused to play the game because a Negro was in the starting lineup. The Rutgers College administration and alumni pressured Coach Sanford and Paul Robeson did not play. He never commented on not playing in the Washington and Lee game, but in 1919 James D. Carr, the first African American to graduate from Rutgers in 1892, wrote a letter to Rutgers College president William H. S. Demarest protesting the exclusion of Paul Robeson in the Washington and Lee game.[5] James Carr had been selected to Phi Beta Kappa as a student at Rutgers, and he later became an assistant district attorney in New York City.

Paul Robeson gained national notoriety on the football field in 1917. He played offensive end, offensive tackle, and defensive tackle and end. In two of the most important games of the 1917 season his play was exceptional. On November 2, 1917, Rutgers played West Virginia University, which was coached by the legendary "Greasy" Neale. Before the game Greasy Neale approached Rutgers coach George Foster Sanford and said: "Foster, you know some of my boys are from the South, and they won't stand for that black man in there. Better take him out." Sanford replied: "What do you want me to do, Greasy—give you the game? I can't play without Robeson. He's the team!" Neale said: "It's up to you. But I warn you, they'll murder him!"[6] Paul Robeson played splendidly against West Virginia, blocking, tackling, receiving punts, and catching passes. At half time Greasy Neale told his team: "See here, boys, any player who can take the beating that Robeson has taken from you, without squealing, is not black. He's a white man! Now go out there and play like hell—and give him a break!"[7] Rutgers and West Virginia played to a 7–7 tie.

On November 24, 1917, at Ebbets Field in Brooklyn, New York, Rutgers played the Naval Reserve football team of Newport, Rhode Island. This team was composed of former college All-Americans, and was coached by Dr. William Bull and Cupid Black. In a review of the 1917 football season published in the *Rutgers Alumni Quarterly* in January 1918, Paul Robeson wrote:

> The Reserve team was composed of the greatest players of the past couple of years. It included Charles Barrett of Cornell University, Black and Callahan of Yale University, Schlacter of Syracuse University, Gerrish of Dartmouth College, all All-American selections; and a number of All-Western men. Here was a team of experienced men, of the highest recognized football ability, in condition, and coached by Dr. William Bull, the famous Yale coach. A team which had defeated Brown, conquerors of Colgate and Dartmouth, by a score of 35–0. And opposing them was "little" Rutgers, with an eleven averaging slightly over nineteen years in age and outweighed at least ten pounds to a man. To all football followers there

13. "Robeson of Rutgers making a long run." Rutgers versus Naval Reserve, Ebbets Field, November 24, 1917. *Robert Smith Collection.*

14. Clipping: "Dashing Robeson Humbles Black's Noted Warriors." New York Tribune, *November 25, 1917. Robert Smith Collection.*

could be but one result. Rutgers didn't have a chance. But Coach Sanford and the Rutgers team felt differently, and the team which trotted on the field in Brooklyn on that Sunday afternoon late in November was full of confidence in their ability to conquer their famed opponents. And they proved it. Never did a team fight like that one. From flag-fall to finish it was all Rutgers, and the final score, 14–0, fails miserably in telling just how superior the wearers of the Scarlet were to the great All-Americans.[8]

Paul Robeson did not mention himself in the review. Against the Naval Reserve he scored a touchdown and played outstanding defense. Rutgers finished the 1917 season with a record of 7–1–1 and the press began to refer to Robeson as "Robeson of Rutgers" or "The Magnificent Robeson." Walter Camp, who coached football at Yale University (1888–1889) and Stanford University (1892, 1894–1895), believed, along with every other football authority in the country, that Robeson should be an All-American in 1917, although in deference to the war effort, Camp published an All-Service team that year instead of a collegiate All-American team.

The following year Rutgers College had a record of 5–2, and he was again selected as an All-American. In addition to playing football at Rutgers he played forward on the

15. Three members of the Rutgers football team, Feitner, Robeson, and Breckley. c. 1917.
Robert Smith Collection.

16. Robeson lined up with team. c. 1918.
Special Collections, Rutgers University Libraries.

17. Group portrait of Rutgers basketball team. Undated.
Robert Smith Collection.

18. Paul Robeson catching on baseball diamond. 1918.
Photo by Jack Abraham. Robert Smith Collection.

basketball team, catcher on the baseball team, and was a javelin and discus thrower on the track and field team. He also played basketball occasionally on the weekends with the St. Christopher Club of New York City while he was a student. During his collegiate career he earned a record twelve letters. By the time he graduated in 1919 Robeson had been elected to membership in Phi Beta Kappa, the national fraternity of scholars; he was also a member of the Cap and Skull Club (a senior honor society) and the Rutgers College literary society, Philoclean. As an orator he won the Edward Livingston Barbour Prize in Declamation, and the Myron W. Smith Memorial Prize in Oratory.

Paul Robeson's athletic career did not end when he graduated from Rutgers College. To pay his way through Columbia University Law School he became a part-time assistant football coach at Lincoln University for one year. His good friend Fritz Pollard, who was selected as an All-American in football at Brown University in 1916, was the head coach at Lincoln. Robeson also became a member of Alpha Phi Alpha, the first all-black fraternity in the country, while he was an assistant coach at Lincoln.

Playing professional football on the weekends while he was attending law school, Paul Robeson was one of the first African Americans to play in the National Football League (which was called the American Professional Football Association prior to 1920) before the ban on African Americans in 1934. He played for the Hammond (Indiana) Pros in 1920, the Akron Pros in 1920 and 1921, and the Milwaukee Badgers in 1922. He was paid between

19. Paul Robeson as member of the Akron Pros of 1920. *Robert Smith Collection.*

$50 and $200 per game. Although Robeson was one of the pioneer players of the National Football League, his career as a professional football player has been largely ignored by professional-football historians.

His professional athletic career ended after 1922, when he began to focus on his career as a stage and movie actor, and as a concert singer. From the late 1940s and throughout the 1950s he was blacklisted for his outspoken views on Civil Rights, his alleged Communist affiliations, and his visits to Communist countries. There was no better example of Paul Robeson being considered a "nonperson" during this period than how he was treated by the Rutgers College Athletic Department. In 1954 the *Rutgers Athletic News* published a list of the sixty-five greatest football players in the history of Rutgers University. Paul Robeson's name did not appear on the list. William McKenzie was the sports information director at Rutgers University in 1954, and he was responsible for the publication. In 1973 he tried to explain the reason Paul Robeson was not included:

20. Group portrait of 1918 Rutgers football squad. 1918.
Robert Smith Collection.

21. Robeson with three other graduates. Cap and Skull Club. c. 1919.
Special Collections, Rutgers University Libraries.

It was a conspiracy of silence. It sounds juvenile now, twenty years later, but he was *persona non grata.* You didn't talk about Paul Robeson. It's very strange but no one ever raised the question (as to why he wasn't on the list). Perhaps I could have, perhaps I should have, I was the editor.

It's very strange to ponder the way things have changed. Fortunately they have. Maybe we have learned something, but how can you explain it intelligently without being stupid? They just didn't consider him in making the list.[9]

For decades he was never considered for induction into the College Football Hall of Fame. Then, in 1970, a committee of Rutgers University and local New Jersey sports people formed, and they nominated him for induction. Although Robeson's name was put forward every year, it was rejected every year until August 25, 1995, when he was inducted into the College Football Hall of Fame, seventy-five years after playing his last collegiate game.

Paul Robeson died January 23, 1976, at the age of seventy-seven in Philadelphia, Pennsylvania. His legacy as a student-athlete is his excellence as a scholar, and outstand-

22. Paul Robeson with varsity baseball team. 1918.
Special Collections, Rutgers University Libraries.

ing sportsmanship despite occasional unsportsmanship from opponents. For African Americans he proved that despite discrimination and segregation an African American could succeed and overcome these barriers. No matter how much success he earned on the athletic field and as an actor and concert singer, he realized the Civil Rights of all African Americans had greater importance. Almost thirty years before Jackie Robinson broke the color barrier in major-league baseball, Paul Robeson established a level of excellence as a scholar-athlete that few others, if any, have ever attained.

23. Paul Robeson. c. 1918.
Special Collections, Rutgers University Libraries.

Derrick Bell

DOING THE STATE SOME SERVICE

Paul Robeson and the Endless Quest for Racial Justice

Paul Robeson's life, like great art, is treasured as much for the images it evokes as for the story it portrays. At one level, one can view the obvious parallel of Robeson's contributions with those of other well-known blacks, Martin Luther King, Jr., Malcolm X, and W.E.B. Du Bois, who paid a large price for their outspoken challenges to racial injustice. At another level, with Robeson's life as model, the significant but less well-known sacrifices of other blacks can be more easily recognized and appreciated.

Consider Tommie Smith and John Carlos. They, you may remember, were the two black athletes who, in accepting their gold and bronze medals in the 1968 Olympics, mounted the victory podium and, as the national anthem played, each bowed his head and thrust high a black-gloved fist in protest against racial strife in America. The U.S. Olympic Committee indignantly dismissed them from the team. Both men suffered through years of job discrimination by employers and boycotts by sports promoters. It was the usual penalty paid by blacks who failed to combine their success with that deference signaling their understanding that triumph has not altered their subordinate status.

Significantly, the retaliatory actions against Smith and Carlos have not dimmed the memory of that event. Back in the early 1970s, I was about to publish the first law-school text devoted to issues of race and racism. As both epigraph and notice that the book would treat discrimination as the evil it is rather than a subject that would be examined "neutrally," I presented a photograph of the Smith-Carlos protest and dedicated the book to all those who throughout this country's history have risked its wrath to protest its faults. I called the black athletes' protest:

The dramatic finale of an Extraordinary achievement
Performed for a nation which
Had there been a choice
Would have chosen others, and
If given a chance
Will accept the achievement
And neglect the achievers.
Here, with simple gesture, they
Symbolize a people whose patience
With exploitation will expire with
The dignity and certainty
With which it has been endured . . .
Too long.[1]

24. Columbia University School of Law graduating class, 1923.
Columbia University School of Law.

The Olympic achievements of Carlos and Smith and the meaning of the nation's reaction to their protest are made clear by comparing them with Paul Robeson's experience. The lesson is clear. No degree of success or superiority in athletics, art, or scholarship insulates black criticism of white racism against swift and certain retaliation. Indeed, the higher the public platform provided by the society's recognition of that success, the more certain that whites will react to criticism, even though undeniably true, as an unforgivable betrayal. Robeson's experience then provides a prophetic paradigm for us all.

And yet, Robeson's outspoken stance against American racism, even his too trusting attraction to communism and Russia, served well both the nation and its black citizens. The process by which this service was rendered is both interesting and instructive.

At least since Abraham Lincoln's letter to Horace Greeley of the *New York Tribune* reporting that, though he hated slavery, his primary goal was to save the Union, and that to this end, he would free all, none, or some slaves, whichever action would best preserve the Union, black people have been on official notice that even as to those policy makers who have sympathy for their plight, relief for racial wrongs will be apportioned out in direct proportion to the degree that interests of whites may thereby be advanced. Entitlement to relief against racial injustice, no matter how blatant or harmful, has never been automatic. In each instance, there has been a direct political or economic benefit to identifiable segments of white society.

The Emancipation Proclamation exemplifies this truth. Lincoln kept his word and freed the slaves when that action would help save the Union. Under severe pressure to turn the tide in the Civil War, he reluctantly issued the order, because it would rally abolitionists in England and France whose influence insured those countries would not enter the conflict on the side of the Confederacy. In addition, the president believed that when word reached the South of the Emancipation decree, it would thoroughly disrupt the South's slave-labor force. He also opened the way for the recruitment of more than 200,000 black soldiers, most from the ranks of escaped slaves.

But just as the Emancipation Proclamation—as a legal document—did not free even one slave because it was addressed to only those sections that had seceded, and over which Union forces and law had no control, so subsequent constitutional amendments and civil-rights laws have been enacted nominally to advance black rights, but actually to serve ends and interests of importance to whites or some of them.

America's victory in World War II did not alter these principles. As in earlier conflicts, blacks had at first been excluded or segregated. The pattern was set at the start of the Revolutionary War when the Continental Congress proclaimed that it would not recruit Indians, vagabonds, or Negroes. When the enemy's challenge became threatening and the number of whites willing to serve proved less than the need, blacks were called upon and responded without rancor or regret. At war's end, the achievements were accepted and the achievers neglected; except that "neglect" inaccurately describes the reign of lynching and

25. Paul Robeson with Eleanor Roosevelt. New York. c. 1942. *Photo by Austin Hansen. Schomburg Center for Research in Black Culture, The New York Public Library, Astor, Lenox and Tilden Foundations.*

terror that was the black man's victory portion after World War I, and which threatened again at the conclusion of World War II.

The war had devastated Western colonial powers. Nonwhite peoples were demanding an end to capitalist occupation and exploitation by Western nations. Communism offered a powerful alternative that both challenged and evoked great fear in this country. Paul Robeson, an international figure, by giving voice both here and abroad to what every black person knew about racism and capitalist exploitation, invested that knowledge with a legitimacy that is the prerequisite for serious opposition.

And, as if that were not enough, Robeson preached the doctrine unholy to guardians of the status quo that the working classes, black and white, were not only brothers, but suffered the same exploitation, a truth quite intentionally (and all too easily) hidden from lower-class whites by appeals to racism propounded by upper-class whites from the earliest days of American history to the present. Any assumption that Robeson's right of free speech encompassed such inflammatory truths proved naive in the extreme. When he proclaimed, as he did in *Here I Stand,* that the enemy is the "white folks on top," and dared suggest that American blacks might not so compliantly fight for America in some future war against a nonracist country,[2] the retaliation that followed became inevitable.

That policy makers in this country recognized and determined to eliminate this formidable black danger to the economic status quo is evidenced by the systematic and blatant violation of Robeson's constitutional rights, admittedly accomplished to shut him up. When Robeson in 1950 demanded to know why his passport had been canceled, State Department officials said it was because he refused to sign the non-Communist affiliation oath.[3]

Robeson was barred from leaving the country, and was denied access to concert halls and speakers' platforms at home. But his message had been heard. And if far fewer rank-and-file Americans heeded his advice than he had hoped, far more policy makers than have

26. Paul Robeson addresses the World Congress of Partisans of Peace. Paris. April 20, 1949. *Courtesy of Hulton Getty/Tony Stone Images.*

ever acknowledged it learned from Robeson that to preserve the Union and their preeminent positions in it, a twentieth-century equivalent of the Emancipation Proclamation might be necessary.

In an effort to limit the effect of Robeson's statement, policy makers and the media recruited well-known blacks to refute it. In an excess of patriotism over experience, some blacks did so. Among them was the baseball hero Jackie Robinson, who had benefited from Robeson's work against discrimination in professional baseball. He testified against Robeson before the House Un-American Activities Committee. The baseball player's prepared statement was carefully worded only to condemn as "silly" Robeson's assertion that blacks would not fight for this country. He defended Robeson's right to his personal views and acknowledged the real injustices blacks suffer. Robeson's enemies really didn't care what Jackie Robinson said. His appearance was comment enough—especially to the press, which eagerly reported the negative in Robinson's remarks, while ignoring the more positive balance.[4] In their turn, the leaders of the major civil-rights organizations deemed it important to prove their own loyalties by condemning Robeson. Walter White, Executive Director of the NAACP, in a devastatingly critical article in *Ebony* magazine, described Robeson as a "bewildered man who is more to be pitied than damned."[5]

To my knowledge, Paul Robeson, while a lawyer, deeply committed to civil rights, never had his name on any of the legal briefs in the school desegregation litigation that led in 1954 to the Supreme Court's decision in *Brown v. Board of Education.* Indeed, as those cases slowly made their way through the courts in the early 1950s, the government's campaign against Robeson had succeeded in turning him into an enemy of his people and a pawn of

27. Walter White. undated.
NAACP Collection, Prints and Photographs, Library of Congress.

Communist Russia. And yet, it is clear today that his strong condemnations of American racism out of court were as effective as any of the arguments propounded by lawyers who have received due credit for their roles in that landmark litigation. Robeson had stated the unstatable. By urging blacks not to reject communism until the free world proves it has a better deal,[6] he enabled NAACP legal-brief writers to warn the Supreme Court that the "Survival of our country in the present international situation is inevitably tied to resolution of this domestic issue."[7]

Consider also the U.S. Government's *amicus curiae* brief before the Supreme Court in *Brown*:

> It is in the context of the present world struggle between freedom and tyranny that the problem of racial discrimination must be viewed . . . [for] discrimination against minority groups in the United States has an adverse effect upon our relations with other countries. Racial discrimination furnishes grist for the Communist propaganda mills, and it raises doubts even among friendly nations as to the intensity of our devotion to the democratic faith.[8]

How important were such arguments to the final outcome in *Brown v. Board*? No less an observer of the American racial scene than W.E.B. Du Bois expressed the view that "No such decision would have been possible without the world pressure of Communism," which, he asserted, rendered it "simply impossible for the United States to continue to lead a 'Free World' with race segregation kept legal over a third of its territory."[9]

And to those for whom even an obvious truth has no validity unless whites embrace it, recourse to the media coverage of the *Brown* decision should be helpful. After summing up the effect of the *Brown* decision on the children in the segregation states, *Time* magazine, in typical *Time* style, observed: "The international effect may be scarcely less important. In many countries, where U.S. prestige and leadership have been damaged by the fact of U.S. segregation, it will come as a timely reassertion of the basic American principle that 'all men are created equal.' "

Time's companion publication, *Life,* supported this position with the assertion that the Supreme Court "at one stroke immeasurably raised the respect of other nations for the U.S." And from *Newsweek* came these words: ". . . the psychological effect will be tremendous . . . segregation in the public schools has become a symbol of inequality, not only to Negroes in the United States, but to colored peoples elsewhere in the world. It has also been a weapon of world Communism. Now that symbol lies shattered."

More pointed is the statement from *Citizen's Guide to Desegregation*: "The Voice of America carried the news around the world. Hundreds of national and international leaders wired congratulations. Only radio Moscow was silent."[10]

A final proof that the *Brown* decision ending official racial apartheid was influenced, perhaps decisively, by the fear that Jim Crow policies might lead black people, far less

28. Paul Robeson is welcomed by W.E.B. Du Bois at the World Peace Congress. Paris. April 1949.
Photo © Bildarchiv Neues Deutschland, Berlin. Courtesy of Julius Lazarus Archives and Collection/ Special Collections/Rutgers University Libraries.

fortunate than Paul Robeson, to follow his example, is found in the *Brown* opinion. Its pages contain no mention of the Communist menace, but catalog the educational and emotional harm of segregated schools, decrying the damage done as so serious as to likely be irreparable. Then, assuming that open acknowledgment was as good as needed action, the Supreme Court deferred any remedy until the next year, at which time it decided that the entitlement of black children to attend desegregated schools need not be granted immediately, and might be delayed until administrative problems were solved—a deferential policy that lasted a full decade.

The Court's unprecedented deferral of a recognized constitutional right presented a perfect parallel between *Brown* and the Emancipation Proclamation. Both documents, as a means of securing and advancing important interests of white society, condemned in symbolic terms obvious and long-standing racial injustice. Both actions were structured so as

Paul Robeson in "Othello"   a Bendiner

29. Paul Robeson as Othello. c. 1945. Lithograph by Alfred Bendiner.
National Portrait Gallery, Smithsonian Institution. Gift of Alfred Bendiner Foundation.

to mask the real benefits to whites behind assurances to the citizenry that the policy or decision is the tardy response to long-ignored petitions for racial reform. Most blacks accepted such assurances without question, and, in both instances, mounted major movements (mass escapes in the nineteenth century and protests in the twentieth) that would have been effective even had no Proclamation or landmark decision prompted them. That blacks responded in this way is fortunate, because the Emancipation Proclamation— as indicated earlier—was unenforceable, and *Brown*'s enforcement was delayed until blacks insisted on it.

By the time black protests and marches of the 1960s made *Brown* more than a symbol, Paul Robeson was on the sidelines, another in a too-long list of blacks sacrificed to the cause of racial equality in a land seemingly determined to destroy those who most believe in its ideals. In his most famous stage role, as Shakespeare's *Othello*, Paul Robeson says in the final scene, "I have done the state some small service. And they know it." Even today, that statement, applied to his life, would not be acknowledged by most Americans whose sense of security seems congenitally condemned to fear any black, particularly one whose achievements have been recognized and who then dares to criticize even the most odious racial problems. Robeson's message to us is that in the face of adverse reaction, we must continue our protests against racial injustice. Ignoring the lessons of history, we hold open the door of fellowship to America's white masses when they discover, finally, that black people are not the cause and racism is not the remedy for their oppression. We blacks may not save this country through commitment of this character, but we will save our souls, and we will have remained true to the rich testament Paul Robeson left us.

VISUAL ARTS, DRAMA, MUSIC, AND FILM CONTRIBUTION

30. K. MacPherson and Pap (two men with movie camera) photographing Paul Robeson. 1930.
Beinecke Library, Yale University.

Deborah Willis

THE IMAGE
AND PAUL ROBESON·

There was always a largeness
about Paul Robeson. . . .
                    Lloyd L. Brown[1]

As I consider the above epigraph as an introduction to the visual construction of Paul Robeson, I am reminded of the myriad images I have observed of Paul Robeson—performer, spokesperson, athlete, and family man.[2] What did Robeson tell us through these images? It is difficult to pinpoint of what exactly Robeson's career consisted. He was all those things mentioned, in addition to being a social activist. His life is divided nearly in half. During the 1920s and 1930s Robeson found wide public acceptance; however, after the Second World War his position would dramatically change. During the reactionary years of the late forties and early fifties, generally known as the McCarthy era, Robeson's left-wing views left him attacked and ostracized from American culture. Certainly Robeson was not the only African American to incur the wrath of American society. However, unlike some other spokespeople—W.E.B. Du Bois, A. Philip Randolph, and leaders within the NAACP—Robeson was a member of an artistic community. His criticisms of U.S. policy and continuing racism were made as a self-appointed cultural spokesperson, and he undertook this path without the benefit of an organization. Fame was a tool to be used for articulating a sociopolitical platform. Yet, because this platform was dependent upon a fickle media, it was not difficult for America to crack down on Robeson by simply removing the platform. By the 1950s, with his passport revoked and living under "house arrest" conditions, television, the medium that forever transformed American culture, was an outlet denied to Robeson. As J. Fred MacDonald observed:

> The decision to ban Robeson from American television had political and racial dimensions. Politically, it was simply too controversial for a commercial network to air the views of an admitted leftist at a time when cold war tensions were nationally unsettling. . . . Without being enunciated, there was a racial component to the Robeson affair. He was an outspoken political activist, a powerful man with deep convictions, he was not content with personal success gained while other Afro-Americans remained deprived. And Robeson was unrelenting.[3]

MacDonald underscores the central tragedy of Robeson: he was a man with a deep commitment to a career that would give him the widest public voice, and transcend the limitations of a racist culture, but he was also a man who was never able to control the means of his own production. Robeson chose a career in performing because it was perhaps the only viable outlet at the time for achieving worldwide recognition. More than being fully cognizant of the use of a public career, points out Martin Duberman, author of a full-length biography of Robeson, the man was endowed with a sense of public destiny, a sense of expectation running throughout his life.[4]

With this in mind, looking at visual images of Paul Robeson, one seeks to find a sense of personal authorship. At first, photographs portray a man who is entirely self-constructed and self-controlled. By sheer force of his will, Robeson seemed independent of external forces— viewed by black people almost as a black man transcending the covert and overt opposition of racism and self-hate of American society. Further, Robeson posed nude or seminude for the established artists and art photographers. This was a radical act when the black, particularly the black male, body represented such a threat to white hegemony. However, when we begin to examine closely the photographic images of Robeson, whether those images are present as publicity stills on stage or in the photographer's studio, they also reveal the construction of the "other," or the state of being seen as outside of dominant culture. The still portraits demonstrate the way in which Robeson did not always resist the stereotypical roles he was portraying. Indeed, at the height of his fame, in 1942, he claimed he would no longer make any Hollywood films after a career marred by social stereotypes, avowing a "simplicity" of character. Similarly, contemporary film historians have found themselves frustrated at encountering the plethora of racist constructions running through his movie career. Thus, the photographs present a difficulty. On the one hand, Robeson is "fully present," a powerful, masculine, and handsome presence. But there are also the photographs of Robeson as the imaginary "Hollywood African savage," in poses that reinforced the inferiority of things African (and African American) and the superiority of those things Western.

What are we to make of these images at the end of the twentieth century? It would be difficult to pinpoint Robeson's thoughts as he did not leave a diaristic record. What we know is mediated through the insights of others and through his own, mediated performances. The study of Robeson offers a perplexing dilemma; he is a fully actualized presence, but he also participates within an ideology that saw those things African as subordinate. Robeson represents a puzzle, a sort of brooding persona, that neither wholly refutes nor resists American racism. Unlike other leading African Americans of the early twentieth century, Robeson was privileged to be photographed from his years as an athletic star in college and after school, as an actor/performer by photographers worldwide. One wonders how much Robeson constructed these images. Robeson is well aware of the camera and its ability to empower its subjects. There are no fixed explanations for the sheer amount and wide range of poses and portraits that are preserved, particularly when considering the outpouring of derision which marked his late career. Under such repression, one would think images of Robeson would be consigned to the trashbin of history. One explanation for the sheer volume of photographic material is that in spite of the severe repression, Robeson endures as a "race man" within the arena of the black viewer/consumer. Indeed his wife, Eslanda Goode Robeson, in her role as his manager at the outset of his career, was well aware of how her

31. Eslanda Robeson. With inscription "To Carlo and Fania Lovingly Essie." London. July 1928.
Photo by S. Georges. Carl Van Vechten Collection, Beinecke Library, Yale University.

husband created a new representative of the black man. Further, later in her life, Eslanda undertook photography. Jeanne Moutoussamy-Ashe, in her study of African American women photographers, notes how Eslanda treated photography as a hobby. However, Eslanda was a close friend of photographer/patron Carl Van Vechten, and they "talked a lot about photography." Moutoussamy-Ashe goes on to make a connection between her seriousness as a photographer and her friendships with Van Vechten and Edward Steichen, a leading photographic proponent and later curator of photography at New York's Museum of Modern Art.[5] (It was Steichen who took the iconic 1933 photograph of Paul as "The Emperor Jones.") Both Robesons understood the power and potency of the image; both were cognizant that visual image could be read as an act of resistance and empowerment. Duberman makes the point in his biography that no study of Robeson is complete without including Eslanda's considerable role in promoting and preserving the Robeson legacy. This would naturally include a visual legacy.

This essay explores the social conditions governing the act of being photographed and the return of the gaze. Within this construct, we encounter the mythos surrounding Robeson which suggests we read his images as defiant. This argument is reinforced by his handsome features, height, voice, smile, and his desires. This reputation has come down through the years—from his first public reception as the celebrated genius destined for glory, to the later period of public attack and a tortured autonomy. In either case, the integrity of the man was left intact. But to what extent does the brooding, black man play into the hands of the racialist? To what extent are these sometimes scowling images controlled by Robeson or controlled by others? To what extent do we find the act of signifying African American masculinity as we look at Robeson on stage and in film? In considering these questions, this essay offers a critical exploration into the least-discussed area of Robeson scholarship, his image in photography. The photographs encompass the entire spectrum of Robeson's life: personal, performative, and political. What follows is an attempt to isolate the characteristics of Robeson's photographic presence. How and in what way Robeson escapes, contorts, appropriates, or falls victim to the dominant racist discourse forms the central issue in uncovering the dilemma and the myth of Robeson.

In the photograph titled "Paul Robeson, Rutgers' All-American," ca. 1918 (see figure 32), a cropped portrait from the full negative, Robeson is pictured in his prime as a football athlete. It is difficult to view this image without comparing it to the way in which photographs of African American athletes are currently used by universities, media, and advertisers to sell products and ideas. Indeed, one could make the case that this is exactly what Rutgers College had in mind with its portraits of Robeson as football star. At the time this photograph was taken, Robeson was only the third African American to attend Rutgers College, and the first African American to be part of the football team. His extraordinary success as a football player, in spite of overt racism and violent hostility, is not necessarily evident in the photograph. Robeson performed under conditions unimaginable by today's sport

32. Paul Robeson, Rutgers' All-American. c. 1918.
Robert Smith Collection.

standards. But what we see is a 6-feet 2-inch 190-pound man, whose hand is nearly the size of the football, clearly a formidable athlete. We see Paul Robeson as manifesting all the attributes of masculine power. Robeson is portrayed as an expression of the ideas of a superlative athletic prowess as well as a strong black presence.

It is interesting that most images we see of Robeson in his years at Rutgers do not portray his work as a scholar, an honor student whose senior thesis was titled, "The Fourteenth Amendment: The Sleeping Giant of the American Constitution," which analyzed civil-rights legislation and how the constitution could be used in the fight for civil rights. Relatively few depict his prominence on the college debating team. Nor do we have a photograph of Robeson's 1918 valedictorian speech, on the "New Idealism," which also argued for the expansion of civil liberties as outlined in the Constitution. What we are readily presented with are the photographs showing him excelling in football and basketball.

Are these athletic images the beginning of the visual construction of Robeson for consumption by white America? To what extent did Robeson believe in the construction of this all-American athletic persona and to what extent did he control these images? It is interesting to note that in other football photographs, Robeson is seen with other players, and he is not holding the ball. Robeson is one of a crowd; he is consigned to the background, not allowed to be seen as the star of the team. Yet, as Francis Harris explains in this volume, it was Robeson who propelled the Rutgers football team to victories unrealized before in the history of the college.[6] This photograph offers up Robeson as a complete physical presence, at the height of his athletic achievement, and not as the lone black figure towering over and surrounded by white men. It is an important indicator in the photographic history of Robeson. His physicality would remain a central element within the picturing of Robeson throughout his entire life.

The dilemma of representation, masculinity, autonomy, and the black presence collide in a 1922 publicity portrait (see figure 33). The photograph was taken of Robeson in *Voodoo*, the English production of *Taboo*, a play written by Mary Hoyt Wiborg, a socialite. The play followed what was essentially the standard plot of a racially "progressive" drama. *Taboo* was set in the antebellum South during a severe drought. Robeson's character intervenes and saves the mute grandchild of the plantation mistress, who was accused by superstitious slaves of causing the misfortune. The point of Robeson's character was not only to save the boy, but to restore the white patriarchal order.

This image of Robeson represents the part of the play in which the character Jim is transformed, through a "flashback," and turns into a "voodoo" king, after which it begins to rain. Because of our knowledge of Robeson, a man of great presence and dignity, this photograph is startling: Robeson is pictured wearing a large hairpiece that towers over his head like a fright-wig. Wrapped around his torso and over one shoulder is a towellike fabric that appears to be of non-African origin. He wears sandals which also appear to be made in the West. Robeson's arms are folded across the front of his body in a self-protective position.

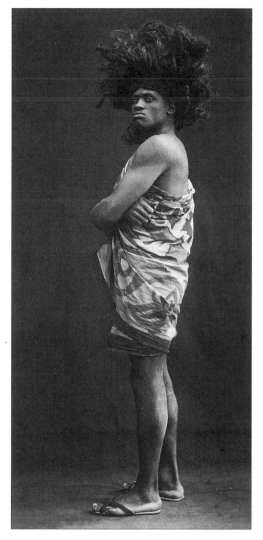

33. Paul Robeson in *Voodoo,* the English production of *Taboo.* 1922. Version II.
Photographs and Prints Division, Schomburg Center for Research in Black Culture, The New York Public Library; Astor, Lenox and Tilden Foundations.

His scowl, meant to be fierce, is almost comical. Certainly, seen today, Robeson's performance in character is a cultural abomination. The costume and posture reinforce the outsider view of African people. Robeson is the "mad primitive." This generic African "warrior" becomes derisively African in general. Tall and childlike, Robeson poses no real danger or threat to any established order. This is a persona ruled by superstition and emotion, an anomaly in modern times. This figure does not cut through racist ideology. In being pictured as such, Robeson subjects himself to a cultural falsity and is eventually undone by the European visual standards. He is the primitive, unable and incapable of effective rational leadership. A social being that must be led or dominated. Aside from this "flashback" there was no reason for Robeson to dress in such a costume. Although the playwright's notion of African culture is not grounded in anything remotely realistic, it does represent the contemporary thinking at the height of the Harlem Renaissance period. Unfortunately, Robeson was not the only performer to go along with such racist portrayals.

34. Paul Robeson autographed photo for Fredi Washington.
"To darling Fredi, Really my 'weakness' Much Love Paul." c. 1926–1926.
Photographs and Prints Division, Schomburg Center for Research in Black Culture;
The New York Public Library, Astor, Lenox and Tilden Foundations.

The untitled studio portrait of Robeson standing, c. 1925–1926 (see figure 34) shows a beaming Paul Robeson. The photograph was most likely taken as a studio publicity portrait for his portrayal of a boxer in Jim Tully and Frank Dazey's play, *Black Boy*. The drama, loosely based on the life of Jack Johnson, costarred Fredi Washington. This particular photograph, part of the Robeson portrait collection at the Schomburg Center for Research in Black Culture, bears the erotic inscription to Washington, "To darling Fredi, Really my 'weakness,' Much Love Paul." Washington, a beautiful, light-skinned actress and dancer from Georgia, later costarred with Robeson in the film *The Emperor Jones*. Her fame came from her role as the tragic mulatto Peola in the 1934 film production of *Imitation of Life*. Duberman reports that Washington and Robeson were "an item" during the production of *Black Boy*,[7] and the photograph's inscription appears to support that assertion. At this time it was common practice for actors to exchange portraits after the run of a production and personalize the portrait through an inscription. Many photo archives of performers are strewn with personalized portraits. It is also important that the performers isolated the image they wanted to use in promoting themselves. Robeson's smiling figure creates a self-confident stance, and barely contains a boyish masculinity. This is an instance of self-definition. The photograph is also significant because it shows Robeson with his Phi Beta Kappa key. One of the first photographs in his early life to provide some visible evidence of his academic skills, it shows his youthfulness off the stage and without an athletic uniform.

35. Paul Robeson, Otto [*sic*] and Liversight and son on stage of *Black Boy*, 1926.
Library of Performing Arts, The New York Public Library, Astor, Lenox and Tilden Foundations.

36. Robeson as Othello. 1930.
Corbis-Bettmann.

As a result of his theatrical experiences and a superior intellect, Robeson thoroughly studied the works of William Shakespeare. He developed a masterful rendition of these works, particularly his strong interpretation of the role of Othello in 1930–1931 (see figure 36). Part of the success of Robeson was attributed to his understanding of Othello's isolation in Italy. Robeson was offered the role of Othello once in London in 1930; and in 1942, Robeson began performing *Othello* in the United States, directed by Margaret Webster, a Shakespearean director, and costarring Uta Hagen and Jose Ferrer, who were married at that time. Robeson had been unhappy with the 1930 production of *Othello* and had spent time in the intervening years studying the part. Figure 36 depicts Robeson as Othello—thinking deeply with hand to the side of his face. He stares away from the camera—an instance of the brooding, dark character. Although the 1942 performance would also have mixed results, Robeson found new meaning in the cultural isolation of the Othello character. Like Othello, Robeson had become a hero. Also Othello was a foreigner, and as such was outside the dominant culture. Yet he rose to public prominence through his military powers, earning the respect and position of a cultural "insider." So too, at this point, in 1942, Paul Robeson was at the height of fame. In spite of segregation color bars and other cultural obstacles, Robeson achieved fame and was an example others would follow. For Robeson, Othello embodied the conditions of black men. Figure 37 offers a candid view of Robeson as Othello.

Caught backstage, Robeson is clearly a leading actor dressed in costume appropriate to this seminal role. As the black Venetian general, Robeson's character has psychological and physical depth which, because it is Shakespeare's, escapes the usual racial limitations. The integrity of the role merges with the spirit of the man. He is allowed to achieve a seriousness of purpose, even though he is dressed in costume. There is nothing degrading about this role. Robeson has the appearance of a self-directed and incisive leader of men. The difference is particularly startling when compared to the voodoo king in *Voodoo*. The photograph points to the cultural extremes Robeson was to negotiate.

37. Robeson as Othello. c. 1943.
Photographs and Prints Division, Schomburg Center for Research in Black Culture, The New York Public Library, Astor, Lenox and Tilden Foundations.

In another studio portrait taken in 1934 (see figure 38), Robeson sports facial hair—a mustache and goatee. He is presented as a contemplative Robeson, different from many of the earlier photographs. At this time, Robeson is living in London, England, a society he found relatively more racially tolerant and open than America. He stares directly into the camera. It is a private view. His facial hair and open collar suggest an easy exchange with the photographer, as yet unidentified. I get the sense of what the sculptor Antonio Salemmé found in Robeson's presence: "You knew you met somebody unusual. There was no mannerism of any sort. Absolute authenticity. He spoke slowly and he took his time about everything. . . . Paul had this air of not going anywhere and yet he traveled fast. . . . He was a born gentleman . . . deeply a man of good will."[8] Salemmé had been working on a full-size statue of Robeson over a two-year period.

Compare this portrait with another London picture, a portrait of Lawrence Brown and Robeson rehearsing for a concert (see figure 39). Both these photographs demonstrate a personable figure. His integrity as a man and as a performer is left completely intact. Two undated photographs (c. 1940) (see figures 40 and 41) taken by black photojournalists Morgan and Marvin Smith for the black newspapers, most likely the New York *Amsterdam News,* offer an alternative view of Robeson. In both, Robeson is performing in concert at Mother A.M.E. Zion Church in Harlem. Significantly, Robeson's brother Ben was the pastor of the church. In figure 40 we can see that the surroundings are the barest necessities needed for the concert, chairs are stacked up under a stairway and behind Robeson. Several members of the audience are visible to the extreme left. Robeson and Lawrence Brown are singing pas-

39. Paul Robeson with Lawrence Brown rehearsing at the piano.
Photographs and Prints Division, Schomburg Center for Research in Black Culture, The New York Public Library; Astor, Lenox and Tilden Foundations.

sionately. Robeson's mouth is open and appears full of voice, his right hand rests as a fist upon the piano. Brown, seated and playing the piano, looks as if he is swaying back toward the audience. The men are connected and appear to be moved by their own performance. It is a measure of Robeson's strength as an artist that he appears as professional, as poised, under the most basic performing conditions. The portrait reads intimate, as the Smiths are able to record the moment at relatively close proximity to Robeson.

Similarly, figure 41 offers Robeson in mid-performance; this time the setting appears to be a stage. There is less light and Robeson's full figure is set against a dark background; directly behind Robeson is Brown at the piano. On the back of the photograph the setting is again described as "Mother Zion Church." And, again, the Smiths had close access to Robeson in making the portrait. What these photographs convey was Robeson's performance of the Negro spirituals. Even more than acting, the spirituals were what defined and distinguished Robeson as a performer. Indeed, no role was considered complete if Robeson did not sing. His rich bass-baritone voice was distinctive and recognizable. These portraits show the power and intimacy of his performance—in both cases for a largely African American audience—and the intensity of purpose not found in his acting stills. Robeson is defined as an individual, and not as a type. It is further significant that these photographs were taken

40. Paul Robeson with Lawrence Brown singing, in mid-performance. c. 1940.
Photo by Morgan and Marvin Smith. Photographs and Prints Division, Schomburg Center for Research in Black Culture, The New York Public Library; Astor, Lenox and Tilden Foundations.

41. Robeson performing. c. 1940.
Photo by Morgan and Marvin Smith. Photographs and Prints Division, Schomburg Center for Research in Black Culture, The New York Public Library; Astor, Lenox and Tilden Foundations.

for black newspapers. The black press would never have reproduced Robeson as seen in *Taboo*. Their editorial philosophy was to depict African Americans with dignity and poise, offering a contrast to Robeson's publicity stills put out by commercial studios. The Smith portraits point to the public identity an African American audience was interested in cultivating and promoting.

In this still from the movie version of *Show Boat* (see figure 42), Robeson is seated in the foreground of a dock on a Hollywood movie set. *Show Boat* is the story of a family who runs a vaudeville traveling show boat throughout the South. Thrown into this milieu are enslaved men and women also helping to work the show boat, whose lives parallel the main characters'. Robeson's character Joe is wearing a plaid shirt with sleeves rolled up to his elbow. He has a small knife in one hand, which appears to be a shaping tool or for shelling peas. The relaxed pose appears as if Robeson were resting between lifting the bales of cotton in the background. This scheme visually epitomizes the theme song that Robeson is known to have performed with distinction throughout his career, "Ol' Man River." As film critic Donald Bogle writes, "when Robeson sings 'Old Man River,' he brings the melodrama alive and even manages to triumph over the images we see as we hear him. When Robeson sings the lyrics about 'toting that barge and lifting that bale and spending another night in jail,' he's seen in the most stereotyped of montage sequences. But one forgets all that."[9] Robeson's constructed image is one of sensitivity and defiance. We see three men working in the background, the wagons full of cotton, and Robeson sitting, looking far off into the distance in what could be read as a contemplative pose. This carefully composed portrait was generated by Hollywood's publicity machine on the occasion of Robeson's first major Hollywood

42. Paul Robeson in a still from the film *Show Boat* (Universal, 1936). *Photographs and Prints Division, Schomburg Center for Research in Black Culture, The New York Public Library; Astor, Lenox and Tilden Foundations. Copyright renewed 1963, Universal Pictures.*

43. Robeson in a still from the film *Show Boat* (Universal, 1936). *Courtesy of the Academy of Motion Picture Arts and Sciences. Copyright renewed 1963, Universal Pictures.*

studio film. Robeson's character is a survivor. Significantly, the $40,000 Robeson received for the part represented a milestone for black actors in the film industry. Ironically, Gary Null cites a perplexing quote from Robeson published in *Film Weekly*:

> The box-office insistence that the Negro shall figure always as a clown has spoiled two Negro Films which have been made in Hollywood, *Hallelujah* and *Hearts in Dixie.*
>
> In *Hallelujah* they took the Negro and his church service and made them funny. . . . Hollywood can only visualize the plantation type of Negro . . . the Negro of 'Poor Old Joe' and 'Swanee Ribber.' It is as absurd to use that type to express the modern Negro as it would be to express modern England in the terms of an Elizabeth ballad.[10]

In *Sanders of the River*, a British film directed by Zoltan Korda, we once again find Robeson as another brooding African man in a faux Zulu costume with too much costume jewelry (see figure 44). In this still from the film, a moment representing the "African" scene, Robeson is poised with spear raised. We encounter the scowl, but it evokes a resignation, a limitation of where to go in such costume. Robeson's gaze is intense, the dramatic lighting of the portrait adds intensity to the eyes. Another publicity still from *Sanders of the River* (see figure 45) portrays a young flirtatious Robeson wearing the same large necklace of "animal-like" teeth. He is seated looking delicately at his fellow actress Nina Mae McKinney. The actress is kneeling, wearing beaded necklaces and arm bangles. She is dressed

44. Paul Robeson in the film *Sanders of the River* (London Film Productions, 1935).
Photographs and Prints Division, Schomburg Center for Research in Black Culture, The New York Public Library; Astor, Lenox and Tilden Foundations.

45. Paul Robeson and Nina Mae McKinney in *Sanders of the River* (London Film Productions, 1935).
Photographs and Prints Division, Schomburg Center for Research in Black Culture, The New York Public Library; Astor, Lenox and Tilden Foundations.

in a grass skirt and posed as if she is thumping a large drum. The pose is full of ironies about the romanticized and savage African. McKinney's hair is "pressed" and eyebrows arched; her breast is covered with a small wrapped fabric. Both Robeson and McKinney seem to be suppressing laughter, an expression that mocks and resists their costumed "primitive" appearance. It is as if both are at a costume party and recognize the level of hypocrisy and hilarity in the Western view of Africa. Neither seems to be working in "character" as was the case in *Voodoo*. Indeed, there is almost an intimacy of expression that reads as a level of communication between McKinney and Robeson. Their expressions offer a contradiction to their public predicament.

Robeson had initially looked forward to playing this role when he discussed the project with the director, ". . . if he could portray an African leader with cultural integrity and accuracy, he would be making a contribution in helping people—especially black people—to understand the roots of African culture. . . ."[11] Robeson was supportive of this film on many levels: he believed the research conducted by the Kordas would enhance an international understanding of the roots of African culture; he felt the music and dance of Africa could be better understood when placed within the context of this movie. He states, ". . . I think the Americans will be amazed to find how many of their modern dance steps are relics of an African heritage—a pure Charleston, for instance, danced in the heart of the Congo."[12] The photograph does not reveal or present the plot, which Robeson eventually rejected because of the glorification of colonialism in Africa. When it premiered in England, he denounced the film and tried to buy the rights to stop its distribution. Robeson, embarrassed by this film, was criticized by both the black and white press for his portrayal of Bosambo—who was viewed as a "loyal lackey, dependent on his white master." Fifteen years later, he stated to a black reporter, "I committed a *faux pas* which, when reviewed in retrospect, convinced me that I had failed to weigh the problems of 150,000,000 native Africans. . . . I hate the picture."[13] Film historian Donald Bogle posits "that Robeson went as far as attempting to buy the rights to the film in order to prevent distribution. Whether or not that is true, the film was released, to the deep and everlasting regret of Robeson."[14]

As we reinterpret these images of Robeson at the dawn of the twenty-first century, I am awed by the continued interest in Robeson's image, both the preservation and reconstruction of the image. In beginning to place Robeson's images in context within the larger picture of American history, I see an obvious shift of experiences documented by black and white photographers whose cameras followed his life. African American photographers working for the black press pictured Robeson in concert, allowing for the sense of dignity and the bearing of Robeson as a man to filter through. This figure was one of power and grace. These few photographs stand in marked contrast to the publicity stills made and manufactured by Hollywood. In those, Robeson performs the "primitive," sometimes resisting, but often conforming to the limitations imposed. There exists a crisis in meaning in looking at the visual evidence and the myth. Robeson's pictured image moves between the harsh and the solemn, paving a path for others to follow. As Harry Belafonte remarked, "It is because Robeson made his protest bitterly that we can be more lighthearted now."[15] There is no easy way out of these images. Robeson used all the means available to move culture toward an egalitarian and fairer place. In the end, we are left with the striking images of a man whose life transformed what would be possible for generations of African Americans.

46. Paul Robeson in the film *Sanders of the River* (London Film Productions, 1935). *Courtesy of the Academy of Motion Picture Arts and Sciences.*

47. Paul Robeson as "The Emperor Jones." 1933.
Photo by Edward Steichen. The Museum of Modern Art, New York. Gift of the photographer. Copyprint © 1998.
Courtesy of Vogue. *Copyright 1933 (renewed 1961) by Condé Nast Publications, Inc.*

Charles Musser

TROUBLED RELATIONS
Paul Robeson, Eugene O'Neill,
and Oscar Micheaux

In two brief years—1924 and 1925—Paul Robeson established himself as a preeminent, multi-talented performer with remarkable achievements in the theater, on the screen, and in concert. Robeson's association with the Provincetown Players and his appearance in two Eugene O'Neill plays—he debuted in *The Emperor Jones* on May 6, 1924, and in *All God's Chillun Got Wings* on May 15, 1924—were crucial to his success.[1] With Robeson performing each play in alternating week-long runs, they became the vehicles that launched him to stardom. Although these plays generated significant controversy from sectors of both the white and African American communities (though generally for quite different reasons), Paul Robeson and his wife, Eslanda (Essie) Goode Robeson, did not apparently share the critics' reservations. Their loyal, ongoing relationship with O'Neill was evident in the actor's various revivals of *The Emperor Jones* and *All God's Chillun,* in his subsequent appearances in O'Neill's *The Hairy Ape,* and in their extensive socializing with the playwright and his friends. This stands in marked contrast to their association with African American filmmaker Oscar Micheaux.

48. Photograph of Eugene
O'Neill in blackface with
Louise Bryant and George
Cram Cook in the 1916
Provincetown Players pro-
duction of *Thirst* at the
Wharf Theatre, Province-
town.
*Beinecke Library, Yale
University.*

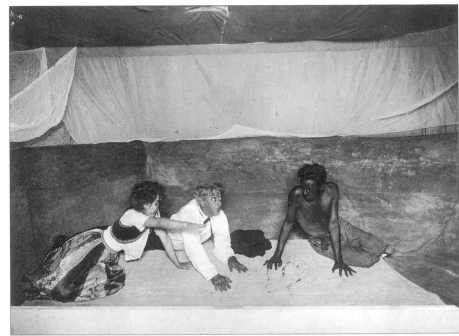

Only a few months after his debut in *The Emperor Jones*, Paul Robeson was appearing before Micheaux's cameras in *Body and Soul* (released in late 1925). Robeson's involvement in this motion picture proved so distasteful, however, that he and his wife avoided mentioning it in writings and interviews. It became a taboo subject. Indeed, for many years people believed that the 1933 film version of *The Emperor Jones* was Robeson's cinematic debut.[2] The Robesons' opposing reactions to these experiences point toward the complex relation-ships between the works, which is the subject of this essay.

WORKING ON *THE EMPEROR JONES*

Robeson's embrace of *The Emperor Jones* can be explained by the pleasures he experienced during its production. Here the actor found a seemingly utopian space in which he could explore his artistic aspirations. In the biography she wrote about her husband, *Paul Robeson, Negro* (1930), Essie devoted most of a chapter to his association with the Provincetown Players, who "wrote and produced plays entirely for intellectual and artistic self-expression and experiment."[3] As she described the nature of her husband's evolving relationship with these new colleagues: "At Jimmy's [James Light], Fitzy's [Eleanor Fitzgerald], or Gig's [Harold McGee] he had long talks with O'Neill about *Jones* and *Chillun*, about the meaning of the plays, about the purpose of the theatre. As he knew them better the talk drifted to the theatre in general, to life in general."[4] After having worked with second-rate theatrical dilettantes, Robeson was enamored with O'Neill and his circle (a feeling that unquestionably went both ways). There were leisurely, fascinating conversations—the very type of interaction that the actor enjoyed so much. "Paul began to sense vaguely how great plays were written," Essie observed.

> When a sensitive, gifted artist like Gene went into a community, or witnessed a human experience, or felt the powerful influences of nature, he reacted emotionally to them; because of his great gift he could go back to the theatre, and, with characters, conversation, scenes and acts recreate that community, or person . . . so successfully that he could make the people who saw his play know and understand and sympathise with that community or person . . . as he did; and perhaps feel, according to their sensitivity, at least some of the emotional reactions he felt. This knowledge gave Paul an entirely new conception of the theatre. As a spectator and as an actor it meant infinitely more to him. He could now get more from a play and give more to a play.[5]

In this process, Robeson came to have a new understanding about art, about life, and about himself. The Provincetown Players, concluded Essie, "were really responsible for Paul's choice of the stage as a career."[6]

49. Paul Robeson as "The Emperor Jones." c. September 1925.
Photo by Maurice Goldberg. The Alain Locke Papers, Moorland-Spingarn Research Center, Howard University.

Working with director James Light, the twenty-six-year-old Robeson felt he was given considerable latitude to make the parts of Brutus Jones and Jim Harris his own. As Essie remarked:

> They tore the lines to pieces and Paul built them up again for himself, working out his own natural movements and gestures with Jimmy's watchful help. "I can't tell you what to do," said Jimmy, "but I can help you find what's best for you." Paul was able to bring to both *Chillun* and *Jones* not only a thorough understanding of the script itself, but a further racial understanding of the characters.[7]

This sense of a true and honest collaboration has all the earmarks of a Stanislavskian approach in which the actor absorbs himself into the role, working from his own personal experience and sense of inner truth. As Constantin Stanislavsky wrote in *My Life in Art*, published in English the same year Robeson appeared in O'Neill's two plays:

> I speak of the truth of emotions, of the truth of inner creative urges which strain forward to find expression, of the truth of the memories of bodily and physical perceptions. I am not interested in a truth that is without myself, but the truth of my relation to this or that event on stage, to the properties, the scenery, the other actors who play parts in the drama with me, to their thoughts and emotions.[8]

Stanislavsky's "creative if" enables the actor to take a playscript, which is "a coarse scenic lie" and transform it into something fundamentally new—something in which the actor can and must totally believe: "the most delicate truth of his relation to the life imagined."[9] This working method helps to account for Robeson's sense of artistic integrity that sustained his devotion to O'Neill and associates. Indeed, given the freedom to interpret and present the role of Brutus Jones, he was quite content to retain the problematic language contained in *The Emperor Jones* playscript. In this he differed from the actor he was intended to replace—and discipline—Charles Gilpin.

Today *The Emperor Jones* is linked primarily to Paul Robeson, due to the 1933 film adaptation in which he starred. In the 1920s, however, the O'Neill play was associated first and foremost with Charles Gilpin, who originated the role and was then generally regarded as the leading black dramatic actor of his day. Gilpin and Robeson offered two quite different interpretations of the part. Robeson's size and charismatic presence made him fit naturally into the role of a larger-than-life dictator. As critic Will Anthony Madden remarked, "To begin with, Robeson has the physical build that makes him look the part of just what the character portrays and with that powerful rich voice and the ease with which he acts, I must say the theatre has gained a great deal by the addition of this sterling and promising actor to its ranks."[10] Gilpin—with his slighter build, older appearance (he was in his mid-forties by 1920), and apparent lack of sex appeal—had had to construct a character who achieved his aim through cunning, deceit, and guile. In the film *Ten Nights in a Bar Room*

50. Charles Gilpin as "The Emperor Jones." c. 1920. *Carl Van Vechten Collection, Beinecke Library, Yale University.*

(Colored Players of Philadelphia, 1926), Gilpin played a character on a steady downhill slide—a trajectory similar to the one he executed in *The Emperor Jones.* To this role he brought a sense of inner struggle and torment that was anguished and intense yet carefully calibrated and controlled.[11] It is this complexity that O'Neill undoubtedly found compelling in his performance, and why he preferred Gilpin to Robeson—despite his praise for the latter's work in that role. O'Neill's "preference" is surprising because the actors "collaborated" or interacted with the O'Neill playscript in quite different ways.

Gilpin had established himself as an important figure in black theater before appearing in *The Emperor Jones.* He had worked on the stage since the 1890s, and Sister Francesca Thompson informs us that he was the first of the Lafayette Players to be given star billing. Retaining a strong sense of independence, he quit that group when he felt his salary was insufficient.[12] According to Thomas Cripps, he lost a job in a major Hollywood production of *Uncle Tom's Cabin* because he played the part of Uncle Tom with too much aggression.[13] Gilpin was never a mannequin who did the producer's or director's bidding.

It is fashionable, and perhaps too easy, for today's critics to lambaste *The Emperor Jones.* Although a controversial work from the outset, and one the African American community found particularly problematic, *The Emperor Jones* did possess significant progressive attributes, if not as an isolated text, then as a piece performed in 1920s America. On the plus side, Jones can be seen as a complex, tragic figure in the tradition of Shakespeare's *Macbeth*—playing such a role was then a rare opportunity for black performers. In fact, the play provided both Charles Gilpin and Paul Robeson, the two great African American actors of the 1920s, with a vehicle for national recognition. Moreover, their casting in the play altered the racial politics of New York theater, where white actors in blackface had routinely played prominent African American characters. This practice disintegrated in the wake of O'Neill's work.[14] Finally, the play not only has one principal character, but also is particularly open to creative remolding by the actor who plays that role, and Eugene O'Neill did insist on a black actor.

O'Neill systematically avoided characters who might be seen as providing positive images, something that made many black critics and audiences unhappy, not only with *The Emperor Jones* but also *All God's Chillun*. As *All God's Chillun* went into rehearsals early in 1924, W.E.B. Du Bois publicly supported O'Neill for this refusal, providing an endorsement that was printed in the Provincetown Players playbill:

> . . . the Negro today fears any attempt of the artist to paint Negroes. He is not satisfied unless everything is perfect and proper and beautiful and joyful and hopeful. He is afraid to be painted as he is, lest his human foibles and shortcomings be seized by his enemies for the purpose of the ancient and hateful propaganda.

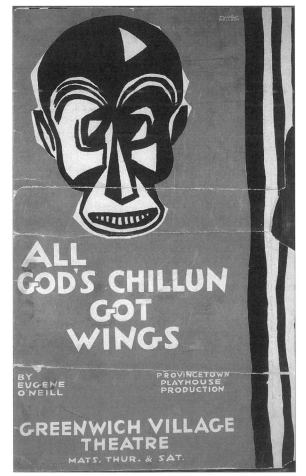

51. Original poster for Provincetown Playhouse production of *All God's Chillun Got Wings*. 1924. Silkscreen.
Library of Performing Arts, The New York Public Library, Astor, Lenox and Tilden Foundations.

Happy is the artist that breaks through any of these shells, for his is the king of eternal beauty. He will come through scarred, and perhaps a little embittered—certainly astonished at the almost universal misinterpretation of his motives and aims. Eugene O'Neill is bursting through. He has my sympathy, for his soul must be lame with the blows rained upon him. But it is work that must be done.[15]

Certainly it would be wrong to dismiss O'Neill's creations as simple, degrading stereotypes. Moreover, Robeson's persona, as it was then emerging, worked off and problematized these characters to a remarkable degree. Although Robeson played Jim Harris, who could not pass the bar exam in *All God's Chillun*, the actor was widely known as a successful graduate of Columbia Law School (albeit one who had found his opportunities in the profession blocked by racism within the legal establishment). Less foreseeable, less public and perhaps more controversial, the desexualized relationship between the Jim Harris character and the white woman who became his wife was not sustained in the backstage world that Robeson actually inhabited.[16] This gap between character and performer foregrounded the play as a construction and emphasized Robeson's talents as an actor.

Nevertheless, Gilpin and many black commentators of the time recognized that the plays' problems went well beyond the question of positive or negative images. There were deeper, less easily articulated issues of racial representation, as well as the more obvious one of language. One offensive aspect of *The Emperor Jones* and *All God's Chillun* was O'Neill's free use of the word "nigger," which he most often put in the mouths of his black characters. Brutus Jones constantly employs the term—referring to "bush niggers" and "common niggers." When talking to himself, he routinely uses this term of address. Once established in the role—if not from the very outset—Gilpin avoided the demeaning term. According to O'Neill's biographer Louis Sheaffer, Gilpin balked at the word "nigger" and changed it to "Negro" or "colored man." He began taking other liberties with the script as well. O'Neill eventually threatened to have him fired—or punch him out.[17] After 204 performances in New York, *The Emperor Jones* went on the road for two years, during which time Gilpin was free from close supervision and presumably adjusted the language to his own taste.

The Emperor Jones, as Gilpin performed it, was the product of a struggle between writer and actor. O'Neill himself was not always sure who had won, claiming that Gilpin "played Emperor with author, play and everyone concerned."[18] Certainly Gilpin felt that he had "created the role of Emperor, . . . [O'Neill] just wrote the play."[19] Gilpin's ability to transform the play, however, was limited. Certainly he could not alter the basic narrative and the assumptions that underlay it. For Gilpin, alcohol was one refuge. And when he reprised his performance in 1926, at least one critic noticed that Gilpin seemed to "lend the impression of a slight loss of enthusiasm in the role."[20] His acting suggested a certain distance between actor and character, at least to those looking for such signs in his rendering of the part.

Certainly this working against the grain was consistent with his treatment of the role of Uncle Tom in the Hollywood movie of Harriet Beecher Stowe's novel. James Baldwin's remarks seem apropos:

> It is scarcely possible to think of a black American actor who has not been misused. . . . What the black actor has managed to give are moments, created miraculously, beyond the confines of the script; hints of reality, smuggled like contraband into a maudlin tale, and with enough force, if unleashed, to shatter the tale to fragments.[21]

In his performance Gilpin resisted, implicitly criticized, and where possible transformed elements of the O'Neill play that he found offensive. Despite their different responses to the script, clearly both Gilpin and Robeson saw the performance of this play as something more than a simple, faithful rendering of a script. It was a creative process in which each brought his own considerable talents to bear. For the young Robeson, eager to make his mark in the world, it was a sudden, very positive opportunity.

WORKING FOR MICHEAUX

Oscar Micheaux, it is clear, dealt with Robeson in a way that was quite different from the Provincetown Players. A man of tremendous energy, Micheaux preferred socially engaged filmmaking to cinematic expression for art's sake. Moreover, given the costs associated with filmmaking, he operated under severe financial restraints where time was money. While working with the black producer-director, Robeson must have found few if any opportunities for leisurely exchanges and speculations about art and life. Certainly Micheaux did not

52. Oscar Micheaux. Undated.
Photographs and Prints Division, Schomburg Center for Research in Black Culture, The New York Public Library, Astor, Lenox and Tilden Foundations.

conceive of the relationship between playwright and actor as an equal one when it came to control over the final representation. His attitude was probably much closer to that of Sergei Eisenstein or Lev Kuleshov, for whom an actor's performance was just the raw material to be transformed by the subsequent processes of cinema. In a Micheaux film, aggressive editing and intertitles frequently changed the meaning and value of an actor's work.

Assuming he saw *Body and Soul*, Robeson must have felt manipulated and used. Micheaux had torn his performance to pieces and built it back up in a way that acquired new and unexpected meanings. Such feelings of alienation were not unusual for actors trained on the stage: Charles Chaplin, for example, was so deeply distressed about his loss of control when moving from stage to screen that he promptly insisted on directing the films in which he appeared. On stage, actors at least retained the illusion of having the final say, of offering the final interpretation. With film, particularly silent film edited in the Micheaux style, the opposite is true. This was doubtlessly a profound source of artistic conflict between Micheaux and Robeson. Micheaux was an auteur—a producer/writer/director. He was, in short, his own Emperor. Correspondingly, perhaps Robeson found concert work so appealing because it gave him full control over his own performance.

Robeson's loss of creative exploration and control was only one reason for the actor's unhappiness with *Body and Soul*. Although the picture was arguably the high point of Micheaux's career, it turned out to be a disaster for just about everyone involved. Panned by the press and attacked by the clergy, the film offended many in the black community. *The New York Amsterdam News* changed Micheaux's name to Mischeaux (as in mischievous) and dismissed all of his pictures as passé.[22] *The New York Age* refused even to mention the film. Here was an obvious reason for the Robesons to quietly forget its very existence.

This denial must have been unexpected, however, for the film had begun as a promising project of cultural significance and political weight. *Body and Soul* was perfectly designed to provide Robeson with a needed counterpoint to his work with the Provincetown Players. The interracial collaborations of Greenwich Village were complemented by an intraracial affiliation with the foremost African American film director of the silent era as well as with an essentially all-black cast. In what must have been seen as a starring vehicle, Paul was to play two roles—that of twin brothers. The first is a decent, hardworking inventor. His more prominent *doppelganger*, however, is a corrupt, womanizing preacher.

This role of a sociopathic clergyman might seem an unexpected choice for the youthful Robeson, whose father had been a minister. Yet it is worth noting that Essie began the opening chapter of the actor's biography with a lengthy and highly critical description of the ways in which black communities turned their preachers into godlike figures and then spoiled them. "Preachers, being human beings, had their failings. Some remained faithful to their great responsibilities and some remained unscrupulous."[23] Here was a topic, perhaps an obsession, that the Robesons and Micheaux seemed to share. Moreover, as Pearl Bowser and Louise Spence have remarked, African American newspapers were running headline stories about

53. Still photograph from *Body and Soul* (1926), Oscar Micheaux's film, showing Paul Robeson as minister. *Courtesy George Eastman House.*

54. Still photograph from *Body and Soul* (1926), Oscar Micheaux's film. Paul Robeson (left) as preacher. *Courtesy George Eastman House.*

the moral transgressions of prominent black clergymen, including their compromising ties to rumrunners in the age of prohibition.[24] Could not *Body and Soul* have been expected simply to add to the chorus of dismay and outrage? As we now know, the answer was a resounding "No." At the very least, the film lacks any counterexamples of honest and self-less preachers (indeed, the deacon seems eager to join the Robeson character in a sur-reptitious drink during his sermon). As Charlene Regester has suggested, in attacking the clergy so relentlessly he had broken an unwritten law.[25] The portrayal must have proved an embarrassment to, among others, the Reverend Benjamin (Ben) Robeson, Paul's older brother.

One other factor contributing to the Robesons' initial excitement with the film proj-ect involved Robeson's contract with Micheaux. Acting as his manager and showing her lack of knowledge of the film business, Essie contracted for her husband to receive a modest $100 per week for three weeks of work on *Body and Soul*. True, Paul was to receive 3 percent of the gross above $40,000.[26] Since the performer provided Micheaux with what is now called crossover potential, that financial participation must have seemed promising. That income became a moot question, however, after the film's critical reception and overall failure at the box office in the black community. The film apparently never reached white-oriented theaters. In retrospect, the Robesons must have realized that Micheaux had the better part of this bargain. The filmmaker had exploited their business naiveté, damaged the actor's image, and harmed his employability. In contrast, the O'Neill connection led to increasingly profitable work opportunities at home and abroad.

FROM THEATER TO FILM

All of Robeson's aforementioned problems and difficulties with Micheaux pale in compar-ison to one previously overlooked factor: Micheaux's picture *Body and Soul* was a profound reworking and critique of O'Neill's plays *The Emperor Jones* and *All God's Chillun*. Moreover, the film was not just an attack on O'Neill; it was a slap at Robeson himself. Once this critical insight is recognized, it solves any number of long-standing mysteries regard-ing the film. Not only does it explain the Robesons' furious silence; this framework for read-ing the text resolves the problem of its narrative incoherence. Although this interpretation of the film might at first glance seem farfetched, it was one I feel that Micheaux expected many in his audiences to grasp. Only the disastrous reception of the film—and perhaps also the changes demanded by censors—obscured this connection.

Body and Soul appeared at a time when the relationship between film and theater was extensive and frequently profound. The man many considered the greatest American actor of his day, John Barrymore, worked alternately in theater and film. (Many of the race films of the 1920s were likewise populated by black actors who had performed or continued to perform at the Lafayette Theater in Harlem, including Lawrence Chenault and Evelyn

Prier.) Film was the younger art, and cinematic adaptations or pirated reworkings of theatrical hits were common. Indeed, Thomas H. Ince had already turned Eugene O'Neill's *Anna Christie* into a film starring Blanche Sweet and directed by John Griffith Wray. Released in late 1923, it was hailed by *The New York Times* as a breakthrough in the history of cinema. "Here is a picture with wonderful characterization that tells a moving and compelling story—a film that is intensely dramatic, and one that will win new audiences for the screen."[27]

Not all filmic engagements with theatrical works in the 1920s were simple or friendly adaptations. In 1925, for example, Ernst Lubitsch directed an audacious reworking of Oscar Wilde's *Lady Windermere's Fan*, which completely avoided Wilde's dialogue. In this artistic duel, Lubitsch challenged Wilde's aphorisms and verbal wit with his own visual dexterity—what critical discourse was coming to recognize as the "Lubitsch touch." Lubitsch, moreover, was not above revising the narrative construction of scenes when he felt that Wilde had handled them awkwardly. For some critics this provided one basis for the film's success. Robert E. Sherwood praised the picture, noting that "Lubitsch filtered Wilde's manuscript through his own exceptionally sensitive mind, and then formed the resultant precipitation into the continuity for his picture."[28] For the *New York Times* critic Mordaunt Hall, this relationship created a kind of interference that made it difficult for him to enjoy the film.[29] Micheaux intended at least some members of his audience to appreciate *Body and Soul* within a somewhat similar intertextual framework. Micheaux did not require these viewers to have an intimate familiarity with the O'Neill plays, though this clearly would be helpful: audience members who had a decent familiarity with theatrical news in the black press would have appreciated much of what Micheaux was seeking to achieve.

Body and Soul calls out for spectators to make specific comparisons with *The Emperor Jones* and *All God's Chillun* at certain moments and encourages them subsequently to reflect on the film in this light. Moreover, Micheaux's employment of Robeson for this 1924–1925 picture was much more than the astute promotional scheme of a showman who hired a rising star cheap: Robeson's appearance in *Body and Soul* helped to forge a crucial intertextual connection between the film and the much publicized and discussed O'Neill plays. Micheaux offered particularly sustained parallels between *Body and Soul* and *The Emperor Jones* even as his radical textual displacements, structural inversions, condensations, and elaborations are extraordinary in their breadth, originality, and critique. These operations rework the play's basic narrative and thematics and result in a sustained engagement with its ideological presuppositions.

Let us begin with the basic, shared narrative of both *The Emperor Jones* and Micheaux's film: Robeson plays an escaped convict—an outsider—who comes to dominate a black community by concealing his past and by creating a new supernatural or religious identity. Brutus Jones, for example, has the local populace convinced that he has divine powers and can only be killed by a silver bullet. The Robeson character in Micheaux's film assumes the identity of a minister whom the women of his congregation treat as a Christlike figure: Martha Jane,

55. Still photograph from *The Emperor Jones* (United Artists, 1933).
Courtesy of the Academy of Motion Picture Arts and Sciences.

for example, cleans the faux preacher's shoes as if she were washing Christ's feet. Ultimately, however, each character played by Robeson is overthrown by his subjects or supporters, whom he has cynically exploited in the course of his stay in those communities. Each then escapes into the woodlands or jungle where he is tracked down by the angry populace. If this is not enough, the surname of the Robeson character in Micheaux's film, Reverend Isiah T. Jenkins, shares the first and last letters with the last name of O'Neill's character, Brutus Jones.

If one still resists Micheaux's linkage between characters and works, further evidence is provided by the two shots following the main title of *Body and Soul*. The first is an inter-title:

The Rt. Reverend Isiah T. Jenkins, alias, "Jeremiah,
The Deliverer"—still posing as a man of God.   —Paul Robeson

The second is a newspaper insert with the following information:

EX-CONVICT MAKES ESCAPE

"Black Carl," noted Negro detective, reports the escape of a prisoner whom he had arrested in Tatesville, Ga. and was bringing North for extradition to England where he was wanted on several charges. When arrested, the ex-convict and a man of many aliases, was posing as a preacher under the title of "The Rt. Reverend Isiah T. Jenkins."

Indeed, the action of *Body and Soul* unfolds in Tatesville, Georgia. The news item offers a kind of alternative closure to the main narrative of the film, which the audience might otherwise dismiss as "just a dream." But why is Black Carl bringing his prisoner north for extradition to England? A bizarre non sequitur until one realizes that Robeson was in London enjoying a much-celebrated appearance in *The Emperor Jones*, just as the film was opening. Ads and promotional copy made much of Robeson's English success, so audiences were prepared to appreciate the inside joke even before they entered the theater.

The full implication of this "joke" becomes evident in the refusal to provide the spectator with Jenkins's real name. Indeed, these cards suggest that Jenkins is just one of *Robeson's* many aliases. Brutus Jones and Jim Harris were two others. What then were the "crimes" of which Robeson was being accused? Undermining Gilpin and his resistant performances was one of Robeson's offenses.[30] Simply acting in the O'Neill plays, which some critics found deeply disturbing, is another starting point. African American theater critic Will Anthony Madden considered O'Neill's race plays to be "genius productions . . . of the most insidious and damaging kind."[31] Robeson's desire to appear in the plays is certainly understandable, but these ideological and ethical issues were exacerbated by Robeson's enthusiastic endorsement of the works in question. As *The Emperor Jones* had its London debut, roughly a month or so before the premiere of *Body and Soul*, Robeson mobilized his Stanislavsky-like outlook to endorse the play in the strongest and most disturbing terms. "O'Neill has got what no other playwright has—that is, the true, authentic Negro psychology. He has read the Negro soul, and has felt the Negro's racial tragedy," the actor remarked. Describing the process of playing a modern Negro who is gradually reduced to primeval man, Robeson added:

> One does not need a very long racial memory to lose oneself in such a part. . . .
> As I act, civilization falls away from me. My plight becomes real, the horrors terrible facts. I feel the terror of the slave mart, the degradation of man bought and sold into slavery. Well, I am the son of an emancipated slave and the stories of old father are vivid on the tablets of my memory.[32]

In this article, which appeared in Reynold's *Illustrated News* (London) and was reprinted in *The Pittsburgh Courier,* Robeson comes across as egotistic, somewhat simple-minded, and an Uncle Tom. In contrast to Gilpin, whose engagement with the playscript precluded "a childlike naïveté and trustfulness,"[33] Robeson wholeheartedly embraces it. If *The Emperor Jones* was insidious, as Micheaux and many African American critics believed, then Robeson's statements were compounding the offense. The actor was also grandstanding, and Micheaux opened the film with two title cards that cut him down to size. They suggest that Robeson is not an actor playing evil roles but is himself a dissembler very much like the characters he plays. Or put another way, Robeson confused the (white) stage with real (black) life.[34] Robeson and his friends were not simple-minded. They must have realized that *Body and Soul* was a not-so-private joke made at his expense. No wonder the performer never mentioned it.

MICHEAUX'S TRANSFORMATION OF *THE EMPEROR JONES*

Micheaux's digs at Robeson must have been added shortly before the film's premiere. Initially the filmmaker was probably more interested in using Robeson to engage O'Neill's depictions of Negro life than in abusing his actor. How then did Micheaux rework *The Emperor Jones*, transforming it into this extraordinary film *Body and Soul*? He began by taking what one Paris reviewer astutely called "an American fantasy,"[35] what Micheaux clearly believed was a white fantasy, and resituated it back in black reality. That is, he saw the clergy as the center of power in many black communities and eagerly explored how such power could be abused by an unprincipled con artist or impostor. In this he was transposing O'Neill via Charlie Chaplin's *The Pilgrim* (1923), in which Charlie is an escaped convict who is forced to play the role of village parson or face exposure and arrest. In contrast to Chaplin's picture, however, Micheaux subsumed comedy under the conventions of drama and melodrama.

In *The Emperor Jones* O'Neill underscores the point of economic exploitation and makes clear that Jones is merely doing what he learned from watching powerful (white) heads of corporations and government, who stole big time. Even though O'Neill's Marxist sympathies are evident, in the end the playwright is not interested in the politics of exploitation so much as the psychological unravelings of an individual.[36] Brutus Jones talks about how he took the islanders' money, but the process is never shown. Micheaux, in contrast, spends most of his film detailing the many ways in which the Reverend Jenkins exploits the black community. The film begins with Jenkins helping himself to a saloonkeeper's hard liquor and then demanding a "donation," threatening the hooch seller with an antiliquor campaign if he protests. The impostor builds his power base by endearing himself to his congregation, particularly

56. Paul Robeson in a scene from *The Emperor Jones* (United Artists, 1933).
Courtesy of the Academy of Motion Picture Arts and Sciences.

57. Paul Robeson on the throne in *The Emperor Jones* (United Artists, 1933).
Courtesy of the Academy of Motion Picture Arts and Sciences.

the older women who fantasize a sexual relationship with him. Martha Jane just represents an extreme case as she seeks to have her unrequited desires played out through her daughter, Isabelle. That is, Micheaux shows us some of the mechanisms whereby the real "Emperors" of the community pull the levers of power. These are not based on the imitation of white capitalists but are embedded in the specific structures of African American communities. Micheaux's "opening up" of the narrative might be compared to the 1933 film adaptation of the play itself. In that film, the filmmakers expanded on the narrative by tracing out the personal life story of Brutus Jones. His arrival at the island is touched upon, but scenes which credibly depict the process of exploitation and make substantial the conditions of the oppressed are absent.

This does not mean that Micheaux was uninterested in psychological issues. The portrait he created of Martha Jane is a remarkably sophisticated study of this woman's pathology: her willful blindness and girlish naiveté in the face of a difficult life of toil. As the dreamer, she is the film's psychological center; she is also the character who changes, who awakens. In contrast, Micheaux rejects the psychological devolution of the Jones/Jenkins character—the stripping away of civilization and his reduction to the primeval state of the jungle. Jenkins is evil: a dissembler from start to finish. When his wicked behavior has been exposed and he is fleeing from the posse, he grovels in front of Martha Jane and convinces her that she has spoiled him and so is responsible for what he has done. Told that only she can save him, Martha Jane hides him and then helps him escape. But Jenkins has not changed. His unraveling is simple play-acting as he exploits—albeit somewhat desperately—her known weaknesses. Although the film does trace a downward spiral, it is not in respect to his psychological unraveling but in the brutality with which he steals and the severity of his crimes.

Micheaux ultimately rejected O'Neill's interior psychological drama and reasserted the melodramatic tradition by reintroducing a series of oppositions: good and evil, victim and victimizer, innocence and corruption, and even women and men. Isabelle is one of the archetypal innocents or long-suffering victims of villainy who, as Peter Brooks suggests, are unable to speak.[37] In this instance, Isabelle cannot speak because she will not be believed by her own mother. Jenkins is clearly on the side of villainy, in ways that Brutus Jones is not. Brutus is in some sense a tragic figure, caught up in a world, burdened with a fate that is beyond his control. Jeremiah ("the deliverer") has no such redeeming qualities. Again consider the transpositions Micheaux introduces when the Robeson character moves through the forest. As Jones flees through the jungle, going in circles, he becomes the victim of his own terror, of his own return to an African primitivism. He wants to go in a straight line to safety but in circling back ensures his own demise. As Jenkins and Isabelle go in circles through the woods during a rainstorm, the circling would appear calculated on Jenkins's part. Isabelle is isolated and cut off, the protection that society offers her is lost, and he is free to rape her. Likewise, when he circles the table to grab Isabelle and force her to hand him her mother's money, Jenkins is reduced to an uncivilized brutality even as he remains self-conscious of his own

58. Paul Robeson as "The Emperor Jones." 1933.
Photo by Edward Steichen. Courtesy George Eastman House. Reprinted with permission of Joanna T. Steichen.

actions (stepping back and finding a sadistic pleasure in Isabelle's pain and greeting her emotional pleadings with clever word games). And when he later flees from his congregation, he may be desperate but he does not lose his head. Rather than being killed, he turns and kills his pursuer. This stands O'Neill on his head. For O'Neill the mechanisms of oppression are the universal ones of white capitalism, but barbarism is tied to the African American unconscious. Micheaux reveals that the mechanisms of exploitation are in some sense specific to small black communities deprived of other forms of leadership (elected officials, legitimate businessmen, and so on). Nonetheless, Jenkins represents a different and unracialized form of barbarism. Jeremiah/Jenkins is a sociopath not unlike Hannibal Lector in *Silence of the Lambs.*

Micheaux's rewriting of O'Neill's play occurs along other trajectories. In *The Emperor Jones*, "the people" are savages effectively outside of civilization and its ethical distinctions. These social decencies are restored in Micheaux's film. Micheaux reminds us how Martha Jane earned the money she saved: picking cotton, ironing other people's clothes, and so forth.

59. Paul Robeson in still from the film *The Emperor Jones* (United Artists, 1933).
Courtesy of the Academy of Motion Picture Arts and Sciences.

60. Paul Robeson in *The Emperor Jones* at the Savoy Theatre, London. 1925.
Photo by Sasha. Courtesy of Hulton Getty/Tony Stone Images.

Their homes and communal spaces—the domestic interiors in which they live—are shown (excepting the opening scene in the palace, O'Neill limits himself to psychological interiority). Likewise, in both *The Emperor Jones* and *All God's Chillun*, it is obvious that O'Neill has an uncomfortable time dealing with black sexuality and avoids it at all costs. In *All God's Chillun*, Jim and Ella live like brother and sister. There is only one female character in *The Emperor Jones* and she is older and clearly of no sexual/romantic interest for Brutus or the audience. Brutus may be a dictator who appreciates high living, but he appears remarkably chaste. His principal preoccupation seems to have been accumulating money. This may have been credible when Gilpin played the role, but when Robeson took over, with his charisma that exuded an intense sexuality, this absence became painfully clear. Micheaux would have none of this. It is Jenkins's attractiveness that binds and blinds the older women, making them his chief supporters. Rape and seduction are Jenkins's métier: prerogatives that come with the office.

French reviewers commented that *The Emperor Jones* seemed too underdeveloped to be a truly satisfying theatrical experience. Where O'Neill is silent or retreats from a fully developed story, Micheaux is ready to confront and elaborate. He also is ready to engage issues of language, something that Gilpin had also found disturbing in O'Neill's work. He does this in two ways. First at judicious moments he counters the associations of white with good,

61. Still photograph from *Body and Soul* (1926), Oscar Micheaux's film. Paul Robeson singing with Bible on his shoulder. *Courtesy George Eastman House.*

62. Still photograph from *Body and Soul* (1926), Oscar Micheaux's film. Paul Robeson singing and gesturing. *Courtesy George Eastman House.*

dark with evil—which O'Neill mobilizes but leaves intact and unquestioned in *All God's Chillun*. Isabelle at one point calls Jenkins "a white-livered, lying hypocritical beast." Such constructions are carefully selected to make audiences sensitive to this use of language and aware of its arbitrariness and potential reversibility. Charlene Regester has also pointed out that Isabelle chastises her mother for using the term "nigga'" which she calls vulgar. Although the word appears in *Body and Soul* rarely, perhaps we might say judiciously, it is significant that the word is always written in dialect and is never literally spelled out. Moreover, her pronunciation of the word matches that of "pastah."[38]

Finally any extended engagement of *Body and Soul* must consider the Robeson *doppelganger* and Micheaux's use of dream, both of which have been much discussed but perhaps little understood. Suggestions that these can be explained as responses to censorship demands miss the point.[39] The playing of double roles at this time was a popular cinematic convention—Marion Davies played a double role in *Lights of Old Broadway* (1924) and dozens of other examples in American cinema of the 1910s and 1920s could be offered. It gave an actor the opportunity to display the full range of his or her acting talents. Again this can be understood as a response to *The Emperor Jones*, which was hailed as a unique opportunity for black actors. Certainly Robeson's performance in *Body and Soul* is, to my mind at least, far more inventive and impressive than his work in the film version of *The Emperor Jones*. It may well be his best screen performance. But the *doppelganger* is more than an artistic trope. These two brothers are linked to the Robeson characters in O'Neill's two race plays. If Jenkins is Jones's alter-ego, then Sylvester is the nonneurotic, healthy counterpart to the tortured Jim Harris of *All God's Chillun*. Indeed, Sylvester is dressed in a suit that appears to be identical to the one worn by Jim Harris.[40] Like Jim, Sylvester is ready to marry and embrace a woman who has been seduced/raped/corrupted by someone else. But here the parallels end. While Jim Harris fails to become a lawyer, Sylvester becomes

63. Brutus Jones costume from the film of *The Emperor Jones*. 1933.
Museum of the City of New York. Gift of John Krimsky and Cochrane Gilford.

a successful inventor. Jim Harris's efforts are undermined by the machinations of his white wife, Ella Downey, while Sylvester's efforts are fostered by the devotion of Isabelle. In *Body and Soul,* as in other Micheaux films, love and marriage become an act of racial solidarity that acts as a necessary defense against societal exploitation.

As has been often noted, Robeson's double role in *Body and Soul* wreaks havoc with any notion of a logical plot. If Sylvester lives in the same town as his brother, then his brother's past and posturing as a minister become impossible. The integration of these two narrative strands is achieved as the result of a metacritical engagement with O'Neill's work and through a character's hallucinatory or dream state. It is Martha Jane's persistent, even absurd, dream state that encourages African American audiences to scream at her to "Wake up!" as the film unspools.[41] Of course, *The Emperor Jones* should itself be understood as an expressionist rendering of its main character's inner state. So there is a parallel and inversion here once again. Martha Jane rather than Jenkins replaces Brutus Jones as the psychological pivot. Yet Martha Jane does finally respond to the audience's cries. She does wake up. And she does do the right thing. In this nonrealist text, Micheaux thus gives us a message echoed seventy years later by several films by Spike Lee, notably *School Daze* (1988) and *Do the Right Thing* (1989).

As a Micheaux character said in *Within Our Gates* (1919), "it is the duty of each member of our race to help destroy ignorance and superstition." For Micheaux, it was the duty of these films to awaken their audiences and to force them to reflect on their predicament. Indeed, this was a message that *Body and Soul* addressed not only to audiences in Harlem and other black urban communities of the 1920s but to Robeson himself. It was a message that Robeson was not then ready to hear. It would be another ten or fifteen years, after a series of unhappy experiences in the British and American film industries, before the performer's viewpoint would begin to change.

64. Paul Robeson in still from *The Emperor Jones*. 1933.
Corbis-Bettmann.

65. Paul Robeson singing at the Civil Rights Assembly. Washington, D.C. January 1949.
Photo © by Julius Lazarus.

Doris Evans McGinty
Wayne Shirley

PAUL ROBESON, MUSICIAN

Of the several aspects of a life filled with outstanding achievements, none is so impressive as that of Paul Robeson, musician. In an early stage of his career as a singer, he performed a historical concert on April 19, 1925, at the Greenwich Village Theatre in New York with Lawrence Brown, an African American, as piano accompanist. The concert was historic not only because it garnered pivotal critical approval for Robeson, but also because it drew attention to the solo vocal program built exclusively around music reflecting black culture. Although Robeson had given a concert devoted to music by African Americans at Boston's Copley Plaza Hotel on November 2, 1924, the program was not exclusively vocal: a lengthy piano solo performance by his accompanist was included. Both concerts were well received. Critics writing for the *Boston Transcript* and the *Boston Post* were highly enthusiastic, but it was probably the overwhelming praise from the New York critics that brought wide attention to Robeson, the musician. He was acclaimed in the *New York Evening Post*, the *New York Times,* and the *New York News*: in the last, Edgar G. Brown called Robeson the

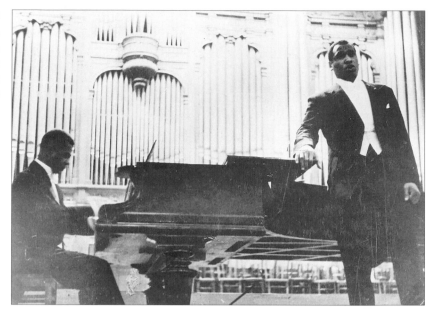

"Embodiment of the New Negro and the next Caruso." This was the beginning of a lucrative and highly successful career as a concert singer.

From Robeson's point of view, embarking on a concert singing career was a leap into a new area of performance. By 1925, he was an established actor, with performances in New York and London to his credit. As a concert singer, however, he was practically a novice: prior to the Boston concert, which developed as a result of encouragement from his wife, Eslanda, and friends—especially Carl Van Vechten—Robeson had sung relatively little in public. Yet he accomplished the transition from theater to concert stage with apparent ease. His extraordinary vocal endowment was, of course, the major factor, but there were others. His experience on the dramatic stage, which included moments of singing, must have been helpful, and it is likely that his singular rapport with the music that he chose to sing was of great importance. He had a deep understanding of and great affection for the Negro spirituals and secular songs which he heard in church and community during his childhood, and he considered them integral to his being. The Greenwich Village Theatre audience overwhelmingly approved the experiment, and Robeson went on to repeat his triumph throughout the United States and in many other parts of the world. Lionized on both sides of the Atlantic, he sang to sold-out houses in the most eminent concert auditoriums such as Carnegie Hall in New York, the Royal Albert Hall in London, and Tchaikovsky Hall in Moscow. He was welcomed just as eagerly in African American churches—large and small—meeting halls of labor unions, and outdoor stadiums where his audiences sometimes numbered in the tens of thousands.[1] Robeson's contribution to rekindling interest in the spiritual, if judged solely by the number of persons who heard him sing, was enormous.

When Robeson sang Negro spirituals on his history-making programs, it was not the first time that the folk song had appeared in concert dress. The world had been awakened to the beauty and appeal of this music by the Fisk Jubilee Singers in their travels across the United States, England, and Europe in the 1870s. Setting out with the purpose of aiding financially beleaguered Fisk University, the singers succeeded in raising over $150,000 for the school. In their performances the Fisk Jubilee Singers modified the folk songs which had been handed down by oral tradition from pre–Civil War days and created the tradition of the concert spiritual. European harmonies were added, and as a result some of the melodic inflections and rhythmic flexibility involved in the original performance practices were inhibited or eliminated. Moreover, the concert hall environment was less hospitable to the freedom and spontaneity that characterized the folk-style performance. The folk tradition did not die out, however, but continued to flourish in communities such as that in which Robeson spent his childhood. In the meantime, choral groups, including professional jubilee groups and choirs of historically black colleges and universities, performed in the concert tradition, often using arrangements supplied by African American composers.

In 1916, composer and baritone Harry T. Burleigh (1866–1949) published a version of the spiritual "Deep River" arranged for solo voice. Burleigh was the first recognized African

67. Paul Robeson. c. 1925.
Photo by Lester Walton. Photographs and Prints Division, Schomburg Center for Research in Black Culture, The New York Public Library, Astor, Lenox and Tilden Foundations.

70. Paul Robeson in concert at Mother A.M.E. Zion Church (church of brother Benjamin) in Harlem. 1956. *Photo © by Julius Lazarus.*

71. Paul Robeson signing autographs for several Black women after singing performance at Mother A.M.E. Zion Church in Harlem. 1956. *Photo © by Julius Lazarus.*

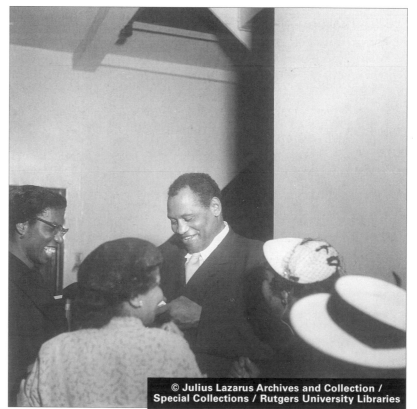

72. Portrait of Roland Hayes by Winold Reiss. 1925.
Pastel on board.
National Portrait Gallery, Smithsonian Institution.

enjoyed and came to expect. Robeson sometimes exercised a prerogative of folk song prac-tice by adding verses or making changes in the words which underlined his struggle for liberation of the oppressed. For example, in "We Are Climbing Jacob's Ladder," the line "Soldiers of the cross" could become "Soldiers in the fight," or the line "Freedom, we must have" could appear in "No More Auction Block for Me."

It did not suit Robeson's aims to study voice extensively as would be expected of a con-cert artist devoted to classical music. However, in 1926, he worked with vocal coach Frantz Proschowskya and studied voice with Teresa Armitage, a high-school teacher, with an eye toward improving his vocal skills and learning to preserve his voice. When in the early 1930s he studied with Jerry Swinford, well-known vocal coach, we may conclude that his purpose was to extend his range as a musician as he expanded his repertoire, an expansion that will be described later in this essay. In 1934, Robeson clearly expressed his artistic aspirations: "I am not an artist in the sense in which they [music critics] want me to be an artist and of which they could approve. I have no desire to interpret the vocal genius of half a dozen cultures which are really alien cultures to me. I have a far more important task to perform."[2]

On the whole Robeson fared well at the hands of music critics who actually faced a chal-lenge when writing about his concerts. Finding it difficult to review a non-traditional recital in the traditional manner, critics often relied upon descriptions of Robeson's stage presence, his dignity, his facial expressions, the affectionate delight he showed in his singing. Almost unfailingly, they were moved by the power of the voice. Robeson's voice, marked by the deep resonance in the lower register that is associated with the true bass voice (although Robeson's was more frequently designated a bass-baritone), sent critics scrambling for adjectives like "mellow," "velvety," "luscious," "smooth," and "rich," and phrases such as "a voice in which deep bells ring," and "deep and rolling bass." Glenn Dillard Gunn of the *Chicago Herald Examiner* pronounced Robeson's voice "one of the most beautiful in the world" (February 1, 1926). Above all, critics responded to an undeniable authenticity in Robeson's rendition of the African American spiritual.

It was inevitable that music journalists would compare Robeson with Roland Hayes, the African American singer who had been acclaimed for his masterful singing of spirituals. At first, critics tended, generally, to prefer the Robeson style, pointing out his naturalness and expressing pleasure in the absence of the effects of formal training. Some, however, found the Robeson recitals lacking in artistry. And while, more often than not, critics expressed surprise that programs of spirituals could provide sufficient variety to sustain interest, a few writers were critical of what they conceived of as monotony in his programs. Appearances on programs with other musicians—violinist Wolfi, pianists Vitya Vronsky, Ania Dorfman, and Solomon, thereminist Clara Rockmore, the Brahms [string] Quartette, to name a few—might have served to answer the criticism of monotony. On one of the occasions when Robeson sang a concert using orchestral accompaniment for the spirituals instead of the piano, a change which might have been thought to create variety, another objection was raised, for critics found his Paris concert with Pierre Monteaux and orchestra somewhat artificial.

From time to time, reviews, even though laudatory, were somewhat condescending in tone, introducing such stereotypical concepts as the naiveté or childlike enthusiasm of the colored race. Even the frequent mentions of Robeson's naturalness, though apparently accurate when applied to Robeson's stage presence, smacked a bit of the oft-repeated notion that African Americans achieved artistic success not through the application of intellect or industry but only as a result of God-given talent.

The addition to his programs of art songs and operatic selections typical of the classical vocal recital seemed to be an obvious next step for Robeson, if he was to grow as a musician, let alone answer his critics. But, as if to emphasize his conviction regarding the value of and the contribution made by the music of black culture, he continued for five years to devote entire programs to Negro spirituals and secular folk songs. He was disappointed that audiences in some African American communities seemed to prefer programs of classical European content; yet he was not deterred from his mission. He stated it thus: "Now, if I can teach my audiences who know almost nothing about the Negro, to know him through my songs and through my roles . . . then I will feel that I am an artist, and that I am using my art for myself, for my race, and for the world."[3] Few, if any, other musicians of Paul Robeson's stature have been able to conduct a career in which the artist's philosophy and mission were reflected so clearly in the content of the music performed.

From 1929 onward, Robeson began to inject more frequent and lengthier comments between songs, discussing the meanings of the spirituals and highlighting their relationship to the universal sufferings of mankind. He also began to incorporate recitations from his famous roles in the theater. By the 1930s, the Negro spiritual was no longer the driving factor in his performances. In fact, neither of the two pieces now most closely associated with Robeson—"Ol' Man River" and *Ballad for Americans*—is a spiritual. We shall come back to these two at the end; first we shall take a general look at Robeson's repertory other than the spirituals.

For most of us the knowledge of Robeson's singing, and of his repertory, comes through his recordings. The late recordings, representing concert appearances, are accurate

73. Paul Robeson listening to latest Marconiphone radio to get English pronunciation in preparation for concert. 1931.
Courtesy of Hulton Getty/Tony Stone Images.

reflections of his repertory of the time. But we should look at the earlier Robeson discography with a certain skepticism. Concert audiences love to hear what a singer does best: thus the repertory of a touring singer changes slowly, and many works remain on the program from season to season. But recordings require constant new repertory: there's no point in rerecording something already on disc. Thus recordings often represent material gotten up for the session and then discarded. For Robeson this is particularly true for the pre-1940 recordings made for the English company Gramophone. Later recordings, done first for Columbia Records and then for a variety of labels including Robeson's own company Othello Records, tend to represent repertory he was committed to.

Among the Gramophone recordings, those with Lawrence Brown represent material Robeson did in concert; those with orchestra are more likely to be material gotten up for recording only. Some of the just-for-recording repertory is fairly routine: beloved hymns ("Nearer, My God, to Thee") and sentimental favorites ("Trees"). Other repertory is more puzzling to those seeking to understand Robeson. This is especially true of the fairly large

74. Paul Robeson in concert at Royal Albert Hall, London. December 13, 1931.
Photographs and Prints Division, Schomburg Center for Research in Black Culture, The New York Public Library, Astor, Lenox and Tilden Foundations.

75. Still from the film *Show Boat* (Universal, 1936).
Courtesy of the Academy of Motion Picture Arts and Sciences. Copyright renewed 1963, Universal Pictures.

number of Dear-Old-Southland numbers he recorded—"Dear Old Southland" itself; "Carry Me Back to Green Pastures," even "That's Why Darkies Were Born." Robeson sings these songs stunningly, but they were not part of his active repertory.

Nor, save for an occasional "St. Louis Blues," were the various blues and jazz numbers he recorded. These recordings are usually seen in the light of Count Basie's statement, "It certainly is an honor to be working with Mr. Robeson, but the man certainly can't sing the blues." Judged by less exacting standards, many of them are worth listening to: certainly they can hold their own against present-day Classical Crossover recordings.

Robeson's film songs are another example of special repertoire. One song Robeson learned for a film—Mendelssohn's "Lord God of Abraham," sung in *Proud Valley*—became a staple of his repertory; but of songs written especially for films, only "I Still Suits Me," written for the film version of *Show Boat,* was much performed by Robeson. Other film songs were duly released on recording—and therefore remain audible to this day—but were not sung by Robeson in concert. Thus for many years we could hear Robeson singing the faintly hilarious "Killing Song" from *Sanders of the River,* but not "O Isis und Osiris."[4]

As we have seen, Robeson's concert programs of the 1920s often contained one set described as "Negro folk-songs." This group would contain secular folk songs—notably "Water Boy"; it would often contain also one or two songs by the pre–World War I generation of African American composers. Robeson continued his loyalty to these composers through the 1930s, regularly performing such songs as J. Rosamond Johnson's "Li'l Gal" and Will Marion Cook's "Down de Lovah's Lane." Later Robeson assayed an occasional song in "Li'l Gal" style by a white composer: Clutsam's "Ma Curly-Headed Baby" remained in Robeson's repertory to the end, and Lily Strickland's "Mah Lindy Lou" was sung fairly often in the 1930s. (Perhaps it was these songs that caused Gramophone to suggest the Dear-Old-Southland numbers: if he sang J. Rosamond Johnson's "Dis Little Pickaninny's Gone to Sleep," why shouldn't he sing "Got the South in My Soul"?)

Late in 1930 Robeson began expanding his concert repertory beyond the spirituals and black secular numbers. In 1931 this expansion took the form of a direct onslaught on the central repertory of the classic Lieder singer: his 1931 programs often started with a group consisting of Beethoven's "Die Ehre Gottes aus der Natur," "O Isis und Osiris" from *The Magic Flute,* "Passing By" by Edward Purcell, and a Schumann song—sometimes "Die beiden Grenadiere," sometimes "Ich grolle nicht." (A second set would lead, by way of two Russian songs, to Robeson's black repertory, usually starting with "Water Boy.")

"Die Ehre Gottes" and "O Isis und Osiris" continue appearing, though not in tandem, on those recitals for which Robeson wanted a majestic opening number, until the early 1940s, when they are replaced by "Lord God of Abraham." But after 1931 he avoided performing an entire group weighted toward the Germanic repertory. During the early 1930s English recital songs—Roger Quilter's "Now Sleeps the Crimson Petal," John Ireland's "Sea Fever"— occasionally took up the slack. But by the late 1930s he tended, for concerts requiring a group from the standard concert-singer repertory, to do a Russian group, sometimes all-Moussorgsky. This allowed Robeson to sing in his beloved Russian: it also tantalized audiences with excerpts

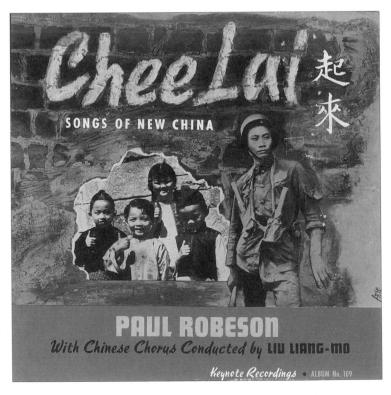

76. *Chee Lai. Songs of New China.* Album cover, Keynote Recordings. 1941. *Charles L. Blockson Private Collection.*

from *Boris Godunov,* causing many to wonder whether Robeson might take on the role on the operatic stage.

In 1934 Robeson began including a general folk-song group in his concerts. English audiences had long been accustomed to such a group; here the audience's expectation and Robeson's interest were one. Early folk-song groups are heavy on folk songs of the British islands—including Cecil Sharp's arrangement of "Oh No, John," which Robeson continued to program throughout his career. In later years he added folk songs of other lands. As his political commitment became stronger these songs were increasingly chosen from radical sources: "Chee Lai," "The Peat-Bog Soldiers." Along with these came more militant African American folk songs—songs from Lawrence Gellert's classic 1936 collection *Negro Songs of Protest* and militant early spirituals such as "No More Auction Block for Me."

In the early 1940s, with the release of his first song album for Columbia Records (his first Columbia album had been *Othello*), Robeson found a phrase for the music he was most interested in performing—*Songs of Free Men.* He explained in the notes to the album:

> The particular songs in this album have . . . folk quality and show in no uncertain way the common humanity of man. Beyond this, they issue from the present common struggle for a decent world, a struggle in which the artist must also play his part.
>
> These songs are a very important part of my concert programs, expressing much of what I deeply feel and believe.

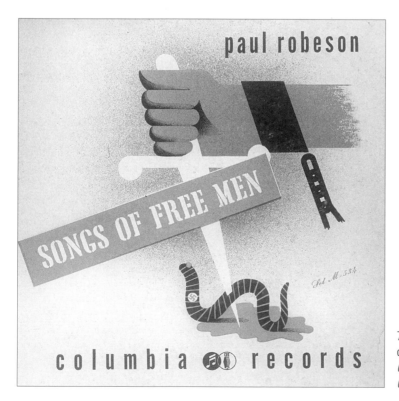

77. *Songs of Free Men.* Album cover, Columbia Records. c. 1944. *Charles L. Blockson Private Collection.*

In fact the album included both folk songs—"The Four Insurgent Generals"; "The Peat-Bog Soldiers"—and songs in folk and popular styles such as Earl Robinson's "Joe Hill" and Marc Blitzstein's "The Purest Kind of a Guy." For the remainder of Robeson's career the "Songs of Free Men" were to be as important as the spirituals: this repertory is, finally, as important to understanding Robeson as musician as are the spirituals.

We rightly see this repertory in terms of Robeson the activist, but it also revitalized him as a musician. And his championing of the repertoire was finally important for the repertoire itself: In a world where status was granted to a piece by its appearance on concert programs, it was more significant that Robeson sang "The House I Live In" than that Sinatra sang it; it was the fact that Robeson sang "Joe Hill" that made it the well-known song it is today.

———

Suddenly, in mid-1935, "Ol' Man River," which had shown up on almost every Robeson program for several years previous, disappeared from his printed programs. It had not dropped

78. Announcement for *Show Boat* London production with Paul Robeson and Alberta Hunter. 1928.
Photographs and Prints Division, Schomburg Center for Research in Black Culture, The New York Public Library, Astor, Lenox and Tilden Foundations.

out of Robeson's repertory, it had just become so inevitable as an encore that it lost its place on the regular program. (Its place as a formal ender was taken by "Joshua" or—for lighter programs—"Shortnin' Bread.")

It was Robeson's voice that suggested "Ol' Man River" to Jerome Kern and Oscar Hammerstein II, and Robeson's association with the song is so thorough that we must be reminded from time to time that he was not the first person to sing the song. The part of Joe, who sings "Ol' Man River," was sung in the original (1927) production of *Show Boat* by Julius ("Jules") Bledsoe. Robeson first sang the role in the 1928 London production. "Ol' Man River" first appeared on his concert programs in 1931; by then he had already recorded it three times.

In later life Robeson found his association with "Ol' Man River" something of a problem: how could he preach the need for action when people would not go home until he had sung this song, with its outer message of human powerlessness? Robeson, who was no stranger to the changing of words (he recorded Foster's "Old Black Joe" as "Poor Old Joe"; in his Carnegie Hall recording of Othello's final monologue "the circumcisèd dog" becomes "the damnèd heathen dog") solved this problem by altering the lyrics to make it a song of determination:

> But I keeps laughin'
> Instead of cryin';
> I must keep fightin'
> Until I'm dyin' . . .

This was a necessary change for Robeson (the alternative was to refuse to sing "Ol' Man River" at all), though it makes for a much more negative version of the song: the river, despite all that determination, just keeps rolling along. The original "Ol' Man River," in fact, carries the powerful subtext that it is Joe, as well as the river, that endures, but Robeson hoped not to endure but to prevail.

If Robeson reshaped one of the two pieces he is most identified with, he was part of the initial shaping of the other. When Earl Robinson rewrote his *Ballad of Uncle Sam* (originally written for a Federal Theater Project revue), for radio as *Ballad for Americans*, he did it in collaboration with Robeson, who made sure that the solos were in keys that could be sung in his person-to-person voice, without the mechanics of "classical" voice-projection, which the microphone had made unnecessary. During 1939–1940 the *Ballad for Americans* swept through America: it was even chosen to be the principal musical work at the 1940 Republican National Convention. (The Republicans hoped for Robeson, but he was elsewhere in New York that night, performing the *Ballad for Americans* in a program that also included the premiere of William Grant Still's *And They Lynched Him on a Tree*.[5]) Through the recording made in 1940 with the People's Chorus it continues to preach its doctrine that America was all Americans.

The *Ballad for Americans* suggests that you need not be of a particular ethnic group to speak for America. But in fact what you had to be to speak for America through *Ballad for Americans* was Paul Robeson. Other well-known baritones essayed the piece (they were wise enough not to record it), but it was only Robeson, who had earlier renounced the career of a strictly classical recital singer, who could do this piece without the artificiality that the classical baritone must impose on his material. Robeson could wear the mantle of classical baritone when he chose—many of us would give a good deal for a record of Robeson singing "Die Ehre Gottes aus der Natur," or for an adequate recording of "Lord God of Abraham." But to speak for all America it required someone who could shed the distancing of the concert artist and summon up instead—both in speech and in song—a seemingly casual but profound personal rapport with the listener—not a recitalist but a *mensch*. Many people will find some other aspect of Robeson's musical activity of more significance than *Ballad for Americans,* yet it does mark a moment when he did in fact do what he always hoped to do: speak for all America.

79. Paul Robeson performing during CBS broadcast of *Ballad for Americans*. November 5, 1939.
Schomburg Center for Research in Black Culture, New York Public Library, Astor, Lenox and Tilden Foundations.

80. Maurice Browne, Paul Robeson, and Peggy Ashcroft in *Othello*. 1930.
UPI/Corbis-Bettmann.

Martin Duberman

ROBESON AND *OTHELLO*

It had long been in the back of Robeson's mind that he would someday like to play Othello.[1] After his enormous success in the 1928 London production of *Show Boat,* the idea entered other minds as well. In the end it was the actor-producer Maurice Browne and his wife, the director Ellen ("Nellie") Van Volkenburg, who put together a production. The couple had founded the Repertory Company in Seattle and the Little Theatre in Chicago, and Browne had recently had a huge success producing R. C. Sherriff's play *Journey's End.* The profits from that venture were so great that he became a partner in the purchase of the Globe and Queens theaters. The press reported that Browne had been able to offer Robeson a contract calling for a three-figure weekly salary—"said to equal the largest ever paid in London to an actor in a 'straight' part—though well below the £1,000 a week understood to be commanded by a musical comedy star like Jack Buchanan." Rehearsals were scheduled to begin after Robeson's return from his 1929 American tour, with an opening planned for London in the spring of 1930, followed by a production in the States. "We are really very excited about it," Essie wrote right after Paul formally signed the contract—"Paul is already working on the part."[2]

He began rehearsals in early April. He had hesitated about signing on for the production—"Am still afraid of Othello but we can talk it over," he had written Maurice Browne when first approached. Browne later commented, "For eighteen months I wrestled with him," and "my persistence broke down his objections." He overcame Paul's qualms with promises of a first-rate director and a first-rate Iago. He got neither. Browne cast himself as Iago and gave the directing plum to his wife, Nellie Van Volkenburg. Both choices were self-indulgent. Browne had aspirations to act ("I had always itched to play Iago," he later confessed) without being an actor, and Nellie had had scant directing experience since her days with Chicago's Little Theatre, and none in Shakespeare. Robeson did get a first-rate Desdemona in the twenty-two-year-old newcomer Peggy Ashcroft. He had seen her in Matheson Lang's production *Jew Süss*, her first major success, and because his contract with Maurice Browne gave him the right to decide who would play Desdemona, asked Ashcroft to audition. She was terrified: "I can't sing in tune," she remembered years later, "and I had to perform the Willow Song in front of Paul Robeson." Nonetheless, he liked what he

81. Peggy Ashcroft and Paul Robeson in *Othello.* 1930.
Carl Van Vechten Collection, Beinecke Library, Yale University.

heard and she was offered the role. Ashcroft was thrilled at the opportunity; "for us young people in England at the time," she later recalled, Robeson "was a great figure, and we all had his records, and one realized that it was a tremendous honor to be doing this." The supporting cast was also well chosen: Sybil Thorndike as Emilia, the then little-known Ralph Richardson as Roderigo, and Max Montesole, an experienced graduate of Frank Benson's famed Shakespeare company, as Cassio. They would prove "supportive" in several needed senses.[3]

At the start, Essie enthusiastically wrote Nellie Van Volkenburg, "I have a feeling that we are going to have a magnificent time with Othello." It proved to be anything but. Robeson realized from the first that his director and his Iago were hopeless, likely to prove actual impediments to his own performance. After the first week of rehearsal, Essie, who had a sharp eye and a short fuse for incompetence, wrote indignantly in her diary, "Nellie doesn't know what it is all about. Talks of 'tapestry,' of the scene, the 'flow,' and 'austere beauty,' a lot of parlor junk, which means nothing and helps not at all. . . . She can't even get actors from one side of the stage to the other. Poor Paul is lost."[4]

Van Volkenburg and Browne were fascinated with the "psychological dimensions" of the play and urged on Paul the theory (both were gay) that Iago's motivation was best explained as the result of his having fallen in love with Othello. When Paul asked for specific direction, he got instead patronization, the more galling for coming from an officious amateur. Nellie had a penchant for standing in the back of the stalls and yelling instructions through a megaphone; one day, while rehearsing the Cyprus scene, Paul paused and asked her a question. "Mr. Robeson," she shouted through the megaphone, "there are other people on the stage besides yourself!" Peggy Ashcroft, horrified at this gratuitous humiliation of Robeson, decided that Nellie was "a racist."[5]

Ashcroft found her entire experience in *Othello* "an education in racism," something about which she had previously been ignorant. "Paul would tell us stories which I could hardly believe. . . . He talked a lot to us, and particularly Rupert [Rupert Hart-Davis, her husband], about his problems in the States," though "he didn't talk politics"—his concern then was with the plight of his people, not with any particular political program for ameliorating it. When queried about "the racial aspect" of the production, Ashcroft was widely quoted in the press as saying, "Ever so many people have asked me whether I mind being kissed in some of the scenes by a coloured man, and it seems to me so silly. Of course I do not mind! It is just necessary to the play. For myself I look on it as a privilege to act with a great artist like Paul Robeson." In fact they were a bit skittish during rehearsals. The press bombardment about "how the public will take to seeing a Negro make love to a white woman" made Robeson somewhat "infirm of purpose"; as he told a reporter fifteen years later, "For the first two weeks in every scene I played with Desdemona that girl couldn't get near to me, I was backin' away from her all the time. I was like a plantation hand in the parlor, that clumsy."[6]

Robeson was sympathetic to Ashcroft's plight under Nellie's direction. While rehearsing the scene where Othello denounces Desdemona as a whore, Nellie insisted Robeson keep slapping Ashcroft to "encourage" her to fall at a particular angle—one that Ashcroft felt "was physically impossible to do in one movement. . . . I think she was a sadist"—bringing her instead to the verge of tears. Without a word, Robeson got up and left the theater. He sent a message to Maurice Browne that he could no longer continue under Nellie's direction, and requested a replacement. When Browne threatened a breach-of-contract suit, Robeson—with his Equity suspension still fresh in mind—returned to rehearsals.[7]

But thereafter, clear that (in Ashcroft's words) "there was no help, indeed only hindrances, from our director," Robeson, Ashcroft, and Max Montesole—with Sybil Thorndike joining them whenever she could—took to rehearsing together evenings in one another's homes. Montesole, with his considerable experience in playing Shakespeare, provided crucial support; according to Ashcroft, he "was the saving of the production—as far as it could be saved." Jimmy Light also pitched in by coaching Robeson privately. "I think Paul would have given up long ago," Essie wrote in her diary, "if it hadn't been for Jim and Max. They have both been working like blazes over him."[8]

But if the cast members did all they could to help one another, Nellie retained final say over staging, lights, and sets—and made a considerable botch of each. Her staging was at once fussy and remote, long on detail (much of it anachronistic, like the introduction of a quasi-Venetian skirt dance) but short on immediacy (in resorting to a series of ascending platforms, she managed to put much of the stage action at the farthest possible remove from

82. Paul Robeson, Anna May Wong, and Mei-Len-Feng. London. 1935.
Photo by Fania Marinoff. Carl Van Vechten Collection, Beinecke Library, Yale University.

the audience). She cut significant passages from the text in favor of highlighting extratextual diversions like dance, incidental music (including a sailor's ditty as Othello lands on Cyprus), and conspicuous set changes. ("It would not have surprised me," one critic later wrote, "if Mr. Paul Robeson had 'obliged' with a negro spiritual too"—unaware that Robeson and Maurice Browne had had a "terrific row" during rehearsals when Browne tried to insist that Robeson arrive at Cyprus *singing*.) Nellie staged the final scene of the play with the bed tucked away in a corner, creating a remote, frigid mood when precisely the opposite effect was called for. Then, in addition, she allowed set designer James Pryde, a well-known painter (with no experience in scenic design), to include an enormously high four-poster bed, which caused such a racket being hoisted into position behind the curtain as Ashcroft and Sybil Thorndike were playing the preceding Willow Scene that Thorndike—the one cast member to whom Nellie deferred—told the stagehands in no uncertain terms that they could not move the bed until after she had begun her long speech: "I can shout my way over it, but Desdemona can't."[9]

As for the lighting, Nellie kept it dim to the point of inscrutability. The subdued effects were necessary, she explained in her program notes, in order to maintain the integrity of Pryde's scenic "paintings," but as James Agate acidly pointed out in the *Sunday Times*, "The first object of lighting in the theatre is not to flatter a scene-painter but to give us enough light to see the actors by." The actors even had trouble seeing one another, yet when one of them complained to Nellie she snapped, "Switch on the exit lights over the doors"—her sole concession. (Later, with the director no longer on hand after the opening, Ralph Richardson kept a flashlight up his sleeve to light his way across the stage.) To complete her miscalculations, Nellie pasted a disfiguring beard and goatee on Robeson and until the final scene dressed him in unsuitably long Elizabethan garments (including tights, puffed sleeves, and doublets), instead of Moorish robes, which would have naturally enhanced the dignity of his performance.[10]

By opening night, Paul (according to Essie) was "wild with nerves." Her own hair went "gray in a patch" during the final ten days of rehearsal, and she clutched Hugh Walpole's hand throughout the opening-night performance as select members of the gala audience—Baroness Ravensdale, Garland Anderson (the black author of the hit play *Appearances*), Lady Diana Cooper, Anna May Wong—came up during intervals to offer moral support and to compliment her on her white satin gown. Paul, by his own account, "started off with my performance pitched a bit higher than I wanted it to be," but by curtain he was recalled twenty times. The critics, however, responded more tepidly than the audience. Browne and Van Volkenburg got a general drubbing—the production "has little to recommend it"; "Maurice Browne cast himself for Iago, and ruined the play." "They caught the hell they so well deserved," Essie wrote in her diary.[11]

Sybil Thorndike came off well, and Ashcroft got a splendid set of notices, but Robeson's own reviews ran the gamut. The virtues of his performance were sharply contested. At one

83. Paul Robeson as "the Moor" in
Shakespeare's *Othello.* 1930.
Carl Van Vechten Collection,
Beinecke Library, Yale University.

extreme, he was hailed as "great," "magnificent," "remarkable"; at the other decried as "prosaic" and "disappointing." A number of critics agreed that he had played the role in too gen-
teel a fashion, as if "afraid of losing himself"; Othello became "a thoughtful, kindly man,
civilised and cultured," rather than "the sort of great soldier to whom the senators of
Venice would entrust their defense." ("Robeson endows Othello with an inferiority complex
which is incongruous," wrote *Time and Tide.*) Putting a direct racial gloss on the same complaint, one reviewer ascribed Robeson's caution and geniality not merely to his own personal
modesty but to his fear that "any assumption of arrogance might be mistaken for the inso-
lent assumptions of the less educated of his race." Another critic, in *The Lady,* suggested
that his "lethargy" was an attribute intrinsic to blacks, and used that as "confirmation" for
the view that the hot-blooded Othello had been conceived by Shakespeare not as an
Ethiopian but as a passionate Arabic Moor. ("There is not a much closer racial affinity between
the Negro and the Arab than between the Arab and the white man, and a far closer cultural
affinity between the last two.") In regard to that view, Robeson's own interpretation of the
play in 1930 was less pronouncedly racial than it would be by the time of the Broadway production in 1943. Whereas he later argued forcefully that debate over whether Shakespeare

intended Othello to be a Negro or a Moor was a nonquestion—by "Moor" Shakespeare meant "Negro"—in 1930 Robeson told a newspaper interviewer, "There are, of course, two distinct schools on the subject, and it is possible to produce a convincing argument for either side. It is possible to prove from the text that Othello was a Negro, but the same argument applies to a Moor. If, of course, Shakespeare intended definitely to write of a Moor, then I am not the man for the part. This, however, I consider doubtful. Anyway, the Moor is chiefly of negro extraction."[12]

Robeson shared the critics' discontent with his technical abilities, yet attempting the role, he told one newspaper reporter, had nonetheless been liberating: ". . . Othello has taken away from me all kinds of fears, all sense of limitation, and all racial prejudice. Othello has opened to me new and wider fields; in a word, Othello has made me free." Even after the

84. Publicity shot of Paul Robeson with Uta Hagen and Jose Ferrer, stars in *Othello*. c. 1943. *Photographs and Prints Division, Schomburg Center for Research in Black Culture, The New York Public Library, Astor, Lenox and Tilden Foundations.*

opening, he continued to work with Jimmy Light, steadily improving his performance. "He is much better now than he was at the opening," Essie reported ten days later. "He has been working steadily at his part, and some changes have been made in his costumes, so that he is 100 percent better." The Van Vechtens came over the following month, saw for themselves, and agreed with Essie's estimate. "He is magnificent, unbelievable," Van Vechten wrote Alfred Knopf, and to James Weldon Johnson he reported, "Paul is simply amazing. . . . He completely bowled me over with surprise. I did not expect such a finished and emotional performance. . . . They stood on chairs and cheered him the night we were there." Du Bois wrote from New York to ask for some pictures for the NAACP's *The Crisis* and to say "how thrilled we are" with his success.[13]

Box-office business was brisk at first, and after Maurice Browne bowed out as Iago (by his own account, he "fled like a frightened rabbit" after the critics drubbed him, turning the role over to his understudy), there was added reason to hope for an extended run. But public interest failed to build, and, given the high production costs—Robeson was paid a reported record salary of three hundred pounds a week—the show closed after six weeks, and then briefly toured the provinces while negotiations proceeded for a transfer to the States. Jed Harris, the American producer who had recently revived *Uncle Vanya* with success, came to dinner at the Robesons', and it was widely announced in the press that he would bring *Othello* to New York the following season with Lillian Gish as Desdemona, Osgood Perkins (who had been hailed in *The Front Page*) as Iago, and Robert Edmond Jones as set designer. It was also rumored that Gish was negotiating to do a film version with Robeson. There were additional soundings from the Theatre Guild and from producers Gilbert Miller and Sydney Ross.[14]

None of this came to fruition. Robeson was under contract for another American concert tour, to run from January to April 1931, which undercut Jed Harris's preferred dates. Apprehension over the likely reception in the States of a black man kissing a white woman also proved dampening. "I wouldn't care to play those scenes in some parts of the United States," Robeson himself told a *New York Times* reporter: "The audience would get rough; in fact, might become very dangerous." One Southern paper editorialized in response, "He knows what would happen and so do the rest of us. That is one form of amusement that we will not stand for now or ever. This negro has potentialities for great harm to his race."[15]

But according to Essie, who carried on the negotiations, it was Maurice Browne who ultimately destroyed the attempt to carry *Othello* to the States. Nobody wanted his production, and he tried to prevent Robeson from appearing in a restaged version by claiming that he alone had the right to "sell" him. He did manage to prevent Peggy Ashcroft from accepting an offer from John Gielgud to appear at the Old Vic, "lending" her out instead—to her anguish—for a Somerset Maugham play. Essie was furious at Browne's manipulations. "He's a rascal indeed. I am surprised he could not play 'Iago' better. He's a real villain."[16]

Paul, too, seems to have blamed Browne far more than Van Volkenburg for the tensions and inadequacies of the production. Once opening night was safely behind him, Paul wrote Nellie a gracious and self-effacing letter thanking her "for the real help you have given me. Under different circumstances you & I would certainly have worked together with much more sympathy. I do feel most of it was my fault, but somewhere in the middle of things Maurice & I suddenly became antagonistic & I'm afraid deep down always will be. . . ." By the time the play closed, in July, Browne (so Essie wrote the Van Vechtens) became "openly nasty," and at the final performance, as Ashcroft remembers it, he gave a curtain speech to the audience in which he "thanked everybody, except Paul and myself."[17]

AFTERWORD

Robeson played the role of Othello twice more in his career; in 1943 on Broadway (and then on national tour), and in 1959 to commemorate the one-hundredth-anniversary season at Stratford-on-Avon in England.

By all odds, the Broadway *Othello* was the most distinguished and historic of the three. It was directed by Margaret Webster and costarring Uta Hagen and Jose Ferrer as Desdemona and Iago. The opening night curtain came down to a thunderous ovation that lasted a full

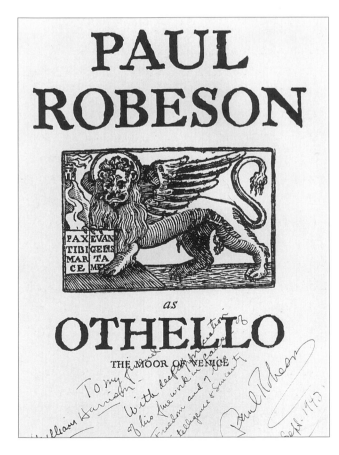

85. Program for *Othello*. 1943. Inscription: "To My Friend William Harrison—With deep appreciation of his fine work in cause of Freedom and of his intelligence & sincerity. Paul Robeson. Sept. 1943."
Special Collections, Rutgers University Libraries.

twenty minutes. The New York critics were somewhat more divided than the audience, but high praise predominated. With 296 performances, this production set an all-time record for Shakespeare performances on Broadway.

Impressive as the Broadway *Othello* was as a theatrical event, it was a major milestone in American racial history. Many years later, when James Earl Jones was about to attempt the role of Othello himself, he paid tribute to the importance of Robeson's 1943 performance (which Jones had seen): ". . . it was essentially a message he gave out: 'Don't play me cheap. Don't *anybody* play me cheap.' And he reached way beyond arrogance . . . way beyond that. Just by his presence, he commanded that nobody play him cheap. And that was astounding to see in 1943."[18]

The 1959 Stratford *Othello* was a far less happy affair. Having been hounded by the U.S. government for more than a decade for his defiant insistence on full equality for blacks, and his outspoken pro-socialist, anti-colonialist views, Robeson first lost his pass-

86. Paul Robeson and Uta Hagen in *Othello* (New York production). c. 1943.
Photo by Vandamm Studios. Library for Performing Arts, The New York Public Library, Astor, Lenox and Tilden Foundations.

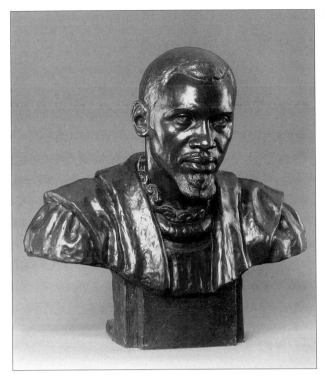

87. Bust of Paul Robeson as Othello by Richmond Barthe. 1974. Bronze.
Photo by Manu Sassoonian. Art and Artifacts Division, Schomburg Center for Research in Black Culture, The New York Public Library, Astor, Lenox and Tilden Foundations.

port, and then his health. At Stratford, he was further handicapped by a gimmicky, flashy production basically at odds with Robeson's own gravity and nobility of presence. Most of the critics congratulated him for having risen above the ill-conceived production. But he was relieved when the seven-month run ended. Though he had never missed a performance, every one of them, he later confessed to his wife, had been "an ordeal." He had gotten through on sheer grit, as was characteristic of a man who throughout his life, and to its end, refused to bow.[19]

88. Paul Robeson. Nude kneeling. 1926.
Photo by Nickolas Muray. Courtesy George Eastman House.

Jeffrey C. Stewart

THE BLACK BODY

Paul Robeson as a

Work of Art and Politics

During my research for the centennial exhibition, *Paul Robeson: Artist and Citizen*, I received a tip from Professor James Smalls, of Rutgers University, that the Carl Van Vechten Papers at Yale University's Beinecke Library contained a set of nude photographs of Robeson taken by the famous celebrity photographer Nickolas Muray. These photographs were filed by Van Vechten in a folder entitled, "Paul Robeson as an Art Object," a striking classification, since the book *The Revealing Eye: Personalities of the 1920s in Photographs by Nickolas Muray and Words by Paul Gallico*, reproduces one of these nude photographs (see figure 88) in a book of celebrity *portraits*.[1] Subsequently, I discovered more nude photographs by Muray in the George Eastman House Collection and in Susan Robeson's book, *The Whole World in His Hands*.[2] The tip, the discovery, and the seeming contradiction between looking at someone as an art object and portraying his or her identity, set my mind to thinking. Why did Muray choose to photograph Robeson in the nude, when most other photographers showed him in full dress, most often in three-piece suits? (See figure 89.) Why

89. Paul Robeson. October 1927.
Photo by James Allen. Carl Van Vechten Collection, Beinecke Library, Yale University.

did Robeson pose for them nude? What do these photographs tell us about why Robeson became an icon of the modernist art movement of the 1920s? What is the meaning of these photographs?

First, I believe there are many potential readings of these photographs, and I do not want to foreclose other interpretations in setting forth my own. Indeed, I believe there are several meanings of these portraits and that such meanings change depending on the interpretive context in which they are placed. For example, there is a long tradition of popular photography and poster art of seminude male athletes, especially boxers. After Jack Johnson won the heavyweight championship in 1908, photographs and posters of the seminude Black champion proliferated (see figure 90). Similarly, there is an Orientalist tradition in late-nineteenth-century European painting and photography depicting naked and seminaked

90. Barcelona fight poster (Arthur Cravan vs. Jack Johnson), 1916. *Photo courtesy of Roger Lloyd Conover for the Estate of Fabian Lloyd.*

Africans as guards of harems and so forth.[3] But since these photographs by Muray were intended as fine art and were part of a portfolio of American portraiture, I would like to situate them within what I believe was a process by which the image of a naked African American could become viewed as an art object, a nude, and as an object for consumption as what would have been called high art. That an African American body could move from being merely an item of sports curiosity to an object of aesthetic beauty suggests a shift in the interpretive context of the Black male body in the third decade of the twentieth century, a shift that nicely parallels the journey taken by Robeson himself from star athlete to artistic celebrity of the Greenwich Village set. In that sense, I believe one way of looking at these photographs is to see them as symptomatic of a broader social and cultural change in the interpretation of Blacks during the 1920s.

Why did such a shift in the valuation of the Black body occur at this time? The cultural shift was linked to a social and economic change in American life during the first two decades of the twentieth century, a change epitomized by the Great Migration that brought hundreds of thousands of African Americans out of the South and into the urban North, and into the frame of attention for educated middle-class Northerners, such as Nickolas Muray and other artists in places like New York.[4] These Black migrants' arrival (see figure 91) coincided with two other monumental cultural changes, which were centered in New York and the 1920s: first, the emergence of a class of African American intellectuals and artists who burst onto the American cultural scene to create the Harlem Renaissance, the Black literary, visual, and performing arts movement; and second, the flowering of a white American modernist literary and artistic movement based on the sexual ideas of Sigmund Freud, the cultural pluralism of William James, and the racial fascination of Carl Van Vechten (see fig-

91. Armistice Day 1919, Lenox Avenue and 134th Street.
The United States History, Local History and Genealogy Division, The New York Public Library, Astor, Lenox and Tilden Foundations.

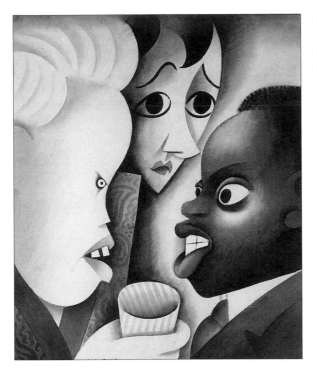

92. Carl Van Vechten, Fania Marinoff, and Taylor Gordon. India ink and wash on paper by Miguel Covarrubias. 1929.
Library of Congress, Prints and Photographs Division, LC-USZ62-86018. Courtesy of the Miguel Covarrubias Foundation.

ure 92) that transformed the image of the Negro from a post–Civil War ward to a twentieth-century American primitive, whose presumed freedom from civilization was positive in the anti-Victorian bohemianism of Greenwich Village.[5] Paul Robeson enters this narrative precisely at the intersection of these social and intellectual currents: he was the son of a Black migrant, a talented young African American intellectual with a Phi Beta Kappa key, a B.A. from Rutgers College, and an L.L.B. from Columbia University, and the possessor of a magnificent body, having been an outstanding athlete at Rutgers. It was partly because of that body that he was cast in the plays by modernists in the 1920s: as Charles Musser suggests in his essay in this volume, Robeson's body was one of the reasons that Robeson became identified with *The Emperor Jones* in the public imagination, even though Charles Gilpin had originated the title role in O'Neill's play of the same name. In short, Robeson's body made him seem more primitive to the white Greenwich Village audience.

Actually, the racial coding of Robeson's body size had begun long before he played Emperor Jones in 1924. When Robeson began to dominate the football field in 1917 as Rutgers's premier player, newspaper commentators invariably linked Robeson's size and race to tell the story (see figure 93). The "Giant Negro," as the *New York Tribune* put it, played a leading role in Rutgers's blanking of Fordham on October 28. "A dark cloud," the *Tribune* continued, "upset the hopes of the Fordham eleven yesterday afternoon. Its name was Robeson."[6] Something of that same sense of Robeson's monumentality also seemed to inspire Mary Wiborg to select him to star in her play, *Taboo* (1922), a fantasy about a white woman's Freudian dream that transports her back to Africa and into the presence of an African

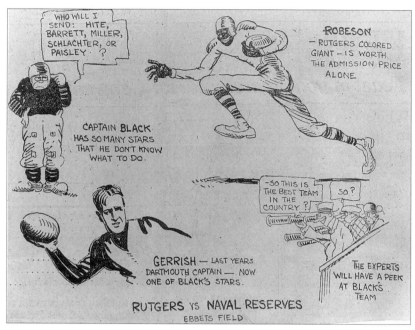

king. Robeson's body (see figure 94) is draped in a pseudo-African garb that emphasizes Wiborg's phallocentric sense of African primitivism.[7] In Wiborg's play, Robeson's big body is majestic and magisterial; in *The Emperor Jones,* commanding but demoniacal; when Robeson is cast in *Black Boy* (1926), Robeson's body is appropriated to present a more contemporary stereotype of African American behavior, the Jack Johnson–type Negro, the threatening Black rapist, an image that Edward Steichen represented in his photograph (see figure 95) from that production. Throughout the plays that Robeson acts in during the 1920s, his particular body comes to signify the gargantuan threat of the Black body to civilization. Moreover, since Robeson possessed a big body wrapped in jet-black skin, his presence in plays like *Black Boy* could epitomize white images of the Black male as utterly Other and different from white men. Those images had their American origin in slavery and continued to shape white reactions to such bodies in the 1920s when, as a matter of fact, urban whites began to notice more Black bodies in their northern midst. Whether Robeson knew it or not, the lens through which he was viewed by many whites in the 1920s was fashioned out of slavery and post-slavery images of the Black man as the strong and dangerous body, images that proliferated in American folklore of the big Negro man who was simultaneously the ideal worker, the powerful, industrious slave, but also potentially the revolutionary whose strength, fearlessness, and courage might overthrow the system.[8]

The historian John Blassingame writes about this figure in *The Slave Community,* where he argues that, in addition to the lazy, sleepy, shiftless Sambo stereotype of antebellum planter narratives, there also existed on southern plantations the big bad Negro, whom Blassingame calls the Nat figure (after Nat Turner, the Virginia slave who led the murderous slave rebellion of 1831).[9] Nat was the strong, hardworking, but dangerous slave who did

94. Paul Robeson in *Taboo,* a play by Mary Hoyt Wiborg. 1922.
Photo by Brugiere. Library of the Performing Arts, The New York Public Library, Astor, Lenox and Tilden Foundations.

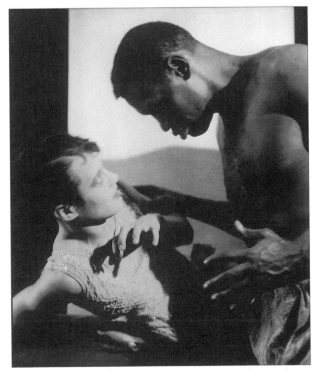

95. Robeson as boxer in *Black Boy,* with Fredi Washington. 1926.
Photo by Edward Steichen. Courtesy George Eastman House. Reprinted with permission of Joanna T. Steichen.

not take whippings and might strike back and risk death rather than be humiliated by his master, who often feared such a slave. In the postbellum world of late-nineteenth-century industrial capitalism, the big Negro image lived on in the myth of John Henry, the steel-driving man who raced a mechanical pile driver and won, only to drop dead afterward. It is worth noting that the myth of John Henry contained or harnessed the potentially explosive sexuality and revolutionary potential of such Black men and directed it toward a challenge against industrialization. As such, once contained in the heroic narrative, the big Black body became something that whites (and Blacks, perhaps for different reasons) could identify with as the representative man who stands in their place and, through his sacrifice, symbolizes the best in humanity. That is perhaps why the folklorist Guy Johnson discovered that the John Henry myth was part African American and part European American in origin—it was a heroic myth that spoke to the crisis of masculinity experienced by all men at the turn of the century who found their masculinity challenged by industrialization.[10] Robeson would play John Henry (see figure 96) as an actor in a play written by Roark Bradford, a white Southern writer who authored an article entitled, "Paul Robeson is John Henry," an article that suggests how unselfconsciously whites could identify Robeson the person with heroic fictional Black characters.[11] That Robeson could play both the primitive and the dangerous Negro, embody the fantasy and the fear of the Negro, suggests one reason for his enormous popularity with white audiences of the period. He, wittingly or not, became a site for the doubleness of white consciousness about the Black male body in the 1920s—that it was both a site of rejection and identification, both completely Other and one's Self.

96. Paul Robeson and Alexander Gray in *John Henry.* c. 1940.
Photo by Lucas and Monroe Studio. Photographs and Prints Division, Schomburg Center for Research in Black Culture, The New York Public Library, Astor, Lenox and Tilden Foundations.

I want to suggest that something similar is going on in Muray's photographs of Robeson. It seems obvious that the photographs inscribe a narrative of Robeson as an erotic exotic, first because of the choice to photograph a major African American intellectual and performer in the nude, and second, to do so from provocative angles that focus the viewer's attention on his sensuality and blackness. These photographs can be read, indeed probably were read, as narratives of the Black primitive whose body is colonized and dissected for white eyes. This became palpable to me when I learned that one of the nude photographs was made into a postcard (perhaps by Van Vechten) that was sent around among friends.[12] (See figure 88.) That this photograph and perhaps others were turned into postcards reminds me of the nude photographs of African women and men that were turned into postcards, which British, French, and German colonizers mailed back home from Africa, and suggests that a colonial narrative operates in these photographs: they are representations of the Other that whites are able to gaze at, fantasize over, and enjoy in the privacy of their homes, away from the contradicting presence of a Black man whose brain and personality are powerful counterweights to merely thinking of him as a body.[13] And when we recall that Robeson's disrobed and imposing body was featured in *The Emperor Jones*, these photographs satisfied what was probably a well-circulating, well-voiced desire—to see more of the magnificent body that was exposed down to his pants in the closing performances of Eugene O'Neill's classic play (see figure 97). Here the Black Other became something more than an abomination: it became something that the audience wished to look at and to appropriate.

Even more, Muray's photographs also suggest a modern, liberal documentary narrative of the Negro situation in twentieth-century America. Figure 88, for example, seems a meditation on the Negro as a slave, a poignant view of him that reminds me of the abolitionist icon, "Am I not a man and a brother?"[14] Here Muray frames Robeson's body not as a caricature but as a modern-day Pietà, without the mother, of course, but with all of the sympathetic smoothness and sorrow of Michelangelo's famous sculpture. We see Robeson posed on his knees and his toes, in a kneeling position, with his wrists crossed over the left side of his body. His head is angled away from the viewer's gaze, almost as if he is ashamed, and his eyes appear closed. Robeson is presented here as a primitive, but interestingly, not as a free one, but in constraints, a bound person though he is not bound by rope or chain; and he seems to be in agony. His wrists are crossed as if they have been tied and only recently released, without the subject seemingly realizing that he is now free of them. This photograph, then, is a visual metaphor of the postbellum African American, who though freed by the Civil War still acts and poses as if still in bondage. That message is reinforced by the Christian imagery operative in the photograph. Robeson is kneeling—a posture evocative of prayer and submission that evokes a Christ-like figure: his wrists form a cross, his head is bowed, and he appears resigned to a fate dictated by a higher power. This and other photographs in the series pull together Christian and racial iconography to emphasize a common

97. Paul Robeson in *The Emperor Jones,* the first act of which he gave at the Savoy Theatre, London.
September 1925.
Photo by Sasha. Courtesy of Hulton Getty/Tony Stone Images.

theme of liberal progressivism: the Negro epitomizes the Christian message that when attacked, the victim should turn the other cheek and submit oneself to God's will as the only assertive act possible for those who are not yet free. When we recall that Muray's photographs were taken just after Robeson—a son of a slave—had launched a concert-singing career (with Carl Van Vechten's assistance) devoted to spirituals and nineteenth-century work songs, then we can see Muray's portrait as an interpretation of Robeson's act, that of a modern Negro identifying with the pain and the sorrow of his people through song.

Interestingly, this photograph was the only one from the series published in *The Revealing Eye,* and is one of only three photographs in the book of men in the nude. The other two male nudes were photographs of dancers, a particular interest of Muray's. This is interesting because most of the men photographed in the book, such as George Bernard Shaw (see figure 98) and Edward G. Robinson (see figure 99), are not only fully clothed, but semi-formally attired in three-piece suits, with strong, powerful demeanors represented. By contrast, Robeson and the dancers are not only nude, but in stylized poses, poses that resemble in their effect those that are struck by the women Muray photographed. Even the photograph of Langston Hughes, a head shot of him fully clothed, has a dreamy quality that makes him look like a girl. As Richard Dyer has remarked, the Muray photographs render Robeson both passive and feminized, a representation that fit notions in the nineteenth and twentieth centuries that Black people were the "female" of the races who were conquered and

98. George Bernard Shaw. Undated.
Photo by Nickolas Muray.
Courtesy George Eastman House.

99. Edward G. Robinson. Undated.
Photo by Nickolas Muray.
Courtesy George Eastman House.

dominated by the "masculine" race, the European.[15] Robeson is separated visually from the world of powerful men whose photographs in the book emphasize their minds—they are originators of ideas (Shaw) or creators of powerful dramatic characters (Robinson). Why photograph one of the most powerfully masculine presences on the American stage as a woman? One answer is that such a posing minimizes some of the threat that a powerful Black manhood poses to the white American psyche. Less threatening than an image of a fiercely proud Black man (see figure 100) are the images of Robeson as the kind of dancer that Muray creates, images that emphasize Robeson's seductiveness and attractiveness to the gaze of whites. Moreover, because Robeson's face is angled away from the viewer, figure 88 is less the portrait of an individual and more a type photograph—less identified than those of the dancers, and more, simply a body, a Negro's body. Without the caption, we would not know that the figure represented is Robeson. The "the-ness" of the Negro[16] seems even more apparent in figure 101. Here Robeson is photographed from the rear, still kneeling, but now uncurled

100. Paul Robeson. Undated.
Photographs and Prints Division, Schomburg Center for Research in Black Culture, The New York Public Library, Astor, Lenox and Tilden Foundations.

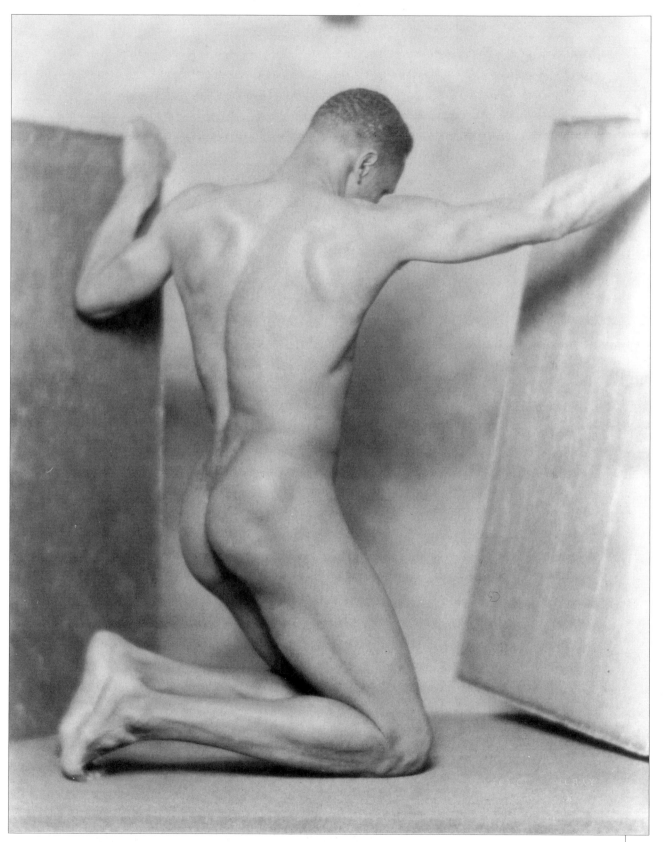

101. Paul Robeson, Nude kneeling, 1926.
Photo by Nickolas Muray. Courtesy George Eastman House.

and rising, his torso upright, his arms extended and holding up two separate boards or walls, while his head remains bowed. Because his face is completely hidden from our view, the subject is even more anonymous than in figure 88. What is now more available to our gaze is Robeson's beautiful body, his magnificent back and shoulders, his buttocks, and his thighs. The photograph could be a pinup, since it functions like soft-core pornography, gratifying a desire to see what cannot ordinarily be seen, the parts of a person's body that are always hidden, even from his or her own view. The body parts in focus are the sexual—the buttocks, the thighs, the back—while the arms, ankles, and feet are blurred. Given that Muray was an excellent photographer, this focusing was obviously not an accident, but an aesthetic choice for aesthetic effect: it presents what is important, suppresses what is extraneous, and conveys the illusion that the figure is in motion, as if he is rising from the posture of figure 88. Perhaps if we titled figure 88 "The Former Slave During Reconstruction"—a period of formal freedom but actual bondage—then we should title figure 101 "The Twentieth-Century Negro"—the African American in the process of rising up, or, as Marcus Garvey would put it, "Up, You Mighty Race!"[17] Moreover, of all the photos, this one has the most homoerotic appeal with its sexual duality: Robeson appears as the masculine ideal, but is also feminine, as the soft focus of the photograph transforms his image into a fantasy of the Black body as erotic. When we recall that Carl Van Vechten was gay, it is quite understandable why this photo was collected and preserved in his collection, along with other photographs of naked Black men.

Figure 102 provides an advance on the reading of these photographs, for Robeson is now standing, as if he struggles to his feet; and figure 103 lets us in, finally, on the series' secret, that this magnificent body belongs to Robeson: his face is turned toward the camera. Simultaneously, his body is more available to us in figure 103, though the pose conceals his genitals with the awkward extension of Robeson's left leg. His strength is shown by the bicep of his left arm, while his power is exemplified by the tightened lower left arm and coiled fist—again blurred because it is in motion. Perhaps figure 103 should have been titled, "The New Negro," who now stands on his own two feet and is able to express, as the New Negro militant migrants of the 1919 race riots did, his anger at the barriers of racism, segregation, lynching—the unyielding wall of white supremacy—that imprisons the African American in twentieth-century America. Here, of course, the ambivalence of Muray's photograph is conveyed at the extremities. Because of the lighting and the printing, Robeson's feet appear enlarged. When we remember what Sander Gillman has said about the Jewish foot as a stereotypical reduction of the Jew to physiological deviance, we can sense here that this representation of Robeson's foot adds a comic element, reminding the viewer of the jokes about Black people's feet and color that were the stock and trade of vaudevillean humor.[18] The power of the figure is undercut by the angle of the figure, the awkwardness of the stance, and the peculiar balance that would be required to hold this pose. The anger of the New Negro is present, but in an awkward posture, with some stereotypical elements present, a subtle reminder that the Old Negro has not been completely transcended.

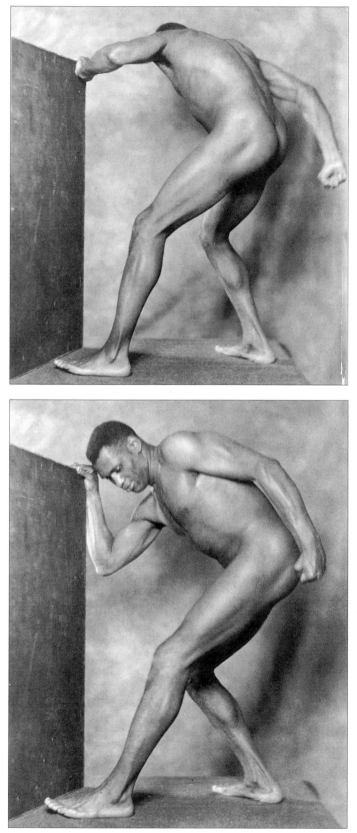

102. Paul Robeson, Nude standing. 1925.
Photo by Nickolas Muray. Carl Van Vechten Collection, Beinecke Library, Yale University.

103. Paul Robeson, Nude standing. 1925.
Photo by Nickolas Muray. Carl Van Vechten Collection, Beinecke Library, Yale University.

At least figure 103 presents us with a recognizable individual instead of a body. We finally have access to his face and the slight smirk of a smile, which gives a hint of his personality and suggests, perhaps, his awareness that he is doing something risqué and vaguely pornographic. The smile also might hint at something else—Robeson's motivation for posing for the nude photographs. Robeson must have known that he had a beautiful body and the nude photographs for Muray, an art photographer, were an opportunity for Robeson to preserve the image of that beauty forever. It would not detract from the dignity and respect we have for Robeson as an artist or an activist to suggest that vanity may have played a part in his decision to pose for these photographs. The slight smirk on his face can be read as a sign of his pride in the body that he reveals in the photographs. The dancers, whom Robeson's photographs resemble, most certainly took pride in their bodies and probably felt that a focus on those bodies was appropriate, a way of honoring the truth that their bodies were beautiful. And like the others, Robeson certainly knew that, like all of our bodies, eventually it would decline. Why not preserve what was exceptional—and what so many praised him for having—at a moment when he was in his prime? Of course, nowadays, after Mappelthorpe, it is difficult to regard such figures without thinking of them as homoerotic. But in Robeson's time that was not a necessary conclusion. Indeed, I doubt that Robeson would have posed for them, had he not had a rock-solid sense of his own heterosexual identity. Given that he and Muray were heterosexual, it seems likely that they interpreted these photographs as celebrating heterosexual desire.[19]

The two final portraits in the Muray series return us to more anonymous renderings of Robeson's body.[20] One seems to continue the racial narrative: the sitting man seems weighted down by the pillar jutting out from the wall. The photograph seems to create a visual representation of the burdens of blackness, that to be Black means to be almost crushed beneath the weight of white attitudes, practices and institutions. But this photograph also serves to remind us of the possibility of other-than-purely-racial interpretations of these photographs. During my research on these photographs I happened to see a copy of Ayn Rand's *Atlas Shrugged* (see figure 104), and it immediately struck me that Muray may have had classical sculpture based on mythological themes in mind when he posed Robeson. The resemblance between his figure and this sculpture of the Atlas figure is unmistakable. The uplifted arms, bent legs, and burdened carrying of something too heavy for any ordinary man is clear in both. It's as if, in seeing Robeson's body, Muray saw classical images of the strong man; indeed the strongest of men—Atlas, who was able to carry the world on his shoulders. Similarly, Robeson seems to be weighted down by the whole world on his shoulders and by burdens too heavy for ordinary men to shoulder. What we have here is a narrative about masculinity, which is being reconstructed in the 1920s, not only in America, but also abroad, as new notions of who is the masculine ideal are being introduced—and Robeson is entering that discourse through these classically inspired images. While hunting around in the Van Vechten collection of photographs at Yale, I discovered another similar photograph of

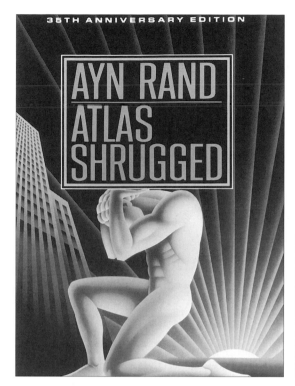

104. Cover of Ayn Rand's *Atlas Shrugged*. 35th Anniversary Edition, New York, Signet Books, 1992. Artwork by Nicholas Gaetano. *Courtesy of the artist.*

105. German poster, *Ideale Nacktheit* (Ideal Nakedness). Zehnter Band Verlag der Schonheit, Dresden. *Carl Van Vechten Collection, Beinecke Library, Yale University.*

a naked man, this one a German poster or advertisement entitled, *Ideale Nacktheit* (Ideal Nakedness) (see figure 105). Of course, on one level this attests to a homoerotic taste, not only in Van Vechten, but also in Germany (and England), where the *Sonnenkinder* rebelled against the traditional mores and traditional definitions of masculinity in the interwar period, when many of the youth believed that aggressive masculinity was responsible for World War I.[21] One replacement for the old notion of aggressively masculine white men was the beautiful male youth who gloried in their physical beauty. But another was to turn to Black men like Robeson as figures of "ideal beauty." Such an analysis revises our usual notion of the kind of cultural work done by white modernist artists in the 1920s in regard to the Black subject. It suggests that Muray's photographs are part of a modernist movement that utilized neoclassical models to reconstruct Black manhood in the 1920s in ways that are not typical. Here the form—neoclassicism—is linked to specific content—heroic manhood, the ideal man—in a way that tranforms the prevailing image of Black manhood in the 1920s.

When I showed the Muray photographs to my graduate seminar in Cultural Studies, the students reacted with a litany of classical, Renaissance, and medieval analogies that jumped into their heads, from images of Hercules, especially Hercules struggling with Anthaeus, to

Michelangelo's *Libyan Sybil* on the Sistine Chapel, to Samson in Milton's *Paradise Regained*.[22] Clearly, those educated in European artistic traditions could see the neoclassical iconography which underpins the Robeson photographs. And I believe that Muray's choice constituted a political act: it dignified Robeson's image by placing it within a European artistic frame, by making his body into an object of fine art, thereby shifting the interpretation of that body away from the narrative of the primitive, the beast, and the animal in which most Black bodies were interpreted in American popular culture. For in the European art tradition, the naked becomes the nude when the body portrayed is linked with a mythological subject whose heroic actions dignify and abstract our gaze from the sexual to that of high moral character. Thus, in posing Robeson as a classical nude, Muray reconstructed Robeson's body as a mythological hero and thereby sought to contain the explosive sexual and racial energy associated with that body by placing an art frame around it. This classical or mythological reading of Robeson was not limited to Muray's photographs. A critic who reviewed Robeson's performance in *Black Boy* praised Robeson's performance and separated it from the primitivist content of the play by describing his "Samson-like presence" on stage.[23] Here the remark about Robeson's "presence" refocuses a key element of Robeson's attraction, that is, his presence, his personality, his character projected on stage. The move from exotic erotic primitive to "Samson-like" hero is a way for European-trained critics to separate Robeson out from the racial metanarrative of American culture. To sum up, Muray's photographs captured and re-presented an image of Robeson as a hero of mythological proportions, whose resemblance to Atlas or Hercules or even Samson transformed Robeson's appeal into that of a universal man, whose masculinity, courage, and nobility constitute his image as a site of identification for all Americans, even white males.

That this is an imperfect or incomplete transformation should be obvious, and suggests why the sexualizing and racializing narratives discussed earlier in this essay continue to operate, despite Muray's neoclassical gaze. A perfect example is the final photograph in the series of Robeson from the rear, standing. After pulling out some snapshots I took of Michelangelo's *David* on a recent trip to Florence, I realized that this photograph of Muray's distinctly resembles that of Michelangelo's magnificent sculpture. The left foot is slightly forward, the left hand rests on the left thigh, and Robeson's right hand is curled, as if he too searches for the rock that will bring down Goliath. But the racial and sexual elements remain here as well. We are distracted from the body of David in Michelangelo's sculpture by the magnificent head, whose eyes look outward with a commanding self-assurance that is often narrated as the essence of the courage and resolve of the democrat. In Muray's photograph, however, the head does not distract us—it is barely visible, again cast downward, its gaze, even Robeson's eyes, hidden from view. Our focus, therefore, falls on his body, again. He could be a hero. He could also be a submitting slave, about to be whipped. The indeterminacy of the image leaves us with an ambivalence about the intention of the photographer and the message of the photograph.

Such a reading suggests that Robeson remained in Muray's gaze as a body; and the function of the neoclassical frame was as much to contain that body, to limit its racial and sexual energy, as it was to free that body to exist as a mind. Containment of the Black body was a precondition of admittance to the realm of high art. And such strategies of containment were not always successful. For example, the sculptor Antonio Salemmé posed Robeson as the classical figure of the "Praying Boy,"[24] with upstretched arms, presumably entreating God to answer those prayers, when Salemmé created his full-size plaster nude sculpture of Robeson, entitled *Negro Spiritual* (see figure 106). But when Salemmé painted it black and sent it to the Philadelphia Art Alliance to be displayed in Rittenhouse Square, the Alliance balked and rejected the sculpture, citing the potential disturbance that his nude might have on race relations! One can only wonder what that disturbance would have been (see figure 107). There was a limit to how effectively the neoclassical frame could eliminate the sexual and racial connotations of the naked Black body in American life in the 1920s. Even here, alternative readings break through the hegemony of interpretation and suggest a return to our earlier observations. Even Kenneth Clark admits that, despite the belief of

106. *Negro Spiritual,* front view. Plaster statue of Paul Robeson by Antonio Salemmé. 1926. *Carl Van Vechten Collection, Beinecke Library, Yale University*

many art critics that the success of any nude sculpture rests on its ability to be appreciated without any sexual arousal, the truth is that any nude is seen as pleasurable because it satisfies our desire to see and feel the sexual on display.[25] Thus, the Muray nudes worked because they accomplished a double task and fed a double consciousness—a desire to see the Black body displayed and revealed, and also a desire to see it revealed in such a way that it was assimiliable into a Western, European sensibility and tradition. The photographs worked because they presented Robeson as simultaneously an Other and an ideal, a neoclassical as well as a modern figure, an art object and a man, an object of curiosity and an object of beauty, a racial inferior and a racial superior to the typical American white man.

Such a recognition of the duality of Robeson's presence in the 1920s art world allows me to assess the combined impact or significance of these photographs. They reveal that for many in the 1920s, not only his modernist friends but also those who attended his concerts and his plays, Robeson's body—and his easy, powerful, majestic use of that body—was one of the most compelling things about his performances. Along with his personality, his body was a key aspect of his presence on the stage and in person. And unlike the use

107. *Negro Spiritual,* side view. Plaster statue of Paul Robeson by Antonio Salemmé. 1926.
Carl Van Vechten Collection, Beinecke Library, Yale University

of the body by Bill "Bojangles" Robinson (see figure 108) and other physical performers of the vaudeville stage, Robeson's body recalled no staccato modernist dissonance of pantomimic theater, but rather classical forms that were inscribed with narratives of the hero and what the ideal male should look and be like. As such, Robeson's popularity existed because it mediated between what was racial (stereotypes of the big Negro, the John Henry character) and what was mythological (classical figures like Atlas, Hercules, and David who were the human equivalents of gods). As such, Muray's photographs reveal Robeson as a man in the 1920s who was able, because of the changing demographics of American race relations and his own dignity and use of his body, to be perceived by both Black and white, men and women, as simultaneously utterly different from and similar to the best in American civilization.

In the 1920s, and for a good part of the 1930s, Robeson became the site where African American and European American aspirations for the ability to cross over came together and fused in his representation. His was a representation that was heavily racial but also, I believe, a contained and domesticated representation of the Black body that fit white expectations.[26] Alain Locke perhaps first codified a truism as old as American segregation: segregation is ultimately self-defeating because, by separating whites and Blacks physically and socially, American society made us desire one another even more than if the "relations of the races" were left alone.[27] Robeson's contained but sexually explosive image made it possible for him

108. Bill Robinson. January 25, 1933.
Photo by Carl Van Vechten. Prints and Photographs Division, Library of Congress, Carl Van Vechten Collection (LC-USZ62-79292).

to cross over into elite white society: it was his *carte blanche* into a transgressive social life which suggests that the body has been a way for the Black man or woman (Josephine Baker or more recently Toni Braxton come to mind) to negotiate white fantasies of crossing to get white society to accept what it has defined as Other. Robeson first crossed over by representing the big Black dangerous man on stage; but as the Muray photographs show, the next step was to move from the inaccessible, sullen, dangerous Negro (such as the photo by Edward Steichen, figure 95) to the accessible African American, who incorporated Western values of heroism, universality, and nobility in his body and his personality. For the Black man or woman, the desire to cross over and simply be regarded as an American is normal, a kind of crossing that the immigrants experienced, but most Blacks have not. Whites, at least elite whites, desire to cross over and experience—sexually, culturally, photographically—something that had been defined as *verboten*. That desire for the Other operated in Robeson's life, and Muray's pictures freeze that moment in time: the Black man portrayed wants to get in, wants to break through the walls (see figures 101–103); he is in the process of standing up, but ultimately, ironically, ends up carrying the white man's burden, the burden of human agency in the face of industrial capitalism. What is not voiced directly but is nevertheless implied in these photographs is that a key to Black success is Black availability to whites, something graphically represented in the Muray photographs. Here the demand is more than the usual, the demand that the acceptable African American be agreeable, impressionable, and nice—he must also disrobe and pose. The message then is that Robeson must be willing to be a commodity of modernist whites, for, after all, in the 1920s, only modernist whites would accept him. While their racialism was less abhorrent than that of white middle America, their fantasies nevertheless constituted a powerful demand that this Black aspirant to crossover access get naked for the modernist gaze.

It seems to me that in the 1930s, Robeson began to rebel against the purely iconic ways in which his image could be used to narrate the fantasies of American culture, whether dreamed up by modernists or popular-culture makers. He began to sense how the photographic lens could be used to detract from his humanity, to pose him as a body without much of a mind, especially as he moved from the realm of art photography into the world of capital-intensive motion-picture production. Especially after making *Sanders of the River* (1935), he learned how editing could trick him into thinking that he had honored the African tradition when the camera showed him as disgracing it. When he was soundly criticized by Blacks and leftists for his role in this movie, he began to see how the easy marriage of the iconic and the heroic that he had sometimes achieved in such high-art circles as the Muray photograph shoot would not necessarily continue in the 1930s. Robeson began to become more guarded in front of the camera. For example, in photographs taken during the 1930s (see figure 109), Robeson's naive openness in front of the camera is gone. He eyes the camera suspiciously. We see this in figure 110, where, standing before a mural of Venice, Robeson holds his arms folded, in a protective position, his face tensed. Again, in figure 111,

109. Paul Robeson. c. 1930s.
Photo by Stella E. Simon. Library of the Performing Arts, The New York Public Library, Astor, Lenox and Tilden Foundations.

Robeson poses in front of a U.S.S.R. poster challenging the gaze of the viewer. In the photograph by Stella Simon (see figure 109), taken during the 1930s, Robeson exudes a seriousness and a profundity not present before. Here is a man of substance and a man with a powerful vision of humanity, captured by Simon in figure 112, where the focus on the head rather than the body states what is most important about this man. Here Robeson has moved from the naive representation of blackness to the threshold of becoming a representative Black intellectual.

I think that Robeson became increasingly sophisticated about his image, and that he began to pose his body in ways that maximized its power as a signature of moral and political leadership, rather than as a fetish of aestheticizing modernist gazes. In the 1930s and 1940s, Robeson reappropriated some of the postures and poses he created in the 1920s and adapted them to his more activist career in the 1930s and 1940s. In the still from *Song of*

110. Paul Robeson in front of mural of Venice.
c. 1933–1935.
Photo by Max Ewing. Carl Van Vechten Collection, Beinecke Library, Yale University.

111. Paul Robeson in front of U.S.S.R. poster.
c. 1933–1935.
Photo by Max Ewing. Carl Van Vechten Collection, Beinecke Library, Yale University.

112. Paul Robeson. c. 1933.
Photo by Stella Simon. Library for the Performing Arts, The New York Public Library, Astor, Lenox and Tilden Foundations.

Freedom (see figure 122), Robeson turns the Emperor Jones–like jacket into an emblem of authority and emerges as a leader of white men. Similarly, in *Proud Valley,* Robeson's seminakedness (see figure 127) is no longer an erotic exoticism, but a working-class male bonding between white and Black in struggle. And during the 1940s, Robeson begins to use his body politically to frame his intellectual challenge to American racial hegemony: In figure 113, he swings his large, commanding body into step with demonstrations against post–World War II racism in America. In figure 144, his body becomes a symbol of African American manhood and self-defense, as he poses against the Lincoln Memorial in the background, just after telling the diminutive President Harry Truman that if Truman would not do something about lynching, Negroes would. Not surprisingly, Truman reacted to the statement—and the large African American who made it—by calling it a threat. Robeson's size, once he was politically engaged, made him seem more of a threat to the hegemonic system of American racism than if he had been smaller and less forceful.

Robeson grew in his ability to use his body politically and forcefully during the campaign of Henry Wallace for President. As his posing here (see figure 114) with Wallace suggests, Robeson's size was an asset to the movement. He was a commanding voice not only for Wallace's anti–Cold War policies and for Wallace's grassroots democratic populism (see

113. Paul Robeson and Louis Burnham picketing the White House to protest discriminatory employment practices of the Bureau of Engraving and Printing. August 4, 1949.
Corbis-Bettmann.

114. Robeson and Wallace backstage at Madison Square Garden. New York. 1948. *Photo © by Julius Lazarus.*

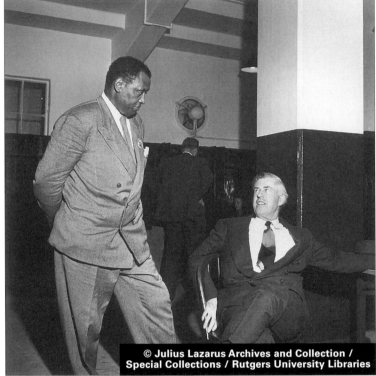

© Julius Lazarus Archives and Collection / Special Collections / Rutgers University Libraries

figure 115). Moreover, while doing his best to help Wallace win the presidency, Robeson remained an independent force, becoming a more and more powerful lecturer, as well as a singer at political events. In figure 116, he shows his kinetic body in action as he conveys a political message through expressive song. And when this large, resolute African American suggested in Paris in 1949 that African Americans wanted peace and not war with the Soviet Union, his remarks had a far greater impact on those American journalists covering the event than similar remarks by W.E.B. Du Bois, partly because Robeson's commanding body had become a virtual symbol of resistance.

Robeson's size and powerful use of his body cut both ways, however. Once his remarks were distorted and turned against him, the man who was loved as a body was hated because he had a critical mind. In the aftermath of that stand in Paris in 1949, Robeson ceased to be an American icon, even though he continued to be a hero for small numbers of Blacks and whites in this country, and much larger numbers of people around the world. In the aftermath of the Peekskill riot on September 4, 1949, the campaign launched against Robeson took its toll on his mind. But his body remained strong and supple, supporting his still-powerful voice, even during his virtual incarceration in the 1950s (see Introduction). After his passport was returned in 1958, Robeson again used the stage with the same style and flair as before. Despite all of the strategies of containment, Robeson had turned his body into a weapon of resistance. His upright body became a symbol of courage and integrity around the world (see figure 117).

115. Robeson stumping for Wallace. Eugene, Oregon. August 26, 1948.
UPI/Corbis-Bettmann.

116. Paul Robeson singing at the National People's Lobby. Washington, D.C. August 5, 1948.
Photo © by Julius Lazarus.

This posture of defiance connects him with contemporary manifestations of the Black body as a site of resistance, one of which is captured in the 1996 documentary film *When We Were Kings.* The title says it all. The movie captures that moment in the 1970s when the promise and the utopianism of the Black Nationalist and Black Arts Movements were still vibrant, when Black men were not only fighting for the heavyweight championship (among our Black selves), but a Black promoter had pulled it off. And this whole spectacle was situated in Africa in Zaire, ironically, where a man who was both a counterrevolutionary and a state murderer walked around as if he were a king. But all of that is background to what is foregrounded in this movie, that is, a discourse on Muhammad Ali and the Black body. Ali is the talking, specifying, intellectualizing, African-bonding Black man from America who constantly displays his body for popular consumption and constantly refers to himself as pretty. Indeed, his performance points up how far we have come in one sense from Robeson's time, since being the Black body no longer requires dark skin color. Being Black is talking Black, having a Black consciousness, a Black identity, something that Foreman lacks in the movie (and in the 1970s) even though he is bigger and darker skinned. He is merely a Black body, simply a Black physical mass. Foreman's massiveness narcotizes the white media, who believe he will pound Ali, the intellectual body, into the floor of that Zairian ring. But while we might want to equate Robeson with Foreman, the real connection is with Ali. Yes, in Ali

117. Paul Robeson singing at Vienna International Youth Festival. August 4, 1959.
Photo © Bildarchiv Neues Deutschland, Berlin. Courtesy of Julius Lazarus Archives and Collection/Special Collections/ Rutgers University Libraries.

118. Paul Robeson at press conference after receiving honorary doctorate from Humboldt University, Berlin. October 12, 1960.
Photo © by Gerhard Kiesling, Berlin. Courtesy of Julius Lazarus Archives and Collection/Special Collections/ Rutgers University Libraries.

there is also a bit of Charles Gilpin, the smaller, more cynical actor of the first run of *The Emperor Jones,* about whom Eugene O'Neill complained that "Gilpin played the Emperor with cast, playwright and everyone involved." Ali certainly played the Emperor with everyone, even Mobutu, in Africa. But Gilpin lacked sexual energy and Robeson, like Ali, exuded it (see figure 174). And Robeson was not as big, as massive, as Foreman: Ali and Robeson were roughly the same height, the same build, though different in personality and politics. But both used the sexual energy of their bodies in their performances, and by doing so also found a way to include their voice, their song, their talk, and their opinions in the presentation of their bodies. They commanded that white people, all people, including dissenting Black people, pay attention to them, and in doing so, turned their bodies and performances into the lightning rods of controversy. Not surprisingly, like Robeson, Ali became a pariah to the nation because he enacted precisely what Robeson implied in his 1949 Paris World Congress of Partisans of Peace Speech—that a self-conscious Black man should not fight for America in an imperialist war. When Ali refused induction into military service, he stepped into Robeson's space. He occupied a political stance of the enlightened Black body, stating implicitly: "Yes, I am strong enough to beat everybody's ass in the ring, but not fool enough to kill fellow brown peoples." That anti-imperialist, internationalist act on Ali's part echoed Robeson who, in 1954, had warned against the coming colonialist war in Vietnam.[28] Now, in the changed historical context of the 1990s, one in which the Vietnam War is generally understood as a huge mistake and conscientious objection as an honorable response to that injustice, Ali has been allowed to return from his pariah state to become an American hero again. Perhaps now at the end of the Cold War, the time is right to welcome back America's best body and one of its best minds—Paul Robeson.

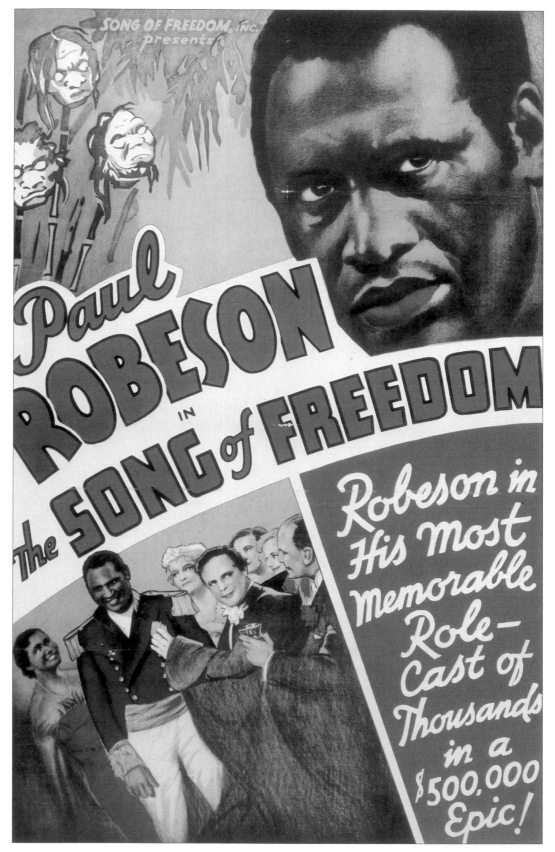

119. Poster, *The Song of Freedom* (British Lion, 1936).
Courtesy of the Academy of Motion Picture Arts and Sciences.

Mark A. Reid

RACE, WORKING-CLASS CONSCIOUSNESS, AND DREAMING IN AFRICA

Song of Freedom and *Jericho*

Paul Robeson appeared in eleven films during his almost twenty-year film career. Oscar Micheaux, an African American filmmaker, cast Robeson in *Body and Soul* (Micheaux, 1924), in which Robeson made his film debut as a corrupt preacher. In Kenneth MacPherson's *Borderline* (Pool, 1930), Dudley Murphy's *The Emperor Jones* (United Artists, 1933), Zoltan Korda's *Sanders of the River* (London, 1935), films made outside Hollywood, Robeson is cast in major roles. In his two Hollywood films, James Whale's *Show Boat* (Universal, 1936) and Julien Duvivier's *Tales of Manhattan* (Twentieth Century Fox, 1942), he appears in secondary or minor roles. Unlike his black contemporaries during the 1930s, Robeson was a featured star in most of his British films.

Robeson's British film roles broadened the casting possibilities for other African American actors such as Sidney Poitier in the fifties and sixties and Denzel Washington in the eighties. During most of Robeson's acting career, Hollywood films offered practically no major roles for black actors. Since Hollywood occasionally cast black actors in nonsubservient roles at least a decade before the United States entered World War II, it is important to mention the few exceptions when Hollywood was not so utterly resistant to change.[1]

During the late 1930s, Hollywood churned out such plantation melodramas as Victor Fleming's *Gone With the Wind* (Metro-Goldwyn-Mayer, 1939), but also produced films that advanced roles for African American actors. Such 1930s Hollywood films with noble black male protagonists include John Ford's *Arrowsmith* (Goldwyn, 1931), Mervyn LeRoy's *I Am a Fugitive from a Chain Gang* (Warner, 1932), and *They Won't Forget* (Warner, 1937). In *Arrowsmith* Clarence Brooks is Dr. Marchand, a Howard University–trained medical doctor, who helps the white hero fight an epidemic that is sweeping through the West Indies. Of minor importance but marking an advance in black screen roles, actors Everett Brown and Clinton Rosemond appear as sympathetic characters in, respectively, *I Am a Fugitive from a Chain Gang* and *They Won't Forget*. Nearly twenty years later, Sidney Poitier appears in similar sympathetic roles that were first introduced in the 1930s. For instance, Poitier appears as a doctor in Joseph Mankiewicz's *No Way Out* (Twentieth Century Fox, 1950), as a stevedore in Martin Ritt's *Edge of the City* (United Artists, 1957), and as an escaped convict handcuffed to a white convict in Stanley Kramer's *The Defiant Ones* (United Artists, 1958). However, it was Paul Robeson, and not Sidney Poitier, who became the first successful African American to achieve leading-man status in major motion pictures.[2]

Robeson was the first African American who consistently received major film roles in which his intelligence was equal to any of the films' white characters'. Admittedly, a few of his British roles featured characters who indirectly supported colonialism, as in Zoltan Korda's *Sanders of the River* and Robert Stevenson's *King Solomon's Mines* (Gaumont British, 1937). Robeson also appears in films that explore the black heroes' "double consciousness" and the shortcomings of romantic idealism in colonial Africa. Many critics chastise Robeson for the stereotypical film roles he performed, but the same critics have not extended their criticism to the systemic realities that determined his roles in American and British cinema. These critics are quick to attack an actor whose screen roles, according to them, contradict his leftist political beliefs. Contrary to this form of film criticism that posits within the individual a sort of power over institutional forces, I would argue that such criticism should also include an analysis of the institution. It is more constructive to view Robeson's dilemma as consistent with the systemic nature of any mass-marketed form of entertainment. Thus, it is quite understandable that Robeson's leftist idealism would have little effect on bettering the general image of blacks in American film. Yet and still, there remains a qualitative difference between the American and British films in which he appears. In surveying Robeson's different roles stateside and across the Atlantic, one discovers that there exist differences which require a reevaluation of some of Robeson's films. This particular reevaluation of Robeson will consider the individual actor as well as the national and international industry he works in, because merely chastising Robeson ignores the formidable, but still indeterminate, nature of a capital-intensive industry that produces mass entertainment.

120. Paul Robeson in still from *King Solomon's Mines* (Gainsborough, 1937). *Photographs and Prints Division, Schomburg Center for Research in Black Culture, The New York Public Library, Astor, Lenox and Tilden Foundations.*

Additionally, the hero-centered approach to film criticism inadvertently posits a utopian understanding of the forces that compel profit-motivated industries to change, for better or worse, their attitude toward racial, ethnic, gender, and sexual imagery. Thus, Robeson's roles are the final product of economic and social forces that affect qualitative and quantitative changes in casting and film production. Again, it is absurd to suggest that an actor, even of Paul Robeson's professional stature, determines the roles that the film industry offers.

Though Robeson's British films tend to support colonialism in Africa, some of these films cleverly contest the contemporary racist ideas of Adolph Hitler's National Socialist Party, the fascist ideas of Benito Mussolini, and the practice of racial segregation in American life. Moreover, all his British films have *mise en scènes* in which black actors perform alongside their white colleagues. Consequently, the films fly in the face of Nazi beliefs about the Aryan race, Italian fascist adventurism in Ethiopia, and American racial segregation. The films provide better roles for Robeson and, by extension, other black actors seeking work in *mainstream* movies.

In British films, Robeson had major roles and, unlike his African American contemporaries in American films, the British filmmakers did not use racially segregated scenes. Moreover, his leading and supporting roles are in racially integrated scenes. In 1936 and 1937, the British film industry cast Robeson in two major movies that move from Western

121. Paul Robeson (fourth from left) in the motion picture production of *The Big Fella* (1937).
Photo by F. S. Johnson. Photographs and Prints Division, Schomburg Center for Research in Black Culture, The New York Public Library, Astor, Lenox and Tilden Foundations.

settings to African locations and explore the character's pan-African consciousness which, according to Harold Cruse, has its roots in nineteenth-century African American political thought. Cruse writes, "Every Pan-Africanist trend of the twentieth century, including [Marcus] Garvey's, had its roots in nineteenth-century American Negro trends. The radical elements in these nineteenth-century trends were not Marxian, but native American, in essence."[3]

Paul Robeson's roles in two British productions dramatize the marriage of pan-African consciousness with seemingly benevolent colonial practices. The remainder of this chapter analyzes how J. Elder Wills's *Song of Freedom* (British Lion–Hammer, 1936) and Thornton Freeland's *Jericho* (Buckingham, 1937) construct the major black protagonist as a wise, democratic, and benevolent leader.

This chapter considers how the two films construct the notion of African independence by positing intelligence and leadership qualities in a Western-born and -bred black protagonist—the role Robeson performs in these particular British films. The main focus of this chapter centers on three issues that trouble artists like Robeson whose livelihood is their work in the entertainment industry. First, what happens to the political importance of pan-African ideas when its spokesman is an American or British black who becomes a wise benevolent tribal leader in an Africa that is still governed by a colonial administration? Second, how does each film use Robeson's phenotypic attributes and skilled performance to conceal the film's *refined* colonial attitude toward black Africa? Granting the aforementioned shortcomings, how might the two films be historically situated to reveal how Robeson's fame, on stage and screen, provides these films with a marketable black star who could contest, through his stage and screen performances, Europe's fascist movements and America's racist practices? In discussing these issues, I will show how the two films construct the black diasporic character as a Western-educated black whose pan-African ideas further the British colonial project and speak not to Africa but to the dilemma of its diasporic people in the Americas and Europe.

J. ELDER WILLS'S *SONG OF FREEDOM* (1936)

J. Elder Wills's *Song of Freedom* is based on a story told by Major Claude Wallace to Paul Robeson when both were working on *Sanders of the River*.[4] The film features Paul Robeson as John Zinga, a British-born stevedore who wants to emigrate to Africa even before he learns that he is a direct heir to the kingship of Casanga, a West African island. Less than fifteen minutes into the film, John has a discussion with his wife, Ruth, in which he expresses his fervent desire to emigrate to Africa.

John: I met a fella in the pub coming home, sailing for Africa tonight.

Ruth: Africa, it's always Africa isn't it, John?

John: After all, that's my home, that's where we come from. I wonder which part.
   . . . What wouldn't I give to know?

Ruth: But you're happy here. The people are kind.

John: Oh, I know. Oh, they're grand people: Bert and Nell and the fellas down at the
   docks. But somewhere in those parts [Africa] are our people, Ruth. And I've
   got a feeling that they're grand people too. The people we belong to.

122. Still from *The Song of Freedom* (British Lion, 1936).
Courtesy of the Academy of Motion Picture Arts and Sciences.

In the same scene, John states that he feels out of place and different from the other white dock workers. He confesses that, "It's funny that [white] fella didn't want to go. Natural. He's leaving his people to go out amongst strangers. He'll be sort of out of place, lonely maybe. And however hard I try, I always feel the same here. Out of place." Ironically, the scene ends with John embracing Ruth and singing "Sleepy River," a lullaby that visually introduces a montage sequence of family-oriented images that links white with black parents and couples. The montage sequence first shows a white working-class woman knitting and rocking her baby to sleep; this scene is followed by another in which a black working-class couple enters a bedroom to observe their three children, who are asleep in one large bed. The montage sequence ends with a return to John and Ruth Zinga embracing at a window that overlooks their working-class interracial neighborhood. John's rich bass voice connects several images of working-class black and white Londoners who share similar experiences of love and parenthood. His singing sutures (connects) the montage sequence of concerned parents with the childless couple John and Ruth. John Zinga's voice-over produces an interracial sharing of parenthood and love. Ironically, it is also John's voice that articulates a contradictory sentiment: he wants to expatriate to Africa and, thereby, leave the familial images of blacks and whites that his voice has earlier connected.

John's African desires express the general sentiments of many first-generation immigrant communities in the European and American metropolis. In particular, John Zinga articulates feelings of blacks and whites who, for various reasons, saw the African emigration movement as the best remedy for the racial problems during the American antebellum and reconstruction periods.[5]

Presently in Western Europe, unemployment is at its highest and conservative political parties, like Jean-Marie Le Pen's Front Nationale party in France, propose repatriation policies for their Turkish, Arab, and black African émigré workers. There even have been moves to repatriate European-born second-generation Turks, Arabs, and black African family members of these émigré worker communities.[6] Thus, John Zinga's expatriation desires, America's antebellum and reconstruction-era African repatriation schemes, and Europe's contemporary repatriation policies, taken together, reveal how Zinga's African dream and its final realization directly support racist policies that would have black diasporic members, émigré workers, and other unwanted exilic groups in constant middle passages—a postmodern condition that is only welcomed and celebrated by those far removed from its detrimental socioeconomic and psychic effects.

John becomes a famous concert singer, leaves his working-class community, and becomes the darling of the upper-class concert audience. Ironically, it is in this exclusively white upper-class milieu that John learns that he is the direct descendant of the deposed king of Casanga, an island off the west coast of Africa. John replaces his ties to the interracial and working-class community that opens the film with professional success, financial rewards, and, later, African nobility.

John and Ruth expatriate to Casanga; they become an Anglo-African royal family that maintains the British Empire. Consequently, John returns for concert performances on the British stage. As an African king on the British stage, he does not don his usual tuxedo, but reveals his massive shirtless chest, because he is a noble Anglo-African subject who receives financial support for Casanga by leaning against wooden African totems on the London stage. He is unarguably the rightful heir and, after World War II, the worthless postcolonial administrator of this West African island. His dream is nothing but a metaphor for all the colonial adventures written and filmed for John Zinga's varied Western audiences.

Similar to the film's abandonment of John's interracial working-class stevedore community for his stage career, the film denies that there exist any benefits in Casangan culture before the arrival of the noble Zinga couple—John and Ruth. Upon arriving with their pan-African dreams, patriarchal rights, and very Western ways, John and Ruth fill a leadership vacuum that has seemingly existed since his great grandparent's political exile. The Zingas also inherit a kingdom of African children, who provide familial closure to the earlier transracial montage of concerned black and white parents. Once again, and reflecting the operatic quality of many of Robeson's film roles, John's basso profundo cements two distant racialized objects—the West (medicine and money) to the Casangan civilization.

John, a British subject by birth but an African in his faith, hope, and charity, is rightful heir to the nineteenth-century civilizing and racially uplifting mission. In patriarchal fashion, he finances the Westernization of his "backward" African family-kingdom. The film concludes with John Zinga's pan-African dream realized, which certain black spectators might view as an instance of nationalistic pride, but such a celebration is negated by the film's racist ideological proposition. In the kingship of black but culturally British John Zinga, the film supports British colonial efforts in Africa.

The film dramatizes John Zinga's contradictory emotions toward his stevedore colleagues, his Casangan kingdom, and his white upper-class audience. *Song of Freedom* presents the Casangans as a superstitious group of primitives who require, like other nations in Africa and Asia, a black leader steeped in Western traditions. Richard Dyer describes how the ethnographic cultural elements such as "song, dance, speech and stage presence are either inflected by the containing discourse as Savage Africa or else remain opaque, folkloric, touristic."[7] Dyer later states,

> Robeson himself is . . . distinguished from these [African] elements rather than identified with them; they remain 'other.' This authentication enterprise also falls foul of being only empirically authentic—it lacks a concern with the paradigms through which one observes any empirical phenomenon. Not only are the 'real' African elements left undefended from their immediate theatrical or filmic context, they have already been perceived through discourse on Africa that have labeled them primitive, often with a flattering intention.[8]

Dyer's observations are of importance to any understanding of Robeson's British film if, and only if, we disregard the fact that most forms of popular entertainment are produced for Western audiences. This does not deny the importance of Dyer's observations that reveal the nature of this capital-intensive system of production, distribution, and exhibition. Robeson unwittingly expresses this narrow vision when he states, "*Song of Freedom* is the first film to give a true picture of many aspects of the life of the colored man in the west."[9] Unfortunately, the film shows both non-Western (the Casanga) and Western (black Londoners') life and experiences. Robeson's comment, however, reveals the Western perspective that generates a narrative which restricts John Zinga's consciousness to missionary-type heroics. He is a black person (a been-to African or an African diasporic individual) who is uncomfortable in "primitive" Casanga until it becomes more like the London he left.[10] Dyer correctly finds that the film is merely a travelogue version of Africa, its people, and their cultural customs. After discussing Thornton Freeland's *Jericho*, I describe, in more detail, the dilemma of double consciousness as represented in both Robeson and Zinga.

THORNTON FREELAND'S *JERICHO* (1937)

Paul Robeson's first visit to Africa occurred during the shooting of exterior scenes in Thornton Freeland's *Jericho* (*Dark Sands* is the American title).[11] The film is set in France and North Africa toward the end of World War I, 1917 to be exact. Robeson stars as Corporal Jericho Jackson, a member of an African American unit of the American Expeditionary Forces stationed at Camp Genicourt in Bordeaux, France. Sergeant Gamey is the highest-ranking black officer of the unit and is also a notorious bully. While on a tour of duty, their battleship is torpedoed and begins to sink. Similar to the stereotypical response of black characters in horror films, these soldiers become irrational. During all this excitement, Jericho pushes Gamey who, in his fall, receives a fatal blow to his head. During an inquiry into Gamey's death, a black private falsely and unwittingly states that Jericho hit Gamey with his fist. The Army court finds Jericho guilty of Gamey's murder and gives him the death penalty. Although most noncommissioned black soldiers in the unit and the commissioned white commanding officers of the battalion feel that Jericho is innocent, they must comply with the court's ruling.

Captain John Mack, a white commanding officer who attended college with Jericho, gives Jericho permission to leave jail and "sing with the boys" during a Y.M.C.A. Christmas Eve concert. During a group prayer, Jericho takes a gun from a guard and escapes into the night. He then steals the clothes off a black African soldier and, when white American military police stop to question him, he replies in French. The white military police allow him to leave. Jericho's foreign attire and language confuse them. He does not fit their expectations though the military police agree that "he's just another dinge."

Jericho steals a sailboat on which a sleeping white soldier has taken refuge. The sailboat will take them to an imaginary North African country where their phenotype no

123. Still from *Jericho* (1937).
*Photographs and Prints Division,
Schomburg Center for Research in
Black Culture; The New York Public
Library; Astor, Lenox and Tilden
Foundations.*

longer marks them as different. Ironically, the same court that sentenced Jericho holds Captain
Mack responsible for Jericho's escape. The court dishonorably discharges Mack and sentences
him to five years in a military prison. In 1922, Mack is released from Leavenworth Federal
Penitentiary and spends the rest of his screen time in pursuit of Jericho Jackson. Finally,
Mack finds Jericho and considers how quickly the North African people protect Jericho because
of the social good he has done for them. Mack abandons his pursuit and returns home without Jericho, who was ready and willing to leave with his commanding officer.

Jericho, who has had three years of medical school, mends the sheik's broken leg. In
return, the sheik offers shelter and sustenance as long as Jericho wishes to stay. Similar to
the medical work and leadership role that John Zinga performed for the Casanga people,
Jericho Jackson establishes a makeshift clinic, where he heals the sick of the sheikdom. He
also becomes the "brave and strong" leader of several North African tribes on a salt caravan.
Like Zinga, Jericho hopes that one day this village will have a hospital equipped with the
necessary instruments and medicine. He marries the sheik's daughter, who is the only dark-
complected person in the sheikdom, and with their son they are the only brown-complected
villagers. After successfully leading several tribes on a salt caravan and warding off bandits,
Jericho becomes the sheik of the village in which he had initially found refuge.

124. Still from *Proud Valley* (Ealing, 1940).
Courtesy of the Academy of Motion Picture Arts and Sciences. Copyright Canal + UK Ltd.

Jericho's pending death sentence forces him to leave the community of noncommissioned African American soldiers and their commissioned white American commanding officers. Where Zinga leaves the West to fulfill his pan-African dreams, Jericho seeks refuge from a death sentence. Jericho is easily integrated into a racially ambiguous North African community in which he, his wife, and son are its only black members. Nevertheless, Jericho never faces hostility from the North Africans as Zinga initially faces with the black Casangans. Jericho and Zinga's Western training provides them with skills that the non-Western tribal communities lack. Both of Robeson's roles present an African diasporic male who leads African people because he has acquired skills. These non-Western locales permit John Zinga and Jericho Jackson's flight from such American and European social inequities as racial segregation and classism. Consequently, the films celebrate the black man's leadership ability and technical skills. These heroic black images, though very individualistic in constitution, portray racial harmony, not racial strife. The films were widely exhibited in England and less widely in the U.S. Robeson's characters mixed with different races and classes, quite a change from America's racial segregation and the German Nazi Party's racist and anti-Semitic policies. Surely, the two films have problems if one considers the primitive and childlike images of indigenous Africans and their seemingly backward culture that required such a Western-educated hero-leader as the Afro-British John Zinga or the African American Jericho Jackson.

SUMMARY AND CONCLUSION

The two films construct the black diasporic character as a universal image of the Western-educated black whose pan-African ideas further the British colonial project. The films speak not to Africa but to the dilemma of its diasporic people in the Americas and Europe.

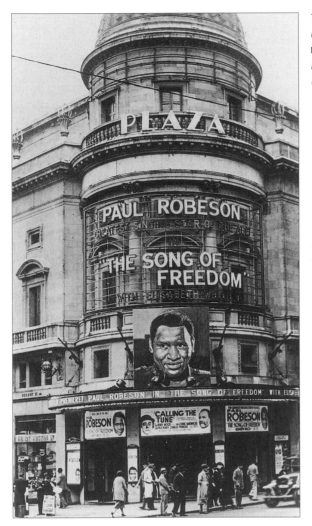

125. Photograph of theater advertising *The Song of Freedom,* including likeness of Robeson on the marquee. 1937.
Paul Robeson Cultural Center Collection, Rutgers University.

Still, J. Elder Wills's *Song of Freedom* and Thornton Freeland's *Jericho* present interesting images of Robeson as a pan-African hero. Robeson's roles in the two films dramatize the inescapable contradictions when a pan-African hero expresses the benefits of Western technology in colonial, as opposed to postcolonial, Africa. Together, the films present what Du Bois refers to as a *double consciousness* and which he explains, "[i]t is a peculiar sensation, this double-consciousness, this sense of always looking at one's self through the eyes of others, of measuring one's soul by the tape of a world that looks on in amused contempt and pity. One ever feels his twoness,—an American, a Negro; two souls, two thoughts, two unreconciled strivings; two warring ideals in one dark body, whose dogged strength alone keeps it from being torn asunder."[12] Robeson's roles in the films present two types of pan-African heroes—African American and Afro-British—whose trajectory, like that of W.E.B. Du Bois's self-imposed exile in Ghana, ends in Africa. The narratives dramatize a diasporic situation rather than an African condition that partially explains the lack of black African leaders in the films.

The films also exhibit a type of *double consciousness* in their purposes. First, movie production requires large capital investments by groups who seek profits. Second, it is far wiser to circulate your message to the largest possible audience, and this is sometimes possible through a mixture of entertainment and social commentary. In the two films, Robeson's voice, acting skill, and physical stature provide auditory and visual entertainment, while his blackness, in communion with nonblacks, and his progressive social observations, when taken together, express antifascist and antiracist messages. Still, the entertainment and educational mix can obscure the film's antifascist and antiracist politics if critics do not consider the historical context—world film history and social history—in which the films circulated. For instance, the protagonist's articulation of pan-Africanism is visually shown through his speech and by his migration to and self-exile in Africa. Both films depict multiracial groups—soldiers in *Jericho* and laborers in *Song of Freedom.* The films present two of the first appearances of a pan-African hero in mainstream world cinema. However, the sub-Saharan African people and their specific ethnic cultures remain unimportant. If you will, Africans are visually present but the film has glossed over the importance of their ethnic culture.

Plate 1. Winold Reiss, Portrait of Paul Robeson as "The Emperor Jones." 1924.
Conte crayon and pastel on board. 30 1/16 x 21 9/16 in. (76.3 x 54.8 cm.).
National Portrait Gallery, Smithsonian Institution. Gift of Lawrence A. Fleischman and Howard Garfinkle
with a matching grant from NEA.

Plate 2. Original poster for Provincetown Playhouse production of *All God's Chillun Got Wings.*
1924. Silkscreen.
Library of Performing Arts, The New York Public Library, Astor, Lenox and Tilden Foundations.

Plate 11. *Here I Stand* book jacket. 1958.
*Charles L. Blockson Afro-American Collection, Temple
University.*

Plate 12. Robeson at New York rally
for Amnesty for Smith Act Victims.
1954.
Photo © by Julius Lazarus.

POLITICAL ACTIVISM
AND FINAL YEARS

126. Paul Robeson singing at "Lift Every Voice" rally to end discrimination in Parkchester housing project in New York, organized by the American Labor party. Alan Booth is accompanist. 1956.
Photo © by Julius Lazarus.

Mark D. Naison

PAUL ROBESON
AND THE AMERICAN
LABOR MOVEMENT

One of the least known, but most significant dimensions of Paul Robeson's political activism was his participation in the American labor movement. From 1939 through the mid 1950s, Robeson defined the interracial unions of the Congress of Industrial Organizations (CIO) as the major vehicle for progressive social change in the United States and urged Black workers to join them and rise to union leadership. For Robeson, involvement in the labor movement was an expression of a broad philosophy of life, embodied in his concert repertoire, his presentation of his personal identity, and his view of American history. When Robeson returned to the United States in 1939, he did so as a partisan of international working-class solidarity, who cherished his working-class roots, highlighted commonalities in the folk culture of different nationalities, and extolled the struggles of working-class people against exploitation and poverty as the great humanizing force in the twentieth century. No cultural figure in modern American history, with the possible exception of Woody Guthrie, so completely identified his life and art with the fate of American labor. In fifteen years of political activism, Robeson spoke and sang at hundreds of picket lines, rallies, and demonstrations organized by unions whose philosophy he shared. Robeson was an honorary member of several left-led unions and regularly spoke at their national conventions. Barred from major concert halls during the Cold War, excluded from film and radio, Robeson still found an audience in the halls of left-wing unions and the African American church.

The depth and character of Robeson's involvement with labor raise intriguing questions about Robeson's political identity. Was Robeson's commitment to labor activism a byproduct of his Communist affiliations or was it reflective of a broad social philosophy of which "pro-Sovietism" was one part? Were his speeches and concerts before working-class audiences dictated by political commissars or shaped by powerful—and often idiosyncratic—experiences as an internationally renowned African American cultural figure? After reviewing Robeson's remarks to labor audiences, I tend toward the latter interpretation. In explaining why he was so comfortable with working-class audiences, Robeson spoke of two major influences—the hardships of his youth, "working in brick yards, in hotels, on docks and river boats," and the transforming effects of contacts with the British working class.[1] Robeson claimed he came to England in the late 1920s as the darling of that nation's elite and left it as a partisan of international working-class solidarity. "In England," Robeson declared, "I had held long sessions with leaders of the Labor Party and had traveled all over the British Isles, visiting with the Welsh miners, railway men, dock workers and textile workers—sharing their griefs and little triumphs, learning their songs, basking in the warmth of their generous friendship and hospitality. I had learned, during these years, an important lesson: that the problems of workers the world over are much the same."[2] Although trips to the Soviet Union played a seminal role in Robeson's political evolution, he developed his persona as a "people's artist" in a British working-class milieu. During his last two years in England

127. Still from *Proud Valley* (Ealing, 1940).
Copyright Canal + UK Ltd. Courtesy of the Academy of Motion Picture Arts and Sciences.

(1937–1939), Robeson gave regular performances in British music halls, helped sponsor a trade-union theater, and lived among Welsh miners while making the film *Proud Valley*.[3] The Welsh experience had a lasting impression on Robeson. The working conditions the miners labored under recalled the experiences of Robeson's relatives in tobacco plantations of North Carolina, and their hospitality toward Robeson evoked images of interracial working-class unity that became a reference point for Robeson's hopes that the United States might transcend its historic prejudices. "It's from the miners in Wales," Robeson declared, ". . . where I first understood the struggle of Negro and white together . . . when I went down in the mines with those workers, lived among them."[4]

When Robeson returned to the United States in 1939, after more than ten years of exile, he was determined to make participation in trade-union causes and the African American struggle for full equality the moral guidepost of his life, a kind of "reality check" to make sure he was not seduced by money and fame. While maintaining a backbreaking (and lucrative) schedule of concerts, recordings, theatrical productions, and films, Robeson found time to participate in the organizing campaigns of the CIO, the insurgent labor federation that was trying to organize basic industry across lines of craft and skill. The CIO had several features that attracted Robeson: its unions welcomed Black workers as members (although they didn't always fight racial hierarchies at the workplace), allowed Communists to participate as organizers and union leaders, and projected an evangelical sense of mission about workers' strivings for personal dignity and civic recognition. Robeson believed that Blacks had to join the CIO to make progress toward racial equality and decided to use his reputation as an artist to help secure Black involvement in one of the most important organizing drives of the prewar period: the United Automobile Workers Union (UAW) campaign to organize the Ford Motor Company. During May of 1941, just prior to a National Labor Relations Board election at Ford, Robeson sang and spoke before an audience of thousands of workers in a rally at Cadillac Square and followed it up with visits to African American churches and Ford assembly plants. In one of these appearances, he spoke passionately of his own stake in the movement:

> I know about the situation at Ford's and I'll be glad to tell you what I think about it. Most Negroes think of me as a football player and song star. They do not know that before I could get through college, I worked as a bricklayer, on an ice wagon, and as a waiter. . . . The Negro problem cannot be solved by a few of us getting to be doctors and lawyers. The best way my race can win justice is by sticking together in progressive labor unions. It would be unpardonable for Negro workers to fail to join the CIO . . . they cannot be a part of American Democracy except through labor unions.[5]

The success of the Ford organizing drive cemented Robeson's identification with the CIO. From the spring of 1941 on, Robeson made regular appearances before union conventions

128. Paul Robeson leads Moore Shipyard workers in Oakland, California, in singing "The Star-Spangled Banner." "This is a serious job," he told them, "winning the war against fascists. We have to be together." September 1942.
Still Picture Branch, National Archives. Courtesy of A.P./White World Photos.

and union rallies, urging labor leaders to fight racial discrimination at the workplace, and urging Blacks to strive for union leadership. Challenging middle-class hegemony in the civil-rights struggle, Robeson argued that an organized Black working class, aware of its rights and linked to "progressive" forces in white labor, was the best hope of progress for the race. In a speech to labor organizers in 1943, Robeson advised Blacks to "view the whole struggle within the Labor Movement as our struggle. We must fight for our rights inside our labor organizations, for here for the most part are our real allies—those who suffer as we, subject to the same disabilities as we."[6]

Robeson affirmed his links to the labor movement, and his own "working-class identity," by becoming an honorary member of several CIO unions. The first organization which conferred this honor on him was the National Maritime Union (NMU), which asked him to speak at its July 1941 Convention. The NMU had a large and active Black membership, a Black secretary-treasurer (Ferdinand Smith), and a leadership group that adhered to the foreign-policy perspectives of the Communist Party. In supporting the NMU, Robeson could endorse interracial unionism and the promotion of Blacks to positions of union leadership without jeopardizing the pro-Soviet sentiments at the core of his political identity. Robeson's speech to the convention called for "complete rights for labor, for complete equality for the colored people of this country," but concluded with the controversial declaration that "the Soviet Union is standing four square for the cause and rights of all the oppressed peoples of the world." As a finale, Robeson took requests from the audience and sang "Bill of Rights, Water Boy, Joe Hill, Fatherland, Old Man River, Jim Crow, It Ain't Necessarily So, Spring Song, Song to Joe, Ballad for Americans." This was a bravura Robeson performance, fusing labor solidarity and an insurgent American patriotism rooted in multiracial unity with a defense of the Soviet role in world politics.[7]

Not all unions were comfortable with the persona Robeson brought to his labor activism. Many American Federation of Labor (AFL) unions excluded Blacks from membership, some CIO unions kept Blacks out of union leadership, and quite a few in both federations remained hostile to Communist participation, even during years (1941–1945) when Communists were partisans of patriotic sacrifice. However, Robeson found many unions in the CIO that embraced much of what he stood for. In New York, he developed close ties with the NMU, the Fur and Leather Workers Union, the Transport Workers Union, the United Electrical Workers Union, and the United Public Workers Union; in the South, with the Food and Tobacco Workers Union and the Inland Boatmen's Union; in the West, with the Mine, Mill and Smelter Workers Union, and the International Longshoremen's and Warehousemen's Union, an organization where Communists were strong at the local level rather than the national leadership.

In his speeches to working-class audiences, during wartime and after, Robeson combined a disingenuous and inaccurate portrait of an international freedom movement under Soviet leadership with a subtle and compelling vision of an America freed from race and class prejudice. The Soviet Union Robeson told workers about was more a projection of his needs and fantasies than an actual country—a place where the people controlled the government, where race prejudice had been conquered, and where the struggles of nonwhite and colonial people were given recognition and support. While the Soviet government *did* treat African Americans with deference and respect and intermittently supported revolutions against Western colonialism, Robeson's sanitized portrait of Communist victories in the postwar world, such as the one he offered to Winston-Salem tobacco workers in 1947, undermined his stature as a commentator on international affairs: "Our national leaders are wasting their

129. Robeson receiving honorary lifetime membership in the International Longshoremen's and Warehousemen's Union (ILWU) from President Harry Bridges. 1950s. *Courtesy of Esther Jackson/* Freedomways *magazine.*

130. Robeson in front of poster "End the cold war—get together for peace!"
Soviet American Friendship conference. New York. 1948.
Photo © by Julius Lazarus.

time trying to break down independent nations in Europe. . . . There's nothing going to happen to Tito, nothing going to happen in the Balkans or in China or the Soviet Union. These people have the land in their hands and they're not going to take it away from them."[8]

But if Robeson's vision was clouded when touching on events in Eastern Europe, it could be precise and even prophetic when focusing on race and ethnic relations in the United States. At a time when racial segregation was still official policy in many portions of the nation, and when immigrants from Asia, Latin America, and Eastern Europe still faced discrimination and contempt, Robeson redefined America as a hybrid product of the world's peoples rather than an embodiment of the Anglo-Teutonic "genius" for self-government. To Robeson, American democracy was a communal product, built on the labor of the oppressed of all nations, and its true custodians were its workers and people of color:

> It is well to remember that the America which we know has risen out of the toil of many millions who have come here seeking freedom from all parts of the world. The Irish and Scotch indentured servants who cleared the forests, built the colonial homesteads, and were part of the productive back bone of our early days. The millions of German immigrants of the mid-nineteenth century, the millions more from Eastern Europe whose sweat and sacrifice in the steel mills, the coal mines and the factories made possible the industrial revolution . . . the brave Jewish people from all parts of Europe who have so enriched our lives on this continent; the workers from Mexico and from the East—Japan and the Phillippines—whose labor has helped make the West and the southwest a rich and fruitful land. And, through it all, from the earliest days—before Columbus—the Negro people, upon whose unpaid toil as slaves the basic wealth of this nation was built! These are the forces that have made America great and preserved our democratic heritage.[9]

By defining labor as the criterion of citizenship, Robeson was reinventing America in a manner that placed African Americans at the center of the nation's culture and history, and transformed immigrants and workers into guardians of the country's best traditions. Moreover, the musical performances that invariably accompanied his speeches, featuring spirituals, folk songs, and songs of political resistance, turned music of the common people into high art, providing a model of cultural democracy for his audiences to draw strength from. Robeson had the power to make the most despised and embattled worker, whether Black, Jewish, Mexican, or Filipino, feel part of a great adventure, the creation of a multiracial, democratic America that would be a beacon to the world's peoples. In Robeson's view, the struggle against race prejudice was the highest form of patriotism, the precondition for victory over fascism and future peace and prosperity.

Before the Cold War reached its peak, Robeson brought this incendiary—and inspirational—message to hundreds of thousands of workers in football stadiums, ballrooms and arenas, and mass meetings outside factory gates. But Robeson also spent time with

131. Paul Robeson (center) at New York Polo Grounds Rally for Free Palestine. Others, left to right: unknown; Leo Isaacson, American Labor party candidate; Mr. Asman, union leader; Glen Taylor, Progressive party vice presidential candidate; and Norman Miller. 1948. *Photo © by Julius Lazarus.*

workers, particularly those belonging to embattled ethnic minorities, in more isolated settings. Throughout the 1940s and 1950s, he gave regular performances at the summer resorts and children's camps of left-wing Jewish workers in upstate New York, places where African Americans were welcome as guests and Robeson's militant pro-Sovietism was echoed by his audience.[10] In 1946, Robeson traveled to the Panama Canal Zone to help the United Public Workers Union challenge segregation and wage discrimination on the part of the United States government against Black Panamanian workers. In 1948, Robeson traveled to the Hawaiian Islands to help the International Longshoremen's and Warehousemen's Union organize plantation workers of Japanese, Filipino, and native Hawaiian descent.[11] Robeson not only spoke and sang about the multiracial character of the American working class, he experienced it first hand, in union meetings, picket lines, church services, meals at workers' homes, and singing sessions around campfires. Even on the political left, few other leaders so appreciated the role of people of color—Mexican, Asian, Polynesian, as well as African American—in developing a modern American economy. His vision of American identity, still compelling fifty years later, was forged more by intimate personal contact than by adherence to an ideological formula. In the tradition of Walt Whitman, Robeson found the true strength of America in the lives of its common people.

Robeson's romantic identification with American workers, however, would be sorely tested in the Cold War years. As relations between the United States and the Soviet Union deteriorated and Communist governments came to power in Eastern Europe and Asia, anti-Communist feeling spread rapidly through American society, shattering the atmosphere of tolerance that had allowed open leftists to function as leaders and organizers in the American labor movement. Although conservatives and elected officials launched most anti-Communist initiatives, some segments of the American working class, operating through churches, veterans organizations, or union locals, eagerly joined the anti-Red crusade. White Catholic workers, who had been one of the bulwarks of the CIO in basic industry, shared the outrage of their clergy over the Soviet occupation of Eastern Europe and helped purge Communist organizers from many unions they had helped to build. In the South, white workers who had reluctantly participated in interracial unions fell prey to an atmosphere of regional hysteria sparked by modest federal initiatives in the sphere of civil rights. By 1948, Robeson, a strong supporter of Henry Wallace's independent presidential campaign, had become *persona non grata* in many trade union circles where he had once been honored as a conquering hero. Leaders of the NMU and the Transport Workers Union, where Robeson held honorary

132. Paul Robeson addressing the Progressive party nominating convention. Philadelphia. June 1948. *Photo © by Julius Lazarus.*

memberships; barred him from their conventions; leaders of the UAW banned him from participating in national union events.[12] More tragically, large numbers of working-class whites joined in the mob attacks on Jewish and Black concertgoers who went to hear Robeson sing in Peekskill, New York, in 1949. Although New York's left-wing unions provided a protective phalanx for Robeson in the second Peekskill concert, blue-collar residents of Peekskill, Catholic and Protestant alike, contributed heavily to the crowd of thousands who hurled rocks and bricks and racist epithets at the 25,000 New Yorkers who came to that community for a day of folk music. In an event which pitted white against Black, Christian against Jew, and veterans organizations against leftists, Robeson's hopes of a united working class reinvigorating democracy seemed relegated to a distant future.[13]

133. Motorist prepares to join 30,000 veterans demonstrating against a concert by Paul Robeson the next afternoon at Peekskill, New York. September 3, 1949.
Courtesy of UPI/Corbis-Bettmann.

134. Interracial audience gathered to hear Paul Robeson at Peekskill concert. Peekskill, New York. September 4, 1949.
Photo by Wally Permiller. Photographs and Prints Division, Schomburg Center for Research in Black Culture, The New York Public Library, Astor, Lenox and Tilden Foundations.

135. Clashes erupt throughout the golf course at Peekskill after the concert. Peekskill, New York. September 4, 1949. *Corbis-Bettmann.*

136. Paul Robeson's records and musical scores are burned on a pile of flaming chairs started by anti-Communist rioters at Peekskill. Peekskill, New York. August 28, 1949. *UPI/Corbis-Bettmann.*

Nevertheless, Robeson continued to express a Whitmanesque faith that America's common people—or at least the left-wing organizations that spoke for their "true" interests—would be Black America's best ally. "To be completely free from the chains that bind him," Robeson told the *New York Age* shortly after the Peekskill riot, "the Negro must be part of the progressive forces which are fighting the overall battle of the little guy—the sharecropper, the drugstore clerk, the auto mechanic, the porter, the maid, the owner of the corner diner, the truck driver, the garment mill and steel worker."[14] Cut off from the mainstream of the labor movement by anti-Communist sentiment, excluded from the commercial media, Robeson defiantly increased his involvement with a small number of CIO unions that stubbornly sustained militant interracialism and a pro-Soviet outlook even at the height of the Cold War. These unions, along with the African American church, became his refuge and his solace during the late 1940s and early 1950s.

Who were these holdouts to the Cold War consensus? For the most part, they were unions with a large Black membership, a large Jewish membership, or a sizable component of Latino and Asian workers. In the first category was the Food and Tobacco Workers Union, which was engaged in a heroic, and ultimately futile, effort to hold on to its predominately Black and female locals in the tobacco plants of North Carolina. Robeson went to North Carolina to address those workers when they were on strike, linking their struggle to the Henry Wallace presidential campaign, which was directly challenging segregation codes during its southern tour. In the second category were the Fur and Leather Workers Union and District 65 of the Distributive Workers Union, which had heavily Jewish memberships and a sizable minority of Black workers and leaders. In the third category were the Mine, Mill and Smelter Workers Union and the International Longshoremen's and Warehousemen's Union, which had large numbers of Mexican and Asian members as well as a sizable Black cadre. Robeson also maintained close ties with Local 600 of the UAW in Detroit, which was able to keep a left-wing leadership group through the mid 1950s. These organizations provided a forum for Robeson as a labor activist, as a critic of American foreign policy, and as an artist. Fending off government investigations, raids from other unions, and efforts by employers to decertify their locals, they welcomed Robeson, in the years of his internal exile, as a symbol of resistance to political repression.[15]

During the 1950s, a defiant Robeson, barred from the largest concert halls and arenas, gave stirring vocal performances to Jewish garment workers in the Bronx, Finnish miners in Minnesota, Black auto workers in Detroit, and multiracial audiences of waterfront workers in San Francisco and Oakland. More than ever, he proclaimed his identification with the poorest and most embattled sections of the American working class—African Americans, immigrants, people of color. "In 1947," he told a labor audience, "I announced that I would put aside my concert career for the time being to enter the day-to-day struggles of my people and the working masses of this country. I meant the struggle for our daily bread . . . on the picket lines of the Mesabi iron range, with the auto workers in Cadillac Square, the gallant tobacco

137. Paul Robeson acknowledges the tremendous ovation given him after introduction by President Reid Robinson (left) to the delegates at the 42nd Convention of the International Union of Mine, Mill and Smelter Workers. Sudbury, Ontario, Canada. February 1, 1955.
*Courtesy of Esther Jackson/*Freedomways *magazine.*

workers in Winston-Salem, the longshoremen, cooks and stewards in San Francisco, the furriers, electrical workers, and a host of others."[16] In 1951, Robeson put these sentiments to the test by joining with a small group of Black workers and union officials to found the National Negro Labor Council, an organization concerned with the exclusion of Black workers from skilled labor categories and advancing their claim to union leadership. In the face of harassment by government investigating committees and large national unions, the Council exposed patterns of economic inequality within American industry that had survived the building of interracial industrial unions, and they organized Black caucuses within unions to demand the promotion and advancement of Black workers on the job. In his speeches to the Council, Robeson defended the organization's program, which twenty years later would be called "affirmative action," as the cutting edge of the civil rights movement, and anointed the Black working class as the repository of the nation's hope for democracy and social justice:

> As the Black worker takes his place upon the stage of history . . . a new day dawns
> in human affairs. The determination of the Negro workers, supported by the whole
> Negro people, and joined with the mass of progressive white working men and

138. Paul Robeson with leaders of the National Negro Labor Council. Left to right: Coleman A. Young, later mayor of Detroit, Michigan; Robeson; William Hood, former president of Ford Local 600, UAW; and William Marshall, actor. 1951.
*Courtesy of Esther Jackson/*Freedomways *magazine.*

women can save the labor movement. . . . This alliance can beat back the attacks against the living standards and very lives of the Negro people. . . . And it can help to bring to pass in America and in the world the dreams our fathers dreamed—of a land that's free, of a people growing in friendship, in love, in cooperation, and in peace.[17]

During the four years of its existence, the Council registered important accomplishments: it fought for clerical and sales jobs for Blacks in the Sears Roebuck chain, opened apprenticeship opportunities in the electric and automobile industries, helped end discriminatory hiring practices in the New York hotel industry, and won jobs for Black workers in the federal government's Bureau of Engraving. But it was unable to survive the continuous pressure placed on individuals and organizations linked to the Left. Two of the small left-wing unions that had supported creation of the Council—the United Public Workers Union and the Food and Tobacco Workers Union—folded during the early 1950s; others shrank drastically in size, while several key founding members of the Council were expelled from the UAW. By 1956, when the Council was designated a "Communist Front Organization" by the Subversive Activities Control Board, the organization lacked the financial resources to contest this designation, and decided to disband.[18]

The Council's dissolution left Robeson as a leader without a movement. Deprived of his passport, excluded from theater, film, and the concert stage, banned from radio and television, Robeson now was effectively cut off from direct personal contact with ordinary workers, an activity that had given his life direction and meaning for over twenty years. For the first time since his early years in England, Robeson no longer had a politically active labor movement as an audience for his music, a sounding board for his ideas, and an inspiration for his dreams. For someone who defined his integrity and honor by his connection to the common people, this had to be a crushing blow.

But the legacy of these twenty years continues to haunt and challenge future generations. Robeson's speeches to labor audiences, and musical performances that accompanied them, invoked an almost biblical transformation of the American social order, elevating those who labored in isolation and contempt to the center of the national pantheon. When Robeson spoke, the African American sharecropper, the Chinese laundry worker, the Mexican fruit picker, the Finnish iron miner, and Jewish garment worker could see themselves as architects of American democracy, heirs of ancient cultures whose labor shaped

139. Members of Peekskill, New York, concert audience displaying rocks with which they were pelted by an angry mob. c. September 4, 1949.
Photo by Perounlan. Schomburg Center for Research in Black Culture,
The New York Public Library, Astor, Lenox and Tilden Foundations.

a modern economy, and whose music, art, and literature helped make American culture vibrant and attractive. More than any artist of his generation, Robeson *experienced* America as a nation of diverse peoples, and used that experience to create a new vision of American identity. By seeking out Americans where they worked, by rejecting hierarchies of class and color, Robeson saw democracy as a living product, re-created every day where its common people, labored, loved, and sang. Even at the height of the Cold War, his speeches to labor audiences had a visionary quality. "I have great confidence," he declared in 1951, "that the working class movement of America, white and black . . . shall labor that our children and their children shall work an American earth . . . a democratic earth that WE have helped to build."[19]

140. Paul Robeson singing at "May Day" Celebration. Union Square, New York. c. 1948.
Photo © by Julius Lazarus.

141. Ben Davis and Paul Robeson in Washington, D.C., demonstration against
the anti-Communist Mundt-Nixon Bill. June 2, 1948.
Photo © by Julius Lazarus.

Gerald Horne

COMRADES AND FRIENDS
The Personal/Political
World of Paul Robeson

Paul Robeson was the "tallest tree in our forest," as is often said. Although he was a brilliant individual, it would be mistaken to see him as *sui generis*, in terms of either his radical vision or his political affiliations. The scholar Daniel Aaron has observed that "Not the 'aberration of individuals' drew men into Communism in the 1930s but the aberration of society.'"[1] Certainly this is true of Robeson and the cohort of activists that surrounded him. As they were coming to political maturity the nation was gripped by a Great Depression that not only was driving millions into impoverishment but was accompanied by a spate of ghoulish and macabre lynchings of African Americans. Such extreme times often call forth radical alternatives and in the 1930s this meant the Communist Party (CP) and organizations within its orbit.

Within the orbit of the CP at that time was the cream of the African American intelligentsia. This illustrious group included not only Robeson, but also the writer Shirley Graham, the activist Claudia Jones, the writer and activist Louise Thompson Patterson, and a number of others. It also included the man who was, perhaps, Robeson's closest friend and political ally—Benjamin J. Davis, Jr. Davis's profile was not unlike that of Robeson. This black man graduated from Amherst College and Harvard Law School in the 1920s at a time when African Americans rarely graced these hallowed halls. Like Robeson the 6-foot tall, 230-pound Davis was a football star, playing left tackle and named to the All-East squad in 1925; next to him on the Amherst line was Charles Drew, an African American who went on to make significant scientific contributions. Davis tutored Drew on the finer points of the gridiron art, but tutoring Davis was his close friend Paul Robeson. As Davis later recalled, "I first met Robeson during my summer vacation in 1923. . . . I sat at the feet of Paul and he used to take me out to a lot to teach me how to protect myself in a game." This skill was necessary because the prevailing atmosphere of racism often meant that African American athletes frequently were targeted for vicious gouging and other tactics designed to maim and injure. As Davis noted ruefully, "At that time it was pretty tough for a Negro to play football and if you didn't know how to take care of yourself you'd be messed up something awful."[2]

In 1964 Robeson recalled that "Ben and I first met here in Harlem some 35 years ago . . . often passers-by on the Avenue would be startled and amused as Ben and I worked out some football tactics on the sidewalk. Again, we would discuss our hopes as future lawyers, and where and how we would work."[3] Davis recalled the infamous game in 1924 with the university in Robeson's hometown—Princeton—where a rumor was floated that the Tigers were going to crucify Amherst's African American players. At the stadium Davis and Drew were told, "We don't allow Negroes in here." This edict did not stand, but experiences such as these ultimately drove Davis to the left and, though he was from one of the staunchest and most affluent Black Republican families in the nation, he joined the Communist Party a few years after graduating from Harvard Law School in 1928.

Working closely with him in his political endeavors was Paul Robeson. They were quite close. Robeson acknowledged bluntly that Davis "influenced my ideological development."[4] In turn Davis told Robeson directly that "a guy like you is born once every century. . . . Every ounce of you is pure gold."[5] Lloyd Brown, the African American novelist and activist, knew both men well. He recalls their relationship as being "very, very important" to both. Robeson, he said, had "great admiration [and] respect" for Davis. Paul Robeson, Jr., concurs with Brown's evaluation. He observed that Davis and Robeson were "really good friends." Davis would frequently visit Robeson's Connecticut home for weeks at a time. At those times he and Robeson, Jr., would play tennis for hours on end and would engage Robeson, Sr., in lengthy games of chess. Davis was considered "part of the Robeson family."[6]

The Davis-Robeson relationship was so close that Robeson drew upon their bond in shaping his work in the theater. For example, in *Othello,* as a device to excite his nightly rage onstage, Robeson imagined that his close friend, Ben Davis, had betrayed him.[7] The prospect of Davis betraying his friend could be a source for dramatic inspiration, but it was far from being realized. Though Davis was a Communist and Robeson too was to be found on the left side of the political spectrum, blandishments and inducements were insufficient to turn one against the other; indeed, as time wore on it seemed that their relationship became even closer.

From the beginning of Davis's affiliation with the Communist Party, Robeson was one of his staunchest supporters. In 1934 Davis was working in Harlem for the party organ, the *Liberator*. He and the staff worked from dawn to late at night and the salary was a none-too-generous ten dollars per week. Yet, even this meager sum would have been much less but for Robeson sending a "few pounds to keep us going."[8]

Yet, despite—or perhaps because of—this friendship, Davis could be unrelenting in his criticism of Robeson's artistic contributions. For example, in 1936 Davis pointed to the boy-cott of Robeson's film *Sanders of the River* and would not accept the excuse that editing had made it a distorted and negative work:

> . . . that explanation may be acceptable, but good faith alone is not enough. The picture was an out and out betrayal of the African colonials, whatever may be said of your good intentions and the imperialist twist came about in more than the cutting of the film. You became the tool of British imperialism and must be attacked and exposed whenever you act in such pictures or plays.

142. Paul Robeson in a scene from *Sanders of the River* (London Film Producers, 1935).
Photo by Turnbridge, London. Photographs and Prints Division, Schomburg Center for Research in Black Culture, The New York Public Library, Astor, Lenox and Tilden Foundations.

Robeson replied wanly, "you're right . . ." and, indeed, such bracing criticism from a respected friend no doubt convinced this leading actor that he had to be more careful in the selection of material; this may help to explain his dwindling appearances on the silver screen.[9]

In 1943 Ben Davis, Jr., was elected to the New York City Council, replacing Adam Clayton Powell, Jr., who went on to serve in the U.S. House of Representatives. Davis received the endorsement of Powell, Richard Wright, and a host of other well-known personalities. The pianist Teddy Wilson was chair of Davis's Artists Committee and along with another key endorser—Paul Robeson—played an important role in getting Lena Horne, Duke Ellington, Count Basie, Mary Lou Williams, Coleman Hawkins, Billie Holiday, Jimmie Lunceford, Art Tatum, Ella Fitzgerald, Lucky Roberts, Josh White, Pearl Primus, Fredi Washington, and a number of others to express public support for Davis. When Davis was reelected in 1945 Robeson chaired the Committee of Artists for Davis's reelection and helped to recruit to the ranks Jose Ferrer, Leonard Bernstein, Frederick O'Neal, Jerome Robbins, Langston Hughes, and many others.[10]

143. Paul Robeson, Adam Clayton Powell, Jr., and Malcolm Ross (chairman of the Fair Employment Practices Committee Campaign), during 3rd Annual Negro Freedom Rally. June 25, 1945. *UPI/Corbis-Bettmann.*

At this historic juncture, what had hampered support for Communists in the past—support for the U.S.S.R.—was not a hindrance, since this nation was allied with the U.S. in a titanic battle against fascism. Thus, during the 1941–1945 era, Robeson's pro-Sovietism, which bedeviled Robeson during a good deal of his life, was viewed not as a handicap or an example of naiveté but as a useful counterweight against the ultraright.

But this benign view of Robeson's attraction to socialism was to change radically with the conclusion of the war. After Winston Churchill's "Iron Curtain" speech in 1946, support for Moscow was seen as perfidy at worst, inanity at best. However, Robeson and Davis refused to retreat from their firmly held convictions. They came to find, however, that others who had joined them in the halcyon days of the war were not so inclined when the Cold War commenced. Quickly, Robeson and his friends on the left found themselves not only isolated politically but disdained. In 1948 Davis was indicted for violating the Smith Act prohibition against teaching Marxism-Leninism; in 1948 he was convicted and, simultaneously, ousted unceremoniously—if not illegally—from his post in the City Council.

These setbacks were costly, but not without consequence: they were viewed as positive by many. For as a *de facto* inducement to get African Americans—who so recently had

144. Robeson standing before the Lincoln Memorial, Washington, D.C., after White House meeting with President Truman on September 23, 1946. *UPI/Corbis-Bettmann.*

supported Robeson and the left—to move away from this tendency, the more egregious aspects of Jim Crow were eased.[11] By 1951 Davis was in federal prison for violating thought-control legislation, but by 1954 the U.S. Supreme Court ruled in *Brown v. Board of Education* that *de jure* racial segregation was no longer the law of the land. However, the eclipsing of the political influence of the left—as has happened globally—set the stage for the rise of various forms of nationalism; and among African Americans this trend had decidedly "antiwhite" emphases.[12]

———

However, this viewpoint was hardly acknowledged as World War II ended and the Cold War was launched. Robeson continued to ally with Davis and others on the left. In January 1946 Robeson joined Davis in the American Crusade to End Lynching; the war's end brought a revival of this atavistic trend of lynching and Robeson was quick to rise in opposition.

The next year Davis and eleven of his comrades were indicted, but Robeson did not desert his friend. Instead, he chose to serve as cochair of the National Non-Partisan Committee to Defend the Rights of the Twelve Communist Leaders. Unlike Davis's races for the City Council, celebrities and artists did not flock to this banner. In part this reluctance was induced externally. According to the *Daily Worker*, "such big agents as Moe Gale, Joe Glaser, the William Morris Agency and other managers had refused to okay the contracting of such stars as Erskine Hawkins, Louis Armstrong, Benny Goodman . . . Count Basie and Billie Holiday . . . [and] threatened the cancellation of contracts for recordings, television, dances and other engagements" unless they all cut ties with the left.[13]

Of course, all did not flee. George W. Crockett, Jr., who was to have a distinguished career as a congressman from Detroit, served as a lawyer during the trial of the Communist leaders and worked closely with his fellow African American leaders, Davis and Robeson. Under Robeson's leadership, the National Non-Partisan Committee published a widely circulated pamphlet entitled "Due Process in a Political Trial: The Record vs. the Press." Here it was noted that during the trial Robeson's fellow Columbia Law School alumnus, Judge Harold Medina, "reserve[d] his most [sharp] shafts for defense counsel George W. Crockett, Jr." Robeson agreed that there was a "dual standard used by the Court in applying the rules of evidence . . . protectiveness toward prosecution witnesses contrasted with badgering of defense witnesses . . . derogation of the defendants' case . . . the judge as prosecutor . . . discriminatory application of rules of evidence . . . deprecation of the defendants' evidence in the presence of the jury."[14] The experience was shocking for Robeson, not least because the victim was his friend, Ben Davis. Robeson, the lawyer, was moved to announce that as a result of this difficult experience, "there I acquired a devastating contempt for [the] court[s]."[15]

This contempt was not alleviated after Davis was convicted and imprisoned. Robeson chose not to abandon his friend, even as pressure mounted to do so. Before leaving for prison

145. Robeson clapping hands at protest meeting against the conviction of the twelve American Communist Party members. New York. c. 1949.
Photo © by Julius Lazarus.

© Julius Lazarus Archives and Collection / Special Collections / Rutgers University Libraries

Davis told him, "everything in the apartment—and the apartment itself—are at your complete disposal. . . . I shall miss you. But as fighters for the working class and people we shall be together again." Robeson was pivotal in organizing the Trade Union Committee to Repeal the Smith Act and other forms of mass support for his friend. In Robeson's newspaper, *Freedom,* Davis was featured frequently. In the July 1952 edition he was compared to anticolonial leaders in Africa. At the 1953 convention of the National Negro Labor Council, which he too had helped to organize, Robeson remarked forcefully, "If we concede that . . . Ben Davis belongs in a Terre Haute Jim Crow jail, then we concede McCarthy's right and [Attorney General] Brownell's right to jail you and me and Harry Truman and to dig up Franklin Roosevelt and put him in jail too!" Even before the House Un-American Activities Committee in 1956, which was aching to find a reason to persecute him further, Paul Robeson would not denounce Ben Davis: "Nothing could make me prouder than to know him. I say he is as patriotic an American as can be."[16]

146. Robeson at New York rally
for Amnesty for Smith Act
Victims. 1954.
Photo © by Julius Lazarus.

This position was maintained adamantly by Robeson until Davis's death in 1964. Although his association with Communists did not endear him to many, Robeson believed that the Communists' advocacy of socialism ultimately was the answer to the scourges of racism and capitalist exploitation that had engendered the slave trade and brought Africans to this hemisphere in the first place. That "Stalinism" marked the Soviet Union did not cause him to jettison this analysis, no more than the "Terror" of the French Revolution caused Thomas Jefferson or Tom Paine to abandon the promise of Paris. His close relationship with Ben Davis then was not just personal—it was ideological as well.

———

Ben Davis was not the only African American Communist whom Robeson befriended. William Patterson was another. Born in the San Francisco Bay Area in the 1890s, Patterson, like Robeson and Davis, was also a lawyer—and a graduate of the law school at the University of California. His radicalism bloomed early. He was arrested in 1917 for protesting World War I, and shortly thereafter he joined the National Association for the Advancement of Colored People (NAACP). The 1919 steel strike in Pittsburgh found attorney Patterson on the case rendering legal assistance. Like Robeson he had an affinity for Africa and moved to London with the intention of returning to the motherland. But in London he was convinced that his fight was in the U.S., so he returned to the land of his birth. He became a partner in a New York City law firm that decades later came to include future U.S.

ambassador to Ghana Franklin Williams and future New York City mayor David Dinkins. It was during this time—the 1920s—that he encountered Paul Robeson. During this period, Patterson became a Communist and a leader of the International Labor Defense, which specialized in defending victims of racist and political repression.[17]

Throughout the years Robeson and Patterson collaborated on a number of worthy causes. One of the most significant but least heralded was the pressure they exerted to force major-league baseball to integrate its ranks. Although columnists with the *Pittsburgh Courier* and the *Baltimore Afro-American* were also instrumental in this process, it was Patterson who set up the historic meeting in 1942 between Robeson and baseball commissioner Kenesaw Mountain Landis that led ultimately to Jackie Robinson's breaking down the barrier of Jim Crow and unleashing events that were to change the face of sports—and the nation.[18]

However, Patterson and Robeson collaborated most fruitfully and directly in their labor with the Civil Rights Congress (CRC). Founded in 1946 as a result of a merger among the International Labor Defense, the National Negro Congress, and the National Federation for Constitutional Liberties, the CRC—though little known today—was undoubtedly the most important organization confronting the Red Scare and McCarthyism after the World War II. For the bulk of its existence, the CRC was headed by Patterson, and during that time Robeson was a top fund-raiser for the organization. At an early 1949 rally for the Trenton Six—a group of political prisoners who came to notoriety not far from his hometown of Princeton—Robeson sang along with Pete Seeger and gave a "generous contribution" as well. Later that year, in Chicago's Tabernacle Baptist Church, Robeson spoke before six thousand

147. Paul Robeson (fourth from left) and Alphaeus Hunton being escorted from Soviet Friendship Rally celebrating the 40th anniversary of the October Revolution. 1957. *Photo by Sam Schulman. UPI/ Corbis-Bettmann*

148. Paul Robeson marches in demonstration of National People's Lobby. Washington, D.C. August 5, 1948.
Photo © by Julius Lazarus.

people—with two thousand huddling outside—and made the call that led to a substantial sum being raised. Just as Robeson attracted celebrities to Ben Davis's electoral campaigns, he was also useful in attracting celebrities to the CRC banner. Just as Robeson's newspaper, *Freedom,* often featured Ben Davis, this journal also featured prominent CRC cases.[19]

Like any sound political relationship, this Patterson-Robeson tie was reciprocally beneficial. In 1949 Robeson was excoriated after raising doubts about whether African Americans would join in war against the U.S.S.R. At this point, many began to flee from Robeson's embrace, but not Patterson. Instead he provided a CRC platform so that Robeson could elaborate on his controversial remarks: "American Negroes must not be asked ever again to sacrifice on foreign shores," said Robeson. He continued, "If we must sacrifice, let it be in Alabama and Mississippi where my race is persecuted."[20] Angry picketers from the Veterans of Foreign Wars circled the site as Robeson's supporters cheered him on. Here is glimpsed the dialectic that ultimately led to the relaxation of the most atrocious forms of Jim Crow: to induce African Americans to join the Cold War crusade, racial conditions in the U.S. had to improve; however, the price paid for this bargain was lessened African American support for figures like Robeson, Davis, and Patterson who, up to that point, had been lionized as the fiercest and most sophisticated fighters against racism.

Patterson and the CRC did not stop there in their support of the increasingly beleaguered Robeson. At its Bill of Rights Conference in July 1949, the CRC issued a statement
of support signed by scores of delegates. When Robeson had to fight the U.S. State Department for the right to obtain a passport, Patterson and the CRC filed a hard-hitting *amicus
curiae* brief. Eventually Patterson personally took over the leadership of this fight.[21]

The Patterson-Robeson relationship received its most severe test during the fabled
Peekskill riot of 1949, when right-wing hysteria led to a physical assault on a CRC rally. But
even before this explosion there had been troubling and worrisome signs. In 1947 there had
been a spate of politically motivated cancellations of contracts at sites where Robeson was
scheduled to sing, most notably in Albany and Peoria. Then Robeson was scheduled to perform on the CRC's behalf in Miami, but opposition was so harsh and unyielding that Patterson
felt duty bound to retreat. Bluntly, Patterson asserted, "Reaction wants the murder of Paul
Robeson. . . . We must have no political[ly] naive outlook on this question." Robeson's appearance was cancelled.[22]

Hence, the CRC and Patterson should not have been surprised by the riot that greeted
their first Peekskill rally featuring Robeson in August 1949, or their second rally there—
designed to show they would not be intimidated—in September 1949. Before the first rally
the local press whipped up emotions about the arrival of the supposedly unpatriotic Robeson,
who was telling Negroes not to join the Cold War crusade. Hundreds of police were present as the CRC assembled but, like the matador that waves the cape as the bull charges by,

© Julius Lazarus Archives and Collection /
Special Collections / Rutgers University Libraries

149. Paul Robeson preparing to
sing at 1949 Paris World Peace
Congress. April 1949.
Photo © by Julius Lazarus.

150. Flyer announcing bus transportation to the Peekskill concert from Harlem. September 4, 1949.
Photographs and Prints Division, Schomburg Center for Research in Black Culture, Astor, Lenox and Tilden Foundations.

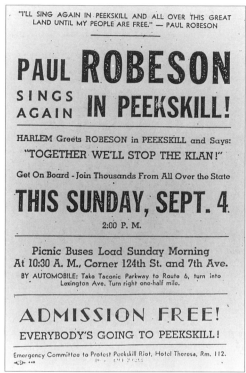

the authorities refused to halt the determined protesters bound on assaulting CRC supporters. This riot was not unexpected as evidenced by the presence of numerous television cameras shooting endless reels of film.

The state estimated that 15,000 people were present at the CRC event; the CRC estimated a crowd of 30,000. In either case, a horrible scene of destruction ensued. Pete Seeger, who also sang there, saw four- to five-inch rocks sailing by and cracked skulls afterward. In sworn affidavits, Albert Spivey swore he saw "four state troopers beating up two of the concert guards." In his affadivit, Leo Stark, who required stitches in his head, saw 150 police and rowdies go wild. Irving Warman was startled by the women cheering on the thugs and underscored the role played by the American Legion in the tumult. Anita Payne recalled frenzied shouts of "nigger" while Dr. Seymour Gladstone heard cries of "kikes . . . nigger lovers." Harold Taylor heard "dirty Jews." Michael Salte saw a burning cross, the calling card of the Ku Klux Klan. Nina Phillips had a finger amputated. Esther Marquit had a tooth knocked out by one of those rocks Pete Seeger saw. One member of Local 65 of the Wholesale and Warehouse Workers Union wound up on the "critical list" with a "blood clot on the brain." Starr Koss submitted a drawing of passengers huddling on the floor of the bus as glass splattered around them.[23]

Along with Robeson, Ben Davis also happened to be at Peekskill. Davis was quoted by a state trooper as saying, "'We are not pacifists and we are going to stand up toe to toe and slug it out . . . we will be prepared to defend ourselves." In an affidavit Davis filed about

151. Female spectators gesture at people walking to attend concert on September 4, 1949. *UPI/Corbis-Bettmann.*

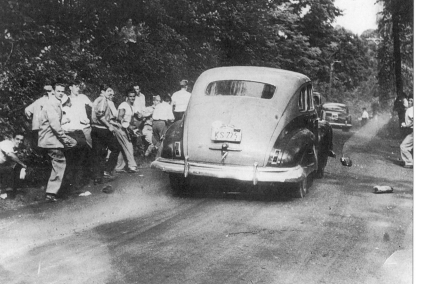

152. Although the concert on September 4 was peaceful, anti-Communist protesters rioted, surrounding cars, preventing occupants from leaving the concert, overturning cars, and attacking occupants.
Photographs and Prints Division, Schomburg Center for Research in Black Culture, The New York Public Library, Astor, Lenox and Tilden Foundations.

153. Members of the Peekskill Protest Committee gather in New York City's Grand Central Station to protest against Governor Dewey's decisions in the recent investigation of the Peekskill rioting. September 21, 1949.
UPI/Corbis-Bettmann.

154. While Paul Robeson sings inside Municipal Auditorium Theatre (background), Sam Cook, Jr., and his wife, Mary, take license numbers of all cars parked in the immediate vicinity. Cook, national director of the Western Nationalist Crusade, an organization with some 100,000 members, had earlier protested Robeson's right to sing in the city-owned auditorium because of Robeson's alleged Communist affiliations. Cook said that he intended to issue the list of license numbers to various investigating agencies throughout California and the United States. Oakland, California. February 9, 1958.
UPI/Corbis-Bettmann.

the second riot in September, Davis vividly recalled what had happened: "I was a passenger in an automobile . . . the car was pelted with rocks and stones . . . shattered the windshield . . . glass splattered upon me and those sitting [next] to me . . . the car swerved again and again." The driver was bleeding. There were shouts: "Hang the Robeson niggers with a rope!" "Get the dirty Jews!" State troopers stood by as this commotion unfolded. The five passengers in Davis's car were injured. Robeson and the Communist leader Irving Potash, both in the car right behind Davis, were also besieged.[24]

Peekskill was a turning point in the Red Scare and the Cold War. It was apparent that those seeking to stand with Robeson and exercise their First Amendment rights and oppose anti-Communism would be repelled—violently if necessary. The stick of Peekskill, accompanied by the carrot of civil rights concessions, guaranteed that African Americans

155. Henry Wallace and W.E.B. Du Bois, during presidential campaign. Harlem. N. Y. 1948.
Photo © by Julius Lazarus.

in particular would be increasingly reluctant to ally with the CRC—or their most well-known supporter, Paul Robeson.

This was not immediately apparent in Peekskill's aftermath, for the response to the riots was swift and immediate. The *Pittsburgh Courier* reflected the view of the black press by denouncing the rioters and hailing Robeson. The American Jewish Congress demanded the appointment of a special prosecutor. But symptomatic of the long-term trend was the fact that the Alabama Klan burned Robeson in effigy and the National Urban League implicitly condemned him at their Denver convention. While Eleanor Roosevelt, Mayor William O'Dwyer, and Jackie Robinson blasted the rioters, A. Philip Randolph castigated Robeson, terming him a "Johnnie-come-lately to the cause of the Negro." The CRC itself launched a multimillion-dollar lawsuit and tried to mobilize in support of it. Its hopes for the grand jury were cruelly dashed, however. There were forty-five morning and twenty-two afternoon sessions, resulting in thousands of pages of testimony being heard by twenty-one jurors. But the talk at these sessions of the CRC being a "group organized for and serving

156. Robeson greeting Dr. W. Alphaeus Hunton, director of the Council on African Affairs, just after Hunton's release from prison for refusing to inform on contributors to the Civil Rights Congress bail fund.
Left to right, Hunton, his wife, Dorothy, Robeson, and Dr. W.E.B. Du Bois. 1951.
*Courtesy of Esther Jackson/*Freedomways *magazine.*

solely the interests" of Communism was a signal that the criminals who had rioted would not be brought to justice. Patterson and his CRC colleague Bella Abzug were among the lawyers for twenty-eight plaintiffs suing under federal civil rights laws for $2.02 million. Ultimately the suit came to naught, as did their meeting with the U.S. attorney general in an effort to press criminal charges and their petition for dismissal of the police and state officials involved.[25]

Despite this crushing blow that Peekskill represented, Robeson continued to stand by Patterson and the CRC. Months later Robeson was in Gary, Indiana, working with the local CRC chapter on various matters. Right after the meeting concluded, according to a local CRC leader, the local newspaper "opened a red-baiting barrage, they managed to get the names of people on the executive committee and printed only the names and addresses of the new people; they tried to intimidate the leaders of the church where the meeting was scheduled." Calls came to the church saying "that a mob was on its way to the church to break up the meeting." Unavoidably, all this led to a "letdown." The chapter vice president "became intimidated" and dropped out. "Other active steelworkers who are shop stewards or planned to run for union office" dropped out. The recording secretary dropped out. But the "continuous red-baiting in Gary's only daily newspaper" did not abate.[26]

Robeson's celebrity was not sufficient to bar the disintegration of the Gary chapter or the CRC itself. By 1956 the organization that had been headed by his good friend, William Patterson, was defunct, a direct victim of pressure from a federal agency, the Subversive Activities Control Board, and a generally unfavorable atmosphere. Although the CRC fell apart, Robeson's friendship with Patterson did not. They remained close during the remaining years of both. However, the marginalizing of figures like Davis, Patterson, and Robeson ultimately did not benefit African Americans or those on the bottom rungs of the socio-economic ladder. Yet, this was the price that was paid for civil rights concessions.

Robeson worked closely with his friend Ben Davis and the Communist Party, and he worked closely with his friend William Patterson and the CRC. Robeson not only worked closely with the Council on African Affairs (CAA), he was its leader. Founded in 1937 to raise awareness about colonialism in Africa and to push for its demise, CAA also was forced out of existence in 1956 as a direct result of pressure from the Subversive Activities Control Board. And just as it appeared that the CAA's demise was no bar to Africa's advance—Ghana's independence in 1957 seemed to indicate this—in the long run it did seem that the CAA's demise hampered the ability to mount effective opposition to overt and covert backing by the U.S. for apartheid and white minority regimes in Southern Africa.[27]

Although Robeson was a leader of the CAA, he was not alone in this capacity. The CAA's other leaders included W.E.B. Du Bois, who moved his office to CAA headquarters in New York City after being sacked by the NAACP in 1948 for his refusal to back the Association's support of President Truman's reelection and his staunch advocacy of the third-party candidacy of Henry Wallace. The other member of the CAA's troika was W. Alphaeus Hunton; like Du Bois, Hunton held a doctorate (his was from New York University); also like Du Bois he had worked for years at a historically black college, in his case Howard University in Washington, D.C.

At a time in the early 1950s when many in the U.S. were shunning Nelson Mandela's African National Congress because of its ties to the South African Communist Party, Robeson and the CAA were among the few that stood by its side. While many in the U.S. who had heard about the so-called "Mau-Mau" revolt in Kenya either supported the colonizing power in London or scorned the Africans who had risen up against colonialism, Robeson and the CAA took the opposite tack. At a time when many Negroes in the U.S. would have opposed calling themselves "African," Robeson and the CAA proudly disagreed. Robeson recognized that there was a linkage between the struggles of Africans and African Americans. He recognized that as the former attained freedom, they would be able to assist the struggle of the latter—and vice versa. This was a strategic conception he shared with Davis, Patterson, Du Bois, and Hunton.

157. Photograph of New York Mayor David Dinkins trying to shape and direct his administration. February 20, 1990. *The New York Times. Neal Boenzi/NYT Pictures.*

Paul Robeson was no doubt a brilliant individual; however, he did not grow to political and intellectual maturity alone. The path trod by Du Bois before him, and Davis, Patterson, and Hunton with him, assured him that the route he adopted was not misguided. Similarly, the repression that befell Robeson was shared by his comrades and friends. Robeson's passport was taken away, but so was Du Bois's. Davis, Patterson, and Hunton all were jailed during the 1950s for their refusal to bow to the prevailing consensus. Thus, when we assess the damage that was done to the nation as a result of the attack on Robeson, we must also take into account the damage that was rendered when the CRC and the CAA were destroyed; and, yes, we must also take into account the damage exacted as a result of the attack on Communists like Davis.

Paul Robeson was the "tallest tree in our forest" but he was far from being the only tree in that forest. Standing by his side were other eminent black intellectuals like Ben Davis and William Patterson.

158. Paul Robeson beneath huge portrait of Soviet Premier Joseph Stalin at Soviet Embassy celebration in Washington, D.C., of 33rd anniversary of the October Revolution.1950.
UPI/Corbis-Bettmann.

David Levering Lewis

PAUL ROBESON
AND THE U.S.S.R.

Paul Robeson made his last visit to the former Union of Soviet Socialist Republics (U.S.S.R.) in late March of 1960. He had been there more than a half dozen times since the first trip twenty-five years before, accompanied by his wife, Eslanda (Essie), and their friend the English journalist Marie Seton. That first trip in late December 1934 had been full of personal and political drama for the Robesons, with a daylong wait to change trains in Hitler's Berlin before rolling into Moscow, where a small delegation, which included among others the brilliant cinematographer Sergei Eisenstein and the acclaimed playwright Alexander Afinogenov, warmly welcomed them.[1] Eisenstein hoped to cast Paul in a film about the Haitian Revolution. Russia for the Robesons was infatuation at first sight. Ensconced at the historic National Hotel, they were guided about by Eisenstein and other Soviet notables, entertained at dinner by the suave Minister of Foreign Affairs, Maxim Litvinov, and his English wife, and the future Marshal Mikhail Tukhachevsky. Essie wrote home almost giddily about the passionate testimonials of racial empathy punctuating almost every champagne and vodka toast.

159. Paul Robeson and Sergei Eisenstein. c. December 23, 1934. *Courtesy of Naum Kleiman.*

Paul was already world famous. His recent role in *Othello* rivaled in acclaim his reputation as a singer. His movie career sometimes evoked a good deal of controversy, but when that happened it was the film in question whose popularity suffered, not Robeson's. For all that, his reception in the Soviet Union outmatched anything he and Essie had ever before experienced. Remarking on the special chemistry, Marie Seton wrote that "Paul got such intense warmth and affection from everybody."[2] Long conversations with Eisenstein about Soviet cultural life and earnest political advice from William Patterson, the black American Communist undergoing medical treatment in Russia, nurtured a fascination for the exuberant Russian people and a determination on Robeson's part to know more about an ideology that claimed to have revolutionized the relations between the U.S.S.R.'s many peoples of different cultures and colors. Their two weeks' sojourn ended, the Robesons returned to London resolved to place Paul, Jr., in a Russian school, an environment that they believed would be incomparably more nurturing of their son's manhood and mind than even the most liberal school in America.

Accounts of the Robesons' decision to have their son educated in the U.S.S.R. were widely disseminated in both the white and black press in the United States. It was the one country in which "Pauli" would be free of racial bigotry, his parents were quoted as saying. Immediately after *The Song of Freedom* and before filming began for *King Solomon's Mines*, Robeson managed to spend a few weeks alone in the Soviet Union during the summer of 1936 in order to make certain that their decision about their son was the right one. He also took what may have been the first of many immersions in the Russian language. Accompanied by his maternal grandmother, the formidable Eslanda "Ma" Goode, the young Robeson arrived in Moscow in late 1936 to enter the Soviet Model School. Among his classmates would be Stalin's daughter and Molotov's son.[3] Uncles Frank and John, his mother's brothers, had worked in the capital for several years, John as a bus driver and the muscular Frank as a circus strong man. After Paul finished the unhappy British film *Big Fella,* he and Essie went again to the U.S.S.R. for a month to see that Pauli and Ma Goode were fully settled, after which Paul's concert tour, beginning in Moscow, took them to Leningrad, Kiev, and Odessa. The visit ended with a warm and well-lubricated "Russian" New Year's Eve family gathering in Moscow, which also included Lawrence Brown, Paul's faithful accompanist, and William Patterson, well on his way up the top leadership rungs of the American Communist Party (CPUSA).

In the short span of two years, Paul's ideas evolved from apolitical generalities about the unfairness of American race relations to a more focused and informed appreciation of what he understood to be the broader implications of the Russian experiment. His biographer Martin Duberman relates that Paul digested Sidney and Beatrice Webb's new book, *Soviet Communism: A New Civilization?,* discussed Marxism with George Bernard Shaw, and began to stretch his political understanding through discussions with two superbly informed West Indians residing in London—the Communist George Padmore and the Trotskyite C.L.R. James.[4] James thought at the time that Paul was advancing steadily but cautiously left: "He was on the side of all who were seeking emancipation. But that wasn't his whole life."[5] Paul's ripening love affair with the Soviet Union was far from unprecedented among his African American contemporaries. The great scholar and civil rights propagandist W.E.B. Du Bois had returned bedazzled from a two-month sojourn in 1926. "I may be partially deceived and half-informed," he wrote in *The Crisis.* "But if what I have seen with my eyes and heard with my ears in Russia is Bolshevism, I am a Bolshevik."[6]

160. Sheet music of Russian folk songs owned by Robeson. 1937.
Charles L. Blockson Afro-American Collection, Temple University.

161. Henry Wallace, the Dean of Canterbury Hewlett Johnson, Rev. Howard Melish, and Paul Robeson at meeting of National Council of American-Soviet Friendship. Madison Square Garden, New York. 1948.
Photo © by Julius Lazarus.

© Julius Lazarus Archives and Collection / Special Collections / Rutgers University Libraries

In the summer of 1932, twenty-two young black men and women had sailed from Brooklyn on the first leg of a trip to the Soviet Union for roles in *Black and White,* a Moscow film project about racial exploitation in the American South. One of them, the poet Langston Hughes, wandered deep into Uzbekistan, where he encountered the writer Arthur Koestler and observed one of the earliest purge trials. Like so many African American admirers of a regime that was bringing literacy, medical care, hydroelectricity, and full citizenship to non-European populations, Hughes told Koestler, deeply troubled by the implications of the purge trial, that he "observed the changes in Soviet Asia through *Negro* eyes." Overlooking the flaws in the Communist judicial system as temporary necessities, Hughes expressed sentiments that Robeson himself would soon fully share after taking Essie and Pauli to see the Uzbek Opera perform in Moscow five years later. What mattered about the Soviet experiment was not the occasional sham trial in a remote territory, but that Uzbekistan "was a *colored* land moving into orbit hitherto reserved for whites," and, Hughes could have added, that no one was lynched in the process.[7] Article 123 of the Soviet Constitution declared as "irrevocable law" the equality of all citizens, outlawing thereby all forms of social discrimination and guaranteeing civil dignity to millions of people whose brown and yellow complexions would have subjected them to social stigma and legal subordination in Du Bois and Hughes's America.

It was the disjunction in their own country between formal ideals and bitter realities that caused Robeson and many other African Americans to become extremely skeptical of Western criticisms of the Soviet Union. In the long Russian summer he and Essie spent together in 1937, Paul also reflected on what seemed to him the majesty of Article 123 ("loftier in principle than ever before expressed") and contrasted the rights of Uzbeks to those of American Negroes. The political system that gave these dark-skinned people back their long-extinguished pride had nothing in common, he thought, with those systems in which "the inferiority of my people is propagated even in the highest schools of learning."[8] When it came to degrees of imperfections, Bilbo's America seemed more than a match for Stalin's Russia. Moreover, Robeson was bound to have derived much satisfaction in praising the Soviet Union the better to shame the United States. What he made of the meaning of the Moscow treason trials of 1936, 1937, and 1938 was at best ambiguous, therefore, even if, as his friend Seton claimed, he admitted that "dreadful things" had taken place.

Nor was public silence or even a wish not to know too much about the Soviet dark side uncommon during the 1930s among a great variety of leftists for whom the threat of fascism seemed infinitely more exigent than allegations about due process and Siberian labor camps. Indeed, the summer of 1937 saw Paul become increasingly committed to socialism and struggles against reaction. Martin Duberman states that Paul interrupted the family vacation to fly to London to join W. H. Auden, Virginia Woolf, H. G. Wells, Sean O'Casey, and E. M. Forster in an Albert Hall benefit for Basque refugee children.[9] His deep, powerful voice reverberating from the walls of the vast auditorium, Robeson declared that "every artist, every scientist, every writer must decide *now* where he stands. He has no alternative."[10] The summer of 1937 was to be the Robesons' last visit to the U.S.S.R. before the outbreak of World

162. Paul Robeson (center) talking with two American volunteers in Spain. Photo from a scrapbook concerning the tour of the Negro People's Ambulance for Loyalist Spain. *Courtesy of the Thyra Edwards Papers, Mss. Department, Chicago Historical Society.*

163. Paul Robeson singing at the 20th-Century German Art Exhibition at the New Burlington Galleries in aid of German artists who had been banned by Hitler. Painting by Max Beckmann on wall behind Robeson. London. April 8, 1938.
Courtesy of Hulton Getty/Tony Stone Images.

War II. When they returned to London (Pauli was to follow shortly), Paul announced that he had to go to Spain. After a profoundly moving concert tour along the front lines being desperately manned by the Republic's fighting forces in early 1938, he and Essie returned to London, where Paul declared that the civil war in Spain had been "a major turning point" in his life.[11] Increasingly, he spoke of fighting for world democracy and of returning to the United States to make an impact. As well, Robeson made it clear that he looked upon the U.S.S.R. as the front-line nation in the looming conflict with world fascism. Unshaken by the announcement in August 1939 of the Hitler-Stalin Nonaggression Pact, he blamed the fecklessness of Western democracies for having forced the Soviets to turn the German war machine away from their country.

When the Robeson family (with Pauli and his grandmother aboard) sailed into New York in mid-October 1939, a month after Poland had been invaded by Germany and Russia, Paul shocked many of his compatriots, black as well as white, by defending Russia's slicing off of the eastern portion of the Polish republic. When the two belligerents invaded Finland that November, Robeson rushed again to the defense of the Soviet Union. Russia's actions were purely defensive, he argued, dictated by the life-and-death predicament forced upon her by the sellout at Munich. In an interesting anticipation of the fateful remarks he would utter after the war about African American participation in a war against the Soviet Union, Robeson called on people of color everywhere to refuse to support the coming crusade against Russia and Germany—such a crusade by the "men of Munich" was really intended to set the German army upon the Russian people, he charged. Yet even as Robeson shocked many Americans, his popularity as an actor and singer rose to unprecedented heights. His recording of the song *Ballad for Americans* was a sensational hit at the end of 1939. *Proud Valley*, opening in 1940, was a considerable success for him, if not a critical one for the film, and his role in *Othello* in Cambridge, Massachusetts, Princeton in 1942, and on Broadway the next year received rave reviews.

But the fate of the Soviet Union was never far from Robeson's vital concerns. He abruptly dropped his opposition to American support for Great Britain and to congressional enactment of military conscription after Hitler's armies invaded the U.S.S.R. in late June 1941. He called for total commitment by all Americans to war production, a no-strike pledge from organized labor, and military assistance to the Russians. In June 1942, he participated in a Madison Square Garden benefit for Russian War Relief, an occasion attended by many leading mainstream political personalities. During the most perilous period in what the Russian people call the "Great Patriotic War," from March to late October 1942, the Wehrmacht's crack Sixth Army and Fourth Panzer division, and legions of Austrian, Italian, and Romanian troops—250,000 in all—pulverized the showcase industrial city of Stalingrad. The fate of the Soviet Union hung in the balance. Desperate to render any and all possible help he could at the peak of the German assault on the city, and quite possibly acting on the encouragement of Soviet officials, Robeson paid an unannounced visit to the Harlem home of Louis T. Wright, the distinguished surgeon and chairman of the board of directors of the NAACP.

164. Paul Robeson in *Othello*. Cambridge. 1942.
Photo by Richard Tucker. Carl Van Vechten Collection, Beinecke Library, Yale University.

Claiming he was authorized to speak for the highest authority, Robeson told Dr. Wright that the Soviet Union would provide material assistance to the NAACP in its postwar struggles in return for the association's sustained public support, or so Mrs. Corinne Wright recalled years later. Wright stated that he would take up the matter with board members and have a response when Robeson again contacted him. On November 11, the Russian Army and Air Force counterattacked the Germans in overwhelming strength. Ten weeks later, in the largest military debacle in history and a decisive turning-point in the war, Field Marshal von Paulus surrendered what was left of his forces to the Russian command. Louis Wright never heard from Paul again about the quixotic proposal of collaboration.[12]

By the time Robeson returned to Russia in June 1949, Winston Churchill had inaugurated the Cold War in the famous "Iron Curtain" speech delivered at Fulton, Missouri. President Truman's infamous executive order 9835 imposing a loyalty oath on federal employees had been followed by the Justice Department's indictment, trial, and imprisonment of the top leadership of the CPUSA. A combination of red-baiting and civil rights promises had destroyed the presidential hopes of Progressive party candidate Henry Wallace in the 1948 elections. Robeson had contributed tirelessly of talent and money to Wallace's cause. Flying into Moscow from Warsaw on June 4, he could not have realized then that his own public career in the United States was virtually finished. Words that he had never spoken in April had been attributed to him by an Associated Press dispatch from Paris. Through painstaking research, Martin Duberman has come as close as is currently possible to retrieving what Robeson actually said before a large audience attending the World Congress of Partisans of Peace. He did *not* say on April 20 at the Salle Pleyel in Paris that American Negroes would never fight against the Soviet Union, as was reported throughout the United States. He merely stated what many other prominent African Americans, Du Bois and A. Philip Randolph included, had said earlier with even greater emphasis: "We intend to fight for peace. We don't want to go off to fight for anybody against anybody. We don't want to make war on the Soviet Union."[13]

He arrived in Moscow exhilarated. The nation was celebrating the 150th anniversary of Alexander Pushkin's birth. Shirley Graham, the novelist, who was shortly to become the second Mrs. Du Bois, remembered Robeson's excitement in Paris after his Salle Pleyel speech. "See you folks back home," he said to Du Bois and Graham, hurrying buoyantly from their dinner table at the exclusive Hotel Claridge. He felt he was on a crusade for peace and could hardly wait to reach the Soviet Union.[14] Robeson was given a Russian welcome that was as warm as the reception awaiting his return to the United States would be hostile. But there were troubling omens. The Jewish accompanist who had taken Lawrence Brown's place after Robeson left Paris had been denied a visa by the Russians. How much Robeson knew of the anti-Semitic purges ordered by Stalin is unclear; he clearly suspected that Jews in Russia were being subjected to intimidation, if not persecution. He and Essie had come to know a great many Russians of the Jewish faith over the years, some, like the recently deceased Eisenstein and Solomon Mikhoels, were among their closest Russian friends. Yet as he moved from one social and official function to another, Robeson realized that Jews were conspicuous by their absence, and he was concerned about the absence of one person in particular. The Yiddish writer Itzik Feffer had accompanied the actor-director Mikhoels on a sponsored visit to the United States in 1943. The Robesons had entertained them. Mikhoels's "mysterious," brutal murder in early 1948 had stunned the Russian Jewish community. Feffer's whereabouts were unknown, but Robeson was adamant with his hosts. He had to see Feffer. Feffer was allowed to see Robeson alone in his hotel room. Drawing a finger across his own neck and writing hurried notes on scraps of paper, the Yiddish writer, who had been in the custody of the secret police since December, let Robeson know that he was doomed.[15]

165. Paul Robeson speaking at the 150th Anniversary Celebration of the birth of Alexander Pushkin, Academy of Science of U.S.S.R. Moscow. June 7, 1949.
Lloyd Brown Collection.

166. Paul Robeson receiving flowers from I. S. Koslovsky, the popular Soviet tenor, upon Robeson's arrival in the Soviet Union. c. 1949. *Lloyd Brown Collection.*

Robeson's concert on the night of June 14 in Moscow's Tchaikovsky Hall was historic. In richly articulated and flawless Russian, he introduced each song with witty or poignant remarks, to the great pleasure of the packed house. There were sixteen songs in all, which Robeson sang in the original English, French, Mandarin, and Italian. "The Four Insurgent Generals" from the Spanish Civil War was enthusiastically received. He sang the fighting American labor song "Joe Hill" twice, and "Ol' Man River," his signature number, moved the audience deeply. Robeson's final number, "Song of the Warsaw Ghetto Rebellion," he sang in Yiddish after paying tribute to his friends Feffer and Mikhoels. "For sure the hour for which we yearn will yet arrive, / And our marching steps will thunder: we survive!" The words of "Zog Nit Keynmol" filled Tchaikovksy Hall as Robeson passed judgment in song on the ignoble policies of the regime to which, for better or worse, he remained wholly committed. Legend, supported by recent scholarship, holds that when he finished, the audience, after a moment of stunned silence, leapt to its feet in thunderous ovation. In fact, the response was both thunderous and divided. With KGB agents scattered about the hall, it was hardly surprising that loud booing, clearly audible on the recording of the concert, arose from a segment of the audience. Those who approved courageously redoubled their applause, while the objectors shouted their disapproval more loudly. The moral confrontation between Muscovites was an extraordinary, if transitory, moment in Stalinism, an evening that must have displeased the Kremlin.

Meanwhile, Robeson had certainly displeased the American State Department. Nearly ten years would elapse before he regained his passport and saw Moscow again. Peekskill, virtual pariah status, and greatly diminished livelihood exacted a psychic toll on a constitution even as hardy as his. Released from bondage, Paul and Essie left the United States for England in July 1958. A month later, much restored by the civil treatment accorded them by British officialdom and the warm welcomes in leftist circles, they landed at Moscow's

Vnukovo Airport on August 15. The welcome was tumultuous, as well it should have been for a towering personality to whom the Soviet government had awarded the 1952 International Stalin Peace Prize and for whom it had named a mountain. Robeson gave numerous press interviews and a televised concert to a crowd of 18,000 in the Lenin Sports Stadium. His elation was evident as he repeatedly thanked the Russian people for the moral support that had made it possible for him and his family to endure.

The Robesons flew to Tashkent, the Uzbekistan capital, aboard one of the new Ilyushin jetliners. The romance of Tashkent and nearby Samarkand evaporated quickly, however, after a few days of sightseeing in blistering heat and hour after hour of watching mostly mediocre movies being screened in connection with the International Festival of Films of African and Asian Peoples. Paul and Essie's good humor seems to have been especially tested by an Indonesian feature dubbed in Uzbek. The last part of their stay was both pleasant and memorable. They quit the Uzbekistan capital for the tropical lushness of Yalta. The modern guesthouse at Orianda was luxurious, and the restful surroundings aided Paul's recovery from a tenacious cold. Within a few days of their arrival, Premier Nikita Khrushchev summoned the couple to join his vacation party. Transported to superb accommodations in the hills above Yalta, the Robesons found themselves in company not only with the boisterous Soviet ruler and the indispensable Anastas Mikoyan and Kliment Voroshilov, but with the Communist party leaders of Italy, Bulgaria, Romania, Poland, Hungary, Czechoslovakia, and the German Democratic Republic. It was a rollicking family affair with volleyball, hunting excursions, and oceans of wine and vodka toasts, all carefully recorded by Vasily Katanian's film crew, who were assigned the duty of documenting the Robesons' visit. Martin Duberman notes that Essie's diary mentioned a farewell toast by Paul that

167. Paul Robeson poses with Soviet Premier Nikita Khrushchev at the Black Sea summer resort near Yalta. August 30, 1958.
UPI/Corbis-Bettmann.

moved them all to tears. They flew back to Moscow on September 12, 1958. A few days later, Paul and Essie returned to London.

Bad weather and a lost passport ruined Paul's plans to appear on radio and television in Prague that December. But Paul and Essie, both somewhat frazzled by eleventh-hour mishaps, emplaned for Moscow on the twenty-ninth just in time to make the Kremlin New Year's Eve party. This time, however, Paul was even more excited about the second leg of his trip, a concert tour of India. He intended to fly from Moscow to New Delhi the second week in January. The Kremlin affair was an elaborate, formal dinner in an imposing hall large enough to hold the cream of the Soviet *nomenklatura*. Among Premier Khrushchev's distinguished guests that evening were W.E.B. and Shirley Graham Du Bois. It had been several months since the two couples had seen each other. The Du Boises had flown into Moscow on November 5 just in time for the commemoration of the fortieth anniversary of the October Revolution. Du Bois had also finally regained his passport after the State Department had refused for eight years to grant one on grounds that the octogenarian cofounder of the NAACP was a Communist. The combative civil rights icon had nearly been sent to prison in 1951 as an "agent of a foreign power." His own treatment was as nothing when compared to Robeson's, Du Bois had observed shortly before sailing from New York for Southampton: "What they have done to Paul has been the most cruel thing I have ever seen."[16] The Du Boises' idylls in Holland and France had been followed by red-carpet sojourns in Prague and East Berlin. Like the Robesons, they had been given a high-profile round of television and radio interviews by the Russians. In a remarkable private meeting in the Kremlin, Du Bois had persuaded Khrushchev to order the creation of an Institute of African Studies to be housed in the prestigious Soviet Academy of Sciences.

Those attending the Kremlin's New Year's Eve banquet witnessed a unique drama. The Du Boises had punctually taken their places at the head table. Khrushchev took his seat at the center of the table and the evening began. The Robesons arrived through a side door a few minutes later. It would be difficult to improve upon the description of what followed in Shirley Graham Du Bois's memoir, *His Day Is Marching On*:

> Obviously because they were late they were trying not to attract attention, and only those nearest them noticed. But Paul immediately raised his head and began searching the crowd. I called their arrival to Du Bois's attention and he lifted his hand to catch Paul's eye. Paul saw him; both men rose simultaneously and began threading their way through the maze of tables toward each other. The going was a bit difficult; chairs were pushed out of the way and waiters with loaded trays had to sidestep them. But the two seemed totally unaware of the commotion they were causing. When finally they did meet, big Paul and small Du Bois threw their arms around each other in a bear hug and Mr. Khrushchev rose to his feet applauding. Then everybody in the hall was up, applauding and shouting their names.[17]

168. Paul Robeson sings at Peace Defense Meeting held at a state bearing plant in Moscow. January 2, 1960.
UPI/Corbis-Bettmann.

Unfortunately, things went badly awry for Robeson shortly after the memorable Kremlin evening. On the day he was to leave for India, January 12, 1959, he was too sick to go. A nagging cold took a dangerous turn, and he was admitted to the Kremlin Hospital. From there, somewhat better, he was sent to convalesce at Barveekha, the exclusive government complex twenty miles outside Moscow. An anxious Essie reluctantly flew back to London, much concerned that Paul might not be well enough to begin rehearsals for the *Othello* production scheduled to open in Stratford-on-Avon in June. He seemed completely restored, though, when he returned to London in early March.

British critics generally disliked young director Tony Richardson's *Othello*, but they praised Robeson's dignified interpretation of Othello, which stood in marked contrast to Sam Wanamaker's hip American Iago. The play behind him, Paul and Essie went again to Moscow in January 1960 for a three-week rest and medical checkup. Essie's examination revealed uterine cancer. The Russian specialists proposed a series of radium treatments, whose results they later assured Essie had been effective. The Robesons flew back to London in late February. They went to Australia on concert tour later that year. Anti-Communist hysteria in the United States was slowly abating. Paul and Essie began to consider returning to New York. All in all, it was a time of anxiety and drift for Robeson. Although he had remained publicly silent about Khrushchev's 1956 revelations of assembly-line murders sanctioned by Stalin, several intimates revealed that Robeson had been profoundly shaken.[18] Friends in London observed a troubling restlessness in him during much of 1960, a penchant for enigmatic political utterances. His biographer cites the apprehensions of Sam and Helen Rosen and several other intimates about the mood swings they detected in Robeson. Helen urged Essie to bring Paul back to the United States. Essie grew more concerned as the year drew to a close.

Abruptly, Paul left alone for Moscow in late March 1961. In the early morning hours of March 27, he locked himself in the bathroom of his hotel and slashed his wrists. Martin Duberman's reconstruction of this puzzling event is that Paul had become increasingly agitated as several people attending a late-night party in his room begged his help for imprisoned relatives.[19] When Paul, Jr., flew into Moscow from New York a few days later, the doctors explained that his father had suffered a bipolar depressive disorder. Pauli became convinced that "Big" Paul had been chemically poisoned by CIA operatives, an explanation he would continue to believe for many years thereafter. The shock and stress caused by his father's suicide attempt temporarily affected Pauli's own mental health. He, too, had to be

169. Paul Robeson on the streets of Moscow. March 20, 1961.
Tass Pictorial Review. Lloyd Brown Collection.

170. Paul Robeson with Essie and his doctors in East Berlin for medical treatment, summer 1963. Left to right: Eslanda Robeson, Professor Rudolf Baumann, Robeson, Dr. Alfred Katzenstein.
Photo © by Franz Loeser. Courtesy of Julius Lazarus Archives and Collection/Special Collections/ Rutgers University Libraries.

171. Eslanda and Paul Robeson in East Berlin hospital, summer 1963.
Photo © by Franz Loeser. Courtesy of Julius Lazarus Archives and Collection/Special Collections/ Rutgers University Libraries.

172. Paul Robeson in East Berlin hospital, summer 1963.
Photo © by Franz Loeser. Courtesy of Julius Lazarus Archives and Collection/Special Collections/ Rutgers University Libraries.

hospitalized. Both Robeson men were transferred to Barveekha after a month, with Essie in watchful attendance. By the end of May, Pauli had recovered fully and his father appeared to be much better. The son flew home to the United States, and Essie brought Paul back to their Connaught Square apartment in London in early June. He seemed to be getting steadily stronger, exercising his still-powerful voice a few hours each day as Lawrence Brown played the old standby songs. But when Paul began to falter after two weeks, Essie decided to fly him back to Moscow without delay.

Shirley Graham Du Bois wrote friends in New York that "whitecoated male nurses" had met the plane at Sheremetyevo Airport.[20] The Rosens flew to Russia to comfort their friends. The nonagenarian Du Bois sent cheerful encouragement from a Romanian sanitorium famous for its claims of being able to prolong life almost indefinitely. Recommending the Aslan Clinic, Du Bois also advised Paul to renounce any plans to go back to America. Du Bois wrote that he hoped to see the Robesons in Ghana soon. Prime Minister Kwame Nkrumah invited Paul to settle in Ghana. Whatever lay in the future, however, had to wait for Paul's recovery. By the second week in September 1961, he seemed much better. Once again, the Robesons returned to London. Tragically, Paul relapsed within forty-eight hours. Twenty-four hours later, Helen Rosen arrived from New York in answer to Essie's frantic appeal. It was decided that Paul should be placed immediately in the Priory, a private psychiatric facility outside London. The ride to the facility took the limousine carrying Essie, Helen, and Paul past the Soviet embassy. As they approached the imposing structure that had served on countless occasions as political haven and social club, Paul became extremely agitated. He forced Helen Rosen to lie down, placing himself over her, shouting, his biographer writes, "You don't know what you're doing, you don't know what you're doing!" "Get down!"[21] Paul Robeson's panic in the rear seat of a car driving past the Soviet embassy implies a great deal, of course, but remains, in the end, poignantly ambiguous. A sick person's momentary commotion can hardly serve as the basis for definitive insight into the state of his or her political beliefs. Certainly, Robeson was never to say or write a single public word at any time to indicate disillusionment with the nation whose political ideology and ruling class he had admired and championed with ever greater fervor and conviction year after year. Moreover, although he would never again set foot in Russia, Robeson entered the noted Buch Clinic in the German Democratic Republic after an extended period of electroshock therapy at the Priory.

Paul and Essie Robeson flew back to the United States on December 22, 1963. While still a patient in the Buch Clinic, Paul had made that decision by himself fifteen days earlier. Thirty-five years after his return, there has slowly come to pass a major reconfiguration of the racial, cultural, and political forces that combined to destroy the health and livelihood of one of the most talented, symbolically ennobling, and courageous Americans of the twentieth century. Belatedly, his university and his nation wish to honor qualities that other nations never ceased to appreciate in Robeson. On the occasion of Paul's sixtieth birth-

173. Paul Robeson returning to the United States. New York. December 22, 1963.
UPI/Corbis-Bettmann.

day, W.E.B. Du Bois offered the best explanation for the long, deep relationship between the man and the people, however troubled that relationship may have become in Robeson's last years. "In America he was a 'nigger'; in Britain he was tolerated; in France he was cheered; in the Soviet Union he was loved for the great artist that he is."[22] If Paul Robeson was also prized, as was Du Bois himself, for his political value to the Soviet regime, that, too, is understandable; nor was it a crime against the United States of America.

174. Paul Robeson. London. 1925.
Photo by Sasha. Courtesy of Hulton Getty/Tony Stone Images.

Charles L. Blockson

PAUL ROBESON

A Bibliophile in Spite of Himself

I am a singer and an actor. I am primarily an artist. Had I been born in
Africa, I would have belonged, I hope, to that family which sings and
chants the glories and legends of the tribe. I would have liked in my
mature years to have been a wise elder, for I worship wisdom and
knowledge of the ways of men.[1]

This chapter memorializes Robeson by focussing on a less-well-known aspect of his
life—his career as a bibliophile and collector of books on the African and global experiences.
An interest in learning and a respect for books were cultivated from Robeson's youth in
Princeton, New Jersey, and his collection reflected a wide range of scholarly interests. Robeson
is known as an orator, athlete, lawyer, writer, singer, actor, thinker, and activist; one of the
threads that ran through all these aspects of his life was his passion for collecting books,
pamphlets, sheet music, and other ephemera on the African global experience.

In the world of intellectual and artistic accomplishment, Paul Robeson looms as one
of those rarest of figures: a man to whom the title of genius can be appended without the
slightest reservation. Though Robeson has been dead for nearly a generation, his legend
resonates today, the tale of a modern-day Da Vinci, a latter-day Imhotep. The time is long
since late and the world so far behind in rediscovering the phenomenon of Robeson, his
individual achievements, and the towering legacy of his uncompromising, dignified quest

to overcome prejudice. While he lived, Robeson was known by millions across the globe for his enormous passion and concern for the struggles of freedom-loving people everywhere.

Even amid the startling lack of familiarity with Robeson's life and legacy, there are aspects of his life's journey which remain underknown even to those who know of the man. Not everyone knows of his unyielding passion for the study of languages. Fewer still know of his appetite for book collecting. Even as a poor minister's son in Princeton, Robeson was exposed to the discussion of books, a discourse that often dominated family gatherings. As a young man, Paul sat in the glow of the parlor's coal stove or amid the breezes of sweet lilac air sweeping the summer porch, listening to his father and various other family members discussing the historical and literary merit of books. He would later recall a household full of "a love for learning, a ceaseless quest for truth in all its fullness."[2]

It was in his father's house that Robeson's intellect grew, his cultural and political mind developing in concert with his broadening creative powers. His father guided him through the study of the tools that would serve him the rest of his life: Greek, Latin, philosophy, history, literature, and the record of the history of the African diaspora as well. Young Robeson displayed an early love for African people.[3]

In what must have been a bold statement for the era, Robeson selected the abolitionist Wendell Phillips's famous oration on the Haitian liberator Toussaint L'Ouverture for his entry in a statewide oratorical contest as a Somerville High School honor student. Though carrying the high hopes and expectations of his friends and family, Robeson fell short of the first prize that day, finishing third but still winning a scholarship to Rutgers College, New Brunswick, New Jersey.[4]

Many years later, in 1936, Robeson performed the role of L'Ouverture in *The Black Jacobins*, a play written by the famous Trinidadian intellectual Cyril Lionel Robert James. Robeson repeated there the words he had uttered so many years before, the fiery words of L'Ouverture: "My children, France comes to make us slaves. God gave us liberty; France has no right to take it away. Burn the cities, destroy the harvest, tear up the roads with cannon, poison the wells, show the white man the hell he comes to make." Even before earning a law degree in 1923 from Columbia University, Robeson began to relentlessly examine the nation's legal system, identifying many of the problems that African Americans shared and tracing their origins to enslavement. For his senior thesis at Rutgers, Robeson selected a topic that culminated in a paper entitled "The Fourteenth Amendment: The Sleeping Giant of the American Constitution." In the document, Robeson declared that "it is the law which touches every fibre of the whole fibre of life which surrounds and guards the rights of every individual."[5]

After earning his law degree, Robeson entered the practice of law. Faced with the very institutional and individual racism that he had decried in his studies, however, he exited the practice, launching instead a career in the arts, letters, and politics. Robeson went on to become one of the most fabulous actors and concert singers of the era. Even the cursory summary of his myriad of personal, literary, and artistic achievements staggers the imagination, though it was never material possessions and fame that drove him but the pursuit of knowledge and racial understanding. The incessant search for truth is reflected in the brilliant polemic of his writing, in his public orations, his music, and the track of his book collecting and reading regimen, an unbroken flurry of fervent movement from the 1920s through the 1960s.

Incredibly, there is more still to Paul Robeson. He was a bibliophile, a man with the marked passion for collecting and possessing books, which indicates the affliction of the insatiable lover of knowledge for knowledge's sake. As a bibliophile, I can yet recall the electric surge of revelation and emotion that coursed through my heart and mind the moment I discovered Robeson's bibliophilia. Many years ago, I read Shirley Graham McCann's (Du Bois's) article in the January 31, 1931, issue of *Opportunity—Journal of Negro Life*, "A Day at Hampstead." The article read in part:

> In a vine covered brick house in Hampstead, one of the world's most beautiful and exclusive suburbs of London, if you are expected, a solemn-faced French butler will conduct you up to a winding stairway to a big library/sitting room on the second floor. Books, books, books, all the books I have wished for and could not buy. Solid big chairs, lovely rugs and pictures and, dominating the room stands in the alcove Antonio Salemmé's bronze head of Mr. Robeson.[6]

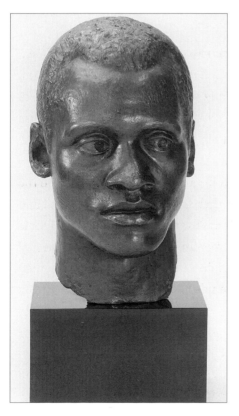

175. Head of Paul Robeson by Antonio Salemmé. 1926. Bronze. 11.5 in.
Jane Voorhees Zimmerli Art Museum, Rutgers, The State University of New Jersey. Gift of the artist.

After reading that article, I felt a new and personally expanding connection with Robeson. I also felt a new link to the world of the New Negro Renaissance Robeson lived through. In addition to the bronze head of Robeson, Ms. McCann no doubt took notice of the impressive Benin bronzes and other African sculptures that must have graced the confines of the Robeson library. Though probably best remembered as the second wife of the internationally known scholar W.E.B. Du Bois, a mentor and friend of the mature Robeson, she was a scholar in her own right, penning a number of books and articles, including biographies of Frederick Douglass and her famous husband as well. In 1946, Shirley Graham wrote a biography of Robeson entitled *Paul Robeson: Citizen of the World.*

A collection of books always reflects the collector of those books to the mind of even the most casual collector. While living in London during the period of Shirley Graham's visit, Robeson and his equally brilliant wife, Eslanda, came into contact with many African students. He studied linguistics and African languages at the London School of Oriental Languages. There he learned Swahili, Zulu, Ashanti, Efik, Yoruba, and Egyptian. To better understand his Nigerian roots, he studied Ibo as well. Many years later, Robeson wrote in his book *Here I Stand* that he felt as one with his African friends, becoming filled with "a glowing pride in these riches, newfound to me. I learned that along with the towering achievements of the cultures of ancient Greece and China there stood the culture of Africa."[7] The British author Marie Seton, a friend of Robeson's, wrote in her biography of him that "his deep need to understand the world around him led him into linguistic studies."[8] Robeson studied Danish, Hindi, Russian, Arabic, German, French, Spanish, Czech, Italian, Yiddish, Hebrew, Egyptian, Chinese, Japanese, Persian, Hindustani, Hungarian, Finnish, Polish, and Norwegian, in addition to many other African languages. Robeson was reported to have possessed one of the finest libraries on the African diaspora in England.

176. Portrait of Paul Robeson by Hugo Gellert. 1928. Lithographic crayon on paper. 15 15/16 x 12 11/16 in. (38.9 x 23.3 cm.).
National Portrait Gallery, Smithsonian Institution.

177. Robeson giving interview using his copy of *Negro Songs of Protest* upon his reception of his honorary doctorate of philosophy from Humboldt University, Berlin. October 12, 1960.
© Gerhard Kiesling, Berlin. Courtesy of Julius Lazarus Archives and Collection/Special Collections/ Rutgers University Libraries.

He also began to study the folk-song traditions of various people, deepening his appreciation of the commonalities of human experience through his grounding with the essence of artistic productions. Thanks to his intensive study of languages, Robeson often displayed the unique ability to speak and sing to others in their native tongue.

Robeson also expressed his opinions in writings and interviews during the periods of nonperformance, commenting on subjects as diverse as "The Source of Negro Spirituals" (*Jewish Tribune*, July 22, 1927), "Paul Robeson Speaks about Art and the Negro" (*The Millgate*, December 1930), and "I Want to be African" ("What I Want From Life," *Daily Herald*, January 5, 1935). On a handwritten note in 1936, Robeson declared that "there can be no greater tragedy than to forget one's origins and finish despised and hated by the people with whom one grew up."[9]

In 1939, Robeson returned to America after twelve years of living in London, largely due to the beginning of World War II and the liberal trends fostered by the presidential administration of Franklin Delano Roosevelt. In that year, Robeson recorded his widely acclaimed *Ballad for Americans*, a patriotic song that was initially broadcast on Columbia Broadcasting System radio. The CBS switchboard was jammed with calls asking where people could obtain the words and music to this piece.

Robeson had become a national celebrity, quickly climbing the ladder to unprecedented fame. He became a model for his race and for American youth everywhere. In 1940, he and his wife purchased a large house with a view of the hills and fields of Enfield, Connecticut. Their home—"The Beeches" as it was called—was furnished comfortably but not pretentiously, complete with tennis court, billiard room, and swimming pool. Over the mantel of the living room were sculptures of Robeson and his son. Both Robeson likenesses, including the

178. The Robeson family on the front steps of "The Beeches," home Paul and Eslanda Robeson purchased in Connecticut in 1942. *Carl Van Vechten Collection, Beinecke Library, Yale University.*

child's sculpture, which was done when he was an infant, were the work of Jacob Epstein, the famous sculptor. Intensely interested in books, Robeson converted one of the house's large rooms into a library for his enormous collection.

In 1943, when he visited Robeson's home, *Look Magazine* writer Avery Strakosh wrote that:

> Robeson made several fortunes during his twenty years of acting and singing. He isn't much for writing and he hardly ever telegraphs. For clothes, Robeson has even less regard than for money. He lets his lawyer and adviser Robert Rockmore handle all of his money for him. He has little regard for it except as it will buy books on sociological subjects, on music and languages. Sometimes the only way that Rockmore can find Paul when he is out of town is to track him down from the postmarks on the boxes of books he sends back home.[10]

While living in London, Herbert Marshall, the well-known British actor, film star, and Robeson friend, was exposed to Robeson's passion for book collecting. Marshall and his wife lived near the Robesons on the edge of Hampstead Heath. Marshall contacted me by telephone in June 1972 while he was visiting the United States, inquiring at the time about Robeson's health. He phoned me because, while visiting Southern Illinois University in Carbondale, Illinois, on behalf of the British Broadcasting Company, Marshall had heard that I had been one of the few people permitted to visit Robeson during the last years of his life, spent in Philadelphia at the home of his sister Marian. Marshall told me that his wife made a sculpture of Robeson and that he and Paul had "helped to found the Unity Theatre, where a group of actors and actresses worked without pay to put on plays of social significance."

Marshall added that he had directed Robeson in his film *Plant in the Sun,* which dealt with a sit-down strike in the United States. When I asked him about Robeson's marvelous library, the one described by Shirley Graham McCann (Du Bois) in 1931, Marshall delivered the most marvelous news. He said that after Paul and Essie returned to the United States at the beginning of World War II, Marshall and his wife had salvaged all of Robeson's books, personal belongings, and papers just before the homestead was bombed out in London. Marshall explained that he had had the books crated and then shipped to the United States. He said that the material became the basis for the Paul Robeson Archives. Before our conversation ended, Marshall said that when his book *Ira Aldridge, the Negro Tragedian* was published in 1958, the same year that Robeson had published *Here I Stand,* Marshall had personally inscribed a copy of his book to Paul. A few weeks later, I was pleasantly surprised to receive in the mail a small package from Herbert Marshall that contained numerous playbills, photographs, and pieces of sheet music inscribed by Paul Robeson.

During the 1970s and 1980s, I received a number of letters about Robeson from Brigitte Boegelsack and Christine Naumann, the curators of the Paul Robeson Archives in Berlin, Germany. The archives exhibited a permanent display of items relating to Robeson's life that included books, broadsides, photographs, sheet music, recordings, and several of the robes

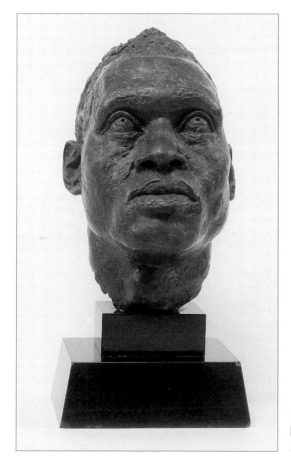

179. Head of Paul Robeson by Jacob Epstein. 1928.
Bronze. 13 1/2 in. (34.5 cm.).
National Portrait Gallery, Smithsonian Institution.

180. Responding to reporter questions as to whether he has changed his mind about the Soviet Union, Paul Robeson recommends that they read his recently published book *Here I Stand* for the answer. Press conference at the Empress Club in West End, London. July 11, 1958.

that Robeson had donned to portray Shakespeare's Othello from the 1930s through the 1960s. In honor of Robeson's sixtieth birthday, the archives published a large poster of the giant's image. The German issue of the poster sold out in a few weeks in the local bookstores.

On October 3, 1988, Christine Naumann sent me an article entitled "Biographical Mosaic Pieces: Books and Music from the London Library of the Afro-American Actor-Singer Paul Robeson at the Academy of Arts of the German Democratic Republic, Paul Robeson Archives." Out of this selection of books and music from Robeson's London library of 490 items, 190 were introduced to the public. Naumann arranged the holdings to correspond to the following areas: drama (Shakespeare editions, introductions, commentaries, contemporary drama); poetry; prose (novels, stories, and epic poems); history, politics, and arts (biographies, autobiographies, essays); music and books on musicology (folk songs, African sources, African American folk songs, Russian and Soviet folk songs, Spanish and Hungarian

181. East German stamp saluting Paul Robeson. 1983.
Charles L. Blockson Private Collection.

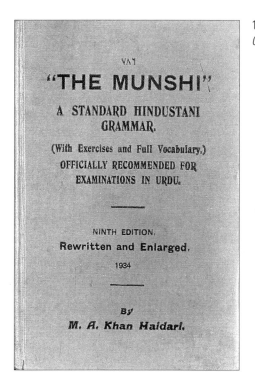

182. *The Munshi: A Standard Hindustani Grammar.*
Charles L. Blockson Private Collection.

composers, operas, church music, African American spirituals); and languages (textbooks, grammars, and phonetics on African, Chinese, Hebrew, Russian, Hungarian, and Welsh languages). Each bibliographical note in the display is followed by the following set of bracketed commentaries: part of Robeson's repertoire; autographed (if so, with address); presentation copy; marginal remarks; or missing pages. After reading Naumann's "Biographical Mosaic Pieces," I recalled Ms. Boegelsack's having told me in 1974 that someone in London had sent her several large containers of Robeson books and papers, which had been rescued from the bombing during World War II.

Robeson did not consider himself a bibliophile. Unlike most collectors and bibliophiles I know, when time permitted, Robeson would add brief annotations to the margins of his books, thereby providing future readers some sense of his mind's index during a particular moment in his life. Through books, Robeson learned how to draw upon inner logic, his own quiet dignity, and a powerful intellectual and spiritual strength to analyze the mysteries of the world around him. Hence, rather than simply collecting them, Robeson read and studied the books that he purchased. One book led to another. Marginal notes and comments written by him give evidence of an erudition comparable to that of a university-trained scholar. Robeson chose the best books for himself with uncanny acumen and for the most part without the advice or guidance of others. His mind ranged over almost the whole field of human intellectual achievement. Reaching into the worlds of words, Robeson forged himself into an instrument of communication whose ability to influence amazingly diverse audiences was unsurpassed.

As a collector for nearly fifty years of books by and about people of African descent, and like any true bibliophile, I am always on the alert for rare items, especially if the items pertain to my hero, Paul Robeson. In 1969, I heard about the sale of Robeson's books at the Argosy Book Store in New York City, unfortunately just one month after the event. I rushed to the scene of the auction, sadly discovering that most of the items had been sold. Looking through miscellaneous volumes, I was able to salvage some of the books of my hero, including *Savage Abyssinia* (London: 1928), *The Tiv Tribe* (London: 1933), *The Story of the Zulus* (London: 1911), and *La Sculpture Nègre Primitive* (Paris: 1929). Over the years, other Robeson books have come my way, a number of which bear his signature. Since my Argosy salvage mission, I have had the good fortune to have purchased works such as *The Munshi*, a standard Hindustani grammar from New Delhi, India, owned by Robeson. Other books in my possession that came from his hands include books on Egypt and Chaldea, a hiero-glyphic vocabulary published in London in 1831, *As it Looks to Young China* (New York: 1932), *The Rise of the Celts, Vols. I and II* (New York: 1934), *Batouala, a Negro Novel in French* (Paris: 1922), and *Tribal Studies in Northern Nigeria* (London: 1930).

As was the case with most liberal-minded book lovers of the day, Robeson was attracted to the international controversy surrounding James Joyce's book *Ulysses,* first pub-lished in Paris. *Ulysses* was considered obscene and was barred from import into the United States. While visiting Paris, Robeson's wife, Eslanda, purchased a copy of the book from Sylvia Beach, the American-born proprietor of the well-known bookshop Shakespeare and Company. Eslanda smuggled the book back to London and wrote later in her diary that "Paul had been tickled to death."[11]

Robeson's pleasure at acquiring unusual, rare, specialty, or otherwise important books is the hallmark of a bibliophile. A few of these types of unusual items have cropped up unex-pectedly during my search for Robeson's books. Merely for the curious will I mention Robeson's copy of his book *Here I Stand* written in German and published in Berlin. Another Robeson gem that I purchased is a book authored by his wife, entitled *Paul Robeson, Negro* (London: 1930). Inscribed in the book is the simple admonition, "Eslanda Robeson, my copy. Please return this book to Eslanda Robeson. It belongs to my basic library and files."

Robeson's book was banned in the United States: no commercial publisher would print it for fear of political backlash. *Here I Stand* was welcomed in laudatory reviews across Europe, Asia, and Africa, once again highlighting through sharp relief the backward and regressive cultural politics that swept the Cold War era sentiment of the United States of America.

Upon his father's death, Paul Robeson, Jr., inherited the vast archival holdings of his parents. The collection contains more than fifty thousand items, including books, unpub-lished manuscripts, legal and financial records, newspaper and magazine clippings, phono-graph and tape recordings, films, awards, memorabilia, and correspondence. The vast collection is currently housed at the Moorland-Spingarn Research Center at Howard

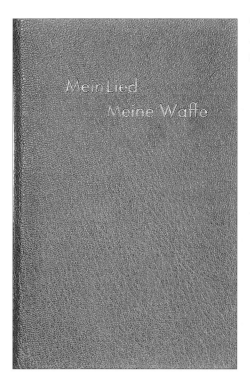

183. *Mein Lied, Meine Waffe* (German translation of *Here I Stand*). Signed. 1958.
Charles L. Blockson Private Collection.

University in Washington, D.C. For nearly twenty years, Paul Robeson, Jr., and I exchanged items from our collections on his father's life and work. As late as June 1996, Robeson, Jr., told me that the major portion of his father's books were at Howard. A number of duplicate copies of books and sheet music have been purchased and resold by various booksellers. Robeson, Jr., told me that his parents, when practicable, made a habit of signing personal copies of books and sheet music in green ink.

Among the high points in the collection are books by and about the Robesons, including Eslanda Robeson's book *African Journey*, and many foreign-language editions of *Here I Stand.* Many of Robeson's personal books are autographed by the authors, including books on the theater, government, politics, and Black liberation.

Other significant books in the Robeson archives are the works of such Robeson friends as the Harlem Renaissance figures James Weldon Johnson, Claude McKay, Langston Hughes, Zora Neale Hurston, Nella Larsen, Jessie Fauset, Countee Cullen, Alain Locke, W.E.B. Du Bois, Walter White, Wallace Thurman, Carl Van Vechten, Rudolph Fisher, and Arthur Schomburg, the famous African American bibliophile and collector.

While touring Europe during the 1930s, Schomburg discovered the sculptor Pietro Calvi's superb marble-and-bronze bust of the nineteenth-century New York native and Shakespearian actor Ira Aldridge. Robeson contributed to raise the funds necessary for the acquisition of the piece by Schomburg. It came to the Schomburg Library in 1936 and, since then, Calvi's sculpture of Aldridge's famous portrayal of Shakespeare's tragic Moor Othello during Aldridge's triumphant tour of Europe in the 1860s has become the centerpiece of the

184. Paul Robeson. Berlin. October 1960.
Photo © Gerhard Kiesling, Berlin. Courtesy of Julius Lazarus Archives and Collection/Special Collections/ Rutgers University Libraries.

185. Paul Robeson. Berlin. October 1960.
Photo © Gerhard Kiesling, Berlin. Courtesy of Julius Lazarus Archives and Collection/Special Collections/ Rutgers University Libraries.

Harlem, New York–based Schomburg Center for Research in Black Culture, the world's largest collection of materials on the subject. Robeson was intimately associated with Aldridge's name and work. Aldridge's daughter Amanda taught Robeson diction while he was performing in *Othello* and he acted in other plays while living in England. The copy of Herbert Marshall's book on Aldridge, inscribed to Robeson, eventually found its way to the Schomburg Collection.

On a cold and depressing December day in 1967, I read a small article on the back page of the *Philadelphia Bulletin* stating that Paul Robeson had been admitted to the University of Pennsylvania Hospital. The article went on to mention that visitors had been prohibited by a doctor's order. That morning, a scant two days removed from Christmas, something stirred deep within me. A stirring in my soul, it seemed, had triggered an almost mystical urge for me to attempt to visit Robeson, so close and yet so seemingly distant. As I drove from my suburban Philadelphia home to the west side of the city, the spirit urged me on, strengthening me to see my quest through. I arrived at the hospital to a quiet reception area, surprisingly unhurried and lacking the bustle and energy that I had anticipated might be associated with the aura of the larger-than-life patient admitted such a short time before. I asked an elderly African American receptionist for the floor that Mr. Robeson was located on. She smiled pleasantly at me, delivering what sounded like a stock answer with a deliberate but friendly tone. "Mr. Robeson is not permitted to see any visitors," she stated. "Although he is not ill, he is receiving a number of medical tests and will be released shortly." Disappointed but undaunted, I hung on the last of her words, almost willing any hint of a different type of response. As if she sensed my desperation, she continued. "However," she said, "I know who you are. I have read about your dedication to our history and your dedication in preserving Mr. Robeson's legacy. Ten minutes, if you promise me that you will not publicize the visit." I quickly regained my composure, assuring her with all the requisite solemnity I could muster that I would not betray her simple but profound kindness. "He is in room 1128 A. His name is not listed on the door."

An electric shower of anticipation rushed down my spine as I walked to the door behind which Robeson was sequestered. I entered the room. Christmas cards, baskets of fruit, and books on the table near his bed immediately drew the attention of my wildly wandering eyes. A large, bright red book seemed to dominate the bed table. As I moved closer to it, the words became legible: *Black Magic: A Pictorial History of the Negro in American Entertainment.* The book had been recently published by Langston Hughes and Milton Melzer. The room, complete with the latest book, smelled of the presence of Robeson, but the man himself was not there.

I was told that he had been taken to another area of the hospital to have a series of X-rays taken. For what seemed like an eternity, I waited in the quiet of the room, hoping against hope to be allowed to remain long enough to meet Robeson, even as I rehearsed again and again what possible lines of greeting and homage I could deliver to convey my humble thanks for the inspiration which he had provided me for the balance of my life. Finally, the door filled with the sound of approaching footsteps and a quiet voice. I saw the wheels of the wheelchair first, followed by the broad form of the chair's occupant and the young African American nurse who was guiding him from behind. Entering the room wearing the wheelchair more than it was carrying him, his still-dominating form hardly diminished by frail health and advancing years, was Paul Robeson, "The Great Forerunner."

Robeson wore a blue-and-white checkered robe. He stood, leaving the chair behind, and advanced toward me. I had enough presence of mind to extend my hand and shake it while introducing myself to him. We were of approximately the same height and build, but he seemed to tower over me. As he shook my hand and smiled, an almost magnetic force spread out from the spot upon which we stood, resonating through the room and filling

186. Paul Robeson in his library.
c. 1943.
Charles L. Blockson Private Collection.

it. As long as I live, I will never forget that moment, the occasion of my first meeting with Paul Robeson.

After shaking my hand, Robeson told me that his sister Marian Forsythe had told him that I wanted to see him, as had his friend Judge Raymond Pace Alexander, the noted Philadelphia African American jurist. Remembering the ten-minute limit placed upon me by the gracious receptionist, I asked him if he would autograph two books that I had brought with me. One was Edwin P. Hoyt's *Paul Robeson: The American Othello*, published in 1967. The other, of course, was a copy of Robeson's own *Here I Stand.* He inscribed the latter "To Charles Blockson, all the best to you. Paul Robeson, December 27, 1967." In the Hoyt book he wrote "Very kind wishes and a Merry Christmas, Paul Robeson."

Before I left the room, Robeson told me that it was "important for you to keep on collecting and preserving our history." In the nine years that he lived in Philadelphia with his beloved sister Marian I was fortunate to visit Paul Robeson at the Walnut Street house. His sister made it a practice to peek through the white Venetian blinds of her home before letting would-be visitors in.

187. Paul Robeson arriving in Berlin. April 10, 1960.
Photo © Bildarchiv Neues Deutschland, Berlin. Courtesy of Julius Lazarus Archives and Collection/
Special Collections/Rutgers University Libraries.

The last time that I saw Paul Robeson before his death was December 17, 1975. On that day, while standing in the doorway of his sister's West Philadelphia home, I caught a glimpse of him sitting at the dining room table, his back toward us. I handed his niece Paulina a book that I had just written, which included a section on Robeson. Turning away, I felt that I had glimpsed him on a bad day; still, his physical presence loomed over the air and filled my soul with the breath of inspiration that I can honestly say I have never quite experienced in the same way in any other context of life. A little over a month later, on January 23, 1976, Paul Robeson died in Philadelphia.

One day, when humanity has matured to the point where it can look back honestly and openly over its struggle to live up to the potential that the Creator meant for it to reach, the example and struggle of Paul Robeson will be fully recognized by all for what it was and is: a blueprint for human existence. Robeson was a man constantly reborn, constantly rising from the ashes of jealousy, race-hatred, and unkindness to triumph again and again. In death, as he was in life, Robeson is constantly reborn in the hearts and minds of every youth or elder who encounters him anew through his books, speeches, recordings, or through someone touched by the ancillary glow of his soul force. I am fortunate enough to have been touched both peripherally and personally by this Renaissance man, the foremost example of such a man to have been born in the twentieth century. My life has been a modest attempt to live up to his example, and to preserve and protect the record of the great people from which he emerged and to which he dedicated in turn the greatness of the spirit that they had bequeathed to him.

ROBESON'S CONTEMPORARY SIGNIFICANCE

188. Paul Robeson speaking at protest against United States policy in Guatemala. June/July 1954.
Photo © by Julius Lazarus.

Julianne Malveaux

WHAT IS ROBESON'S CONTEMPORARY LEGACY?

Shall Negro sharecroppers from Mississippi be sent to shoot down brown-skinned peasants in Vietnam—to serve the interests of those who oppose Negro liberation at home and colonial freedom abroad?
—*Paul Robeson, 1954* [1]

I ain't got no quarrel with them Viet Congs. They don't call me a n———r.
—*Muhammad Ali, 1967* [2]

We were taking the young men who had been crippled by our society and sending them eight thousand miles away to guarantee liberties in Southeast Asia which they had not found in southwest Georgia and east Harlem. And so we have been repeatedly faced with the cruel irony of watching Negro and white boys on TV screens as they kill and die together for a nation that has been unable to seat them together in the same schools.
—*Rev. Martin Luther King, Jr., 1967* [3]

M any of Paul Robeson's positions on issues maintain a currency in contemporary political analysis. Whether he is addressing Vietnam, African independence, the rights of workers, or the development of democracy, statements that he made in the early to middle twentieth century often represent current progressive thinking. When Robeson described himself as one of "Africa's children in America," [4] he shaped the discussion that would later take "Africa's children" from Negro to black to African American. When he gleefully reveled in his blackness ("Sometimes I think I am the only Negro living who would not prefer to be white" [5]), he portended the Afrocentricity of Stokely Carmichael, [6] Maulana Karenga, [7] Molefe Asante, [8] and others. When he spoke of peace, his words foreshadowed those of generations of peace activists who used arguments similar to those he offered to oppose U.S. involvement or intervention in Vietnam, El Salvador, Iraq, and other countries. Robeson's influence was diminished when his right to travel was curtailed; he was effectively muzzled by the House Un-American Activities Committee (HUAC). His treatment raises questions about the perversion of the First Amendment in the name of Cold War solidarity. As historical revisionism focuses on the horrible toll that HUAC took on the lives of hundreds of American artists and the devastating impact it had on our democracy,[9] it is important to focus on the artistic and sociopolitical legacy Paul Robeson left.

Deconstructing Paul Robeson's enigmatic life seems as unachievable as grasping hold of an evasive apparition. The most definitive biography of Robeson's life, by Martin Duberman, is not without controversy.[10] The most comprehensive compilations of Robeson's speeches and writings reveal a man who cannot be reduced to a bumper sticker.[11] Indeed, the opening words of the collection *Paul Robeson Speaks* recall Mrs. Ogden Reid, publisher of the *New York Herald-Tribune,* describing Robeson as having "distinguished himself in four separate fields—scholar, athlete, singer and actor."[12] For all the good will that accompanies her statement, Mrs. Ogden incompletely describes Robeson. To be sure, he achieved distinction as "scholar, athlete, singer and actor." He was also a Rutgers College graduate and a Columbia University–educated lawyer and activist whose voice on issues of racial and economic justice emerged early in his career.[13] He realized his acting and sing-

189. Chinese calligraphy by Paul Robeson.
c. 1950s.
Lloyd Brown Collection.

ing made him something of a racial ambassador and noted, "The talents of the Negro are being brought to the fore and at last the shackles of intellectual slavery are being severed."[14]

Robeson's work might be more easily categorized if racial barriers had not defined his opportunities for achievement in so many areas. He achieved as an athlete despite the negative racial attitudes of his colleagues. He excelled as a scholar despite the fact that he had only limited affiliation to academic institutions after his undergraduate and legal studies at Rutgers and Columbia. In some ways, Robeson's life was scholarship in action. He fashioned a self-directed curriculum that included the mastery of more than a dozen languages, the investigation of political and economic relations on the African continent, and queries about the status of workers in the United States, in Europe, and in the Soviet Union. Robeson did not practice law because he learned that racial barriers would prevent it. Race specifically shaped Robeson's career as a singer, which thrived partly because he claimed his heritage, presenting the earliest concert programs comprised wholly of spirituals, called "Negro music," in the 1920s.[15] As an actor, Robeson hoped to influence the manner in which popular culture presented images of African American people. Because he was treated as an actor, not as a multifaceted actor-scholar-activist, his influence in the movie business was minimized and his intentions to present the African content in a more balanced way were unrealized.

Robeson's range of professional experiences as actor, singer, scholar, and athlete uniquely shaped his activist vision. Much of the work that he did in the activist realm revolved around his attempt to connect aspects of the worldwide oppression that was an inevitable result of capitalism and imperialism. From Robeson's perspective, working-class people in London had much in common with disenfranchised Negroes in the United States, who had much in common with the colonized on the African continent. His awareness of these connections was neither popular, nor well accepted. Still, the fallacy of American racial attitudes was well-illustrated by Robeson's commentary, by the artist's use of his music, theater, and public appearances to heighten political awareness. As his recent biographer Lloyd Brown wrote:

> He sings the songs of the peoples of the world in the languages of those peoples and touches their hearts; they call him brother, son. And what is the primary source of his universal art? His people. His art is great for it has a great foundation—the rich national culture and psychology of the Negro people: sorrow song and jubilee, work song and dance song.[16]

His brother, the Reverend Benjamin C. Robeson, describes his brother's performance so well you can almost hear his deep, rolling voice:

> Have you ever heard Paul sing "Witness"? He is there the personification of his father with his own personality added. He is singing then for his Lord and Master. . . . Here lies the heart of his singing and acting, too. He visions himself

190. Paul Robeson singing in preparation for appearance in the Stratford-on-Avon production of *Othello*.
London. March 1959.
Courtesy of Hulton Getty/Tony Stone Images.

breaking down the barriers that have imprisoned his race for centuries. He knows that hidden away in the teeming millions of African extraction there are others who, if favored by fortune, would be out there in the swim, making a healthy contribution to the progress of humanity.[17]

The richness of Robeson's cultural message softened the sting of his harshest criticism of our nation's racial reality. The fact that Robeson used the cultural context to explore political commentary may explain why his detractors did not focus on the content of his message until the Cold War era. Robeson's message was consistent. Despite his material success during the 1930–1946 period, he recognized the influences of his early life in shaping his views: "My career as an artist in America and abroad, my participation in public life, and the views I hold today all have their roots in the early years."[18]

Some aspects of Robeson's life must be viewed through lenses that reflect the way that institutional racism shapes response to freedom-loving, independent-thinking African American people, especially men, who are neither "grateful" nor supplicant, whose opinions have not been blunted by their awareness of the inevitable consequences of their audacity. Whether we view Robeson as actor or scholar, as activist or athlete, one thing is clear. We must view him as an African American man whose integrity was so unassailable that our nation's treatment of him may well have had a chilling effect on other artists' willingness to use their popularity to deal with issues of global oppression and economic injustice.[19] An examination of the way the United States government treated Robeson during the Cold War may explain why so few who followed Robeson have been willing or able to develop positions that transcend the confines of their professional work, and make key connections between capitalism, oppression, and international affairs. Dr. Martin Luther King,

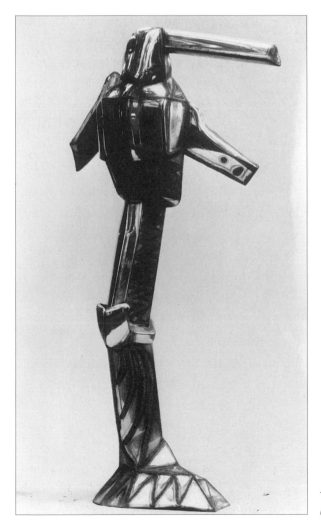

191. Ed Love, *Robeson, Totem.* 1974. Steel.
Collection of the artist.

Jr., certainly transcended the role of civil rights leader when he began to examine the connections between racism and global oppression, to speak out against the war in Vietnam, and to view economic relationships outside the racial context. In some ways, he paid a similar price as Robeson when he found the patronage, acceptance, and credibility he had developed around race matters dissipate when he connected the issues of peace and economic justice. Celebrated entertainer Harry Belafonte's involvement with a range of progressive causes is reminiscent of Robeson's. Belafonte's work has included advocacy for the elimination of apartheid in South Africa, statements on injustice in Central America, and involvement with the Institute for Policy Studies in Washington, D.C.

In the remainder of this essay I will first explore Robeson's positions on race, the rights of workers, colonialism, and global capitalism, and the type of political and economic relationships that his positions assailed. Then, I will discuss Robeson's audacity and his depiction by many as an "ungrateful Negro" who apparently infuriated HUAC, and unleashed that committee's venom against him. HUAC's attempt to humble him was as much about the Committee's negative racial attitudes as it was about his principled resistance. Finally, I shall discuss the implications of the Robeson legacy in a contemporary context. Who are Robeson's inheritors? Are there scholars, artists, and celebrities who have used their acclaim as a platform to address both sociopolitical causes and the oppressive connections that are a result of economic exploitation?

HERE I STAND: PAUL ROBESON'S PHILOSOPHY

What did Paul Robeson stand for? Contemporary historians know him most for his avid interest in the peace process and his opposition to any war with the Soviet Union on humanistic grounds. The words that attracted the enmity of HUAC, misquoted from his actual words as spoken at the 1949 Paris World Peace Conference, were ultimately embraced and defended by Robeson as a simple affirmation of his perception of the Negro commitment to peace: "It is inconceivable that American Negroes would fight with those who have oppressed them for generations against the Soviet Union which, in a generation, has raised them to a position of equality."[20]

Paul Robeson told a California legislative committee that he was "not a Communist" in 1946.[21] He declined to answer the question in subsequent testimony because he thought the question unconstitutional. Robeson's support of the Soviet Union, then, had less to do with communism than it had to do with his support for freedom, for labor, for people of color, and for working people around the world. Much of his focus had been on the dignity of working people. Like Dr. Martin Luther King, Jr.'s, Robeson's focus began with that of African American people. In his writing, speaking, and song, he celebrated the dignity and spirit of African American work and culture. During the years that he spent in England, Robeson became aware of the plight of the English working class and championed the cause of British

192. Essie Robeson, Paul Robeson, and Nnamdi Azikiwe (Nigerian president) at anniversary celebration of Nigerian independence. London. September 1960. *Courtesy of Esther Jackson/Freedomways magazine.*

workers, and by extension, workers around the world. Convinced that capitalism led to an unequal division of resources, he studied socialist tenets. Part of his interest, as the historian Sterling Stuckey indicated, was his conviction that "Africans could learn from an experiment that had brought many formerly backward people of color into the scientific/industrial world of the twentieth century."[22]

Robeson's interest in African liberation (which was based in scholarly study, the exploration of language at the London School of Oriental Languages, and investigation of African culture and politics with some of the leading scholars of the day[23]) led to his participation in the founding of the Council on African Affairs. The Council was described by some as "the most important organization in the United States working for African liberation."[24] Its sixfold program included the "advancement of freedom and international peace," the elimination of "schemes for intensified imperialist exploitation of Africa," and the strengthening of "the alliance of progressive Americans, black and white, with the peoples of Africa and other lands in the common struggle for world peace and freedom." Robeson's

193. Flyer for mass meeting for famine relief in South Africa, featuring Marian Anderson, Paul Robeson, and others. Monday, January 7, 1946. *Lloyd Brown Collection.*

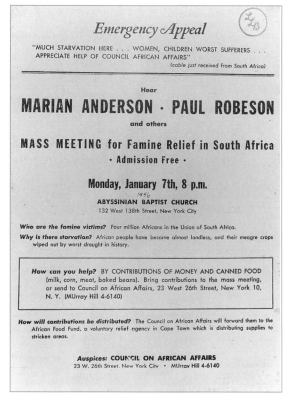

work with "mass rallies, conferences, workshops, cables, declarations, press releases and advertisements, through financial and food aid to alleviate famines in Africa, by hosting nationalist leaders and delegations, and meetings with members of the U.S. government and of the UN secretariat" contributed much to the cause of African freedom.[25] The extent to which he connected the African cause to that of the struggle of American Negroes and other oppressed people illustrated his commitment to issues of freedom. Addressing these issues, Robeson wrote,

> What future can America have without the free and unfettered contributions of our sixteen millions? What place of honor can our country have in the new world a-borning if our heritage is still denied? I speak as an American Negro whose life is dedicated, first and foremost, to winning full freedom, and nothing less than full freedom, for my people in America. In these pages I have discussed what this fight for Negro freedom means in the crisis of today, how it represents the decisive front in the struggle for democracy in our country, how it relates to the cause of peace and liberation throughout the world.[26]

Furthermore, Robeson's personal integrity fueled his belief that his involvement in progressive causes was mandatory, and that his positions were inflexible. In his autobiography, *Here I Stand,*[27] Robeson reminded readers that "my views on world affairs are nothing new," and that before the Cold War his views were considered so admirable that he was awarded the NAACP's Spingarn Medal because of his work for "freedom for all men." The "I Take My Stand" chapter of Robeson's autobiography is a reminder of his professional and activist contributions, and the ways that racism impacted on his career and limited his opportunities.

Robeson wrote that he pursued his career in Europe partly because "opportunities for Negro artists are very limited in our country."[28] He noted that he had been asked to bring his influence to bear on behalf of views he opposed, both by Republicans in the United States, who asked him to oppose Franklin Delano Roosevelt in exchange for the privilege of writing his "own ticket" in Hollywood,[29] and by artistic agents who promised him long-term contracts in exchange for total control of his career. Robeson's response was that "no one was going to lead me around by a golden chain or any other kind." His independence and integrity contrast sharply with that of today's artists, many of whom seem unable to resist placing their integrity and artistic image on the auction block for the highest bidder.

Robeson's study of race and capitalism led him to reject the gradualism that typified U.S. race relations in the mid-twentieth century. At that time, black organizations were strangled by the "paradox of loyalty,"[30] willing to accept the notion of gradualism, and intimidated by the long reach of the HUAC. Robeson, on the other hand, roundly rejected gradualism and wrote that "developments at home and abroad have made it imperative that democratic rights be granted to the Negro people without further delay."[31] Robeson asserted that "segregation must go" and argued that "the viewpoint that progress must be slow is rooted in the idea that democratic rights, as far as Negroes are concerned, are not inalienable and self-evident as they are for white Americans."[32]

194. Paul Robeson joins the NAACP picket line in front of theater in protest of its policy of racial segregation. Left to right: Mrs. Ada Jenkins, Paul Robeson, Earl Robinson, Dr. J.E.T. Camper, Paul Kaufman, Rhonda Pearson, Dan Atwood. Baltimore, Md. February 1947.
Photographs and Prints Division, Schomburg Center for Research in Black Culture, The New York Public Library, Astor, Lenox and Tilden Foundations.

Robeson identified economic forces as a key part of the disenfranchisement of the Negro and advocated scientific socialism, or democratic socialism as a remedy for the economic inequality that African Americans experienced. He explained his position in a 1958 interview with Pacifica Radio:

> If we were free in the South today to carry our weight, to vote . . . would we look around and try to find the ten billionaires among our people? Would we attempt to build them up, or would we try to answer the needs of the great millions of our people?
>
> And so I see other ways of life—Socialism—as trying to solve the problems of millions, of tens of millions at once.[33]

Robeson was also a firm believer in the power of united action, of organization. He advocated organizational unity, suggesting that the many African American organizations come together around selected issues. Further, he was a staunch supporter of the trade-union movement, and used his platform to support unions while at the same time chiding them to include African American unionists in leadership positions. Robeson's prescriptions for "Negro Action" included the development of a central fund, the development of "effective (Negro) leader-

195. Paul Robeson in Harlem. 1955.
Courtesy of Esther Jackson/
Freedomways *magazine.*

ship," and a commitment to black independence. Often critical and occasionally harsh, Robeson's analysis was always offered through the loving perspective that focused on the improvement of the African American economic status as an outcome. And even when Robeson became the target of criticism from African American leaders, he managed to take the "high road" in his responses, often refusing to be as cutting as his critics were. In his well-publicized interaction with Jackie Robinson, for example, he responded to Robinson's (perhaps forced) description of him as "silly" with a dispassionate observation, "We (black people) could take our liberties tomorrow if we didn't fight among ourselves."[34] Contrast this with the manner in which some of today's African American leaders rush to condemn each other, often to curry favor with whites.[35]

Issues of integrity and loyalty were a key part of Robeson's defining philosophy. A less-principled artist might have backed off from strongly held positions, and Robeson certainly had sufficient incentive to do so. Or, Robeson might simply have remained silent rather than affirming his views at every opportunity. The history of equivocation during the Cold War and the HUAC witch hunt clearly reflects the number of "principled" artists who balanced self-interest with integrity. (Today's athletes, who hawk the brand-name shoes that are fuel for significant inner-city violence, stand in stark contrast to Robeson. The fact that these shoes are manufactured for pennies an hour by workers in developing countries would have been a compounding reason for Robeson to refuse to endorse such products. Issues of international labor exploitation, though, are ignored by most people today.) Instead, Robeson was unabashedly both artist and political activist,[36] prepared to pay the price for his views. He defiantly clung to the Ten Principles of Bandung, detailed below as "my viewpoint in world affairs":

1. Respect for fundamental human rights and for the purposes and principles of the Charter of the United Nations.
2. Respect for the sovereignty and territorial integrity of all nations.
3. Recognition of the equality of all races and of the equality of all nations large and small.
4. Abstention from intervention or interference in the internal affairs of another country.
5. Respect for the right of each nation to defend itself singly or collectively in conformity with the Charter of the United Nations.
6. (a) Abstention from the use of arrangements of collective defense to serve the particular interests of any of the big powers.
   (b) Abstention by any country from exerting pressures on other countries.
7. Refraining from acts or threats of aggression or the use of force against the territorial integrity or political independence of any country.
8. Settlement of all international disputes by peaceful means, such as negotiations, conciliation, arbitration, or judicial settlement as well as other peaceful means of the parties' own choice, in conformity with the Charter of the United Nations.
9. Promotion of mutual interests and cooperation.
10. Respect for justice and international obligations.[37]

When one considers today's parochialism and world insularity, it is remarkable that Paul Robeson was able to develop such a profound understanding of international issues. Some of this understanding evolved from his travel and some from reading, but much had its genesis in Robeson's empathy and basic egalitarianism. It was Paul Robeson's unapologetic assertion of international rights, along with his ability to transcend petty domestic nationalism, that made it important for the United States government to silence him.

UNBROKEN, UNBOWED: ROBESON AND THE HUAC

> But I keeps laughing
> Instead of crying
> I must keep fighting
> Until I'm dying
> And Ol' Man River
> He just keeps rolling along[38]

Paul Robeson was first asked to testify before a government body in 1946, when he told the California Legislative Committee on Un-American Activities that he was not a Communist, but an antifacist. At the time, he also praised Communists as fighters for democracy, and indicated he could "just as conceivably join the Communist Party, more so today, than I could join the Republican or Democratic Party."[39] By then, some right-wing organizations had begun to target Robeson with pickets and the organized cancellation of meetings to which he had been invited. In response to the racism he experienced, Robeson indicated, in 1947, his intention to give up the theater and concert stage for two years to "talk up and down the nation against race hatred and prejudice."[40] He said he would sing only for unions and college groups, a statement that interested J. Edgar Hoover, who ordered the Federal Bureau of Investigation to attempt to prove Robeson's affiliation with the Communist Party.

When Paul Robeson attracted the attention of the HUAC in 1948, he was a much-acclaimed international actor and singer with an annual income that exceeded $150,000 (nearly a million of today's dollars). By the time the HUAC was finished harassing him, blocking his right to travel, manipulating his image, and blackballing his work, Robeson was earning about $3,000 per year.[41] Throughout his ordeal, however, he exhibited the integrity that was a defining part of his personality, an unwavering commitment to issues of racial justice, and a consistently dignified posture toward the pathetic group of inquisitors who had distorted the nature and purpose of our nation's Constitution. In many ways, Robeson exhibited the spirit of Ol' Man River, rolling along, despite adversity.

A review of the many verbal skirmishes that Robeson had with members of the HUAC shows that Robeson was unintimidated, unafraid, and often the victor in those ver-

196. Paul Robeson testifying before HUAC (House Un-American Activities Committee). Washington, D.C. June 12, 1956.
UPI/Corbis-Bettmann.

bal confrontations that attempted to get him to change his position or admit wrongdoing. He questioned the HUAC's legitimacy and legality, and described the proceedings as "nonsense" even as members of Congress asked him questions.[42] In response to questions, Robeson attempted to insert statements that dealt with American racism, and with the cause of peace and freedom. In contrast to some of the sessions where witnesses were cooperative and obsequious, Robeson was contentious, focused, and principled. His attitude is best summarized in his autobiography:

> Let me make one thing very clear: I care nothing—less than nothing—about what the lords of the land, the Big White Folks, think of me and my ideas. For more than ten years they have persecuted me in every way they could—by slander and mob violence, by denying me the right to practice my profession as an artist, by withholding my right to travel abroad. To these, the real Un-Americans, I merely say "All right—I don't like *you* either!"[43]

His work during this period reveals a similar focus and public optimism. In his speeches during this period, Robeson insisted on his patriotic right to criticize racial injustice. His spoken and written work from the 1940s, when reviewed as a body, is very reminiscent of the sentiments explored by W.E.B. Du Bois in *The Souls of Black Folk*:

197. "Was FBI involved in attempts to murder Paul Robeson?"
World Magazine. 1979. *Photo © Bildarchiv Neues Deutschland, Berlin. Courtesy of Julius Lazarus Achives and Collection/Special Collections/Rutgers University Libraries.*

198. HUAC members (left to right: Edwin Willis (D, La.), James B. Frazier, Jr. (D, Tenn.), Clyde Doyle (D, Calif.),
Morgan Moulder (D, Mo.), Francis Walter (D, Pa.), Chairman Gordon H. Scherer (R, Ohio),
Bernard Kearney (R, N.Y.), and Frank Tavener, Jr. (Committee Counsel) after voting
to cite Robeson for contempt, Washington, D.C. June 13, 1956.
UPI/Corbis-Bettmann.

It is a peculiar sensation, this double-consciousness, this sense of always looking at one's self through the eyes of others, of measuring one's soul by the tape
of the world that looks on in amused contempt and pity. One ever feels his
twoness,—an American, a Negro; two souls, two thoughts, two unreconciled strivings; two warring ideals in one dark body, whose dogged strength alone keeps it
from being torn asunder.[44]

One gets a sense of Robeson's "dogged strength" in his speaking and writing of this period.
Despite the fact that he cannot travel because the government revoked his passport,
Robeson's public statements remain those of a dedicated freedom fighter anxious to offer
his voice under less than ideal conditions whenever it was requested. In *Here I Stand,* Robeson
recounts instances of setting up international recordings in lieu of participation at meetings he could not attend.[45]

Documentation of the HUAC's work suggests that it was a brutal, nonconstitution-
ally constituted body designed to elicit the worst in human behavior, including the incrim-
ination of colleagues as a way of ensuring favorable treatment. An oral history of the
period, *Red Scare,*[46] makes it clear that Robeson was not the only victim of the HUAC's
venom. I wonder, however, how much of the HUAC's (and the FBI's) vituperation toward
Robeson was the result of his unwillingness to play the stereotypical role of subservient Negro,
the role that so many other subpoenaed African Americans played. In the context of the

199. Eslanda Robeson testifying before Joseph McCarthy–led Senate Investigations Subcommittee. Washington, D.C. July 8, 1953. *UPI/Corbis-Bettmann.*

late-twentieth-century deconstruction of history by race, class, and gender, one might also speculate about the extent to which Robeson's image of intelligent, focused, and physically superior black masculinity was problematic for the white men on the HUAC.

The members of the HUAC may have been individually weak and morally bankrupt, but they had been given enormous power for more than twenty years, not disbanding until the 1960s. Their consolidation of power partly empowered the FBI to destroy radical organizations (like the Black Panther Party) through the counterintelligence programs of the 1960s and 1970s. One wonders if HUAC-directed FBI activities provided a blueprint for subsequent activities, especially when the black community's shunning of Paul Robeson during this period is reviewed. Imagine the psychological burden that Robeson, once revered, must have shouldered when faced with his own community's scorn? Whatever private demons Robeson fought, though, his public stance was unbroken, unbowed, and proudly committed to the causes to which he had dedicated his life. It is clear, as well, that while Robeson was unable to earn a living during his exile, he maintained the affection of the world progressive community, as evidenced by the reviews and sales of *Here I Stand*, the autobiography virtually ignored by the majority press in the United States, though reviewed warmly in the black press (except in the NAACP's *Crisis Magazine*, which described the book as "disorderly and confusing" in 1958).[47]

There are parallels in the black community's treatment of *Crisis Magazine*'s founding editor, W.E.B. Du Bois, and the treatment of Robeson, and the two men were apparently advocates for each other. In his autobiography, Du Bois describes the persecution of Paul Robeson as "one of the most contemptible happenings in modern history."[48] In *Here I Stand*, Robeson describes Du Bois as "one of the truly great Americans of our century" and goes on to write:

> How monstrously evil it is, then, that the little men in high places have dared to say that such a man is not entitled to a passport, that he cannot travel abroad in a world that knows and honors him.[49]

It is likely, then, that Robeson shared Du Bois's sentiment about the period:

> It was a bitter experience and I bowed before the storm but I did not break. I continued to speak and write when and where I could. I faced my lowered income and lived within it. . . . I lost my leadership of my race. It was a dilemma for the mass of Negroes; either they joined the current beliefs and actions of most whites or they could not make a living or hope for preferment. Preferment was possible. The color line was beginning to break. Was not the sacrifice of one man small payment for this? Even those who disagreed with this judgment at least kept quiet. The colored children ceased to hear my name.[50]

WHO CARRIES ON THE ROBESON LEGACY?

Few of today's African American artists have attained the world attention and affection that Robeson amassed in his career as a singer, actor, and activist. Boxer Muhammad Ali has Robeson's world reach and popularity, as does pop singer Michael Jackson. Others, like basketball's Michael Jordan, also have a world following because of their television presence. With rare exception, those with influence similar to Robeson's have neither the knowledge nor the inclination to use their celebrity to lift up the range of issues that Robeson tackled. It may seem harsh, but it is not inaccurate, to suggest that most who have attained world popularity willingly accept the "golden chain" that Robeson refused.

Perhaps our nation's treatment of Robeson has become a cautionary tale for those actors, athletes, and artists who might be inclined to use their celebrity to engender social change. Robeson paid dearly for his commitment, and our nation paid even more dearly. Sterling Stuckey has described our nation's losses from Robeson's "virtual confinement" as incalculable: "No one of comparable artistic ability has been denied freedom for so long. . . . One must consider Robeson's genius as an actor as well as a singer in determining the scope of the crime that was committed against humanity, against world art."[51]

Since Robeson, few artists (or others) have been willing to deal comprehensively with issues of capitalism, poverty, imperialism, and world oppression. Indeed, the public climate

200. Flyer for $1 Edition of *Here I Stand*. c. 1958.
Lloyd Brown Collection.

201. Pablo Neruda speaking at World Peace Congress. Paris. April 1949.
Photo © by Julius Lazarus.

has been to ignore many of these issues and to reduce activism to an episodic experience, so that Hollywood "types" are often willing to attend a rally or champion a cause, but far less willing to make connections.

There have been exceptions. Dr. Martin Luther King, Jr.'s opposition to the Vietnam War cost him the support of many mainstream organizations in the United States. Eartha Kitt's anti–Vietnam War remarks at a White House luncheon in 1968 caused her to be blackballed for nearly a decade. Others, including Tracy Chapman, Danny Glover, Maya Angelou, Nikki Giovanni, Harry Belafonte, Sidney Poitier, Arthur Ashe, Ruby Dee and Ossie Davis, have used their celebrity to advance specific causes, or to address sociopolitical issues in their art. Belafonte's work stands out because of his affiliation with the Institute for Policy Studies, a Washington, D.C.–based progressive think tank concerned with many of the causes that Robeson championed. Despite that similarity, no contemporary figure comes close to Robeson's commitment, unwavering support, and dedication to making the connection between racism, economic justice, and world oppression.

Among the youngest entertainers, those rap artists who have not embraced the genre of nihilistic antiwoman gangsta rap perhaps have the opportunity to use their music much as Robeson used his folk songs to galvanize young people around progressive causes.

Perhaps it is unfair to compare contemporary artists and athletes to Robeson, since Robeson was more than artist, athlete, activist. He was a scholar, lawyer, and so much more, a person who saw his views, his work, his life as "all of one piece." Compartmentalization and individualism are particular features of the late twentieth century; in today's context the necessary conditions to replicate Robeson's contributions are probably absent. However, it is important to examine the stellar example that Robeson offered as a model of the positive possibilities of celebrity, activism, and advocacy. It must be an activism infused with a faith, much like Robeson's "in the whole people, the emergence into full bloom of the last estate, the vision of no high and low, no superior and no inferior—but equals, assigned to different tasks in the building of a new and richer human society."[52]

202. Paul Robeson singing at Vienna International Youth Festival. August 4, 1959.
Photo © by Julius Lazarus.

203. Paul Robeson as Othello speaking just after having killed Desdemona (Uta Hagen)
in the Margaret Webster production of *Othello*. c. 1943.
*Photo by Vandamm Studios. Photographs and Prints Division, Schomburg Center for Research in Black Culture,
The New York Public Library, Astor, Lenox and Tilden Foundations.*

Ed Guerrero

BLACK STARS IN EXILE

Paul Robeson,
O. J. Simpson,
and Othello

From the jump, the American star system is a fickle game demanding some serious personal tradeoffs and sacrifices in order for one to succeed even marginally and thus enjoy its substantial rewards and privileges. And judging from those famous faces pilloried in the supermarket tabloids or on the evening TV entertainment journals, more than anything, stardom looks like a twisted maze of tricks, illusory gratifications, and betrayals that almost always ends in the spectacle of some sort of public torture. Moreover, all aspiring stars should be aware of some of the system's fundamental rules. By generous estimates the average celebrity has a shelf life of about five years. And since stars, celebrities, and people whose sole occupation is their fame are industry-constructed icons serving the profit and needs of huge entertainment and media conglomerates, they have no real power in America.[1] Even after considering the mandatory celebrity charity endorsement or guest appearance for the establishment-sanctioned cause, stars are particularly marked by their lack of social depth. It is exactly that flattened-out, one-dimensional persona of the "intimate stranger," so

204. Paul Robeson. 1925.
Photo by Sasha. Courtesy of Hulton Getty/Tony Stone Images.

familiar to audiences, which makes famous faces so valuable to sponsors. It follows, then, that stars are definitely discouraged from exercising politically dissenting voices or taking complex intellectual stances on any issue. But perhaps most importantly, all stars reign at the whim of an ambivalent audience driven by a scandal-hungry media apparatus. Therefore, the consumer fan is just as likely to be "entertained" by a celebrity's public ruin as by his or her success.

This being the predicament for those the star system was designed to showcase at its highest levels, i.e., superstar whites and those super-rich, black brand names like Cosby, Jordan, and Oprah, the children of celebrities and of entertainment and so on, then the non-white *other* who takes up the quest for stardom armed only with hopeful ambition, raw talent and a few meager connections faces a bumpy, treacherous ride. Beyond the business, public-relations, and status games that the mainstream, white star must play to survive, add into the mix the political complications of being an African American icon held up as role model and activist spokesperson for an oppressed racial formation, and it isn't hard to figure out why Paul Robeson's "case," from his brilliant rise to public renown to his fall into political disfavor, internal exile, and non-personhood, tells such an important and particularly American tale.

In terms of his fate, Paul Robeson has never been alone. Many talented, expressive black people have preceded him. And considering the way racial dialog with any sense of social justice is coopted, skewed, or totally repressed in this society, many will follow. But then all black people in America amount to "cases" of some sort, simply because all are subjected to the panoptical, surveilling gaze of white supremacy and its attendant power relations. Paradoxically, that is our collective fate and distinction here. In a society with such an intense racial hierarchy, African Americans are indelibly marked as the most unassimilated and historically resistant, the most not-white of all non-whites. In a phrase, blacks are the talismans of *difference*. And yet simultaneously, black people are America's uniquely eminent cultural producers (and product), and therefore its deliverance. So one way to understand Paul Robeson's "case" is to locate him in a long trajectory of gifted black artists and creative intellectuals who have contributed much to the nation's development, but who have in complex ways been both celebrated and ignored, exiled or e-*raced* from American public culture for various reasons of *race*, social consciousness, or political commitment. Certainly those names would include Bert Williams, Josephine Baker, Richard Wright, James Baldwin, Chester Himes, W.E.B. Du Bois, Dorothy Dandridge, Ben Webster, and Eartha Kitt. The list is long and it goes on.[2]

At the contemporary moment, the mass media is especially charged with the stormy "cases" and issues of black celebrities, and in the hierarchy of psychic disturbances and threats to the peace and order of *whiteness*, black males top the list. Thus, one cannot escape comparing the case of the most controversial black man of his time, Paul Robeson, with that of the most media-hyped and infamous black man of our time (or perhaps *any* time), O. J. Simpson. While the media construction of Robeson's and Simpson's celebrity reveals many similarities, the two men, their ideals, the distinct meanings and significations of their personas and personal lives, turn out to be radically different. In the physics of fame, ultimately, Paul Robeson stands out as a sort of "anti-O. J." particle. Nevertheless, each in his own style served, finally contradicted, and was banished from, the realm of the celebrities by the same social, political, and media forces that initially found so much ideological utility in his talent and fame.

Paul Robeson, like O. J. Simpson, was an outstanding, celebrated football player at the top of his game and times. And like Simpson's, Robeson's persona and career transcended the football field. However, far beyond his athleticism, Robeson was a gifted intellectual, scholar, and an accomplished actor with one of the finest bass-baritone voices of his generation. Paul

205. Paul Robeson at press conference following attack on fans at scheduled appearance in Peekskill, New York, on August 27, 1949. New York. August 28, 1949.
UPI/Corbis-Bettmann.

Robeson was always on tour, with as much or more of an audience abroad than at home. Everything that Paul Robeson did was marked with his excellence, showed the results of his tremendous intellect, his gifts and diligence. O. J. Simpson, on the other hand, while quite intelligent, lays no claim to the creative life of the mind. Even after having gone through the University of Southern California on full scholarship, Simpson was particularly unmarked by the influences of higher learning in the way that we as an adoring sports audience like to imagine our star jocks. Hence, to the media and his fans, Simpson came off as "a regular guy." If anything, U.S.C. served as a finishing school where he dropped the last traces of his impoverished background, and, from his prosperous school chums, picked up the social and business skills that would later serve him so well.

After football, everything Simpson achieved in terms of fame and material success was the result of his shrewdly focused business instincts at working the star system. Rather than being known for any particular talent of stage or screen, he largely devoted his post-football energies to cultivating, and enjoying, the lucrative activity of being a famous person. In fact, Simpson was the first black superjock to cross over to big-time commercial acceptance as a pitchman on a national scale. O. J. made an easy transition from the sports team to becoming the ultimate, black "company man." Like total yards gained, his seventeen-year run as celebrity spokesperson for Hertz Corporation stands as yet another one of his records. "Just being O. J.," as his friends recall that blissful, pre–Bundy Drive state, amounted to spending out the perks and profit of an eternally compounding celebrity interest rate at the end of a spectacular football career.

But everyone pays to play. So however complex, refined, or popular, the celebrity personas of Paul Robeson and O. J. Simpson (as of all black stars) performed a number of necessary ideological and discursive labors for the dominant social order. In their glory, both were perceived by whites as "safe" or domesticated black men, as the tame exceptions to their more numerous, stereotypical counterpoint: the insurgent, unruly, black male criminal. They were necessary psychic charms against the likes of Nat (or Ike) Turner, Willie Horton, and King Kong.[3] More importantly though, the success and celebrity of both men

206. Paul Robeson in football uniform. c. 1918.
Special Collections, Rutgers University Libraries.

argued against the impossibly long odds stunting the success of the great majority of blacks in America. Robeson and Simpson's spectacular examples validated the system, saying that black people could make it and be fully accepted at the highest levels of power and privilege in white society. This is one of the reasons why their falls from celebrity grace were interpreted by dominant media as such stinging betrayals. With a doublethink logic that implicitly understands the limitations placed on blacks while explicitly arguing that they can succeed, dominant society perceived it as the deepest ingratitude that Robeson and Simpson had acted out in ways that destroyed a privileged status afforded few whites and almost no blacks. They should have been more appreciative of getting what they were never supposed to have had in the first place, or so this twisted line of reasoning goes. This view, of course, conveniently overlooks the discursive machinations of a star system and racial order so heavily invested in the exploitation of Robeson and Simpson's symbolic meaning as successful blacks.

From the beginning, Robeson and Simpson were broadly constructed in the media, in films, photos, interviews, etc., in predictable ways, as big, affable black men, with powerful athletic bodies, domesticated and packaged for the gaze of an admiring public. While the meanings associated with the persona and images of Paul Robeson, according to his many talents, are varied and complex, the impression of a powerful, sometimes eroticized but always

207. Paul Robeson stops in at Les Ambassadeurs in Paris to see film *Show Boat* and signs autographs after being recognized by spectators. Paris. August 27, 1936.
UPI/Corbis-Bettmann.

208. Paul Robeson. 1941.
Photo by Yousuf Karsh. Collection of Yousuf and Estrellita Karsh. Courtesy Museum of Fine Arts, Boston.

contained black body is clearly conveyed in a number of materials, such as Nickolas Muray's series of "classical" nude photos, or those shirtless, well-oiled, muscular glimpses of him singing while shoveling coal or busting rocks in *The Emperor Jones* (1933) and other films like the avant-garde *Borderline* (1930), where his "exotic" blackness is emphasized. Similarly, after football, the most familiar image of O. J. Simpson was on the tube as that record-breaking, superjock body in a three-piece suit jumping obstacles and running through airports to make that perennial business connection in the Hertz commercials of the 1970s.

In Robeson's films, though, one could usually detect a black alliance, a "smuggled-in reality," as James Baldwin would say, in his performances. In *The Emperor Jones*, Robeson as Brutus Jones has ambitions far beyond those permitted the blacks of his times. He even outsmarts a railroad president to cash in on a stock deal. And while Robeson is trapped as a simple "folk Negro" in *Tales of Manhattan* (1942), he manages to smuggle in a rousing speech about social equality. Moreover, Robeson's presence as master thespian in *Othello* provided him with the confident "talented tenth" patina of an educated, accomplished black man that, by example, was purported to benefit all blacks. Over time, though, Robeson became increasingly wary, disenchanted with the media's general exploitation of him, including its focus on his body and voice, disassociated from his intellect, social consciousness, and political activism. By contrast, O. J. Simpson eagerly plunged headlong into the fame game, polishing his crossover smile and broadening his opportunities as a commercial pitchman and celebrity actor, hyping everything from health drinks to exercise videos on cable, serving on corporate boards, golfing and power lunching with company heads. And the focus on the athletic body persisted, as O.J. Simpson the B-movie actor appeared in one-dimensional action or comedy roles in a string of medium-budget features such as *The Klansman* (1974), or *Capricorn One* (1978), or perhaps most memorably, from the late 1980s into the 1990s, in self-parody as Norberg in *The Naked Gun* flicks.

So, both men deployed the public spotlight, yet they pursued quite different paths and career goals. In common, though, they negotiated the generic traps of stardom that confront white celebrities in addition to that special overlay of racial tangles and "double-consciousness" reserved for black stars. Of course, one can extrapolate the Du Boisian notion of "double-consciousness," of having to think as a minority while contending with a world controlled by dominant values, to a vast number of *other* groups outside the norm of star system *whiteness*, such as gays and lesbians, Native Americans, Asian Americans, women, poor people. But because *blackness* represents the most visible and challenging social formation of *difference*, "double-consciousness" reveals itself perhaps most clearly in the careers of black stars and a set of abiding unresolvable contradictions. Beyond the rhetoric of corporate multi-cultural consumerism, all black stars must play to the expectations of a dual audience, of blacks and whites, even if some of those stars would strategically, or foolishly, pretend otherwise. The black celebrity's star potential is largely based on his or her "crossover" appeal to the

209. Paul Robeson and Gavin Arthur in *Borderline.*
1930.
Beinecke Library, Yale University.

vast white spectator/consumer audience held in tenuous balance with the ability to maintain at least the semblance of identification with African Americans. This, however, turns out to be a tricky, perilous maneuver, and a burden which no white star has to bear. The black star, while a wealthy, privileged symbol of equality and showcase success for white folks, is at the same time expected to exemplify and speak for the social aspirations of an oppressed racial formation, i.e., black folks. In wrestling with these two conflicting sets of expectations, Paul Robeson and O. J. Simpson evolved in radically different ways.

Being profoundly socially conscious, multitalented, and intellectually gifted, Paul Robeson never considered his celebrity as an end in itself. Thus he took more political risks during the intimidating frost of the Cold War than most people, black or white, and especially those who viewed stardom as their sole occupation, or ego gratification, or the expression and exploitation of one talent, or merely as a meal ticket in the white world. Throughout his career Robeson was dedicated to, and persistently outspoken on, a number of insurgent issues including racial injustice, decolonization, labor rights, and Pan-Africanism. And if nothing else, he was always acknowledged (and was relentlessly surveilled) for his honest, uncompromised political views and stances. Regardless of his associations with Communism, or how naive or guarded his opinions on the crimes of Stalin, Robeson's identification with the travails and struggles of black people at home, and people of color around the world, were a genuinely felt, evolving, lifelong commitment. In a strategic sense, Robeson's affiliation with Communism was not the real threat. The great danger to the system had more to do with the way Robeson's interpretation and articulation of fame challenged the rigid barriers of stereotype and political silence imposed on black stars, and implicitly, the way his celebrity questioned the "place" of all blacks. As a "hero of the race," Paul Robeson was a premier black internationalist with a worldwide audience. He toured constantly and was as much applauded for playing Othello on the New York and London stages as speaking at a workers' rally in Prague or a peace conference in Paris.

But because he met "double-consciousness" head on, Paul Robeson moved out in front of the racial protocol and power relations of his day. He was point man on patrol in

210. Paul Robeson with cap in *Borderline.* 1930. *Beinecke Library, Yale University.*

America's racial jungle and he suffered the dire consequences of the inevitable ambush. Robeson would not "wear the mask" so poetically described by Paul Laurence Dunbar. He would not fragment his talent by confining his career to any single gift and showing a one-dimensional, grinning star face to his public. He refused to be merely an ex-football star, or movie actor, or singer-entertainer, or socially safe, public intellectual. In a final editorial effort to steer him away from what his crossover audience was beginning to perceive as the dangerous mix of politics and art, *The New York Times* opined that Robeson should not "devote his life to making speeches." The paper suggested that he could best help the cause of blacks

211. Still from *Tales of Manhattan* (Twentieth Century Fox, 1942). *Courtesy of The Academy of Motion Picture Arts and Sciences. Copyright renewed 1970, Twentieth Century Fox.*

by "being an outstanding human being" in the style of Ralph Bunche, Joe Louis, and Jackie Robinson, and by expressing the gifts of the star persona cherished by whites. The paper concluded that "we want him to sing, and to go on being Paul Robeson."[4] As a "race man," a celebrity, and a creative intellectual who was forthright in his opinions, and in possession of a large following, Robeson contradicted white expectations about even a famous black's "place." Consequently, his Red associations did come in handy, as a convenient way to alienate his crossover public and discredit him with the country's "accepted" black leadership without having to confront him on the issues that he found most relevant, the abolition of white supremacy and the promotion of social justice for black people in America.

Robeson and Simpson lived out their star moments on opposite ends of the great paradigm shift in post–World War II, American social consciousness: the Civil Rights Movement. Paul Robeson's activism anticipated the social struggle to come; O. J. Simpson's media persona reaped that struggle's resulting benefits. A generation later and in diametric contrast to Robeson, Simpson played his "double-consciousness" with the depth and skill of a master chameleon acutely sensitive to the shadings, color combos, and expectations of every social moment. To the adoring fans and his inner circle of well-to-do friends, O. J. was all mask. He was the ultimate, empty celebrity persona, an image-conscious shell, appearing apolitical and intellectually hollow on all but the most establishment-sanctioned issues. But of course to be black in America, inescapably, is to be political, for only whites can ignore (or pretend to ignore) the politics and perils of *race*. And it was exactly the ferment and tension of the open black rebellion in the late 1960s that greatly facilitated Simpson's contrasting rise as a media superstar. He was a likable, nonmilitant, black man whom whites could feel comfortable with in very uncomfortable times.[5]

212. Sen. Glen Taylor, Henry Wallace, and Paul Robeson sitting during meeting at Progressive party nominating convention. Standing, left to right: Rexford Tugwell, Clark Formann, Bini Baldwin, and Albert Fitzgerald. Philadelphia. July 1948. *Photo © by Julius Lazarus.*

While not often spoken, Simpson's political stratagems were stated boldly enough in his showcase lifestyle, the pad, the cars, the blonde trophy wife, the endless days on the golf course, all of which exemplified an extreme celebrity assimilation that was supposed to render invisible, or transcend, his *blackness.* During the late 1960s, when asked by a *New York Times* reporter about the mounting social struggles of black people, seemingly transfixed by his celebrity and narcissism, Simpson answered "I'm not black, I'm O.J." And eleven days after the murders on Bundy Drive, the first of what would be a deluge of over fifty books on the case quotes Simpson as telling a reporter in 1976 that, "People like me and I don't think I'm offensive to anyone. . . . People have told me I'm colorless. I stay out of politics."[6] Before the crash, in the great American entertainment tradition, Simpson was a superstar persona who hyped and sold everything, but behind the mask stood for practically nothing.

Although their much-debated transgressions were markedly different (with Robeson's considered political and Simpson's criminal), when the bitter turn of the wheel came, Robeson and Simpson met the same fate. For certain, both were demonized and socially punished with internal exile, made public examples of the power of dominant society over black people, and black men in particular. But that exile has an ironic, differential quality to it reflective of each man's "case" and times. Paul Robeson was exiled and silenced for his political voice, his outspokenness on behalf of the human rights of non-white people at home and abroad. Paul Robeson was made a non-person in America, shut out by the media, shunned by the public. He never really recovered from that condition. And compared to *Circus O.J.,* it's doubtful that the mass media ever made much money from his fate. Conversely, in one of those judicial concoctions possible only in a society fed a constant fix of electronic spectacle and facing racial gridlock, while widely known for scenes of domes-

213. Paul Robeson upon landing in Moscow after eight years' exile in the United States. August 17, 1958. *UPI/Corbis-Bettmann.*

214. Paul Robeson speaks at Humboldt University, Berlin, upon receiving an honorary doctorate. May 10, 1960.
Photo © Bildarchiv Neues Deutschland, Berlin. Courtesy Julius Lazarus Archives and Collection/ Special Collections/Rutgers University Libraries.

tic violence and acquitted of the criminal charge of double murder, Simpson was found civilly liable for the same events. Moreover, the sensation of Simpson's infamy, fed by the shadow of dominant fears surrounding desire, black sexuality, and miscegenation, has made his "case" one of the most sustained money-making media events ever, for all involved. While Simpson was formally found "not guilty," he has also been found "not innocent," by an increasingly skeptical public. Unlike Paul Robeson, who was rendered invisible to the public, O. J. Simpson has been made hyper-real, the indispensable enemy, and probably the most recognized and commodified black man in the history of electronic, mass communications.[7]

Finally, while endless variations on the theme of the black male bogeyman punished by a righteous society are abundant enough today, it's worth noting that Paul Robeson and O. J. Simpson are caught up in a discursive, representational system that was in place to define black men in the white, social imagination at least several centuries ago. The most obvious, yet subtly complicated of ironies about their "cases" concerns the way that both men's star careers cover the range of consonant, overlapping, and contradictory significations about black masculinity gathered around the black protagonist of Shakespeare's play *Othello*. Considering the character Othello, and the plot, from a dominant social perspective, the play reads as a cautionary tale about what happens when white women hang out with successful but "uppity" black men. Note that "uppityness," or nobility, is one of the

215. Robeson at Blaine, Washington–Canada border, January 31, 1952, under sign reading "Immigration" where Robeson attempted to cross into Canada to give speech to meeting of Mine, Mill and Smelter Workers Union in Vancouver, B.C., but could not, so sang to them by telephone from Seattle.
Photographs and Prints Division, Schomburg Center for Research in Black Culture, The New York Public Library, Astor, Lenox and Tilden Foundations.

main Aristotelian criteria of tragedy. So Robeson and Simpson sit balanced at opposite ends of the black star spectrum, with Othello, eternally, poised at the fulcrum. Paul Robeson always struggled either against, or to expand, the stunted conditions of his representation and thus the way all black people are portrayed. While equally aware of the racially proscribed limits of his representation, Simpson has opted to exploit rather than challenge them. Evoking the "positive image" of an exemplary black man, Paul Robeson was acclaimed for playing Othello on the stage. The role was considered one of the marks of his erudite sophistication and talent. Grimly, on the other end of the balance, O. J. Simpson has come to literalize the role and myth. But perhaps more important are the workings of the pervasive racialized, socially and historically determined "way of seeing" that defines and contains both men, and that has led them to their complex fates.

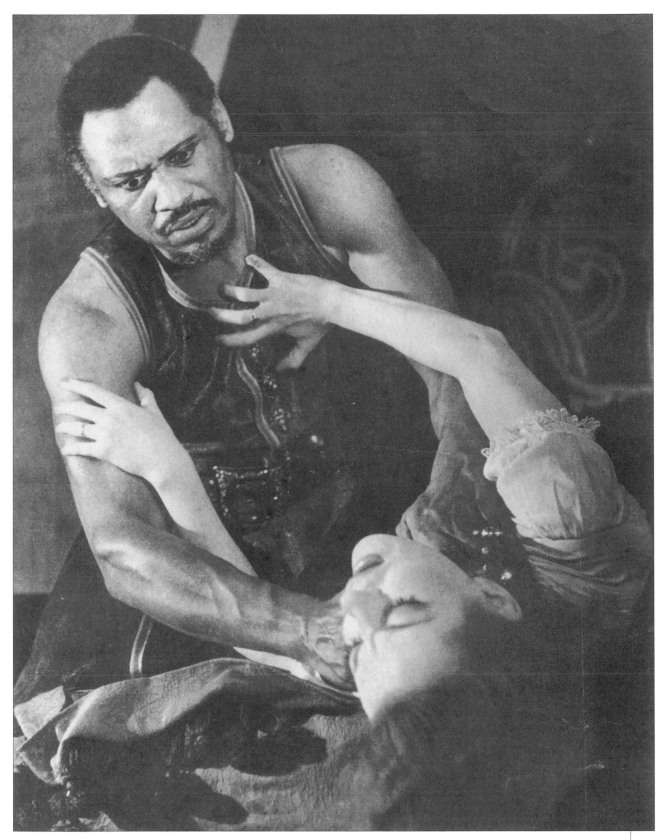

216. Robeson as Othello choking Uta Hagen as Desdemona in *Othello*.
Life, November 22, 1943. *Photo by Herbert Gehr, Life Magazine. © Time Inc.*

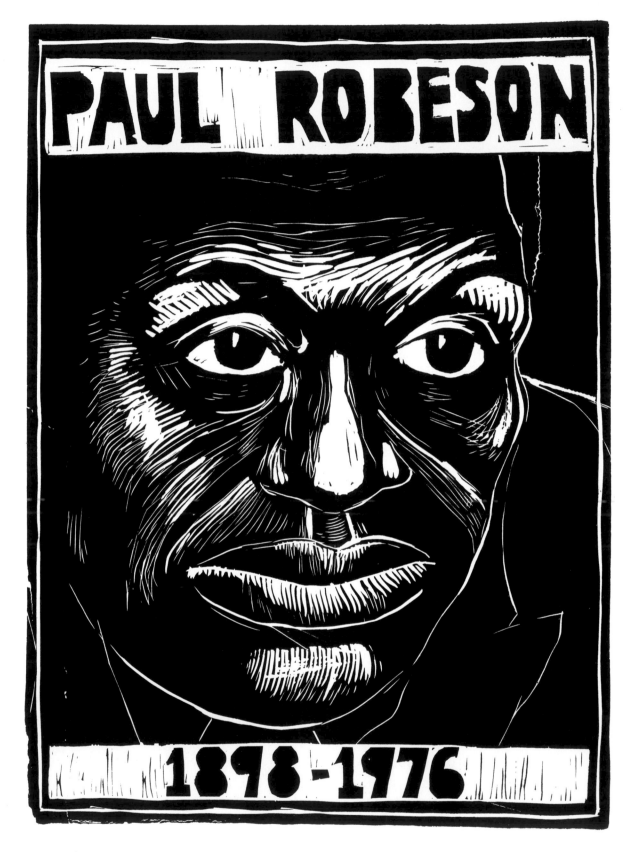

217. "Paul Robeson, 1898–1976." Poster by Leon Klayman in collaboration with Rachael Bell [San Francisco], Wilfred Owen Brigade. 1976. 54 x 40 cm.
Prints and Photographs Collections, Library of Congress.

John Hope Franklin

PAUL ROBESON, ICON FOR THE TWENTY-FIRST CENTURY

One of the first significant events of the bicentennial year of American independence was the death of Paul Robeson on January 23, 1976. Here was an extraordinary, quintessential American hero by any standards. He was an All-American football star and a varsity member of several other sports teams at Rutgers College, and he was the Phi Beta Kappa valedictorian of the class of 1918. Then he went on to graduate from the Columbia University Law School. With a bounty of talents, he became the star of the theater and concert stage as well as an idol of the motion-picture screen. His fellow Americans might well have concluded that he epitomized everything that they held dear. They could have regarded him as the very incarnation of the independent American spirit that they would celebrate in the bicentennial year.

Instead, too many Americans made begrudging concessions to his genius even at his death. *The New York Times,* commenting on his career at the time of his death, lamented the fact that Robeson was "under a cloud during the cold war as a political dissenter and

218. Robeson with United States servicemen. 1943.
Photo by John W. Mosley. Charles L. Blockson Afro-American Collection, Temple University.

an outspoken admirer of the Soviet Union."[1] The editor went on to observe that these circumstances as well as the award in 1952 of a Stalin Peace Prize combined to close many minds to his artistic merits as a singer and actor. These American minds were doubtless closed without attempting to understand what forces and impulses influenced his conduct in World War II. Consequently, it would not be possible for them to grasp the impulses that governed his conduct during the years following the close of hostilities.

The minds that were closed even to less glamorous black Americans during the war were represented by the post–Pearl Harbor white military establishment that rejected highly trained black volunteers for military service by explaining to them that they had everything but color. They were represented by the official Red Cross policy of segregating blood and blood plasma on the basis of race, in the face of the enormous contributions to the very development and deployment of blood banks by the eminent African American hematologist Charles R. Drew. They were represented by the millions of white Americans who literally gloried in the widespread practice of degrading and dehumanizing black Americans by subjecting them to every conceivable form of humiliation including jim crow in transportation, in the recruiting stations, in the barracks, and even on the fighting front. They were represented by the unwillingness, until January 13, 1997, to consider seriously a single one of the million black Americans who served in World War II as worthy of the Congressional Medal of Honor.

If, during World War II, Paul Robeson enjoyed some personal professional success, he did not overlook the predicament of other, less-fortunate African Americans. "Racial and religious prejudices continue to cast an ugly shadow on the principles for which we are fighting," he told the Morehouse College graduates in the spring of 1943.[2] Nevertheless, Robeson urged blacks to support the war effort, warning them that the victory of fascism would "make slaves of us all," and he called on the government to eradicate all of those un-American practices of discrimination that were so common in the factories and the armed forces.[3] Perhaps it was his assertion that the supporters of racial discrimination and racial antagonism were "first cousins if not brothers of the Nazis" that infuriated many white Americans.[4] His holding up the Soviet Union as the example of a nation opposed to racial exclusiveness and in favor of equality of nations must have driven his adversaries to the brink of madness. It surely closed their minds to any possible good that he might offer in any sphere of activity.

Those who survived Paul Robeson and witnessed the observances of the bicentennial during 1976 were moved to recall all too often his words of warning during and after the war. The postwar battles for racial justice were essentially the same as those for which Robeson fought during the war; and the prospects for victory were almost as dim as ever. There was Judge John Sirica of the United States District Court of the District of Columbia ordering the United States Department of Health, Education, and Welfare to begin proceedings

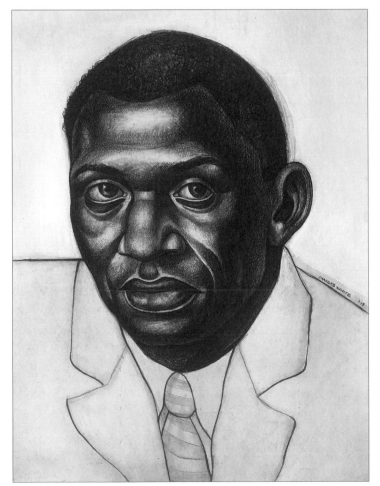

219. Charles White, *Head of a Man II: Portrait of Paul Robeson.* 1943. Charcoal and white gouache. 68.5 x 53.4 cm.
The Art Museum, Princeton University, Museum purchase, Kathleen Compton Sherrerd Fund for Acquisitions in American Art. Photo by Clem Fiori.

220. Group portrait of (left to right) Lawrence Brown, Joe Louis, Marian Anderson, Bill Robinson, Paul Robeson, unknown man, and Olivia de Havilland. c. 1940.
Photo by Sonny Edwards. Photographs and Prints Division, Schomburg Center for Research in Black Culture, The New York Public Library, Astor, Lenox and Tilden Foundations.

against schools in the area that were not complying with the desegregation requirements that had been established. There were numerous allegations of racial discrimination by banks, hotels, schools, orchestras, police departments, prisons, utility companies, beaches, real estate dealers, restaurants, and others where any American might expect to receive equal treatment. It appeared that black issues had been relegated to an insignificant place during the nation's bicentennial year. One can be certain that, had he lived, Paul Robeson would have been one American whose voice could have been heard above all others in that bicentennial year in his condemnation of the practices of racial and all other forms of discrimination.

Almost a quarter of a century has passed since Robeson's death. There have been some developments that would have warmed his heart. Distinguished African Americans grace the faculty of Rutgers, his alma mater, and many other colleges and universities of the first rank. Hundreds of thousands of African American students attend colleges and universities that were closed to them during most of Robeson's life. African Americans have climbed the pinnacle of success in their chosen fields, many more in the sports world, however, than in business and many more in the entertainment world than in education. Most distressing of all is that today there are more young black men in jails and prisons than are in colleges and universities. And if some blacks had attained success in politics and won elections as mayors, members of state legislatures and the federal Congress, and high appointive offices, the flip side was bleak indeed. Millions of African Americans declined to bother to vote, despite the fact that the ballot was won by the struggles of the likes of Paul Robeson and James Farmer and the martyrdom of the likes of Medgar Evers and Martin Luther King, Jr. Consequently, elections that should have been won and agendas that would have given hope to the downtrodden and underprivileged were, through the dereliction of nonparticipants in the electoral process, handed on a platter to the opponents of justice and equality.

The remarkably wonderful thing about the principles for which Paul Robeson stood during his lifetime is that they remain relevant and even urgent today. These principles should not be obscured, moreover, by the caustic and bitter criticism heaped on him by the Cold Warriors. There is no evidence whatsoever that Robeson was ever a part of any subversive group or that he cherished the hope that one day the United States would be under the control of some other power with a different form of government. What he did hope for was that one day the United States would extend to *all* of its citizens the rights and privileges guaranteed in the Constitution.

If Robeson was unable to persuade his contemporaries to join him in his crusade for a better America, he did not give up easily. In October 1949, I was present when he gave a concert in Washington, D.C. It was a unique experience to hear him for the first time in my life; and it was an extraordinary experience to hear an artist "lace" his recital of songs with political and social commentaries. He declared, once more, that there could be no question about his loyalty to the United States, but he made it clear that there were individuals and groups within the United States for whom he had no respect and that he would not trim his comments to curry favor with them or attempt to placate them in any way. I had heard him sing over the radio and on phonograph records, but I had never heard him speak, and I have seldom if ever heard such eloquence, such passion, and such obvious sincerity as he gave his audience that evening. I was persuaded then as I continue to be convinced, even now, that Paul Robeson had a message for his time and for later generations.

Many can utter truths that reflect the consensus of their fellows. Some can speak seriously and even persuasively on controversial questions about which there is honest, but civil,

221. Henry Wallace, Dr. Frank Kingdon, and Paul Robeson visit supporter Albert Einstein at Princeton University. Wallace, editor of the *New Republic,* was touring New Jersey under the auspices of the New Jersey Independent Citizens League. Einstein expressed "great admiration for Wallace's courage and devotion" in the fight for world peace. Princeton, New Jersey. September 21, 1947. *UPI/Corbis-Bettmann.*

222. Paul Robeson singing at Madison Square Garden. New York. 1948.
Photo © by Julius Lazarus.

disagreement. Very few, however, have the courage to speak out in support of unpopular causes when the stakes are high and the risks are many. In taking his stand, Robeson was such a person; and although his stands caused him much anguish and even pain and physical suffering, he saw no alternative. Some of Robeson's gifted predecessors and some of his contemporaries took the position that it was useless to fight the racial bigotry that was so pervasive in the United States. Consequently, they chose to become expatriates and live abroad, where their talents were fully appreciated and where they were not treated as second-class citizens or pariahs. Although Robeson lived and worked abroad for long stretches of time, there is no indication that he ever seriously considered expatriation. To him, this was no solution even for him; and it surely was no solution for the millions of his fellow African Americans who did not have that option and to whom he was as loyal as he was to his country. No, he would return here as frequently as he could, take up the cudgel, and fight the good fight.

Paul Robeson possessed the qualities that made it possible for him to speak to later generations, particularly since the problems with which his generation grappled persist and show no signs of disappearing altogether. That is why he has much to say to those who come after him, and especially to those who look to the next century as an age in which the problems that he faced may be significantly mitigated if not solved altogether. At a time when isolationism, if not downright xenophobia, is casting a shadow over much of our relations with other countries, it is well to remember that Robeson had much to say in support of an internationalism that embraced not only cultural communication but economic and political cooperation as well.

Here, then, are suggestions from Paul Robeson about how in the next century we can live at home and work for its improvement and, at the same time, cultivate the healthiest possible relations with the peoples of the world. Robeson declared that,

> To achieve the right of full citizenship which is our just demand, we must ever speak and act like free men. When we criticize the treatment of Negroes in America and tell our fellow citizens at home and the peoples abroad what is wrong with our country, each of us can say with Frederick Douglass: *"In doing this, I shall feel myself discharging the duty of a true patriot; for he is a lover of his country who rebukes and does not excuse its sins."*[5]

Loyalty, then, is an important ingredient in citizenship, for it gives meaning and substance to any critical position that a person might take. Intolerant observers who shout to a nation's critic that he should love it or leave it cannot understand that the critic shows his

223. Paul Robeson leads pickets at the White House as members of Henry A. Wallace's Progressive party demonstrate in support of the Fair Employment Practices Commision (FEPC) bill. May 24, 1950.
Photo by Al Muto. UPI/Corbis-Bettmann.

224. Flashing a big grin, Paul Robeson holds a youngster during a visit to Budapest, Hungary, on his way to visit Romania. August 30, 1959.
UPI/Corbis-Bettmann.

love of his country by pointing out ways in which it can and should improve itself. One who views flaws in the body politic with silence or indifference obviously has no interest in assisting in the nation's improvement. One who believes that there is no chance for improvement reveals an indifference that borders on cynicism. One who cannot bring himself either to lead in an effort to improve his country or to participate in such an effort reflects a timidity or fear of censure that makes constructive improvement impossible. The example of Robeson in this regard is as clear as it is courageous. When Representative Gordon Scherer asked him, in Robeson's celebrated 1956 appearance before the House Un-American Activities Committee, why he did not remain in Russia, he retorted, "Because my father was a slave, and my people died to build this country, and I am going to stay here and have a part of it just like you. And no fascist-minded people will drive me from it."[6] Anyone who sought to impugn Robeson's loyalty risked becoming a victim of his wrath.

The crusade to eradicate every semblance of racial discrimination and degradation was central to Robeson's fight for a better America. That is why he transformed his concert appearances into a combination of music and lectures on urgent public questions. That is why he wrote letters, essays, and speeches and made scores of public appearances in the cause of racial equality. That is also why his message found a favorable response in the African-American community.

It would not be too much to say that, were Robeson among us as the century ends, and that faraway time has arrived, he would express the same impatience and urgency that he did many years ago. That in itself is an important legacy for the twenty-first century.

225. Paul Robeson clapping. Berlin. 1960.
Photo © Bildarchiv Neues Deutschland, Berlin. Courtesy of Julius Lazarus Archives and Collection/Special Collections/Rutgers University Libraries.

Robeson's wide travels and his familiarity with many peoples and cultures made his name both a household word around the world and a stranger in his own land. He was painfully aware that there were wide gaps between the haves and the have nots in many parts of the world. He also knew that class and racial oppression was not confined to the United States but, indeed, thrived in many places that he had visited in Asia, Africa, and Europe. If he was less critical of some places than he was of the United States, it was because he was impatient with the exaggerated claims of self-righteousness on the part of his fellow countrymen. His level of expectation was high for a land that lived with the exalted principles expressed in the Declaration of Independence and equal justice under law set forth in the Constitution. Therefore, he would press his own country to become the beacon of light for other countries to follow and provide for generations beyond the twentieth century a challenge to transform tensions of race, class, and nationality into the American ideals we hold to be true and honorable.

In pressing this point as he did with ever-increasing vigor, he caused the more narrow-minded in his own country to doubt his allegiance to his native land. However, Robeson wished the best for his own country as he wished for countries everywhere. It was his failure to be a narrow-minded nationalist that led many of his fellow Americans to turn against him. But it was this world view that placed him ahead of his time and, perhaps, made him more tolerant of other systems of government than he was of his own. And, as if to mitigate the extreme positions held by Cold War critics, most of those who sought to make Robeson a pariah are today trading and/or social partners with the Russians and the Chinese. Even some of the lesser xenophobes are beginning to modify their earlier claim that Cuba and the subversives within this country were on the verge of dismantling the United States.

This world view is one of Robeson's major legacies and, indeed, could facilitate our effort to improve our relationships with other peoples and cultures. In an age of sophisticated global communications, the theme of today's generation is that the world has become smaller. Yet, Paul Robeson had long recognized the interconnectedness of the world community. The ever-increasing economic, political, and social interaction and dependency has made Robeson's ideals of openness and tolerance ever more essential to the coming millennium.

Paul Robeson was one of the great icons of his own time. He was a force to be reckoned with and even his severest critics recognized that indisputable fact. Indeed, Robeson remains a powerful icon today. It is clear that he would urge Americans to create relationships beyond their borders, demand that they uphold the ideals of democracy and equality, and challenge this generation to accept this torch as we approach the next century.

NOTES

Jeffrey C. Stewart
INTRODUCTION

1. When referring to people of African descent, Black is capitalized here because it refers to a recognized ethnic minority in America, as is Jewish, Chicano, etc. White is not capitalized because it does not refer to such an ethnic minority. In the essays that follow, each of the authors has made his or her decision about capitalization of ethnic names, as well as their preference for which particular names they use for each group.
2. See James Earl Jones and Penelope Niven, "The Robeson Ruckus and Ad Hoc Art," in *James Earl Jones: Voices and Silences* (New York: Touchstone Books, 1994), chap. 17, 243–263.
3. Harold Cruse, "A Review of the Paul Robeson Controversy (Part II)," *First World* 2 (fall 1980): 26–28. Also see "'I want to be African': Paul Robeson and the Ends of Nationalist Theory and Practice, 1914–1945," in Sterling Stuckey, *Going Through the Storm: The Influence of African American Art in History* (Oxford: Oxford University Press, 1993), 187–227.
4. Sarah and A. Elizabeth Delany, with Amy Hill Hearth, *Having Our Say: The Delany Sisters' First 100 Years* (New York: Kodansha, 1993), 149–150.
5. For Raymond Williams's comments, see Williams, *The Politics of Modernism* (London: Verso, 1989), 151–162.

6. Eric Bentley, ed., *Thirty Years of Treason* (New York: Viking, 1971), 783–784.

EARLY LIFE, ATHLETICS, AND CITIZENSHIP

Lloyd L. Brown
HAPPY BLACK BOY

This essay, with the addition of a brief introduction, is Chapter 4, "Happy Black Boy," of my book *The Young Paul Robeson: "On My Journey Now"* (Boulder, CO: Westview Press, 1997), 31–40, and is reprinted by permission of the publisher.

1. Paul Robeson, *Here I Stand* (New York: Othello Associates, 1958; reprinted, Boston: Beacon Press, 1971, with Preface by Lloyd L. Brown; and 1988, with Introduction by Sterling Stuckey), 23.
2. Paul Robeson, "Here's My Story," *Freedom*, New York, April 1952, 5.
3. Paul Robeson, *Here I Stand*, 17.
4. When William Robeson named his son after that seventeenth-century, nonconformist English preacher and author, he could never have imagined how much of a nonconformist that boy would become.
5. Reeve moved to Detroit, where he is said to have gone into business. The nature of that business is not known, and when Paul met Reeve there in later years he tactfully did not ask about his brother's enterprise.

6. Paul Robeson, *Here I Stand*, 21.

7. William D. Robeson's change of denominations was effected on April 11, 1906. (Letter from Gerald W. Gillette, Research Historian, Presbyterian Historical Society, Philadelphia, December 16, 1971.)

8. *Princeton Press*, February 16, 1901.

9. That church still stands on Downer Street at the corner of Osborn Street.

10. Paul Robeson, "Here's My Story," 5.

11. Interview with Benjamin F. Gordon, New York, June 16, 1971.

12. *Princeton Press*, February 16, 1901.

13. To persons acquainted with William Robeson's gentle and retiring daughter that trait of being "too kind" was seen as the most outstanding characteristic of Marian herself.

14. Interview with Mrs. Marian Forsythe, *Philadelphia*, August 13, 1971.

15. Benjamin C. Robeson, "My Brother Paul," in *Here I Stand*, Appendix A, 120.

16. Interview of Paul Robeson by Pearl Bradley, March 21, 1944.

17. *Somerset Democrat*, Somerville, NJ, June 30, 1911.

18. Interview with Mrs. Margaret (Potter) Gibbons, New York, March 9, 1970.

Francis C. Harris
PAUL ROBESON:
AN ATHLETE'S LEGACY

1. Muriel Freemen, "Somerville Alma Mater Plans Hometown Tribute to Robeson," *Somerset Messenger-Gazette*, Somerville, NJ, April 19, 1973. For an overview of the history of African Americans in football, see Arthur Ashe, Jr. (with the assistance of Kip Branch, Ocania Chalk, and Francis Harris), *"A Hard Road to Glory": A History of the African American Athlete* (New York: Amistad Press, 1988, 1993). The most extensive biographies of Robeson are by Lloyd L. Brown, *The Young Paul Robeson: "On My Journey Now"* (Boulder, CO: Westview Press, 1997), and Martin Bauml Duberman, *Paul Robeson: A Biography* (New York: Alfred A. Knopf, 1988).

2. Paul Robeson, *Here I Stand* (New York: Othello Associates, 1958; reprinted, Boston, MA: Beacon Press, 1971), 22.

3. Fred Stern, "12 Letters & A Two-Time All-American," *The Rutgers Daily Targum*, April 10, 1973, 6.

4. Robert Van Gelder, "Robeson Remembers— An Interview with the Star of 'Othello,' Partly About His Past," *Sunday New York Times*, January 16, 1944.

5. The following is the text of the letter, protesting Paul Robeson's jim-crow treatment in the Washington and Lee football game in 1916 (as cited in George Fishman, "Paul Robeson's Student Days and the Fight Against Racism at Rutgers," *Freedomways*, vol. 9, no. 3 [Third Quarter, 1969], 227–228):

City of New York Law Department
June 6, 1919
President William H. S. Demarest, LL.D.
Rutgers College
New Brunswick, New Jersey

Dear Sir:

During the celebration of the one hundred and fiftieth anniversary of Rutgers College, a statement appeared in the public press that Washington and Lee University, scheduled for a football game with Rutgers, had protested the playing of Paul Robeson, a regular member of the Rutgers team, because of his color. In reading an account of the game, I saw that Robeson's name was not among the players. My suspicions were immediately aroused. After a considerable lapse of time, I learned that Washington and Lee's protest had been honored, and that Robeson, either by covert suggestion, or official athletic authority, had been excluded from the game.

You may imagine my deep chagrin and bitterness at the thought that my Alma Mater, ever proud of her glorious traditions, her unsullied honor, her high ideals, and her spiritual mission prostituted her sacred principles, when they were brazenly challenged, and laid her convictions upon the alter [sic] of compromise.

Is it possible that the honor of Rutgers is virile only when untested and unchallenged? Shall men, whose progenitors tried to destroy this Union, be permitted to make a mockery of our democratic ideals by robbing a youth, whose progenitors helped to save a Union, of that equality of opportunity and privilege that should be the crowning glory of our institution of learning?

I am deeply moved at the injustice done to a student of Rutgers, in good and regular standing, of good moral character and splendid mental equipment—one of the best athletes ever developed at Rutgers— who, because guilty of a skin not colored as their own, was excluded from the honorable field of athletic encounter, as one inferior. . . . Not only he, but his race as well was deprived of the opportunity of showing its athletic ability and perhaps, its athletic superiority. Can you imagine his thoughts and feelings when, in contemplative mood, he reflects in the years to come that his Alma Mater faltered and quailed when the test came, and that she preferred the holding of an athletic game to the maintenance of her honor and principle?

I am provoked to this protest by a similar action of the University of Pennsylvania, heralded in the public press less than two weeks ago. Annapolis protested the playing of the Captain of one of the athletic teams of the University of Pennsylvania, a colored man. Almost unanimously his fellow athletes decided to withdraw from the field and cancel the contest. In this, however, they were overruled by the athletic manager. Such prostitution of principle must cease, or the hypocrisy must be exposed.

The Trustees and Faculty of Rutgers College should disavow the action of an athletic manager who dishonored her ancient traditions by denying to one of her students, solely on account of his color, equality of opportunity and privilege. If they consider an athletic contest more than the maintenance of a principle, then they should disavow the ideals, the spiritual mission and the lofty purpose which the sons of Rutgers have ever believed that they cherished.

Very respectfully yours,
James D. Carr
Rutgers '92

6. "When Paul Robeson Starred Afield," *Westfield (NJ) Leader,* November 18, 1943.
7. Ibid.
8. Paul Robeson, "Review of the 1917 Football Season," *Rutgers Alumni Quarterly,* vol. 4, no. 2, January 1918, 71–72.
9. William Harla, "A Conspiracy of Silence? Notable Omissions Raise Query," *The Rutgers Daily Targum,* April 10, 1973, 1, 9.

Derrick Bell
DOING THE STATE SOME SERVICE

1. Derrick Bell, *Race, Racism, and American Law* (Boston: Little, Brown, 1973), Dedication page.
2. Paul Robeson, *Here I Stand* (New York: Othello Associates, 1958; repr. Boston: Beacon Press, 1971), 36, 49.
3. Dorothy Gilliam, *Paul Robeson: All-American* (Washington, DC: New Republic Books, 1976), 158.
4. Martin Bauml Duberman, *Paul Robeson: A Biography* (New York: Alfred A. Knopf, 1988), 360–361.
5. Duberman, *Paul Robeson: A Biography,* 394.
6. Robeson, *Here I Stand,* 45–46.
7. *Brown v. Board of Education,* Brief for Appellants, 194.
8. *Brown v. Board of Education,* Amicus Curiae Brief for United States, 6.
9. W.E.B. Du Bois, *The Autobiography of W.E.B. Du Bois: A Soliloquy on Viewing My Life from the Last Decade of Its First Century* (New York: International Publishers Co., 1968), 333.
10. Albert Blaustein and Clarence Clyde Ferguson, *Desegregation and the Law* (New Brunswick, NJ: Rutgers University Press, 1957), 11–12.

VISUAL ARTS, DRAMA, MUSIC, AND FILM CONTRIBUTION

Deborah Willis
THE IMAGE AND PAUL ROBESON

1. Lloyd L. Brown, *The Young Paul Robeson: "On My Journey Now"* (New York: Westview Press, A Division of HarperCollins Publishers, 1997), 3.
2. For an extensive pictorial treatment of Paul Robeson, see Susan Robeson, *The Whole World in His Hands: A Pictorial Treatment of Paul Robeson* (Secaucus, NJ: Citadel Press, 1981).
3. J. Fred MacDonald, *Blacks and White TV: Afro-Americans in Television since 1948* (Chicago: Nelson-Hall Publishers, 1983), 55.
4. See Martin Bauml Duberman, *Paul Robeson: A Biography* (New York: The New Press, 1995), 122.
5. Jeanne Moutoussamy-Ashe, *Viewfinders: Black Women Photographers* (New York: Dodd, Mead & Company, 1986).
6. See Francis Harris, "Paul Robeson: An Athlete's Legacy" in this volume; Duberman, *Paul Robeson: A Biography,* 573.
7. Duberman, *Paul Robeson: A Biography,* 103.
8. Duberman, *Paul Robeson: A Biography,* 68.
9. Donald Bogle, *Toms, Coons, Mulattoes, Mammies, and Bucks: An Interpretive History of Blacks in American Films* (New York: Continuum, 1989), 190.
10. Gary Null, *Black Hollywood: The Negro in Motion Pictures* (Secaucus, NJ: Citadel Press, 1980), 43.
11. Null, *Black Hollywood,* 181.
12. Duberman, *Paul Robeson: A Biography,* 170.
13. Duberman, *Paul Robeson: A Biography,* 180.
14. Donald Bogle, *Blacks in American Films and Television* (New York: Garland, 1988).
15. Duberman, *Paul Robeson: A Biography,* 467.

Charles Musser
TROUBLED RELATIONS:
PAUL ROBESON, EUGENE O'NEILL, AND OSCAR MICHEAUX

1. "All God's Chillun Got Wings," *The New York Times,* May 16, 1924, 22.
2. The claim that *The Emperor Jones* was Robeson's cinematic debut has been reiterated as recently as Patricia King Hanson and Alan Gevinson, eds., *American Film Institute Catalog of Motion Pictures Produced in the United States,* vol. F3: *Feature Films, 1931–1940* (Berkeley: University of California Press, 1993), 573. This assertion not only negates the Micheaux film, it further valorizes Robeson's connection with O'Neill, since both Paul and Essie appeared in the avant-garde film *Borderline* (Kenneth Macpherson, 1930).

3. Eslanda Goode Robeson, *Paul Robeson, Negro* (New York: Harper & Brothers, 1930), 77. In fact, Essie is quoting here from a 1929 Provincetown Players Manifesto.

4. Robeson, *Paul Robeson, Negro*, 78.

5. Robeson, *Paul Robeson, Negro*, 79–80.

6. Robeson, *Paul Robeson, Negro*, 76.

7. Robeson, *Paul Robeson, Negro*, 81.

8. Constantin Stanislavsky, *My Life in Art* (Boston: Little, Brown, and Company, 1924), translated by J. J. Robbins, 466.

9. Stanislavsky, *My Life in Art*, 466–467.

10. "Paul Robeson Rises to Supreme Heights," *Pittsburgh Courier*, May 17, 1924, 8.

11. Charles Gilpin's only known screen appearance was in *Ten Nights in a Bar Room*.

12. Sister Francesca Thompson, "The Lafayette Players, 1917–1932," in Errol Hill, ed., *The Theater of Black Americans*, vol. 2 (Englewood Cliffs, NJ: Prentice-Hall, 1980), 211–230.

13. Thomas Cripps, *Slow Fade to Black* (New York: Oxford University Press, 1977), 159.

14. The demise of blackface in American theater at this time was heavily indebted to the extraordinary performance of Charles Gilpin, who originated the role. This was part of a larger transformation of American theater, a change that was preceded and facilitated by the establishment of a serious black theatrical repertory company, the Lafayette Players. In addition, the Lafayette Players mounted a play in Harlem using an integrated cast at virtually the same moment that *The Emperor Jones* was staged in Greenwich Village. ("'Justice' to Be Presented at Lafayette With a Mixed Cast," *New York Age*, November 27, 1920, 6).

15. Provincetown Players, playbill no. 4, 1923–1924 season, cited in Louis Sheaffer, *O'Neill, Son and Artist* (Boston: Little, Brown, 1973), 138.

16. Martin Duberman's biography devotes substantial attention to Robeson's extramarital romances with white women. Martin Bauml Duberman, *Paul Robeson: A Biography* (New York: Alfred A. Knopf, 1988).

17. Sheaffer, *O'Neill, Son and Artist*, 35.

18. Sheaffer, *O'Neill, Son and Artist*, 36–37.

19. Duberman, *Paul Robeson: A Biography*, 62.

20. "Gilpin Again Stars in The 'Emperor Jones,'" *Pittsburgh Courier*, March 24, 1926, 10.

21. Cited in Richard Dyer, *Heavenly Bodies: Film Stars and Society* (New York: Macmillan, 1986), 71. It is a fascinating contradiction, therefore, that Gilpin's one surviving film role—apparently his only film role—is in *Ten Nights in the Bar Room*, a black-cast rendering of a European-American play. And yet the use of mainstream white plays in which the question of racial politics at least appeared to be absent or peripheral was, according to Sister Francesca Thompson, one of the hallmarks of the Lafayette Players. It certainly had advantages to the playing of black roles as conceived by white playwrights and was consistent with one strand of Gilpin's work both before and after *The Emperor Jones*.

22. "About Things Theatrical," *New York Amsterdam News*, December 23, 1925, 5.

23. Robeson, *Paul Robeson, Negro*, 8–9.

24. Pearl Bowser and Louise Spence, *In Search of Oscar Micheaux: Five Essays and an Epilogue* (New Brunswick, NJ: Rutgers University Press, forthcoming).

25. Charlene Regester, "Oscar Micheaux's *Body and Soul*: A Film of Conflicting Themes," in Phyllis Klotman and Gloria Gibson, eds., *In Touch with the Spirit: Black Religious and Musical Expression in American Cinema* (Bloomington: Black Film Center, Indiana University, May 1994), 59–71.

26. Duberman, *Paul Robeson: A Biography*, 77.

27. "The Screen," *The New York Times*, December 10, 1923, 20.

28. "The Film of the Month," *McCall's Magazine*, April 1926. (Clipping, Irene Rich Collection, Academy of Motion Picture Arts and Sciences.)

29. As Hall remarked about *Lady Windermere's Fan*, "Those who have seen or read the play will be disappointed in the pictorial results." (Mordaunt Hall, "The Screen," *The New York Times*, December 28, 1925, 19.)

30. Micheaux must have known Charles Gilpin through the Lafayette Players, whose members he employed on his films.

31. "Paul Robeson Rises to Supreme Heights," *Pittsburgh Courier*, May 17, 1924, 8.

32. "Paul Robeson, Son of Slave Parents, Reaches Pinnacle," *Pittsburgh Courier*, November 7, 1925, 10.

33. Stanislavsky, *My Life in Art*, 466.

34. Marcus Garvey would also come to criticize Paul Robeson in terms similar to Madden and Micheaux. For these individuals, Robeson's uncritical association with white cultural producers was highly problematic. See *Black Man*, October 1935, 10–11, 32; and "Grand Speech of Hon. Marcus Garvey at Kingsway Hall, London, Denouncing Moving Picture Propaganda to Discredit the Negro," *Black Man*, June 1939, cited in Tony Martin, *Literary Garveyism* (Dover, MA: The Majority Press, 1983), 117–118. *Black Man* was a Garvey newspaper published in England. Jeffrey Stewart kindly brought this information to my attention. Since Brutus Jones was generally assumed to be modeled on Garvey, Robeson's appearance in the play and movie version of *The Emperor Jones*, as well as his long-standing defense of O'Neill's work, made the actor a likely target for Garvey.

35. Quoted in "Gilpin Again Stars in 'The Emperor Jones,'" *Pittsburgh Courier*, March 24, 1926, 10.

36. This stripping away of the facade of civilization, which certainly resonates with the experience

of World War I, was first and foremost a crisis in European life, and so we—like Micheaux—might wonder about the suitability of its transposition. See Joel Pfister, *Staging Depth: Eugene O'Neill and the Politics of Psychological Discourse* (Chapel Hill: University of North Carolina Press, 1995).

37. Peter Brooks, *The Melodramatic Imagination* (New Haven: Yale University Press, 1976), 56–80.

38. Although Micheaux uses the term in *Body and Soul*, it is never the white racist word "nigger," but as an African American student once pointed out to me, a different if perhaps related word—"niggah."

39. Cripps, *Slow Fade to Black*, 191–193.

40. See the illustration in Robeson, *Paul Robeson, Negro*, opposite page 102.

41. The "call and response" that black urban audiences often mobilize to engage the screen has been frequently commented upon. When I showed *Body and Soul* to a class on "Race and Representation in American Cinema" for New Haven Public School teachers, half of whom were African American, their active response to the film yielded this refrain. In our discussion of the film, several participants argued that this response was dictated by the film, though it would have been articulated somewhat differently if the audience were exclusively black.

Doris Evans McGinty and Wayne Shirley
PAUL ROBESON, MUSICIAN

1. In the 1940s, at the peak of his career, Robeson drew crowds of 20,000 at Lewisohn Stadium in New York (1943 concert); 30,000 at the Hollywood Bowl; 160,000 at Grant Park in Chicago; and 22,000 at a Watergate Sunset Series concert in Washington, D.C. See Gloria Francis Dunn, "Paul Robeson's Career as a Musician: Implications for Music Education" (Ph.D. Dissertation, University of Michigan, 1987), 92. In 1952, during the time that Robeson's passport was denied to him, 30,000 Canadians heard him at Peace Arch Park on the border between British Columbia and the state of Washington. See Paul Robeson, *Here I Stand* (Boston: Beacon Press, 1971), 55.

2. *Chicago Defender*, May 19, 1934, 10.

3. Eslanda Goode Robeson, *Paul Robeson, Negro* (New York: Harper & Brothers, 1930), 97.

4. In 1992 Paul Robeson, Jr., produced a CD (Omega Classics OCD 3007) containing, with other material, a private recording of "O Isis und Osiris," made in the 1950s.

5. Robeson was not involved in *And They Lynched Him on a Tree*, although he did offer to coach the hapless narrator.

Martin Duberman
ROBESON AND *OTHELLO*

This article, with a few slight changes, and the addition of an Afterword, is taken from my book, *Paul Robeson: A Biography* (New York: Alfred A. Knopf, 1988, reprinted by The New Press: 1995), 122–123, 133–139.

1. As early as 1915, a youthful Paul Robeson had performed a burlesque version of *Othello* when a student at Somerville High School in New Jersey. And as early as 1922, when performing the play *Voodoo* in England, his costar, Mrs. Patrick Campbell, the legendary theatrical star, had told him, he "would make a marvelous Othello." After seeing Robeson perform in O'Neill's *Emperor Jones* in England in 1925, Amanda Ira Aldridge, the second daughter of the great black actor Ira Aldridge, was so impressed with Robeson's "magnificent performance" that she presented him with the earrings her father had worn on stage as Othello and expressed the hope that he would one day play the role and wear her father's earrings. (For source citations, see my biography, *Paul Robeson: A Biography*, 570–571, 584, 597.)

2. Philip Merivale to Paul Robeson (PR), June 6, 1928 (Othello offer); Merivale to Eslanda Robeson (ER), June 22, 1928; Maurice Browne to PR, February 14, 1929, Robeson Archives, Moorland Spingarn Research Center, Howard University (henceforth RA); PR to Maurice Browne, October 6, 1928, Browne and Van Volkenburg Papers, University of Michigan Labadie Collection (henceforth UM: Browne/Van Volkenburg). Browne had had the financial backing of Dorothy Straight and Leonard Elmhirst (the innovative couple who had founded Dartington Hall), and they were his partners in the theater purchases as well (Michael Young, *The Elmhirsts of Dartington*, (London: Routledge and Kegan Paul, 1982), 217–219; interview with Michael Straight, April 3, 1985). *Daily News* (London), September 4, 1929 (contract); ER to Stella Hanau, September 10, 1929, courtesy of Richard Hanau ("very excited"). "We all feel that it will be a great event," Essie wrote to Kahn (ER to Kahn, October 7, 1929, Princeton University: Otto Kahn Papers). Ten years later Merivale again approached PR about an *Othello* production, with himself as Iago (Merivale to PR, February 17, 1940, RA). Robeson told a reporter that Othello was "one role I have always wanted to play. . . . This may be because most of the Othellos I have seen, with blacked faces, have been unsatisfactory to me" (*Lantern*, Ohio State University, December 13, 1929).

When *The New York Times* announced that Robeson's portrayal of Othello would "probably" mark the first time a black had done the role, James Weldon Johnson (JWJ) wrote the

Times to say the news came as a surprise to a group of American blacks who had "recently subscribed $1,000 to endow a memorial chair in the Shakespeare Memorial Theatre" at Stratford to Ira Aldridge, who had played the role in London and on the Continent, with Edmund Kean (among others) playing Iago (JWJ to The Editor, *Times*, September 6, 1929).

3. PR to Browne, October 6, 1928, UM: Browne/Van Volkenburg ("afraid"); Browne, "My Production of *Othello*," *Everyman*, May 15, 1930; Maurice Browne, *Too Late to Lament* (Gollancz, 1955), 323 (itched); *Daily Express*, May 21, 1930. Hannen Swaffer, the influential *Daily Express* columnist, who knew Robeson personally, offered an intriguing anecdote about the reaction Paul and Essie had to *Jew Süss*:

> Paul Robeson and his wife had one of their little arguments.
>
> The only thing I found them disagreeing about, hitherto, was Marcus Garvey, the Negro spell-binder, who was in London not long ago. Paul believes in him. His wife does not.
>
> It was when they saw 'Jew Süss,' however, that the other argument began. When they came out Mrs. Robeson said, 'Now, don't agree with me this time. I hope you do not think what I thought.'
>
> 'I thought that Peggy Ashcroft ought to play Desdemona,' said Paul.
>
> 'That is what I thought,' said his wife, 'but I hoped you would not see it.' That is how Peggy was chosen.

Outside of this brief mention by Swaffer, there is no other evidence that I have found of PR's having any interest in Marcus Garvey. Swaffer, of course, may have gotten it wrong. In her unflattering portrait of him, Ethel Mannin accuses him of being "savagely intolerant" toward blacks and, specifically, "patronising" toward Robeson (*Confessions and Impressions* [London: Jarrolds, 1931], 153–156). Interview with Dame Peggy Ashcroft [Paul Robeson, Jr. (PR, Jr.), participating], September 9, 1982 (hereafter Ashcroft interview); and a four-page typewritten memoir of the production which Dame Peggy kindly prepared for me, August 1984 (hereafter Ashcroft Memoir).

4. ER Diary, April 15, 16, 1930, RA; ER to Van Volkenburg, n.d. (May 1930), UM: Browne/Van Volkenburg.

5. Ashcroft interview, September 9, 1982; Ashcroft Memoir, August 1984.

6. Ashcroft interview, September 9, 1982; *Daily Sketch*, May 21, 1930 (kissing); *The New York Times*, January 16, 1944 ("clumsy"). "This in itself made it more than a theatrical experience, it put the significance of race straight in front of me and I made my choice of where I stood" (Ashcroft Memoir, August 1984).

7. Ashcroft interview, September 9, 1982.

8. Ashcroft interview, September 9, 1982; Ashcroft Memoir, August 1984; ER Diary, May 13, 1930, RA.

9. *Daily Telegraph*, May 20, 1930 (skirt dance). *Time and Tide*, May 31, 1930 (spiritual); the "terrific row" was told by PR to Vernon Beste and described in a letter from Beste to Ann Soutter, May 14, 1985, courtesy of PR, Jr.

10. Agate, *Sunday Times*, May 25, 1930. The reviewer for *West Africa* (May 24, 1930) took particular exception to Robeson's costume, pointing out that when he was finally allowed to wear flowing white Moorish robes in the last scene, he not only looked but also sounded his best; Ashcroft Memoir, August 1984 (Richardson); Ashcroft interview, September 9, 1982 (costume).

11. ER Diary, May 19, 20, 1930, RA; *The World* (New York), May 21, 1930 ("started off"); *Illustrated London News*, May 31, 1930 ("little to recommend"); *Truth*, May 28, 1930 (Browne). Browne and Van Volkenburg were additionally drubbed in the *Evening Standard*, the *Daily Mail*, the *Manchester Guardian*, the *Daily Telegraph*—all May 20, 1930; *The Saturday Review*, May 24, 1930; *Everyman*, May 29, 1930; *Time and Tide*, May 31, 1930; and *Sphere*, May 31, 1930. Hannen Swaffer recorded a touching episode in his *Variety* column (June 4, 1930): "I think Paul performed a very kindly act the other night. He called to see me at my flat to ask me to say that the actor who played Cassio [Max Montesole] had been unfairly criticized by some of the critics, who did not know that his part had been cut on the afternoon of the performance, and that, indeed, he had been going out of his way for days to help Robeson, perhaps to the detriment of his own job." Swaffer also reported that "One London editor walked out during *Othello* because there were Negroes around him in the stalls."

12. *Week-End* Review, May 24, 1930 ("great"); *Daily Mail*, May 20, 1930 ("magnificent"); *Evening News*, May 20, 1930 ("remarkable"); *News of the World*, May 25, 1930 ("prosaic"); *Daily News*, May 20, 1930 ("disappointing"); *Christian Science Monitor*, June 2, 1930 ("losing"); *The New Statesman*, May 24, 1930 ("kindly"); *Reynolds News*, May 25, 1930 ("great soldier"); *Time and Tide*, May 31, 1930 ("inferiority complex"); *Country Life*, May 31, 1930 (arrogance); *The Lady*, May 29, 1930 ("affinity"). Also *The Tatler*, June 4, 1930: "the Moor was not an Ethiopian." Two additional examples of laudatory reviews are the *Daily Telegraph*, May 20, 1930 ("a fine presence, a beautiful voice") and *The New Yorker*, June 21, 1930 ("a great personal triumph for Paul Robeson"). As *The New Yorker*'s summary comment indicates, the New York press reported capsule versions of the London reviews and, surpris-

ingly, leaned with inaccurate one-sidedness to the positive view of Robeson's reception (e.g., *Herald Tribune*, May 21, 1930). Moreover, the American critics who attended the performance praised him more fully than did their English counterparts (e.g., G. W. Bishop, *The New York Times*, May 20, 1930; *Christian Science Monitor*, June 2, 1930; Richard Watts, Jr., *New York Herald Tribune*, May 29, 1930). See *Pearson's Weekly*, April 5, 1930, for PR's view of *Othello*. It's possible that *Pearson's* misrepresented PR's views of the play. Either that, or his views soon evolved. In two subsequent statements he sounded less ambivalent. "There are very few Moors in Northern Africa without Ethiopian blood in their veins," he told *The Observer* (May 18, 1930), and in a radio broadcast in June entitled "How It Feels for an American Negro to Play 'Othello' to an English Audience," he asserted, "In Shakespeare's time . . . there was no great distinction between the Moor and the brown or the black. . . . Surely most of the Moors have Ethiopian blood and come from Africa, and to Shakespeare's mind he was called a blackamoor. Further than that, in Shakespeare's own time and through the Restoration, notably by Garrick, the part was played by a black man" (as reported in the *New York Herald Tribune*, June 8, 1930).

13. *Daily Express*, June 4, 1930 (liberating); ER Diary, May 20, 1930, RA; ER to Carl Von Vechten (CVV) and Fania Marinoff (FM), May 29, 1930, Beinecke Library, Yale University: Carl Van Vechten Papers (henceforth Yale: Van Vechten). CVV to ER, June 22, 1930, RA ("Paul's performance is still with us"); CVV to Knopf, June 27, 1930, University of Texas, Ransom Humanities Center, Alfred and Blanche Knopf Papers (hence forth UT: Knopf); CVV to Johnson, June 21, 1930, Yale: Van Vechten. Essie had gotten hold of a pair of opening-night tickets for the Van Vechtens— "All London is trying to buy them"—but they couldn't get over in time (ER to CVV and FM, March 25, 1930, Yale: Van Vechten). Du Bois to ER, July 10, 1930, RA.

Roger Quilter congratulated PR on his "great achievement" (Quilter to PR, June 22, 1930, RA). Aldous Huxley wrote that, after seeing his "beautiful and illuminating performance," he often found himself thinking back on it "with the most profound satisfaction" (Huxley to PR, July 5, 1930, RA). The writer William Plomer was so moved by his "splendid Othello, in spite of the handicap of bad costume and lighting," that he was "hardly in a fit state" to come backstage (Plomer to PR, May 21, 1930, RA). The explorer Vilhjalmur Stefansson was a bit more backhanded in his compliment— "Shakespeare is stilted and hard to believe but you got more out of your part than any actor whom I have seen" (Stefansson to PR, July 6, 1930, RA)—and Bryher was downright truculent: "I see no reason for acting Shakespeare now. Still I forgot these very strong views whenever I was listening to Othello last week and they only emerged into consciousness during the other sections of the play. I hope this is a road to your working in plays linked to modern consciousness." (Bryher to PR, May 26, 1930, RA).

In retrospect at least, Peggy Ashcroft was one of the enthusiasts of Robeson's performance. Given the fact that he "had to endure great difficulties," she feels "his performance was indeed very, very memorable" (Ashcroft interview, September 9, 1982). "He was a natural and instinctive actor, with imagination, passion and absolute sincerity, and those factors made up for what he lacked in technique" (Ashcroft Memoir, August 1984).

14. Browne, *Too Late to Lament*, 323; *Time and Tide*, June 7, 1930; *Morning Post*, June 18, 1930 (salary); ER to CVV and FM, May 29, 1930, Yale: Van Vechten. *Othello* drew large audiences on its brief tour, due in part to reduced prices (*Sunday Express*, Oct. 13, 1930). ER Diary, May 13, June 3, 1930 (Harris), RA; *The New York Times*, June 8, 1930 (Harris); *The Film Weekly* (England), June 7, 1930 (film). A telegram from Walter White to PR in RA, March 25, 1930, apparently at the behest of Harris, conveyed the offer, adding, "Miss Carrington, who coached Barrymore, to coach in Diction." Noel Sullivan, the wealthy San Franciscan liberal who was a sometime patron to Langston Hughes and whom Robeson and Larry Brown had stayed with during their 1931 cross-country stopover in San Francisco, was apparently also involved in efforts to bring Robeson's *Othello* to the U.S. (PR telegrams to Sullivan, Feb. 14, March 13, April 14, 1931, University of California, Berkeley, Bancroft Library: Noel Sullivan Papers).

15. *The New York Times*, May 22, 1930; *Times Enterprise* (Thomasville, GA), May 27, 1930; Ashcroft interview, September 9, 1982; interview with PR in the *Leeds Mercury*, November 21, 1930: "In New York one is quite safe, but touring the country one visits spots where shooting is a common practice."

16. ER Diary, June 10, July 7, 1930, RA; ER to CVV and FM, July 8, 1930, Yale: Van Vechten. Apparently there was also talk of filming *Othello*, but Robeson turned Browne down on that score. "He feels," Essie wrote Browne, "as I do, that a film will be made forever, and all its faults will mock us in the future, and so he must be careful. . . . He says his performance must be much better than it is now for a permanent record, and I think perhaps he is right" (ER to Browne, June 28, 1930, UM: Brown/Van Volkenburg). For a more positive

view of Browne, see Maurice Evans, *All This . . . and Evans Too!* (Columbia: University of South Carolina Press, 1987); in reference to the 1930 *Othello*, Evans merely comments, "the less said about that the better" (43).

17. PR to Ellen Van Volkenburg, n.d. (June/July 1930), UM: Browne/Van Volkenburg; Ashcroft interview, September 9, 1982.

18. Interview with James Earl Jones, *The New York Times*, January 31, 1982. For more detail, and accompanying source citations, on the Broadway *Othello*, see Duberman, *Paul Robeson: A Biography*, 263–265, 268–281, 295, 661–664, 667–668.

19. For additional information on the Stratford *Othello*, see Duberman, *Paul Robeson: A Biography*, 466, 474–478, 482, 519–520, 733.

Jeffrey C. Stewart
THE BLACK BODY: PAUL ROBESON AS A WORK OF ART AND POLITICS

1. Nickolas Muray, *The Revealing Eye: Personalities of the 1920s in Photographs by Nickolas Muray and Words by Paul Gallico* (New York: Atheneum, 1967), 239.

2. Susan Robeson, *The Whole World in His Hands: A Pictorial Treatment of Paul Robeson* (Secaucus, NJ: Citadel Press, 1981), 43–44.

3. Hugh Honour, *The Image of the Black in Western Art*, Vol. IV: *From the American Revolution to World War I*, Part 2: "Black Models and White Myths" (Cambridge, MA: Harvard University Press, 1989), 174–179. I am indebted to the work of Black feminist critics on the use of the Black body, especially Claudia Tate, Marilyn Mobley, Fath Davis Ruffins, and bell hooks. Hooks's "Feminism Inside: Toward a Black Body Politic," in *Black Male: Representations of Masculinity in Contemporary American Art*, ed. Thelma Golden (New York: Abrams, 1994), 127–140, is very wise.

4. For the Great Migration and its interpretation, see Jeffrey C. Stewart, *1001 Things Everyone Should Know About African American History* (New York: Doubleday, 1996), 52–60, and "(Un)Locke(ing) Jacob Lawrence's Migration Series" in *Jacob Lawrence: The Migration Series*, ed. with an introduction by Elizabeth Hutton Turner (Washington, DC: The Phillips Collection and the Rappahannock Press, 1993), 41–51. The best comprehensive examination of the Great Migration is James R. Grossman's *Land of Hope: Chicago, Black Southerners, and the Great Migration* (Chicago: University of Chicago Press, 1989).

5. For an interesting examination of this idea, see Ann Douglas, *Terrible Honesty* (New York: Farrar, Straus, and Giroux, 1995).

6. "Rutgers Blanks Fordham. Robeson, Giant Negro, Plays Leading Role. . . ." *New York Tribune*, October 28, 1917.

7. Program for *Taboo*, 1921. New York Public Library for the Performing Arts, Theatre Collection.

8. Sterling Brown, "Strong Men" in *Southern Road* (New York: Harcourt, Brace and Co., 1932), 51–53.

9. John Blassingame, *The Slave Community* (New York: Oxford University Press, 1974).

10. Guy Johnson, *John Henry: Tracking Down a Negro Legend* (1929; New York: AMS Press, 1969), 8–26.

11. Roark Bradford, "Paul Robeson is John Henry," January 13, 1940, *Collier's Magazine*. Cover features Roark Bradford, the author, Jacque Wolfe, the composer, and Paul Robeson.

12. The Schomburg Collection for Research in Black History and Culture, New York Public Library, holds a copy of the postcard.

13. For an interesting discussion of colonial representations, see James Clifford, *The Predicament of Culture* (Cambridge, MA: Harvard University Press, 1988).

14. "Am I not a man and a brother?" was the motto used by the English Committee for the Abolition of the Slave Trade and later by U.S. abolitionists. See the entry on Patrick Henry Reason in the *Dictionary of American Negro Biography*, ed. Rayford W. Logan and Michael R. Winston (New York: W. W. Norton, 1982), 517–519.

15. Richard Dyer, *Heavenly Bodies: Film Stars and Society* (New York: St. Martin's Press, 1986), 120–122.

16. The "the-ness" of the Black experience of the white gaze was elaborated brillantly by Herman Beavers in his W.E.B. Du Bois Lecture, "There's More than One Way to Look at a Black Man: Gender Politics and Maculinity," February 4, 1997, George Mason University, Fairfax, VA. Beavers quoted from a poem that epitomized his concept: ". . . The-ness froze him / In a dance. / A-ness never / Had a chance / . . ." where "A-ness" represents the possibility of individuality.

17. For a provocative discussion of Garvey's public attack against Paul Robeson for his representation in such films as *The Emperor Jones*, see Tony Martin's *Literary Garveyism* (Dover: The Majority Press, 1983), 117–118.

18. Sander Gilman, *The Jew's Body* (New York: Routledge, 1991), 38–59.

19. For contrasting views of the impact of Robert Mapplethorpe's photographs of nude Black men, see bell hooks, "Feminism Inside: Toward a Black Body Politic," in *Black Male: Representations of Masculinity in Contemporary American Art*, 136–140, and Kobena Mercer, "Skin Head Sex Thing: Racial Difference and the Homoerotic Imaginary," *New Formations* (1992): 1–23. I thank Cynthia Fuchs for bringing the latter article to my attention. Information on Muray gained from an interview

with friend of Muray's, Blanche Thieman, November 13, 1996.

20. See Susan Robeson, *The Whole World in His Hands* (Secaucus, NJ: Citadel Press, 1981), 43–44, for the photographs discussed.

21. For a discussion of the Sonnenkinder, see Martin Green, *Children of the Sun: A Narrative of Decadence in England After 1918* (New York: Basic Books, 1976).

22. On April 3, 1997, I presented slides of the Nickolas Muray nudes of Robeson to the Cultural Studies 808 Colloquium, at George Mason University, which I team-taught with Cynthia Fuchs. The responses from students wcrc cxccllcnt and informative, especially those on e-mail afterward from Kathy McGill and Howard Hastings.

23. Review of *Black Boy* in *New York American*, October 1926, as quoted in Martin Bauml Duberman, *Paul Robeson: A Biography* (New York: Alfred A. Knopf, 1988), 103.

24. An excellent example of "Praying Boy" (Berlin) can be found in Arnold Walter Lawrence's *Classical Sculpture* (London: J. Cape, 1929), plate 102(a).

25. Kenneth Clark, *The Nude* (Middlesex: Penguin, 1976), 6–7.

26. I am indebted to John Tagg for his discussion of the concept of crossover in "Running and Dodging: Culture and Mobility in the U.S., 1941–43," which he presented before the Cultural Studies Colloquium at George Mason University on February 6, 1997.

27. Alain Locke, *Race Contacts and Inter-racial Relations* (Washington: Howard University, 1992), 48–58.

28. See "Ho Chi Minh Is the Toussaint L'Ouverture of Indo-China," in *Freedom*, March 1954; reprinted in *Paul Robeson Speaks*, ed., with an introduction and notes, by Philip S. Foner (New York: Brunner/Mazel, 1978), 377–379.

Mark A. Reid
RACE, WORKING-CLASS
CONSCIOUSNESS, AND
DREAMING IN AFRICA:
SONG OF FREEDOM AND *JERICHO*

1. During the 1940s, the United States' war efforts would pressure the American film industry to better the film characterizations of African Americans. See Donald Bogle, *Toms, Coons, Mulattoes, Mammies, and Bucks: An Interpretive History of Blacks in American Films* (New York: Viking, 1973), 136–137; Thomas R. Cripps, *Slow Fade to Black: The Negro in American Film, 1900–1942* (New York: Oxford University Press, 1977, repr. 1993), 375–389.

2. Thomas R. Cripps, "Paul Robeson and Black Identity in American Movies," *The Massachusetts Review* 11 (Summer 1970): 468–485.

3. Harold Cruse, *The Crisis of the Negro Intellectual: From Its Origins to the Present* (New York: William Morrow, 1967), 129.

4. Peter Noble, *The Negro in Films* (London: Skelton Robinson, 1948), 115. Also see Thomas R. Cripps, *Slow Fade to Black*, 317.

5. Wilson Jeremiah Moses, *The Golden Age of Black Nationalism, 1850–1925* (New York: Oxford University Press, 1978), 33. Moses argues that,

> The colonization movement must be distinguished from black nationalism, not because whites were involved in the movement as is sometimes suggested, but because many black nationalists refused to leave American soil. Nonetheless, the colonization schemes had among their advocates some black nationalists, as well as whites. The whites may be divided into two categories. . . . Some were benevolent conservatives who were sympathetic to black people and hoped to see them become free and prosperous people—far from the shores of America. Other proponents of colonization were hostile to the libertarian aspirations of Afro-Americans. These men, led by their spokesman Henry Clay, forced the Society to include an anti-abolitionist plank in its constitution. . . . The founding of the [African Colonization] Society [c. 1816] led to the establishment of Liberia [c. 1818], and to thirty years of half-hearted experimentation in African Colonization.

African American leaders who have echoed John Zinga's African repatriation hopes include Henry McNeal Turner (c. 1834) and the Jamaican Marcus Garvey. Garvey was a contemporary of Robeson and was one of his most ardent critics. Thus, John Zinga's feelings and the film's repugnant images of Africans should be seen as carrying mixed signals that may be read as racist as well as a sincere response on the part of blacks to escape racial oppression.

6. Robert Miles, "Racism and Nationalism in Britain," in Charles Husband, ed., *'Race' in Britain: Continuity and Change* (London: Hutchinson and Co., 1982), 286. Miles writes that,

> throughout Western Europe, migrant labour, which is in almost all cases phenotypically distinguishable from the indigenous population, is employed predominantly in the semi- and unskilled sectors of the economy. This is so not because of their 'race' but, *inter alia*, because *beliefs about* 'race' structure the position that the migrants occupy in the process of material production, bringing about an apparent correlation between phenotypical variation and position in production relations.

Thus, the constructed, phenomenal realities of 'race' and 'nation' reflect back the ideologies of racism and nationalism, appearing to validate and verify them. These 'realities' become the material for people's everyday experience, with the result that the categories of 'nation' and 'race' come to play a useful interpretive role in their attempt to make sense of and act within the social world. . . . The notions of 'race' and 'nation' remain available to classes and class fractions as a means of structuring their interpretation of the material problems they face. These notions can therefore become the means by which class interests, which have material basis, are expressed and pursued.

7. Richard Dyer, *Heavenly Bodies: Film Stars and Society* (New York: St. Martin's Press, 1986), 90.
8. Dyer, *Heavenly Bodies*, 90.
9. "Paul Robeson Introduces *Song of Freedom,*" *Film Weekly*, May 23, 1936, 17.
10. In *Paul Robeson: A Biography* (New York: Ballantine Books, 1989), 204, Martin Bauml Duberman writes, "Even the black press . . . agreed he should be satisfied: the *Pittsburgh Courier* welcomed *Song of Freedom* as 'the finest story of colored folks yet brought to the screen . . . a story of triumph.' Langston Hughes wrote to Essie [Eslanda Goode Robeson], 'Harlem liked *Song of Freedom.*'" Although the film and Robeson had their black well-wishers, the black nationalist leader Marcus Garvey constantly criticized Robeson for demeaning the character of the black man. See Marcus Garvey, "Paul Robeson and his Mission," *The Black Man* 2:5 (January 1937): 2–3, and Marcus Garvey, *A Grand Speech of Honorable Marcus Garvey at Kingsway Hall, London, Denouncing the Moving Picture Propaganda to Discredit the Negro*, pamphlet (London: Black Men Publishing Co., 1939). For one of the most trenchant observations on the black and white filmgoer's reception of Robeson's film roles, see Richard Dyer, *Heavenly Bodies*, 68–71.
11. Dorothy Butler Gilliam, *Paul Robeson, All-American* (Washington, DC: New Republic Books, 1978), 88. The author writes, "For . . . *Jericho*, he got a chance to go to Egypt, where some of the scenes were shot. It was an important trip for Paul, who, at thirty-nine, set foot on African soil for the first time." As early as 1936, Eslanda and Paul, Jr., Paul's wife and son, spent three months in Africa while, beginning in the spring of 1936, Paul was busy acting in *Song of Freedom* and within a few months after the shooting finished, he began his role in *King Solomon's Mines*. In commenting on Robeson's absence from his family's African trip, Martin Bauml Duberman, in *Paul*

Robeson: A Biography, explains, "The interval was so brief that he decided not to accompany Essie and Pauli on their long-hoped-for trip to Africa that same summer, especially since 'both the British and South African authorities opposed his going'" (204–205). Duberman also adds that their marital situation may have been an additional reason for Robeson's return trip to the Soviet Union while his wife and son went to Africa.
12. W.E.B. Du Bois, *The Souls of Black Folk* (New York: New American Library [Signet], 1969), 45.

POLITICAL ACTIVISM AND FINAL YEARS

Mark D. Naison
PAUL ROBESON AND THE AMERICAN LABOR MOVEMENT

1. Philip S. Foner, ed., *Paul Robeson Speaks: Writings, Speeches, Interviews, 1918–1974* (New York: Brunner/Mazel Publishers, 1978), 331.
2. Foner, ed., *Paul Robeson Speaks*, 340.
3. Charles H. Wright, *Robeson, Labor's Forgotten Champion* (Detroit: Balamp Publishing, 1975), 9.
4. Foner, ed., *Paul Robeson Speaks*, 364.
5. Foner, ed., *Paul Robeson Speaks*, 135.
6. Martin Bauml Duberman, *Paul Robeson: A Biography* (New York: Alfred A Knopf, 1988), 652.
7. Foner, ed., *Paul Robeson Speaks*, 137–139.
8. Wright, *Robeson, Labor's Forgotten Champion*, 59.
9. Foner, ed., *Paul Robeson Speaks*, 244.
10. Arthur Leibman, *Jews and the Left* (New York: John Wiley and Sons, 1979), 323–324. Robeson's visits to Jewish left-wing summer camps, particularly Camp Kinderland and Camp Wo-Chi-Ca, are also described in detail in chapter 5 of Paul Mishler's unpublished manuscript of 1990, "The Littlest Proletariat, American Communists and Their Children, 1922–1950."
11. Wright, *Robeson, Labor's Forgotten Champion*, 52–55, 62–66.
12. Wright, *Robeson, Labor's Forgotten Champion*, 39; Robbie Lieberman, *My Song Is My Weapon: People's Songs, American Communism and the Politics of Culture, 1930–1950* (Champaign: University of Illinois Press, 1989), 98.
13. On Peekskill, see Howard Fast, *Peekskill, USA* (New York: Civil Rights Congress, 1951); Duberman, *Paul Robeson: A Biography*, 363–380; and David King Dunaway, *How Can I Keep From Singing: Pete Seeger* (New York: McGraw-Hill, 1981), 13–23. For a picaresque literary treatment of the riots, see T. Coraghessan

Boyle, *World's End* (New York: Penguin Books, 1987).

14. Wright, Robeson, *Labor's Forgotten Champion,* 127.

15. On Robeson's appearance for Winston-Salem Tobacco Workers, see Junius Irving Scales and Richard Nickson, *A Cause at Heart* (Athens: University of Georgia Press, 1987), 162–167, and Wright, *Robeson, Labor's Forgotten Champion,* 58–62. On the rise and fall of left-led unions, see Steve Rosswurm, ed., *The CIO's Left-Led Unions* (New Brunswick; Rutgers University Press, 1992).

16. Foner, ed., *Paul Robeson Speaks,* 383.

17. Foner, ed., *Paul Robeson Speaks,* 251–252.

18. On the National Negro Labor Council, see Philip S. Foner, *Organized Labor and the Black Worker* (New York: International Publishers, 1974), 293–311. On the role of the United Public Workers Union, and left-wing activists generally, in fighting racial discrimination in Washington, D.C., in the late 1940s and early 1950s, see Carl Bernstein, *Loyalties: A Son's Memoir* (New York: Simon and Schuster, 1989).

19. Foner, ed., *Paul Robeson Speaks,* 293.

Gerald Horne
COMRADES AND FRIENDS: THE PERSONAL/POLITICAL WORLD OF PAUL ROBESON

1. Daniel Aaron, *Writers on the Left* (New York: Harcourt Brace, 1961), 33.

2. On Davis generally, see Gerald Horne, *Black Liberation/Red Scare: Ben Davis and the Communist Party* (London: Associated University Presses, 1994), 30.

3. Paul Robeson, "Speech Delivered at the Funeral of Benjamin Davis," in Philip S. Foner, ed., *Paul Robeson Speaks: Writings, Speeches, Interviews, 1918–1974* (New York: Brunner-Mazel, 1978), 470–471.

4. Foner, ed., *Paul Robeson Speaks,* 22.

5. Ben Davis to Paul Robeson, undated, Ben Davis Papers, Schomburg Center for Research in Black Culture, New York Public Library.

6. Horne, *Black Liberation/Red Scare,* 59–60.

7. Martin Bauml Duberman, *Paul Robeson: A Biography* (New York: Alfred A. Knopf, 1988), 264.

8. Horne, *Black Liberation/Red Scare,* 44.

9. *Daily Worker,* December 27 and May 10, 1936.

10. Horne, *Black Liberation/Red Scare,* 155.

11. Gerald Horne, *Black and Red: W.E.B. Du Bois and the Afro-American Response to the Cold War, 1944–1963* (Albany: State University of New York Press, 1986), passim.

12. Gerald Horne, *Fire This Time: The Watts Uprising and the 1960s* (Charlottesville: University Press of Virginia, 1995), passim.

13. Horne, *Black Liberation/Red Scare,* 110.

14. National Non-Partisan Committee to Defend the Rights of the Twelve Communist Leaders, "Due Process in a Political Trial: The Record vs. The Press," 1949, Reel 4, Eugene Dennis Papers, State Historical Society of Wisconsin-Madison.

15. Paul Robeson, "The Trial of Judge Medina," August 26, 1949, Box 2, Folder 2/9, Paul Robeson Papers (Berlin).

16. Horne, *Ben Davis,* 257.

17. Gerald Horne, *Communist Front? The Civil Rights Congress, 1946–56* (London: Associated University Presses, 1988), 33–35.

18. Horne, *Communist Front?,* 350.

19. Horne, *Communist Front?,* 235.

20. Horne, *Communist Front?,* 236.

21. Ibid.

22. Ibid.

23. Horne, *Communist Front?,* 237.

24. Horne, *Ben Davis,* 216.

25. Horne, *Ben Davis,* 237–238.

26. Horne, *Ben Davis,* 270.

27. See generally Penny M. Von Eschen, *Race Against Empire: Black Americans and Anti-colonialism, 1937–1957* (Ithaca: Cornell University Press, 1997).

David Levering Lewis
PAUL ROBESON AND THE U.S.S.R.

1. See Marie Seton, *Paul Robeson* (London: Dennis Dobson, 1958), 83; Martin Bauml Duberman, *Paul Robeson: A Biography* (New York: The New Press, 1989), 185.

2. Seton, interviewed by Duberman, *Paul Robeson: A Biography,* 186.

3. Duberman, *Paul Robeson: A Biography,* 208.

4. Quoted material, in Duberman, *Paul Robeson: A Biography,* 191–192.

5. Duberman, *Paul Robeson: A Biography,* 197.

6. Du Bois, "Russia, 1926," *The Crisis,* November 1926, cited in David Levering Lewis, ed., *W.E.B. Du Bois: A Reader* (New York: Henry Holt and Company, Inc., 1995), 582.

7. Hughes, quoted by David Levering Lewis, *When Harlem Was in Vogue* (New York: Penguin Books, 1997. Orig. pub. 1981), 292.

8. Duberman, *Paul Robeson: A Biography,* 211.

9. Duberman, *Paul Robeson: A Biography,* 221.

10. Duberman, *Paul Robeson: A Biography,* 212.

11. Duberman, *Paul Robeson: A Biography,* 220.

12. Account of Robeson's discussion with Louis T. Wright given to David Levering Lewis by Mrs. Louis T. Wright (May 1977) in taped interviewed deposited as part of the collection, *Voices of the Harlem Renaissance,* Schomburg Center for Research in Black Culture of the New York Public Library. For vivid discussion of Stalingrad, see also Donovan Webster, *Aftermath: The Remnants of War* (New York: Pantheon Books, 1996), 98.

13. Quote, cited by Duberman, *Paul Robeson: A Biography*, 343; see also Duberman, *Paul Robeson: A Biography*, endnote 15, 686.
14. Robeson, quoted by Shirley Graham Du Bois, *His Day Is Marching On: A Memoir of W.E.B. Du Bois* (New York: J. B. Lippincott Company, 1971), 118.
15. Duberman, *Paul Robeson: A Biography*, 353.
16. Du Bois, quoted by Duberman, *Paul Robeson: A Biography*, 473.
17. This memorable scene is reconstructed by Shirley Graham Du Bois, *His Day Is Marching On*, 270.
18. Duberman, *Paul Robeson: A Biography*, 506.
19. Duberman, *Paul Robeson: A Biography*, 499.
20. Duberman, *Paul Robeson: A Biography*, 501.
21. Helen Rosen's extraordinary quote is cited by Duberman, *Paul Robeson: A Biography*, 502.
22. Du Bois, "The Real Reason Behind Paul Robeson's Persecution," *National Guardian*, April 7, 1958, in Lewis, *Du Bois Reader*, 799.

Charles L. Blockson
PAUL ROBESON: A BIBLIOPHILE IN SPITE OF HIMSELF

1. Personal note written by Paul Robeson, Paul Robeson Archives, Moorland-Spingarn Research Center, Howard University, 1936.
2. Paul Robeson, *Here I Stand* (New York: Othello Associates, Inc., 1958), 18.
3. Robeson, *Here I Stand*, 18.
4. Robeson, *Here I Stand*, 26.
5. Philip S. Foner, ed., *Paul Robeson Speaks* (New York: Brunner/Mazel Publishers, 1978), 53.
6. Shirley Graham McCann, "A Day at Hampstead," *Opportunity—Journal of Negro Life* (January 31, 1931): 15.
7. Graham, "A Day at Hampstead," 35.
8. Marie Steton, *Paul Robeson* (London: Dennis Dobson, 1958), 77.
9. Robeson, from handwritten notes, 1936.
10. Avery Strakosh, "Born Lucky," *Look Magazine* (March 10, 1942): 65.
11. Eslanda Robeson's diary, "James Joyce's *Ulysses*" (August 28, 1925 entry).

ROBESON'S CONTEMPORARY SIGNIFICANCE

Julianne Malveaux
WHAT IS ROBESON'S CONTEMPORARY LEGACY?

1. Robeson, quoted in Philip S. Foner, ed., *Paul Robeson Speaks: Writings, Speeches, Interviews, 1918–1974* (New York: Carol Publishing Group, 1978), 18.
2. Muhammad Ali, in Justin Kaplan, general editor, *Bartlett's Familiar Quotations*, 16th ed. (Boston: Little Brown, 1992), 772.
3. King, quoted in James M. Washington, ed., *A Testament of Hope* (San Francisco: Harper and Row, 1986), 635.
4. Paul Robeson, *Here I Stand* with Preface by Lloyd L. Brown and Introduction by Sterling Stuckey (Boston: Beacon Press, 1988), 33.
5. Robeson, quoted in Foner, ed., *Paul Robeson Speaks*, 11.
6. Carmichael is credited with the first use of the term "Black Power" (see Mary Frances Berry and John Blassingame, *Long Memory: The Black Experience in America* [New York: Oxford University Press, 1982], 295–341), but Robeson referred to black power in the 1950s (see Paul Robeson, *Here I Stand*).
7. Maulana Karenga, Chairman of the Black Studies Department, California State University at Long Beach, is author of *Introduction to Black Studies* (Los Angeles: University of Sankore Press, 1992), the most widely used Black Studies text in the United States.
8. Molefe Asante is former Chairman of African American Studies at Temple University in Philadelphia and author of a number of books. His most important work may be the *The Afrocentric Idea* (Philadelphia: Temple University Press, 1992).
9. See, for example, Griffin Fariello, *Red Scare: Memories of the American Inquisition: An Oral History* (New York: Avon Books, 1995).
10. Martin Bauml Duberman, *Paul Robeson: A Biography* (New York: Ballantine Books, 1989). See also the more recent biography of Robeson's early years by Lloyd L. Brown, *The Young Paul Robeson: "On My Journey Now"* (Boulder, CO: Westview Press, 1997), from which one chapter is included in this volume.
11. Foner, ed., *Paul Robeson Speaks*, 11.
12. Foner, ed., *Paul Robeson Speaks*, 3.
13. Robeson never took the bar examination or practiced as a lawyer after 1923, when he encountered significant racial obstacles as a legal associate at the New York–based firm of Stotesbury and Meyer (Duberman, *Paul Robeson: A Biography*, 55).
14. Foner, ed., *Paul Robeson Speaks*, 72.
15. Duberman, *Paul Robeson: A Biography*, 87–105.
16. Lloyd L. Brown, in Preface to Paul Robeson, *Here I Stand*, xxxv.
17. Benjamin C. Robeson, in Paul Robeson, *Here I Stand*, 112.
18. Paul Robeson, *Here I Stand*, 27.
19. Celebrities have certainly been willing to lend their influence episodically to important causes through attendance at rallies, testimony to government bodies, and endorsement of issues.

Few, however, have had the consistency of involvement and leadership (which included cofounding the Council on African Affairs) that Robeson had.

20. *The New York Times*, April 21, 1949 (quoted in Paul Robeson, *Here I Stand*, xvii).
21. Duberman, *Paul Robeson: A Biography*, 308.
22. Paul Robeson, *Here I Stand*, xiii.
23. Paul Robeson, *Here I Stand*, 34–35.
24. Foner, ed., *Paul Robeson Speaks*, 9.
25. Foner, ed., *Paul Robeson Speaks*, 10.
26. Paul Robeson, *Here I Stand*, 3.
27. Paul Robeson, *Here I Stand*, 29.
28. Paul Robeson, *Here I Stand*, 32.
29. Paul Robeson, *Here I Stand*, 30.
30. Berry and Blassingame, *Long Memory*, 295–341. Berry and Blassingame coined this phrase to discuss the dilemma that many black men have found themselves in—attempting to prove their manhood by their willingness to fight the wars of a racist America. Throughout our nation's military history, African Americans have had to fight for the right to fight on equal (and even on unequal) terms.
31. Paul Robeson, *Here I Stand*, 77.
32. Paul Robeson, *Here I Stand*, 76.
33. Foner, ed., *Paul Robeson Speaks*, 454.
34. Duberman, *Paul Robeson: A Biography*, 362. Robeson additionally described himself and Jackie Robinson as "brother victims of this terror" imposed by the HUAC.
35. The fact, for example, that several members of the Congressional Black Caucus voted to condemn Nation of Islam minister Louis Farrakhan is remarkable (many made lengthy televised comments about their distaste for his views). While many of Farrakhan's statements are debatable, and some of his views are reprehensible, he is the only person that the United States Congress has ever voted to condemn!
36. Foner, ed., *Paul Robeson Speaks*, 12.
37. Paul Robeson, *Here I Stand*, 46–47.
38. "Ol' Man River" lyrics, cited in Foner, *Paul Robeson Speaks*, 482.
39. Foner, ed., *Paul Robeson Speaks*, 35. See also 180.
40. Duberman, *Paul Robeson: A Biography*, 317.
41. Foner, ed., *Paul Robeson Speaks*, 4.
42. Foner, ed., *Paul Robeson Speaks*, 417.
43. Paul Robeson, *Here I Stand*, 4.
44. W.E.B. Du Bois, *Souls of Black Folk* (Chicago: A. C. McClurg, 1903), 16.
45. Paul Robeson, *Here I Stand*, 59–62.
46. Griffin Fariello, *Red Scare: Memories of the American Inquisition, an Oral History* (New York: Avon Books, 1995).
47. Lloyd Brown, quoted in Paul Robeson, *Here I Stand*, xxvi–xxx.
48. Lloyd Brown, in the Preface to Paul Robeson, *Here I Stand*, xxx.
49. Paul Robeson, *Here I Stand*, 72.
50. W.E.B. Du Bois, Herbert Aptheker, ed., *Autobiography* (New York: New York International Publishers Company, Inc., 1968), 595.
51. Sterling Stuckey, in the Introduction to Paul Robeson, *Here I Stand*, xxii.
52. Robeson, quoted in Foner, ed., *Paul Robeson Speaks*, 164.

Ed Guerrero
BLACK STARS IN EXILE: PAUL ROBESON, O. J. SIMPSON, AND OTHELLO

1. Robert L. Dilenscheneider, *On Power* (New York: Harper, 1994), 167–174. Richard Schickel, *Intimate Strangers: The Culture of Celebrity* (New York: Fromm, 1986), 121–124.
2. Tyler Stovall, *Paris Noir: African Americans in the City of Light* (Boston and New York: Houghton Mifflin Co., 1996). Here Stovall gives the most complete and fascinating account of African American artists in Paris, how they formed an influential community, and why they chose exile over racism in America.
3. John Fiske, *Media Matters: Race and Gender in U.S. Politics* (Minneapolis: University of Minnesota Press, 1996), 256–260. Richard Dyer, *Heavenly Bodies: Film Stars and Society* (New York: St. Martin's Press, 1986), 115–116. Ed Guerrero, "The Black Man on Our Screens and the Empty Space in Representation," *Callaloo*, vol. 8, no. 2 (1995): 395–400. However, it must be noted that even before the tragic events on Bundy Drive, O. J. Simpson bore more than a passing resemblance to the media construction of Ike Turner in that he had a well-documented history of domestic violence that was glossed over by the celebrity system.
4. *The New York Times*, April 25, 1949, 22. For an excellent discussion of this editorial and the turn in Robeson's celebrity fortunes see: Martin Bauml Duberman, *Paul Robeson: A Biography* (New York: Alfred A. Knopf, 1988), 336–362.
5. Leola Johnson and David Roediger, "'Hertz, Don't It?' Becoming Colorless and Staying Black in the Crossover of O. J. Simpson." Toni Morrison, ed., *Birth of a Nation 'hood: Gaze, Script, and Spectacle in the O. J. Simpson Case* (New York: Pantheon Books, 1997), 197–209.
6. As cited in Jeffrey Toobin, *The Run of His Life: The People v. O. J. Simpson* (New York: Random House, 1996), 49, and Marc Cerasini, *O. J. Simpson: American Hero, American Tragedy* (New York: Pinnacle Books, 1994), 196.
7. Bill Carter, "The Simpson Verdict: A Circus of Many Rings," *The New York Times*, February 6, 1997, B11.

John Hope Franklin
PAUL ROBESON, ICON FOR THE
TWENTY-FIRST CENTURY

1. *The New York Times*, January 24, 1976, 1.
2. Speech by Paul Robeson at Morehouse College, spring 1943. Quoted in *The New York Times*, June 2, 1943, 46.
3. Ibid.
4. Ibid.
5. Paul Robeson, *Here I Stand* (Boston: Little Brown, 1971), 73.
6. Hearing of the Un-American Activities Committee, United States House of Representatives, 84th Congress, 2d Session, 4505.

ABOUT THE CONTRIBUTORS

RAE ALEXANDER-MINTER has served as Director of the Paul Robeson Cultural Center at Rutgers University since 1993. As a result of her vision and direction, the Paul Robeson Centennial Project was planned in 1994 and realized in 1998. Her experience as a scholar and author, educator, exhibition curator and developer of museum- and community-based public humanities and arts programming spans over twenty years. Her contributions to scholarship on African American culture and education include landmark studies of women who graduated from the Hawthorne School in the District of Columbia, and of a 200-year-old Black community in northeast Philadelphia. She is the author of *Children's Books and the Search for Black Identity, What Is a Racist Book?,* and editor of *Young and Black in America.* Her research on Henry Ossawa Tanner, an important African American artist of the nineteenth century, led to a national tour of the artist's work in major museums and an extensive catalog in 1991.

DERRICK BELL is a professor and educator, writer, lawyer, and activist. Credited with advancing the academic study of race and racism as a legal issue, he wrote a standard law-school text on the subject, *Race, Racism and American Law.* In 1969 Bell joined the Harvard Law School faculty where, in 1971, he became that school's first Black tenured law professor. He was dismissed after protesting for two years in support of student efforts to achieve more racial and gender diversity on the faculty. He is now a visiting professor at New York University Law School. His numerous books published in the 1990s stretch the bounds of legal discourse and utilize allegorical fiction to make the intersections of law and race more accessible to the public. In the late 1950s, he worked with the Civil Rights Division of the Justice Department, and was later recruited by Thurgood Marshall to the legal team of the NAACP Legal Defense and Educational Fund.

CHARLES L. BLOCKSON is the founder and Curator of The Charles L. Blockson Afro-American Collection housed in the Temple University Libraries. Amassed over forty years, the collection contains over 150,000 books and documents and artifacts relating to Black history and traditions from the sixteenth

315

century to the present. He is also the author of seven books and numerous articles pertaining to people of African descent, including *The Underground Railroad: First-Person Narratives of Escapes to Freedom in the North*, which was made a Book of the Month Club selection. He is a former president of the Pennsylvania Abolition Society and is currently chair of the National Park Service Underground Railroad Advisory Committee.

LLOYD L. BROWN is a distinguished writer, editor, and activist who became a trade-union organizer and published his first book in the 1930s (*Young Workers in Action: The Story of the South River Strike*), while still a teenager. He was a founding member of the Negro American Labor Council organized by A. Philip Randolph, served as Managing Editor of the literary-cultural weekly *New Masses* in the 1940s, and wrote for the Harlem newspaper *Freedom*, founded by Paul Robeson in 1950. Brown's novel *Iron City* has been published abroad in twelve foreign languages. He collaborated with Robeson in the writing of Robeson's book *Here I Stand*, and wrote the preface to the 1971 edition. Brown wrote the biography *The Young Paul Robeson: "On My Journey Now."*

MARTIN DUBERMAN is Distinguished Professor of History at Lehman College and the Graduate School of the City University of New York. He is the founding Director of the Center for Lesbian and Gay Studies and the author of seventeen books, including *Paul Robeson: A Biography, In White America, Black Mountain, Cures, Stonewall*, and, most recently, has edited the two anthologies *A Queer World* and *Queer Representations*. As both historian and playwright, he has received numerous awards, including the Bancroft Prize, two Lambda awards, the George Freedly Memorial Award, and a Special Citation from the National Academy of Arts and Letters for his "contributions to literature."

JOHN HOPE FRANKLIN is the James B. Duke Professor of History Emeritus at Duke University and for seven years was Professor of Legal History in the Law School there. Professor Franklin's numerous publications, during an active career of nearly sixty years,

include *The Emancipation Proclamation, The Militant South, The Free Negro in North Carolina, Reconstruction After the Civil War,* and *A Southern Odyssey: Travelers in the Antebellum North.* Perhaps his best-known book is *From Slavery to Freedom: A History of African Americans*, now in its seventh edition. In 1990, a collection of essays covering a teaching and writing career of fifty years was published under the title *Race and History: Selected Essays, 1938–1988.* His most recent book is *The Color Line: Legacy for the Twenty-First Century*; his current research deals with "Dissidents on the Plantation: Runaway Slaves." He is the recipient of numerous awards, distinctions, and appointments, and has served as president of the Phi Beta Kappa Society, The Southern Historical Association, the American Studies Association, the Organization of American Historians, and the American Historical Association.

ED GUERRERO is Associate Professor of Cinema Studies at New York University, where he teaches film and literature, with an emphasis on Black, ethnic, and third-world film and literary theory. His book *Framing Blackness: The African American Image in Film* was awarded honorable mention by the Theater Library Association in 1994, and has contributed to the critical reconsideration of Black images in American film, both past and present. An active speaker and writer, he is Associate Editor of *Cinéaste* and a member of the Executive Council of the Society for Cinema Studies. He is co-curator, with Charles Musser and Mark Reid, of the Robeson film retrospective developed as part of the Paul Robeson Centennial Project.

FRANCIS C. HARRIS is an author and historian with a focus on the history of African Americans in sports. He is the author (with Charles F. Harris, Jr.) of *The Amistad Pictorial History of the African American Athlete*, a two-volume series documenting the history of African American participation in sports at the collegiate and professional levels. He served as a senior researcher for Arthur R. Ashe, Jr., in the 1980s and designed and organized the reference format for the three-volume work *"A Hard Road to Glory": A History of the African American Athlete.*

GERALD C. HORNE is Professor and Director of the Institute of African-American Research at the University of North Carolina at Chapel Hill. An experienced labor lawyer and legal historian, he has been engaged as a teacher, writer, and legal and political rights advocate for over twenty years. He is the author of ten books, including *Fire This Time: The Watts Uprising and the 1960s; Black Liberation–Red Scare: Ben Davis and the Communist Party;* and *Black and Red: W.E.B. Du Bois and the Afro-American Response to the Cold War, 1944–1963.*

DAVID LEVERING LEWIS is Martin Luther King, Jr., University Professor at Rutgers University. His 1994 study *W.E.B. Du Bois: Biography of a Race* was awarded six distinguished prizes, including the Pulitzer Prize in Biography, the Francis Parkman Prize in History, the Bancroft Prize in American History and Diplomacy, and the Book Award of the Black Caucus of the American Library Association. His major books include: *King: A Biography; Prisoners of Honor: The Dreyfus Affair; When Harlem Was in Vogue;* and *The Race to Fashoda: European Colonialism and African Resistance in the Scramble for Africa.*

DORIS EVANS MCGINTY is Professor Emerita of Musicology of Howard University, having served on the music faculty from 1947 to 1991. A leading expert on the history of African American men and women in music, and African and African American musical history, especially with reference to Washington, D.C., she has been a central force in shaping our understanding of the history of African American music in a cultural context over the past five decades. Her bold interpretations and tireless archival research have been published in monographs, scholarly articles, and in major dictionaries and encyclopedias of music history, including *The New Grove Dictionary of American Music* and the *American Dictionary of Negro Biography.* She was a Contributing Editor for *Black Perspective in Music* from 1975 to 1991. Most recently, her "'As Large as She Can Make It': Black Women Activists in Music" appeared in the book *Cultivating Music in America.* Her knowledge of the extensive music collections in the Moorland Spingarn Research Center at Howard was crucial to the development of the Paul Robeson Centennial Exhibition and curriculum for school-aged youth.

JULIANNE MALVEAUX is a Washington, D.C.–based economist, writer, syndicated columnist, and television and radio commentator. Her work focuses on politics, economics, work, gender, and race. She writes weekly columns for the King Features Syndicate and the *San Francisco Sun Reporter,* and is featured regularly in *USA Today* and *Black Issues in Higher Education.* A selection of Malveaux's columns was collected in 1994 in the book *Sex, Lies and Stereotypes: Perspectives of a Mad Economist.* Julianne Malveaux was Editor-in-Chief of the National Council of Negro Women's compendium on African American women's issues, *Voices of Vision,* and president of the National Association of Negro Business and Professional Women's Clubs, Inc.

CHARLES MUSSER is Associate Professor of American Studies and Film Studies at Yale University, where he directs the Film Studies Program. He has taught cinema studies at New York University, the University of California at Los Angeles, and Columbia University, and serves as Film Historian for the Thomas A. Edison Papers at Rutgers University. He has curated film programs for the Museum of Modern Art and the American Federation of the Arts, as well as for the New-York Historical Society—working with Rae Alexander-Minter on the series "American History/American Film" and "Race and Class in New York." His books include *Before the Nickelodeon: Edwin S. Porter and the Edison Manufacturing Company, High Class Moving Pictures: Lyman H. Howe and the Forgotten Era of Traveling Exhibition, 1880–1920* (with Carol Nelson), and *The Emergence of Cinema: The American Screen to 1907,* which was awarded several national prizes in the field of film and media studies. In 1996 he received the Prix Jean Mitry for his contribution to the study of silent film.

MARK D. NAISON is Professor of American History and Afro-American Studies at Fordham University, where he has been a member of the faculty since 1970. An accomplished historian of New York City, the tenants' rights movement, and the history of the Communist Party in the U.S., he has written *Communists in Harlem During the Depression* and *The Tenant Movement in New York City, 1904–1984.* Naison is the recipient of numerous awards, including the Ralph J. Bunche Award of the American Political Science Association, for the Outstanding Scholarly Work in Political Science that Deals with the Phenomenon of Ethnic and Cultural Pluralism in the U.S. Also knowledgeable about the history and politics of sports, he has chaired the boards of the Center for Athletes' Rights and Education and Sports for the People, Inc. He has also served on advisory boards of the Oral History of the American Left Collection and the American Labor History Series.

MARK A. REID is Professor of English and Film at the University of Florida at Gainesville, where his focus is on African and African American film and literature, including Black women writers and writers of the Black Diaspora. His recent scholarly publications include, as author, *Redefining Black Film, PostNegritude Visual and Literary Culture,* and, as editor, *Spike Lee's "Do the Right Thing."* One current project is focused on "Post Negritude Aesthetics and Womanism: Black Diasporic Film and Video." He has served on the editorial boards of four film journals: *Cinema Journal; Wide Angle: A Quarterly Journal of Film, History, Theory and Criticism; JUMP CUT: A Review of Contemporary Cinema;* and *Black Film Review.* He is co-curator, with Charles Musser and Ed Guerrero, of the Robeson film retrospective developed as part of the Paul Robeson Centennial Project.

WAYNE SHIRLEY has been Reference Librarian/Music Specialist in the Music Division of the Library of Congress since 1965, and brought extensive knowledge of scripts and recorded sound music collections of Robeson and his contemporaries to the development of the Paul Robeson Centennial Project. Author, editor, and compiler of important source materials in American musical history, he was Editor of *American Music* from 1990 to 1993, and has served in the leadership of the American Musicological Society's publications committees and governing council over the last twenty years. His major publications include the book-length *Modern Music: An Analytic Index* and the *Repertoire Internationale des Sources Musicales,* for which he served as American Editor from 1963 to 1965.

JEFFREY C. STEWART is Associate Professor of History at George Mason University. He served as curator of the Paul Robeson Centennial Exhibition and editor of this volume. In 1989, Dr. Stewart curated the Smithsonian National Portrait Gallery exhibition, *To Color America: Portraits by Winold Reiss,* and wrote the catalog biography of that artist. He was previously Director of Research of the Anacostia Museum of the Smithsonian Institution. He has edited two books, *The Critical Temper of Alain Locke: A Selection of His Writings on Art and Culture* and *Race Contacts and Interracial Relations: Lectures by Alain Locke.* His most recent publication is *1001 Things Everyone Should Know About African American History.* He is currently completing *Enter the New Negro: A Biography of Alain Locke.*

DEBORAH WILLIS is Exhibitions Curator/Museum Specialist for the Center for African American History and Culture of the Smithsonian Institution. Previously, Ms. Willis served as Curator of Photographs and Prints/Exhibition Coordinator at the Schomburg Center for Research in Black Culture of the New York Public Library. Her numerous publications and photographic exhibits (as participant and curator) focus on major male and female artists, movements in African American history and art of the nineteenth and twentieth centuries, and African communities in the U.S. and the Caribbean. Her recent books include *The Family of Black America, Visual Journal: Harlem and DC in the Thirties and Forties,* and *Picturing Us: African American Identity in Photography.*

MEMBERS OF
THE ADVISORY COMMITTEE
FOR THE PAUL ROBESON
CENTENNIAL PROJECT

DR. RAE ALEXANDER-MINTER
Director
Paul Robeson Cultural Center, Rutgers,
The State University of New Jersey

MR. CHARLES L. BLOCKSON
Curator
Charles L. Blockson Afro-American
Collection, Temple University

MR. PHILLIP DENNIS CATE
Director
Jane Voorhees Zimmerli Art Museum,
Rutgers, The State University of New
Jersey

DR. SPENCER R. CREW
Director
National Museum of American History,
Smithsonian Institution

DR. MARTIN DUBERMAN
Distinguished Professor of History
Lehman College/The Graduate Center,
City University of New York

MS. CHERYL FINLEY
Consultant
Arts Resource Consortium

MS. PAULA J. GIDDINGS
Professor, Department of Women's
Studies
Duke University

DR. JANET GREENBERG
Robeson Centennial Project Manager

DR. ED GUERRERO
Associate Professor of Cinema Studies
New York University

DR. GERALD HORNE
Professor and Director of the Institute of
African-American Research
University of North Carolina at Chapel
Hill

DR. HELEN ARMSTEAD JOHNSON
Director
Armstead-Johnson Foundation for
Theater Research
Professor Emerita
York College, City University of New
York

DR. DAVID LEVERING LEWIS
Martin Luther King, Jr. University
Professor
Rutgers, The State University of New
Jersey

319

DR. DORIS EVANS MCGINTY
Professor Emerita of Musicology
Howard University

MS. LESLIE MITCHNER
Editor in Chief
Rutgers University Press

DR. CHARLES MUSSER
Associate Professor of American Studies
and Film Studies
Yale University

DR. MARK D. NAISON
Professor of American History and Afro-
American Studies
Fordham University

DR. CLEMENT ALEXANDER PRICE
Professor of History
Rutgers University

DR. MARK A. REID
Professor of English and Film
University of Florida, Gainesville

MR. WAYNE D. SHIRLEY
Reference Librarian/Music Specialist,
Music Division
Library of Congress

DR. JAMES SMALLS
Assistant Professor of Art
Rutgers, The State University of New
Jersey

MR. ROBERT SMITH
Sports Information Director (retired)
Rutgers, The State University of New
Jersey

DR. JEFFREY C. STEWART
Associate Professor of History
George Mason University

MS. DEBORAH WILLIS
Coordinator of Collections and Museum
Specialist
Center for African American History
and Culture
Smithsonian Institution

CREDITS

Photographs from the Julius Lazarus Archives and Collection were acquired by Rutgers, The State University of New Jersey, in 1995 and now comprise the Julius Lazarus Archives and Collection, Special Collections, Rutgers University Libraries. The Julius Lazarus Archives and Collection of Rutgers has contributed all photographs free of charge to *Paul Robeson: Artist and Citizen,* edited and with an introduction by Jeffrey C. Stewart, and retains copyright © to those images. The efforts of the Paul Robeson Cultural Center at Rutgers University to include his photographs in this book were supported exclusively by grants from the National Endowment for the Humanities, a federal agency; The Vice President for Academic Affairs and the Provost's Fund of Rutgers University; and by the photographer himself. Additional photographs from the Julius Lazarus Archives and Collection appeared in a special exhibition on Paul Robeson's activism at the Stedman Gallery, Rutgers University–Camden Center for the Arts from March 9 to May 2, 1998, as part of this centennial project. Funding for this special exhibition was provided by the William Penn Foundation and the New Jersey State Council on the Arts/Department of State.

226a–b. Julius Lazarus during his working years as a photographer.

226c–d. Julius Lazarus on Paul Robeson-Strasse, Berlin.
November 1996. *Photos © by Thomas Aurin, Berlin. Courtesy of Julius Lazarus Archives and Collection/Special Collections/Rutgers University Libraries.*

INDEX

(Page numbers in italics refer to illustrations.)

227. Paul Robeson and Eslanda Robeson in *Borderline*. 1930.
Beinecke Library, Yale University.